Partners of the Imagination

The Lives, Art and Struggles of
John Arden and Margaretta D'Arcy

Robert Leach

indigo dreams
publishing

First Edition: Partners of the Imagination

First published in Great Britain in 2012 by:
Indigo Dreams Publishing Ltd
132 Hinckley Road
Stoney Stanton
Leics
LE9 4LN

www.indigodreams.co.uk

ISBN 978-1-907401-75-6

A CIP record for this book is available from the British Library.

Designed and typeset in Minion Pro by Robert Leach/Nicholas Leach.

Cover design by Nicholas Leach.

Printed and bound in Great Britain by Imprint Academic, Exeter.

Papers used in this publication are recyclable products made from wood grown
in sustainable forests following the guidance of the Forest Stewardship Council.

By the same author:

Theatre
The Punch and Judy Show: History, Tradition and Meaning
Revolutionary Theatre
Stanislavsky and Meyerhold
Makers of Modern Theatre
Theatre Workshop: Joan Littlewood and the Making of Modern British
    Theatre

Travel
The Journey to Mount Kailash

Poetry
Boy and Baggage
Dustprints
Sour Cream
After the Storm

Partners of the Imagination

Contents

List of Illustrations

Introduction

John Arden dedicated his *Two Autobiographical Plays* to
>   . . . all those nosey-parkers who prefer
>   To know the poet's life and what he does
>   Rather than read his words upon the page
>   Or listen to them spoken on the stage.

Specifically:
>   I specially desire this dedication
>   To warm the hearts of those whose cold devotion
>   In setting down the facts and piling archives
>   Within an air-conditioned Institute
>   Produces, for themselves, a Doctorate:
>   And for the poet, death – while he still lives.[1]

I trust the following pages do not spring from a 'cold devotion In setting down the facts', or that they result from my being simply the 'nosey-parker' whom he castigates. On the contrary, what I hope is that I will stimulate my reader into reading some of the work of my subjects, or watching a play by them. This will produce *life*, not death, for them and their work, and that's my aim.

This book attempts to plot the development of a political, philosophical, social and artistic stance. And how the discovering of that stance took a long time, and many twists and turns, before some sort of solution was found. That solution was what Margaretta D'Arcy was to call 'loose theatre'. The book therefore follows the search for this artistic and social (or political) formulation.

In the quest for 'loose theatre', Arden and D'Arcy moved away from what was easily accessible to the critics, both physically accessible in terms of venue (no more West End of London premieres with special seats reserved for critics with mighty and fearful pens); and intellectually accessible in terms of form and content (no more conventional 'challenges' to flatter the critics' self-serving specialisms). Consequently their work became less known than it should have been. This is acknowledged by all who have studied the work. Jonathan Wike, in his Introduction to *John Arden and Margaretta D'Arcy: A Casebook* notes 'the need for more study of their work at this time',[2] and in his appraisal of Arden's work, Javed Malick begins by explaining that his book 'is partly an attempt to correct the critical neglect of John Arden's work'.[3] Yet Arden's, and Arden and D'Arcy's, genius is widely agreed. One example will be sufficient here, since there are many more later in these pages: the radical publisher, John Calder, says, almost offhandedly, 'Of that generation of playwrights (Arden) was the most talented. He is a British Brecht'.[4]

Part of the difficulty seems to have sprung from a writing career which began as Arden's, became Arden and D'Arcy's, then D'Arcy and Arden's, then dissolved into both individual and collaborative works, which were more or less comprehensible as literary work, but which seemed to move increasingly into political or social dimensions. And no sooner had Arden become Arden and D'Arcy or D'Arcy and Arden, than the critics seemed lost. For some reason, in this case, the collaboration of two artists seemed baffling; yet there are far too many pairs of writers and artists who have worked together for there to be any excuse for those who couldn't cope with Arden and D'Arcy: Keith Waterhouse and Willis Hall; Rodgers and Hammerstein; Beaumont and Fletcher; Gilbert and George; Charles Rennie Mackintosh and Margaret Macdonald. Arden himself refers to Robert Graves and Laura Riding. This is the merest tip of the iceberg.

One reason why the Arden-D'Arcy partnership may have discomforted critics and observers is that Arden tends to be the bookish partner and D'Arcy the more outspoken and even aggressive. This is not how male-female partnerships are supposed to work. Arden's natural caution is illustrated by a story D'Arcy tells: 'John is the only child of elderly parents ... His mother put him into a playpen. When the playpen was removed, John was still there, on the spot'.[5] D'Arcy appears much more forceful and even impetuous. One University professor tells of how he invited them to do some work on the campus of the University where he taught. He was only able to obtain from his Finance Office a single cheque, made out to 'John Arden', in payment for their work. D'Arcy immediately marched into the Finance Office and demanded a cheque for herself, which the officer was soon cowed into providing. She achieved, in other words, what the highly-regarded professor had been quite unable to achieve. Male critics or other cultural arbiters do not like to be browbeaten by a woman.

This book concentrates on the public lives of John Arden and Margaretta D'Arcy: their private lives are only mentioned when it seems relevant to their work. They are unusual for their generation in that they have stayed together for well over fifty years and are still, at the time of writing, collaborating and performing together. And they have brought up four children, if unconventionally, at least comparatively successfully.

In earlier ages, Arden, and Arden and D'Arcy, and D'Arcy and Arden, and D'Arcy herself, would have been supported by a thoughtful publisher, one concerned about our culture and heritage, who would have published these authors' 'Complete Works' in a series of uniform volumes. This seems to be impossible in today's over-hyped and over-accelerated world. But such a 'Complete Works' would enable us to read and study at our leisure not simply those plays, novels and other writings which have been published, but also the unpublished work, including the radio plays, which contain some of the authors' finest writing. I hope I have managed to do some justice to some of these barely-known works. Even today, one

iv

might hope that someone somewhere will bring out, say, *Three Radio Plays* by John Arden: *Garland for a Hoar Head, Woe, Alas, the Fatal Cash Box* and *Poor Tom, Thy Horn Is Dry*. This would make a more satisfying book than many play collections by lesser authors which are currently in print.

As it is, the influence of Arden and D'Arcy is still pervasive. We see it in unexpected places, perhaps subliminally, but still clearly, as in some of the finest contemporary drama, such as Jez Butterworth's *Jerusalem*, or Lee Hall's *The Pitmen Painters*. And Martin Lynch has recorded how the moment he realized theatre was for him was when

> I was sitting in the audience at Turf Lodge Social Club in 1975 watching a play called *The Non-Stop Connolly Show* by John Arden and Margaretta D'Arcy. A character from the play – an English yeoman with a gun – was chasing an outlaw from the Land League around the main body of the hall and the crowd was loving it, roaring and cheering on the outlaw. It was that moment when I saw an audience not only captivated but involved.[6]

It is easy to argue, therefore, as I do, that we need to know more about the work of Arden and D'Arcy, and we need to acknowledge their significance more generously.

In the book I have indicated my sources wherever possible in the list of references at the end of the book. I hope the numbering in the text of this system of reference will be unobtrusive enough for the general reader not to feel harassed by it, but that it will be clear enough for those who wish to follow up my sources to be able to do so.

Acknowledgements

A work of this nature puts its author in debt to many people. I gladly offer my sincere thanks to all those actors, students or professionals, as well as stage crew, front-of-house staff, and others, who have worked with me on plays by Arden and D'Arcy: *Live Like Pigs, The Business of Good Government, Ars Longa, Vita Brevis, The Royal Pardon, The Hero Rises Up, The Non-Stop Connolly Show* and *The Little Gray Home in the West.*

Thanks, too, to the always-helpful staff at the National Library of Scotland, Edinburgh, and to the staff at the British Library in London, especially Ike Egbetola, Yadley Day and Rod Hamilton of the British Library Listening Service. Others I am indebted to, and whom I wish to thank, are: Mr M. J. Glen, Headmaster, Terrington Hall Preparatory School; Mr C. H. Hirst, Headmaster, and Ms Katy Iliffe, archivist, Sedbergh School; Michael Moore, MP; Claire Poyner of *Peace News*; Nancy Coughlan, Emma Campbell and Noëlle O'Hanlon; Albert Hunt, Tamara Hinchco and Kika Markham; Finn Arden; and Professor Peter Thomson.

For incalculable amounts of help with computing, editing, the design of the cover, and much more, I wish to thank Nicholas Leach. His patience has been immeasurable, and his help indefatiguable. He has amazed even his father! And a very warm thanks, too, to my publisher, Ronnie Goodyer, for all his support throughout the project.

I offer a very special thanks to the following people, who kindly read the book or parts of the book, in earlier draft form, and made comments, criticisms and suggestions from which the final work has undoubtedly benefitted: Angela Bull, Olga Taxidou, Joy Parker, Tamara Hinchco, Albert Hunt, Nicholas Leach and John Topping.

For the illustrations in this book, I am primarily indebted to Finn Arden, who has supplied the photograph on the cover of this book, and those on pages 9, 29, 31, 49, 112, 129, 158, 198, 263, 269, 285, 321, 322 and 323. Other photographs have been supplied by Adrian Godfrey (page 86), *The Scotsman* (page 96), Mary Evans Picture Library/Roger Mayne (page 105), Albert Hunt (page 117), Bob Quinn (page 216) and Aosdána (292). I am grateful to all of these.

My final thanks go to John Arden and Margaretta D'Arcy, who have not only allowed me to poke about in the dusty corners of their lives, but have barely ever lost patience with me. I know that many biographers fall out with the subjects of their studies; I trust this will not be the case in this instance, because my aim throughout has been to present their ideas and achievements in the clearest possible light. I am an admirer, if not a wholly uncritical one.

R.L.

Prologue

One evening in early November 1956, a young would-be playwright and an aspiring actress sat together under a mulberry tree in an Earls Court garden. It was moist and warm, and there was the sweet smell of rotting leaves. They talked energetically of poetry, the theatre, a new beginning. And they made a promise to each other. They would change the world of the theatre so that all the lumber of decades, the stuffy escapism and the timid placating of 'Aunt Edna', the rigid conventions of theatre-as-an-after-dinner-entertainment, and the smug self-satisfaction which settled like dust on virtually every Green Room in the country – all this they would overturn. They would find a form of drama which would answer to the cry of the imagination, and which would loosen up the tight little, shallow little world of British theatre in the middle 1950s. They would find ways to make a theatre big enough, and welcoming enough, to accommodate what they wanted to achieve.

And that this could be something they could so exactly agree on, that they both could so ardently desire, was in itself remarkable. For he was a staid and respectable Yorkshireman, public school and Cambridge University educated; while she was the daughter of a Russian Jewess and an Irish freedom fighter. Their paths to that garden in Earls Court could hardly have been more different. But from 1955 they were to stand and fight shoulder to shoulder to liberate British theatre, to take it beyond its shallow parochialism and to open it up to the dangerous winds blown in by hard political struggle and by the joyous, noisy, poetic, inconvenient and audacious theatrical ways which Britain had largely lost.

He was the poet and playwright, John Arden, she the actress and idealist, Margaretta D'Arcy. And their story is an extraordinary, instructive and at times almost unbelievable peregrination through the art, culture and politics of Britain and Ireland in the second half of the twentieth century.

One : A Yorkshire Boyhood

John Arden was born on 26 October 1930, of traditional English yeoman stock. His ancestors may be traceable to the Norman Conquest or even earlier, and there is some evidence that he is related to the family of Shakespear's mother. His nearer ancestors came from Beverley in Yorkshire, perhaps the most significant of whom was the local medical practitioner in the early decades of the nineteenth century. This Dr Arden was also a wine merchant and the owner of the Beverley Arms, and he seems to have bribed his way to the mayoralty of the city no fewer than nine times: his most telling achievement as Mayor having been to abolish bull baiting in the market place.[7]

Later Ardens were pillars of the Conservative Party, and John's own Great Uncle Charlie was another Mayor of Beverley. This great uncle's brother, John's grandfather, was also a wine merchant, and seems to have been something of a domestic tyrant. He fathered eleven children, no fewer than ten of them daughters, and just one son, Charles, who became John Arden's father.

Charles Alwyn Arden was born in Beverley in 1891. He worked in the offices of the East Riding of Yorkshire County Council, and about 1911 he joined the cyclists' battalion of the Territorial Army. Consequently, when war was declared in 1914, he was immediately mobilised into what became the Army Corps of Cyclists. The most dramatic moment which confronted this Corps came when they were fighting alongside a group of newly-arrived Portuguese conscripts, who appeared almost mystified by their own presence in the trenches. When the Germans attacked, they fled. Threequarters of a mile down the road they lighted upon the Cycle Corps' parked and guarded bikes. Without ado, they shot the guards, grabbed the cycles and pedalled off into the hinterland of France!

Charles Arden fought throughout the war, ending as a Sergeant-Major. He was never wounded, though his front line experiences left him with a pernicious poisoning of the blood which lasted for over twenty years.. Ironically, on the day he was demobilised he contracted Asian flu. He left France feeling perfectly well, but sickened on the boat, was worse on the train, and was so ill by the time he reached Grantham on his way to Yorkshire that he left the train, and found a boarding house where he was extremely poorly. One of his ten sisters eventually arrived to take him home.

Back in Beverley, Charles's council job had vanished. His father suggested he join the family wine business, but Charles declined unless the terms of the business were changed so that wine could be sold from the shop. As things stood, customers could sip a sample, but nothing was sold over the counter. For the elder Arden, this would be 'common': 'We don't run a pub', he said. So the first acceptable opportunity which presented itself to Charles Arden was in glass manufacturing. He joined the firm of Wood Brothers, makers of bottles, tumblers and other glass products. They sent him for training to Sheffield, and when he returned he found his foot on the management ladder. He was to become, first, assistant manager of Wood Brothers, and later manager.

Once settled in employment, Charles Arden joined a tennis club (where he amused his fellow members by continuing to wear his army boots when out and about), and there he met Annie Elizabeth Layland (known as Nancy), a Primary School teacher five years his junior who had also, coincidentally, trained in Sheffield. In 1924 they were married.

The Laylands were a reasonably well-to-do Methodist family from Otley in Wharfedale, whose Liberalism, however, was not much to the taste of the better-descended (as they imagined themselves to be) Tory Ardens. Nancy's father, an insurance salesman, had been injured by a stone thrown during a demonstration he took part in against the Boer War. His progressive politics were further manifested in his support for striking miners, though they were severely tested when his daughter Nancy voiced her support for the suffragettes: that seems to have been a step too far. When he died suddenly before the outbreak of war, he left his family of five daughters and three sons not only bereaved but insecure, both financially and psychologically. The mother compensated for her husband's absence by assuming a domineering role in the family, from which the children obviously found it difficult to escape. Arden therefore grew up with well over a dozen aunts (including the ten Arden women), nearly all of them spinsters. As he himself wrote, both his parents came from 'awe-inspiring lower-middle-bourgeois matriarchal establishments'.[8]

Nancy inherited something of her mother's pride and subtle ability to control, and she retained the Layland's progressive ideas all her life. She was vehemently against the Empire and its exploitation of colonial peoples; and later, in her old age, she was similarly vehemently opposed to Mrs Thatcher. She practised as a schoolteacher in Barnsley, but seems to have been happy to give it up. She was stocky but diminutive (less than five feet tall), and at first some of her pupils' parents wondered if such a youthful-seeming person could be a teacher. Shortly after she arrived in Barnsley, her landlady tried to gas herself. The gas leaked all over the house, and Nancy had to stay with her headmistress, Miss Turner, until other lodgings could be found.

Barnsley, set in the heart of the Yorkshire coalfield, was still able to offer a young boy growing up there something to stir the imagination. J.B.Priestley's 1933 account conjures up this town where Charles and Nancy lived and where their son John first became aware of the world.

> We were now in the true north country. One glance at the people, with their stocky figures and broad faces, humorous or pugnacious, told you

that. On the road to Barnsley the stone walls began, settling any possible doubts ... Along this road to Barnsley the sun flared hugely before finally setting. All the western edges of the slag-heaps were glistening. I saw in one place a great cloud of steam that had plumes of gold. In another, we passed under a vast aerial flight of coal trucks, slowly moving, in deep black silhouette, against the sunset. It would not have made a bad symbolical picture of the end of one phase of industrial England. When we looked down upon Barnsley, we sàw it for a moment dimly ranged about an ebony pyramid of slag. When we stopped in the town for tea, the sun had gone and the air was nippingly cold. In the café where I ate my toasted tea-cake, a young man was being funny to his girl about somebody's bad elocution. (I suspect that the somebody was a local bigwig.) 'He said "lor" for "law,"' said the young man, 'and "dror" for "draw." Honestly, he did. "We will now dror to a conclusion," he said. Yes, really.' And as they were in that stage of courtship in which each finds the other's least remark a miracle of apt speech, they were very happy, two refined but humorous souls in a wilderness of clods. It was almost dark when we left Barnsley for Huddersfield. The hills were now solidly black; their edges very sharp against the last faint silver of the day. They were beginning to take on, for me, that Wordsworthian quality which belongs to the North. The factories might be roaring and steaming in the valleys, their lighted windows glaring at us as we passed, but behind were those high remote skylines, stern enough and yet still suggesting to me a brooding tenderness.[9]

This was the myth-stirring Barnsley, whose vernacular proved a lasting inspiration to Arden: even after he had lived in Ireland for thirty years, it was likely to creep into his writing. In *Cogs Tyrannic*, for instance, published in 1991, he refers to a 'ginnel-entry', ginnel being Yorkshire for a narrow alleyway.[10]

The town had another side, however. Politically, because of the coal mines, it was a one-party council. However arrogant or sloppy, the Labour Party's power was never threatened, and corruption was well nigh endemic. Whatever the circumstances of particular firms, employees seemed more dangerous and sometimes more threatening than in most towns in the hungry thirties. It is notable . that the managing director of Wood Bros kept a pistol in the drawer of his office desk in case his workers should feel provoked. And Charles Arden had on several occasions to intervene (though not physically) between the workers and the boss when relations were becoming difficult. The level of animosity, or class warfare, in the town may also be judged from the fact that later, when the Labour Council recommended the middle class Nancy Arden for a medal for her work in the Citizens Advice Bureau during the war, she refused it because so much of her work had, she believed, been obstructed by them. And to her, her class background, her

Liberalism, and the fact that the Bureau's chief was an Anglican clergyman, were why they had made her life unnecessarily complicated in the first place.

The Ardens lived in a neat terraced house in Guest Road, just off the main Huddersfield Road. Complications at his birth meant that John was an only child. The *petit bourgeois* outlook of the neighbourhood, shared at least to some extent by the Ardens, cast as the 'prime social crime' 'brawling on the doorstep',[11] while the making any sort of 'personal' comment was wholly unacceptable.[12] Of John, his mother was extremely possessive, taking care to organise him at all points. Thus, he went to school when he was four, but well before that she had taught him to read and write, and even do simple arithmetic. She did not return to work till John was well settled at school. The family asserted its values through christening mugs, 'best' knives and forks (which were only brought out to be polished, and then were put carefully away again) and the portraits of Arden and Layland forebears and worthies. Conversation at meals was literate and polite, and concerned politics or – more usually – church affairs. For a small boy, it was clearly supportive, perhaps protective, possibly even repressive.

But Arden was a child with a powerful imagination. The grotesque medieval church carvings in Beverley Minster transfixed him when he was very small. Once, when out shopping with his mother, he saw a group of discontented men with banners. He was alarmed, though he did not know who they were. We may speculate: was it a political demonstration, or perhaps they were hunger marchers? The fact of them was what was disturbing to the young Arden. He was not only imaginative, he was also clever, as he showed when he watched his great aunt pouring tea, and asked her: 'Do you make the stream of tea shake on purpose, so we can see how you never spill it?' His chosen toys were Hornby trains, Meccano and, later, model aeroplanes. Surprisingly, for those who know the plays he was to write, he never owned a toy theatre, his first experience of toy theatre being when he bought one for his own children in the early 1960s.

He listened to *Children's Hour* on BBC radio – he first encountered the stories of King Arthur when this programme broadcast an adaptation of Sir Thomas Malory's stories around 1938: 'I found it all rather strange, but quite haunting', he remembered.[13] He also owned a children's book of tales of King Arthur, perhaps given to him by an aunt: aunts from both sides of the family gave him books from an early age. The Ardens of Beverley especially had shelves full, and the young Arden gobbled up many pages from volumes of *The Children's Encyclopaedia*, a set of which he found there. His father also possessed a set of a magazine issued in parts before the First World War, *History of the Nations*, which attempted to provide sympathetic illustrated histories of every country in the world, avoiding the easy clichés of British imperialism.

His parents, like many of their social class at the time, belonged to societies and other local organizations. While his mother was active in church affairs, his father, who was a Major in the Home Guard during the Second World War, offered the Boy Scouts secretarial assistance. They were also members of a Playgoers Society, which visited theatres in Sheffield or Leeds from time to time, but also read aloud plays by authors such as Galsworthy and Shaw at society meetings. The Arden parents took their young son to the pantomime, and once to *Alice in Wonderland*, which he hated. The fact that the characters kept spilling the tea at the Mad Hatter's Tea Party upset his notions of propriety, and the descending curtain terrified him. 'Don't like that curtain!' he bawled, and his parents were forced to take him home. He also disliked *Peter Pan*, unhappily identifying the downtrodden Mr Darling with his own father. *The Yorkshire Post*, conservative but decidedly anti-Fascist, was Charles Arden's preferred newspaper, and his son was early aware that Hitler was 'a bad man' – though Dr Goebbels (despite his pretty daughter) was worse. Arden also knew that the Italians were being bad in Ethiopia, as were the Japanese in China. He even vaguely remembered Ramsay MacDonald as Prime Minister.

When young Arden was four a friend of his mother named Mrs Dobson opened a kindergarten nearby, and he was in the initial intake of eight or nine children. After Arden left, the school built up to be quite sizeable, and was obviously successful. In the late 1950s, Arden was surprised to receive several hundred pounds, which Mrs Dobson had left to him, along with similar amounts for the other original pupils, when she died.

When he was six, Arden was transferred to St Mary's Church of England Elementary School, an altogether tougher proposition for the bespectacled, bookish and somewhat mollycoddled little boy. The other pupils all seemed bigger and they also seemed 'rough': the playground was fraught with unpleasantness. Though some of the teachers were sympathetic enough, others were not. After a year or two, Arden, clearly intelligent, was promoted to a class with a teacher who enjoyed practising his sarcasm – as well as his cane – on his charges. He decided that Arden was not careful enough with his pen, and made him come to the front of the class and hold up his inky fingers. 'Professor Inkblot!' he called him gleefully, an epithet he continued to use. 'Have you solved this problem yet, Professor Inkblot?' he would scowl, or 'Professor Inkblot knows, don't you, professor?' thereby upsetting his pupil and at the same time retarding his learning. This teacher seemed to consider all middle class boys 'stuck up', and treated them accordingly. We may perhaps discern something of him behind Mr Miltiades in *Ars Longa, Vita Brevis* as well as the cruel politician in *The Bagman*.

Arden's class background did not help, and matters were exacerbated for him by the existence of a Catholic school down the road, where the boys, many of whom were of Irish origin, seemed even rougher and more frightening than those at St

Mary's. They had a practice of waylaying boys from St Mary's on their way home, and fighting them. Arden was a particular target for these ambushes, since he had to walk home alone without the company of his friends who lived in other districts. His cause was not helped either by the way his mother, pampering him as always, dressed him: for instance, in rainy weather, she insisted on his wearing a sou'wester, which was the cause of much hilarity among the tougher sort of his contemporaries.

So that when war was declared in 1939, and his parents, fearing that Barnsley might be a target for German bombers, decided to take him away from St Mary's and send him to a boarding school, Arden was extremely happy. The school they settled on was Terrington Hall Preparatory School, fifteen miles north of York. Still a highly respected school of its sort seventy years later, with 170 pupils – boys and girls – and twenty-two members of staff, Terrington Hall was then smaller, but its standards were high. At the time it had 65 boys and one girl, the daughter of the recently-widowed matron. The only drawback for young Arden was his school cap, with 'THPS' emblazoned on it: at home in the holidays, when he walked down the street in it, he was again pounced upon by those 'roughs' he thought he had left behind, who grabbed it and barked 'What's this mean?' in his face.

Arden was only able to attend Terrington Hall because his godfather, an uncle married to one of the Arden sisters and living in the south of England, offered to help to pay the school fees. But he was happy there, and his parents were happy for him. They supported him, as when his father played for the parents' cricket team against the pupils, even though Arden himself did not represent the school. Arden, who was made a prefect before he left, appreciated the fact that the teachers were young and interested. Even the head, Mr P.G.A.Clementson, was not much above thirty. Many of the staff seem to have been exempted from military service, either for medical reasons; or because they were between leaving school (or University) and joining up; or because they were Irish, as the exotic but much-liked Mr Eoin O'Keefe from Limerick, was.

Arden discovered Shakespeare here, but also discovered perhaps a more practical form of playmaking: puppetry. He remembered trying – and largely failing – to make sense of Collier's version of *Punch and Judy*, published in 1828. But there were more successful forays into the form: the school magazine records him as one of a group who successfully presented a puppet show (not *Punch and Judy*) to the school at Christmas in 1943. He also recalled watching some other boys present a short play called *The Late Orlando Madden*, when he discovered that the word 'late' had more than one meaning. And he found his own talent as a teller of tales, making up adventures of German servicemen and other villains:

> discovering the excitement, the exploration, the unbelievable personal
> extension of making up stories in all sorts of different voices, telling them
> to my friends, receiving attention and response and laughter and

sometimes flat dissent as rude as it could come ('Oh no I don't believe *that*, Arden, far-fetched, Arden's far-fetched, tell him to shut up, put the cork in, fizzle! – whoever's in the next bed, tell him! nobody believes *that!*'); all this in the dormitory, after lights out, and very strictly out, the blackout pulled back from the windows to give us air, so that any light shown would immediately signal the Luftwaffe as well as the school staff. Talking itself was anyway forbidden. Telling stories with any sort of dramatic climax – shouts, screams, cackles of laughter, volleys of what we presumed to be oaths, associated vocal sound effects of blood, bombs and burst – was very highly dangerous. Has it ever been so dangerous since? If we were heard the headmaster would flagellate our bare behinds with a flat-backed varnished wooden hairbrush, or a stick like a Regency buck's walking-cane. Voluptuous peril gladly risked for the sake of nightly narrative-drama; indeed almost *welcomed*.[14]

The Arden family, c.1936. John stands in front of his father and mother, right; his grandparents in the centre of the front row. Ten aunts are also present.

Arden was also by now reading books: Dr Doolittle, Biggles, Arthur Ransome and Percy F.Westerman, as well as 'the savage' *Struwwelpeter*, with its relentless stories of punishing naughty children, such as Little Johnny Head-in-the-Air, whom his aunts identified with him, who fell into the water because he didn't look where he was going.[15] There were also myths and legends, for which his imagination always had a particular affinity. At the age of eight he was given a book of Irish legends, stories of Cuchulainn and the Red Branch Heroes, the spirit of which he entered into energetically, triggering a lifelong fascination with Irish myth and culture.

The world of myth seemed to surround him even more closely when he went on to Sedbergh School in the very north west corner of Yorkshire, on the outskirts of the Lake District, when he was nearly fourteen in the autumn of 1944. He had gained an exhibition (less than a full scholarship, but a useful reduction in the school fees demanded), which made his attendance possible. In many ways Sedbergh, founded in 1525, was typical of the British boys' public school of the time. It maintained a heavy emphasis on games in general, rugby and running in particular, mixed with a strong dose of muscular Christianity. Chapel services were held twice every Sunday, led either by the mock-hearty school chaplain or by the headmaster, John Harold Bruce Lockhart. Bruce Lockhart had himself been a pupil at Sedbergh, where he had been extremely successful, and captain of both the cricket and the rugby teams. Indeed, he went on to play for Scotland at both sports. He returned as headmaster in 1937, little inclined to change the Victorian ethos which had moulded him so successfully. A Scottish Presbyterian, he exhorted the boys – future leaders of their generation – to remember they were being trained 'not to lead, but to serve'.[16] Quite a large minority of the boys were Scottish, and the Moderator of the Church of Scotland appeared from time to time to prepare boys for entry into the kirk. There was also, as at other public schools, a Junior Training Corps (later re-named Combined Cadet Force). Joining was compulsory. Arden reached the rank of corporal, though he admitted that his own record was 'something of a joke'.[17]

He later claimed that he was 'no rebel' against the regime, and indeed asserted, 'I personally think it is a very good school'.[18] But some of his contemporaries remember him typically clad in what they took to be a duffle coat, which was actually a long purplish overcoat, worn in all weathers – a strong sign of dissidence! He also stood in Hart House's mock election as the socialist candidate. The school magazine's report after the poll begins baldly enough: 'The House is solidly Conservative.' But in its comments it notes that 'the socialist candidate, J.Arden, had the hardest job of all for he had to atone for the sins of the present Government at a job which, together with persistent well-aimed heckling, was eventually his undoing.' The 'heckling' was in fact the beating of a Cadet Corps drum by some cheerfully mischievous saboteur. In the event, Arden came last in the ballot, with just three votes.

The mythic world which he found attractive and absorbing, and which he related to the Arthurian romances especially as created by Thomas Malory, began at the school gates. Some days during term time Bruce Lockhart would announce an 'extra half', which meant that for half that day the boys would be permitted out of the school grounds to wander at will through the dales and fells of the surrounding countryside. They had to go in pairs or threes, and they had to inform the school where they intended to walk. But then they were free. They explored a landscape which somehow conjured the untamed ruggedness of the medieval tales:

> barren benty heathery hills crowded in over narrow valleys which were
> filled with tangled woods and noisy with the roar of brown rivers among
> boulders and fallen tree trunks. It rained nearly every day. When it did
> not rain the hills could be seen extending for miles in a precise clear blue

air, greeny-brown with black patches, dotted here and there with white sheep. Curlews called continuously above the mosses. Huddled in some of the river valleys were small stone chapels, over-shadowed by thick hawthorn trees and often close to the narrow high-arched bridges that intermittently carried the winding valley roads from one bank of the stream to the other. The place-names were in them-selves suggestive of the wildness of the locality – Black Force, Cautley Spout, Baugh Fell, Briggflats, Winder Fell ...

Arden also noted how 'the grim abrupt manners of the north Yorkshire dalesmen seemed also in keeping with the murderous courtliness of the characters of the (Arthurian) romance'.[19] These 'manners' were revealed on those same walks, for the boys often stayed out for tea at a country farmhouse or local pub.

Certainly these walks were better than his initial acquaintance with the countryside, when he was faced with his first experience of the Sedbergh cross country run.

I wasn't too worried at the start, but all the other boys started off at a hell of a pace. I couldn't keep up. Within a hundred yards I'd all but lost sight of them. I staggered along, just catching sight of the last boy as he went round the corner ahead but I ended up totally lost on a bit of rain-swept moor. I went through a muddy farmyard where I was assailed by a dog, crossed a field full of suspicious bullocks and finally turned up at school about half an hour behind everybody else, soaking wet and cov-ered in mud from head to foot where I'd fallen down. After that, I'd take a bit more care – I'd find out where the bloody run was going to go ...[20]

It was not long before Arden discovered that by choosing to do pottery or painting, he could escape the rigours of the run or the rugby field. This alternative was more than mere truancy, however, and he said later that 'there was a good deal of sensible work done in the arts' at the school.[21]

His academic career at Sedbergh began somewhat problematically. He started an option of Ancient Greek, but was unable to respond to the teacher, Rev J.P.Newell, who seemed to him to assume that anyone who had difficulties with Greek was either lazy or stupid. He changed to German, and found the teacher here, Mr A.E.Hammer, much more enlightened. In his Introduction to *Ironhand*, his adaptation of Goethe's *Goetz von Berlichingen*, Arden pays a notably warm tribute to Mr Hammer, 'under whose supervision I first read the original ... and who managed to preserve interest and enthusiasm for it throughout the protracted routine of studying it as an examination "set book".'[22] As he progressed up the school, and gained in confidence, he was excited by courses on Roman history and art which he pursued in the year after his School Certificate, and also a history course remembered fondly because it was not only taught in a stimulating manner, but also because the boys sat round large tables in the school library, rather than in a conventional classroom! He became Head of his House and an assistant librarian, and his final Higher School Certificate success was in English, French and German. He gained an Exhibition to King's College, Cambridge.

By the time he reached the sixth form, he seemed to know his future path. The work in the Art Room, according to the school magazine for March 1948, included 'a project for a village with designs for its principal buildings by Arden.' Architecture fascinated and attracted him, and he was determined to go further in the subject. It was what he would study at Cambridge and in which he would later become fully qualified.

But he also discovered that he had a talent not just for telling stories, as in the dormitory at Terrington Hall, but for the sterner discipline of writing. He won not only the VIth Form English Prize and the Rankin Shakespeare Prize, but also the Sterling English Verse Prize. He was the only boy during his years at the school to have a poem published in the official school magazine, *The Sedberghian*:

The '9.15'

With a hum and a jerk and a greasy slip
Of slithering motion, where the side-bars dip,
And a shoot from the whistle and a belt from the stack,
And wet, hot steam on the rust-red track,
And a flash of the sun on the cylinder-case,
And a silvery sheen on the smoke-box face ...
The Walschaerts valve-gear, inhuman and strong,
Turned in its frames with a low, deep song,
With the song of revolving eccentrics and cranks,
And of gleaming steel on the oil-smoothed flanks
Of the simmering locomotive, which eased
Her great bulk forward on her axles greased ...
And fiery cinders fell on the sleepers,
Fell on the sunburnt, creosoted sleepers,
Fell on the sleepers in a showery glow,
Fell from the sagging firebox low,
Fell and spluttered and rattled on the ballast,
Spat and sparked and tumbled on the ballast,
Staggered along in the course of the brake-van –
Red-hot cinders falling from the ash-pan,
Fallen from the ash-pan as the engine swung,
Swung, to the roar of the exhaust flung
High in the air from the quivering funnel,
Shot to the sky from the thundering funnel,
Roared to the clouds at the mouth of the tunnel,
At the black, deep, sinister mouth of the tunnel,

As the train fled, gibbering, into the smoke-veils,
Rattling in with its high-pitched wails,
And the sun reflected in the rear-lamp's bull's-eye,
Vanishing inwards,
Into the blackness,
Vanishing, vanishing,
Past the signal, the red-armed signal
That jerked to its danger position –
Click …

And in his House magazine, *The Jay*, of which he became editor in his last year, he published other poems. One was a mock Chaucerian description, *The Preyfecte*, which begins:

A preyfecte was ther, and that a dirtye knave,
That from the tymé that he first beganne,
To beaten hardé, haddé loved to tanne
Hys fagge, and eke they of common sorte.

In these two poems, we can already see, if only perhaps in embryonic form, Arden's command of sprung rhythm, his typically energetic syntax and vocabulary, as well as a sense of his subjects' social reality and a glimmer of ironic humour. Other poems he published in *The Jay* included an account of the Junior Training Corps's rainy 'field day' in June 1947, with some rather banal imitations of Wilfred Owen mixed with some vigorous description; a short, almost Tenysonian reflection on Robin Hood's Bay; and a would-be humorous sonnet. He also published other pieces in prose: a lively depiction of a storm, for instance, and a description written in mock seventeenth century English of the school itself.

His intellectual fare varied between his favourite reading – Malory, the traditional ballads, Shakespeare – and the films shown in school, such as *Lady Hamilton*, *A Yank at Oxford* and *The Prisoner of Zenda*. Sometimes visiting theatre companies appeared, such as the Adelphi Players, noted for their 'commitment to theatre as a means of social progress and human enlightenment',[23] who presented Ibsen's *An Enemy of the People* in 1946. Perhaps these helped to inspire Arden to try writing plays himself. His early efforts, he said, tended to be unfinished: he used to 'fill up a couple of exercise books, then it would get left'. 'The Middle Ages had a fascination for me in those days', he remembered. 'I was always writing plays about the Crusades and things'.[24] Of those plays from his teens which we know about, one in mock-Elizabethan verse was on the Gunpowder Plot, and another described the end of a group of villainous Nazis somewhat in the style of T.S.Eliot.

Dramatically, though, the high point of his school career came in his final year when he acted the part of Hamlet in his House play. His House Tutor, Paul Day, decided to produce a Shakespeare play, which he discussed with the young Arden. Their first choice, *Richard III*, was ruled out on grounds of cost, and *Hamlet* (in more or less modern dress) was chosen. Arden says he was surprised to be cast as Hamlet, but he attacked the part with vigour and imagination, and created a performance which made a strong impression. Two reviews of it survive in school publications. In *The Sedberghian*, we are told that

> Hart House aimed high in their choice of play, but fortunately knew just
> where to limit their aspirations. They were content with making it a really
> enjoyable and exciting performance without delving into the depths of
> psychological analysis – an excellent decision, in view of the pitfalls
> which await overambitious amateur, and especially schoolboy,
> productions … If the reflective Hamlet tended to disappear amid the
> bustle he was no great loss … Arden took the part with great energy and
> made light of the countless difficulties. He displayed at times a flair for
> comedy which destroyed any dignity which the Prince might have
> possessed, but his performance was none the less impressive.

Here we have in little some of Arden's later theatrical trademarks: speed of performance at the expense of over-subtle psychology, energy and a flair for comedy. *The Jay* also noted the production's 'emphasis on swiftness and melodrama' which resulted in the play 'grip(ping) its audience from start to finish and fulfil(ling) the first function of the theatre by providing enjoyment'. This reviewer stated that 'Arden knew exactly what kind of man he wanted to portray, and he portrayed him with excellent dash and appropriate movement.'

Evidence of the deep impression the production made on its audience came decades later: in the 1970s, Arden had occasion to write to a contemporary from Sedbergh, Robert Rhodes James, by then a historian of some note and a Conservative M.P., about British policy in the six counties of northern Ireland. James mentioned in his reply how he clearly remembered Arden as Hamlet. Arden's parents, who also saw the production, were delighted by it, though they also worried about its effect on his academic work. The play indeed became a high point for all the pupils during that term, and another writer in *The Jay* noted that

> The production of 'Hamlet' absorbed most of our spare time until half-
> term, but, in the general opinion, it was worth it, if only for the
> Gargantuan feast which Mrs Day afterwards provided for the cast.

At the end of the academic year, however, Mr Day and his wife returned to New Zealand.

So, a multiple prize-winner, a school prefect who performed Hamlet memorably, and a promising writer with his eye fixed on a career in architecture, Arden should have left Sedbergh in Caesar-like triumph. In fact, the final episode of his school career was not so happy. As noted, he was the editor of his house magazine, *The Jay*, for which boys paid a small subscription. Arden was in charge of this money, which was kept in a special cash box. One morning, he left the cash box with perhaps twenty pounds in it in his study room. When he returned, it was gone.

Mr Newell, the teacher with whom Arden had clashed over Greek lessons years earlier in his school career, seized on this to accuse Arden of embezzlement. He threatened to bring Arden's parents to the school and somehow denounce him. Arden, sensitive at any time, was in despair, terrified. He even seriously considered suicide. It was only when his housemaster – and the headmaster – agreed that Newell had gone too far, that there was in fact no evidence of Arden's guilt, that the matter was allowed to fizzle out, and Arden was able to put it behind him.

But not entirely. Decades later, when he was in hospital in 1996 following a heart attack, his mind muzzy with anaesthetic or illness or perhaps just overwrought by his condition, Arden dreamed, or re-lived, half conscious, half asleep, the episode of the stolen cash box – an experience he was to dramatise in a particularly memorable radio play, *Woe, Alas, The Fatal Cash Box.*

Two : Soldier, Student, Architect and . .

Within two weeks of leaving school, John Arden was conscripted into the British Army. For the first time in her history, by the National Service Act of 1948, Britain was to maintain a conscripted standing army in peacetime, and all young men were required to do eighteen months full time service, and four years part-time in the reserves.

National Service became a quintessential fact of postwar Britain's social reality, and was only phased out at the end of the 1950s. It was part of the drabness and austerity usually associated with those years, along with food rationing, cities bombed and derelict, and heavy industry clanking along with Victorian machinery. Even the Empire was crumbling: as India followed Ireland to freedom and nationhood, Britain's international standing seemed inexorably to be slithering away from Great Power status. What was her position *vis-a-vis* the Iron Curtain across which the Soviet Union faced the United States with H Bombs for weapons and 'small wars' – like the Korean War – for tactics? She had to try very hard to keep up. And on 18 September 1949 it seemed that the realisation of British's relegation was virtually complete when the Chancellor of the Exchequer, Sir Stafford Cripps, devalued the pound from an exchange rate of $4-03 to one of a mere $2-80. This may have laid the foundations for the economic boom in the 1950s, but at the time it seemed piercingly to illustrate Britain's reduced role in world affairs. It was a paradox. If Britain was so dull, insignificant, played out, why did she need a conscripted standing army?

Arden described his first twenty-four hours as a soldier in a letter to his old school magazine, *The Sedberghian*, which he entitled 'Into Khaki! or *A Grand Career for a Young Man*' (echoes of *Ars Longa, Vita Brevis* again):

> 'Report for immediate call-up … armed forces of the Crown … Park Hall Camp, Oswestry … between 12 noon and 4 pm …', the half-seen sentences of that long-dreaded buff document conveyed one fact to my fearful mind – in twenty-four hours I would be a soldier, in the soulless grip of military authority for many months to come.
> The train to Oswestry (for those who, as was the case with me, have never heard of the place, Oswestry is the primary training depot of the Royal Artillery, and situated sadly and alone in Shropshire) was crowded with dispirited but forcedly cheerful youths, whose con-versation (except for certain compensations for weak vocabulary) resembled that attendant upon the commencement of a House Run. Rain was falling as we arrived, but it did not dampen the spirits of the heavy Sergeants and Bombardiers ('not Corporal, you ****** – this isn't the Infantry') who superintended the em- and de-bussing at the station and camp entrances respectively.

A huge hall was laid out for our arrival with tables where cutlery and mugs were drawn, documents distributed, and suitcases deposited ('All right, lad, you'll get it back!'). A technical hitch occurred here, for the army papers of many of us had not turned up, and we stood around for half an hour, rather pleased at causing trouble for this so efficient seeming machine. A delightfully P. G. Wodehouse Captain apologised continually, telling us it wasn't the depôt's fault, you know, it was those chappies at the Ministry of Labour or somewhere who were actually to blame.

After this little difficulty was put to rights, and a frugal meal consumed by the 'new intake', as we were officially described, we went to draw kit and clothing. The spectacle of several hundred members of an age-group, clad in very diverse garb, entering one end of a big shed in single file, and re-appearing at the other end in uniform, shapeless, khaki, and standardised, was too suggestive of some outsize sausage machine to be emotionally satisfying.

The introduction to our Squad Bombardier proved a pleasant surprise, for, although he had served numerous years in the Army, he still seemed to retail some few small drops of the milk of human kindness. He showed us to our beds in a draughty hut, where the socially-important problem, 'pyjamas or no pyjamas,' presented itself to those who possessed such delectable but unsoldierly night-wear, bade us a personal 'good night', and re-appeared (apparently only a few minutes later), hammering a bedstead with a stick and roaring that it was already 0600hrs, and time to 'Wakey-wakey, and get your feet on the floor!'

The cheeriness evident in this account, written during the first two weeks of basic training, was not to last. Arden the recruit, perhaps still exhausted from the combined effects of playing Hamlet, taking a scholarship examination for Cambridge and being accused of thieving money from the fatal cash box, was passed fit only for 'lines-of-communication' service, not service on the front line. Consequently, he was recommended for a desk job and did not receive the com-mission his mother had hoped for. He was put into a 'holding troop' in Oswestry, which felt like being little better than a slave, and he spent uncounted hours on jobs such as cleaning obscene graffiti from latrine walls. 'I never at any other time felt quite so forgotten, quite so useless, quite so cut off from all normal human inter-course',[25] he recorded later. It can be neither excuse nor consolation that this feeling was shared by so many conscripts of the time. Karl Miller reports that 'the initial humiliations appeared to be contrived to break you and toughen you simultaneously. The result was that the more impressionable members of each intake, sitting in their "spiders" or huts, began to feel like displaced persons, subject to unbearable sanctions and controls, miserable and desperate'.[26] Miller goes on to speculate about how many may have committed suicide. There is no evidence that Arden was anything like as desperate as that, but he did remark that the conscript army in which he served seemed an 'insane institution', and everyone in it 'either daft or crooked or pissed off'.[27]

Finally he was transferred to the Intelligence Corps at Uckfield in Sussex. Towards the end of his training here, he went on a route march with his unit to Pevensey Beach in hot sunshine and was knocked out by sunstroke. He fainted on parade, and was hospitalised for three days. While thus incapacitated, he missed the final elements of the training, and consequently his army career took another turn and he was posted to Edinburgh Castle, where he remained until he was demobbed in the summer of 1950. He obviously did well enough here, since he was promoted to Lance Corporal after some months. And clerking for the Army in Edinburgh Castle provided a comparatively easy – if somewhat tedious – life: it only involved one hour per week drill with a Sergeant-Major who knew his men were never likely to be 'real' soldiers, and therefore never made unrealistic demands on them. Once a week he had to spend the night in a bunk in the key room, next to the cleaners' cupboard, where every morning at about 5 o'clock the cleaning women would arrive. Their animated conversations, carried on while they drank their morning cup of tea, was loud, convivial and good tempered, until suddenly truncated when it was time for the women to gather up their mops and buckets and make off to their respective places of work. Privately, remembering Chaucer, he thought of this as 'the Parliament of Fowls'! Arden was also somewhat shocked by his older colleagues from some of the Scottish regiments, 'veterans', who talked knowingly of pillage and even rape in the ravaged Germany of 1945. They told disturbing stories, too, of small colonial wars.

Nevertheless, on Saturdays the office staff were permitted to come to work in 'civvies', because in the afternoon they were free to enjoy themselves. For Arden, this meant indulging in the theatres, concerts, cinemas and public libraries of Scotland's capital city. At the 'art' cinemas he saw classic as well as foreign films. The main Edinburgh theatre, the Lyceum, provided a comparatively progressive repertoire, with plays by dramatists such as Christopher Fry and T.S.Eliot; the Lyceum was also the Edinburgh home of the Wilson Barrett Company, with its solid repertoire of strong but conventional dramas. Other theatres presented contemporary Scottish plays, and Arden also caught a production of Eugene O'Neill's *Mourning Becomes Electra*. And at the Assembly Rooms at the two Edinburgh Festivals held while he was in post at the Castle he saw, in 1949, Tyrone Guthrie's version of David Lindsay's *Ane Satire of the Thrie Estaitis*, and the following year George Devine's production of *Bartholomew Fair* by Ben Jonson, about which he was later to write. These both hugely impressed him, partly because of the use of the open stage: he was at the time trying to write a play about Guy Fawkes, and wondered how he could use what he learned from these productions in his work.

Meanwhile, the Korean War broke out, and the terms of national service altered: young men were now required to complete two full years in the armed forces. One man stationed with Arden at Edinburgh Castle, when threatened with the possibility that he might now have to go to Korea, tried to hang himself in the bathroom of the castle. Because he had a place at King's College, Cambridge, Arden should have been exempt from the new extension of service. But the expected notification of demobilisation failed to arrive. With Korea looming, Arden's father contacted Frank Collindridge, the M.P. for Barnsley, who was able to track down the paperwork – mislaid by an incompetent bureaucrat – and Arden was discharged.

Arden's attitude to soldiering and war seems to have been consistent for the rest of his life, though it caused some drama critics problems which did not help in the reception of his plays. In a sentence, Arden was anti-war but not anti-soldier. And he was always fascinated by the highly theatrical rituals of military life. We can detect the inherent drama in Wes Magee's observation that the sergeant-major's 'stream of invective and vituperative language showed an almost poetic quality', as well as in Michael Holroyd's objection: 'I could see no reason for calling a tree a "bushy top object" in order to achieve what was termed simplicity'.[28] Arden himself recorded the ritual for receiving pay:

> One pace forward, two-three, salute, two-three, take-pay-and-paybook-
> in-right-hand: open-left-top-pocket-with-left-hand, say 'Pay and
> Paybook Correct, SIR!', place-pay-and-paybook-in-left-top-pocket, two-
> three, salute, two-three, about turn, left right left right left right LEFT ... [29]

The works of Arden contain a small battalion of soldiers, none of them wholly bad, and all of them conceived with a sympathy and understanding presumably derived from this two year experience of living in khaki. There is the fanatical Serjeant Musgrave, and the charismatic hero of *Soldier, Soldier*; then there are the automata-like Territorials in *Ars Longa, Vita Brevis*, the merry, competent, capable, home-returning Luke in *The Royal Pardon*, the Roman soldiers in *Whose Is the Kingdom?* ('Mars Mars rules the wars') and of course James Connolly himself, who 'joins the army and is sent to Ireland', there to discover his destiny, and its relation – and the Army's relation – to the intractable question of colonialism.

Arden went up to King's College, Cambridge University, in the autumn of 1950. Though he obtained his exhibition in English Literature, his intention had always been to read architecture: he and his teachers at Sedbergh had felt, probably correctly, that English maximized his chance of a scholarship or exhibition. His progress through his three years as an undergraduate in Cambridge to obtain his B.A. seemed to be tranquil enough. Perhaps its high point came when he submitted designs for an Italian Garden for the prestigious Tite Prize, for which he was shortlisted, but he did not win the prize.

He would have liked to enter the University's sometimes self-regarding but always high-powered theatre world. In his first term he auditioned for the Amateur Dramatic Club (A.D.C.), the central University student theatre. He was – along with all the other aspirants – given two contrasting speeches to prepare, and then deliver, which he did. The undergraduates who were running the club that year were Peter Hall and John Barton, already garnering all the power they could in the world of the theatre. Unfortunately for Arden, they rejected him, so that his University dramatic career was effectively stopped before it had started. However, Arden was able to see plenty of interesting drama, often in original or idiosyncratic productions, at the A.D.C. and elsewhere in Cambridge: for instance, Hall's highly-charged production of *Saint's Day* by John Whiting was a powerful experience, vividly remembered.

He also continued writing while at Cambridge, including his first 'soldier' play, about military life in Edinburgh. This he entered into a competition sponsored by the A.D.C., and although it failed to gain the first prize, it was commended. He was also encouraged by a complimentary reference made to it in *Varsity*, the University newspaper. Writing occupied much of his time away from academic study: he belonged to his college's literary society, in which the students read and discussed their own poetry and plays, and to a similar University-wide society which operated out of Trinity College, and these seem to have given him support as well as ideas.

Probably the most significant discovery for Arden during his years at Cambridge was *The White Goddess* by Robert Graves. Published in 1948, Arden described this book as 'intricate, enormous and (to me at that time) extremely disorientating'.[30] Interestingly, Graves's work was also picked up at almost the same time and with similar eager astonishment by Ted Hughes, who was brought up only a few miles from Arden's Barnsley. In 2009 Arden said he still believed *The White Goddess* was 'absolutely basic for western culture'.

The central argument of *The White Goddess* concerns the cultural subjugation of the primordial 'white goddess' to the fierce power lust of the forces of aggressive patriarchy. In prehistoric times, Graves attempts to demonstrate, Europe and the Middle East were the seat of matriarchal cultures, which worshipped a supreme goddess. In this culture, the male's significance was merely as her consort, or son, or victim. But at the dawn of recorded history, this system was in the process of being overthrown, and the male consort was being elevated culturally to a position of supremacy. From here, male domination was able to modify and reconstruct the ancient myths so as to deny that the goddess had ever held the supreme place which Graves asserts was once hers. The argument then extends to the realm of poetry: Graves believed that the goddess, whose symbol is the moon, is the true inspiration for poetry. The secret world which poetry opens up was sometimes, in some places, and over varying stretches of time, protected and enhanced by schools of poets, sort of secret societies, which guarded their own mysteries. Even today, Graves suggests, poets intuitively reassert the goddess in often-unacknowledged (because unsuspected) ways. Finally, and perhaps most significantly, according to Graves, this matriarchal culture, which is embodied in poetry, offers better, more fluid, more humanly rewarding life possibilities than the aggressively rigid patriarchal society in which we actually live.

The White Goddess is, according to its latest editor, Grevel Lindop, 'a fascinating labyrinth of poetry, myth and erudition', which makes 'a plea for a return to imaginative, mythopoeic or poetic forms of thought'. Such a plea may still find a willing response in an imaginative mind, but there are other aspects of Graves's thought in this book which perhaps seem less attractive. There is a sense, for instance, that the true poet must be male, and that he accesses the White Goddess through the passionate sexual possession of a particular woman in the here and now. This passion drives the poet towards spontaneity, a poetry of feeling perhaps, at the expense of more formal qualities or a poetry of the intellect. But in the stuffy Cambridge of the early 1950s, this problematic strand was largely overlooked, or perhaps was accepted unthinkingly, and when Graves gave a series of lectures in Cambridge in 1954, later published as *The Crowning Privilege*, they were extremely popular.

Graves also propounds an English poetic tradition far other than that taught by the Cambridge English school, as embodied in the dominant liberal humanist tradition of F.R.Leavis: 'The only two English poets', Graves wrote, 'who had the necessary learning, poetic talent, humanity, dignity and independence of mind to be Chief Poets were John Skelton and Ben Jonson.' Furthermore, Graves continues, 'the only poet, as far as I know, who ever tried to institute bardism in England was William Blake'.[31] The effects of all this on Arden – and on Hughes, who gave up English Literature as a study at Cambridge in favour of Anthropology in consequence of it – were far-reaching, and affected virtually everything that he wrote thereafter, even if in obscure or almost invisible ways. One obvious sign of the long-lasting influence of Graves's work (among other influences, of course, and other purposes) was Arden's fiercely powerful radio play, *Garland for a Hoar Head*, an exploration of the life and ideas of John Skelton. More certainly, it was under the influence of *The White Goddess* that Arden began, as an undergraduate, to write a play on Arthurian themes, which he wrestled with for another two decades until it emerged as *The Island of the Mighty*, co-authored with Margaretta D'Arcy.

For an aspiring writer, Graves's book is studded with provocative possibilities. Thus, when he discusses the ancient Welsh bard, Gwion, whom he calls 'no irresponsible rhapsodist, but a true poet', he notes that his verse hides 'an ancient religious mystery ... under the cloak of buffoonery'.[32] The conjunction was to be significant in Arden's work, and is more clearly set out in another critical approach subversive of that usually associated with liberal humanism. This was S.L.Bethell's

Shakespeare and the Popular Dramatic Tradition. Bethell takes Sir Philip Sidney's 'What child is there that, coming to a play, and seeing *Thebes* written in great letters upon an old door, doth believe that it is *Thebes*?' and Samuel Johnson's reply, 'The truth is, that the spectators are always in their senses, and know, from the first act to the last, that the stage is only a stage, that the players are only players' as his starting point.[33] He then develops the theory that theatre audiences, especially popular theatre audiences, have a dual awareness of the play-world and the real world at all times, and that they are able to respond to whatever is put before them on the stage on more than one plane of attention spontaneously and unconsciously at the same time. He suggest that a sequence in a Harold Lloyd movie, for instance, is appreciated on at least three levels simultaneously: we admire Lloyd as an equilibrist; we see the scene as farce; and we link the action to the character's romance in the story. This theory was to be tested to the limit in Arden's own later plays.

Arden enjoyed life in Cambridge, yet the experience of being a student was not one which he chose to explore imaginatively in his later writing, unlike his experience as a conscripted soldier. There are virtually no memorable students in his later work, though there are a few scenes early in the novel *Jack Juggler and the Emperor's Whore* which have something to say about student life. Despite this, his next move was back to Edinburgh as a postgraduate student, to complete his training as an architect at the Edinburgh College of Art.

He arrived at the Art College in the autumn of 1953, but found the going hard, partly because the Scottish system of training was not exactly the same as that pursued in Cambridge, but partly also because of a somewhat abrasive teacher who was responsible for teaching the technical side of the subject, which in any case was not Arden's *forté*. Consequently, he took time to settle into this course, and especially in the first year his work was probably marred to some degree by his real fear of failure. What he did was not particularly well received by his teachers and he became somewhat depressed. However, his final design was a bold idea to put a theatre on Edinburgh's famous Calton Hill. Partly using his recollections of the Festival productions he had seen at the Assembly Rooms, he created a large, open stage theatre, which even contrived to incorporate the famous landmark Calton Hill porticoes in its frontage. The boldness of the conception and the finesse with which it was carried out clearly impressed the examiners – though they doubted whether planning permission would be granted for the work – and Arden passed the course to qualify as an architect.

Perhaps Arden's unhappiness in this second stint in Edinburgh was compounded by his unsuccessful love affair with 'a large blonde beautiful' Scottish woman. There is not much detail available on this romance, but Arden tells us that he wrote a number of poems for her, and that she was not displeased with them. He showed her some of his other writing, too, about which she was less complimentary:

'Oh dear ... you really mean all this, don't you?' he reports her as saying. However, the affair proceeded until Arden asked her to marry him, when she rejected his offer. Why? 'Because you are a poet,' she said, simply enough. The fact that much of his recent verse had been, as it were, in her honour apparently made no difference, and when he asked her if she expected him to become a staid business type, with a steady income and a respectable job, she told him, perhaps a little ruefully, that that was indeed what fate held in store for him. The affair cooled, and the young woman finally became engaged to an older man, who seemed to the young Arden 'sinister', but whose charm was undeniable.[34]

Meanwhile, and perhaps more significantly for his future, Arden became more involved in student theatre here than he had at Cambridge. The Art College had its own theatre club, and in his first year, he auditioned and was cast as Old Capulet in *Romeo and Juliet*, a more substantial and challenging part than is often realized. The production was directed by the College's painting teacher, Alan Clarke, and with imaginative costumes and decor, designed by students for whom it was a course assignment, the production, and Arden's performance in it, were very successful.

The next year, 1955, the group presented *All Fall Down* by John Arden, his first performed play. This he had begun to write while still at Cambridge and he was inspired to finish it for this performance in Edinburgh. It was a somewhat stylised Romantic Victorian comedy 'very much in the style of John Whiting's *A Penny for a Song*,' though 'there was no connection between the two - it was just the *zeitgeist*'.[35] The action was set around the building of a railway, and was populated by architects and railway engineers. The central relationship concerned a somewhat gauche navvy and an unscrupulous though wellborn young lady. The production was another clear success. Arden himself acted in it, and the railway navvy was played by Donald Douglas, later a prominent Scottish actor on television and film, as well as at the Glasgow Citizens Theatre. The production helped to remove at least some of the disappointment caused by Arden's failure in the Cambridge theatre world, and encouraged him to write more.

But first he had to find work, and this he managed to do with the firm of Ronald Ward and Partners, architects, in Belgravia. Later he tended to downgrade the firm's importance – 'a large private office which was putting up a lot of these nasty office blocks that one sees: not a very ethical office', he said. But this is a misapprehension, and Arden undersells himself. Ward and Partners are, and were, a prestigious firm. They may have built some 'nasty office blocks', but their creations also included the Millbank Tower, the Nestlé Tower in Croydon and the Marine Engineers Memorial Building. They had also recently completed the commercial premises at 219 Oxford Street with its unique Festival of Britain friezes. Admittedly it was unfortunate for Arden that the partners largely kept the design work for themselves, while the other staff had to concentrate on more humdrum development work. And even where this was concerned, outside visits tended to be carried out by the more senior staff. There was therefore minimal scope for Arden, who nevertheless completed his full qualification as an architect after one year there. He also acknowledged that it was 'a pleasant place to work' and that he 'liked the people'. Soon the whole experience was feeding into his writing, and he clearly enjoyed lampooning the office – or, at least, architects' offices in general – in at least two of his plays, *The Waters of Babylon* and *Wet Fish*.

The undemanding nature of the work was useful in that it did leave time for him to continue writing, and now he entered a script called *The Life of Man* for the north region of the BBC's New Play competition. The idea for this play had originated with a fellow-student in Edinburgh, Margaret Proudfoot, who had suggested transferring the legend of Dionysus from Homer's Greece to a more recent period. But Arden did not write the play until after he left Edinburgh. And then, one morning in early 1956, he received a telephone call to tell him he had won the competition, and the play would be broadcast in the spring.

He was allowed a day off from the office to go to Manchester to collect his prize (though he had to make up the time at the next weekend). Just before the prize-giving ceremony and the celebratory dinner, Arden was taken confidentially aside and informed that parts of the play, though no doubt dramatically telling, could not be broadcast as written – there were obscenities which would have to be rectified. There was a scene, for instance, between a sailor and a prostitute in Liverpool, in which the dialogue was distinctly vulgar, and this would have to be re-written. Also … Annoyed though he was, Arden immediately volunteered to do the rewrites himself to prevent 'them' doing them; but he could not help feeling that the prize had been somehow downgraded.

The play itself was a brilliant debut. As noted above, it was a reworking of the myth of Dionysus. Set in the Victorian period, it retells the experiences of the crazed sailor, Bones, on a packet ship, perhaps too symbolically named *The Life of Man*. During the voyage out of Liverpool, the ship's Captain Anthract, a sort of precursor to Black Jack Musgrave, victimizes a wretched Welsh member of his crew, a former shepherd, who is in fact the Dionysus figure. But as in the myth, the pirates do not recognise this manifest god, and they hang him from the yardarm. Inadvertently, Anthract then manages to set the ship on fire: only Bones has lived to tell the tale. The main action – Anthract's feud with the poor Welsh shepherd – is thus 'distanced' by being told by Bones to his female auditor. Such a summary of course does little justice to the living excitement of the piece as it unfolds (despite Arden's later comment that 'it had a little too much of Moby Dick in it'.[36]) Francis Dillon, listening to a repeat broadcast fifteen years later, wrote:

> The crimp gang, the god, devil, or saint shanghaied aboard a cruel coffin-
> ship, tarts, witches, mermaids, a roaring Bible-hard captain, a bunch of

fables and parables – perhaps one found more than had been written in – were all woven into an exhilarating radio play, radio of a quality we get very rarely these days. Where the story went by dialogue, the talk was taut and authentic; where it broke into verse, it flung itself into the magic winds. The elements of black superstition, a ship sailing on a Friday, whistling on deck and so on were only an evocative frame: the power came from the fine writing.[37]

John Russell Taylor identified several features of the piece which were to become familiar in Arden's later dramatic work, including 'the unpredictable alternation of racy, idiomatic prose and quite highly wrought formal verse, the extensive use of traditional song and ballad, and in the Welsh sailor Jones's evocation of his roaming shepherd life an interest in the bold, free, nomadic life of the "sturdy beggar"'.[38]

The play was directed by Vivian Daniels, later better known for his television work. Arden was not present during either the rehearsals or the recording. When it was broadcast on 16 April 1956, he felt that the casting had been somewhat unsatisfactory, one actor in particular not playing his part as Arden had wanted, and also that the sound effects were sometimes too loud, at which points they obscured the dialogue. The chief lesson learned from this experience was that he needed to be present himself when a radio play was being recorded. It was the same lesson which had to be learned later, and in harder ways, in both the television studio and the theatre. For a satisfactory performance, Arden discovered, and thereafter passionately believed, it was necessary for the author to be present throughout the process.

For now, however, it was clear that the drama was taking over from architecture as the centre and focus of John Arden's life.

Three : An Irish Girlhood

Margaretta Ruth D'Arcy was born on 14 June 1934. Her earliest days were blighted with pyloric-stenosis, a blockage of the gastro-intestinal tract, which is marked by violent vomiting, dehydration and other symptoms. She seemed to be rejecting her mother's milk, and in the most frenzied manner. An operation to clear the passage was performed on the infant, with apparently total success.

The mother, whom she might have been thought to be rejecting in this earliest act of her infancy, was the child of Russian Jewish émigrés, Barnet and Millie Billig. Born perhaps a year or two before 1870, this couple, D'Arcy's maternal grandparents, had grown up in Odessa on the Black Sea until, sometime around 1890, they had left for Austria; that is to say, Millie had left with her three sisters. Barnet seems to have stayed behind, or perhaps been detained for army service. The story is less than wholly clear, and one may suspect that the departure of these Jewish people was likely to be the consequence at one or two removes of the raging pogroms in Russia in the later 1880s. Whatever the reason, not long after she had gone, Barnet assumed Millie's surname (Billig) and smuggled himself across the border to join her. They tried to settle in Austria, but for some reason – again, probably anti-Semitism – were unsuccessful. So they continued on to Britain, where they arrived in 1898 and found a home in Hanbury Street, off Brick Lane in the East End of London. They were part of a wave of immigration: in 1881, the Russian population in England and Wales numbered just over three thousand; by 1901, that number had risen to 61,789.[39]

Barnet and Millie Billig spoke not a word of English, and seem to have had no craft or trade either. They scraped a living making and selling confectionery and Barnet's hand-rolled cigarettes and cigars from a handcart. He was a serious, bookish sort of man, but with a strong personality which his children did not question. Throughout their childhoods, after school and after tea, they had to spend their evenings not playing out in the street like other children, but studying in the front room of their house, which consequently reminded visitors of a library. Barnet Billig was a faithful attender at the synagogue, and taught other Jewish people Hebrew. Millie, his wife, did the cooking and cleaning. In later years, she became somewhat deaf and used an ear trumpet; she also wore a brown wig. She lived into her nineties, and only died in 1963.

Of their children, Esther, the eldest, was unable to take up a scholarship she won because of the family finances, though she did become a nurse, and later a governess. Levi, the eldest son, was considered academically brilliant. He obtained a scholarship to Cambridge University where he read Arabic and Hebrew, and later taught at the Hebrew University in Tel Aviv. There, he worked for an independent socialist state in Palestine, which would see equality between Jews and Arabs, but sometime in the mid-1930s he was shot by an extremist. His dream was never realized.

The next two children, Hannah and David, and Rebecca, the youngest Billig child, all qualified as doctors. Hannah was to gain considerable fame later as 'The Angel of Cable Street'. Born in 1901, she gained a scholarship from Myrdle Street Elementary School to London University to read medicine. She trained at the Royal Free Hospital and qualified in 1925. Though her parents had by now moved out to Burdett Street in Tower Hamlets, Hannah took a job at the Jewish Maternity Hospital in Whitechapel, and two years later in 1927 was able to set up her own practice in Watney Street, just off Cable Street. In 1935, she moved her surgery to 198 Cable Street, where a blue plaque still commemorates her work. She was renowned for tending anybody who was sick, whether they could pay her or not, and was a familiar sight cycling to patients' houses with her black doctor's bag slung on the handlebars, though she later drove a Morris Cowley car. She also helped to teach the local children to read and write.

In the Second World War, Hannah Billig was made medical officer for Wapping Air Raid Shelters. On 13 March 1941, she was helping the victims of German bombing when she was herself blown out of the shelter. Picking herself up, bandaging her own painful ankle, she continued for hours working for the injured. Only after she had helped the last patient did she bother to look at her own ankle, which she then discovered was badly broken. She was awarded the George Cross for her bravery. Soon after this she joined the Army Medical Corps and was posted to Calcutta, where she not only tended the wounded soldiers from the grizzly Burma Campaign, but also flung herself into famine relief work, for which she was awarded an M.B.E. After the war, she returned to Cable Street, and carried on where she had left off. She welcomed the introduction of the National Health Service in 1948, and when she retired in 1964, she emigrated to Israel. But it was not long before she was working as a doctor here, too, treating Israelis and Palestinians without distinction until she was a very old woman. She died in 1987.

Miriam, Hannah's younger sister and D'Arcy's mother, did not – at least initially – go into the medical profession. Born in 1907, she was awarded a scholarship to the London School of Economics, which she attended in the late 1920s. Though during Margaretta's adolescence and in her early adulthood, she would from time to time suffer from her mother's unexpected and apparently irrational 'blitzes' (as she called her outbursts), she also came to recognise her mother's courage and determination, both in her attempts to free herself from the domination of her orthodox Jewish upbringing, and for her belief in 'Mother Nature'. 'We were brought up with no fear of thunderstorms, lightning, rain, or swimming out of our depth', Margaretta records. Miriam also had useful practical skills: 'We had no running water or electricity, my mother knew how to clean the well, how to stop the oil-lamp smoking, how to get the fire burning with wet sticks we had gathered: she knitted our swimming-togs, she would make a summer dress for each of us all in one night'.[40] Miriam Billig (or D'Arcy) was a free spirit, unconventional, and uncowed by the demands of respectability. She was also, again according to D'Arcy, 'naïve, romantic, idealistic, enthusiastic and very impressionable'.[41] Her naïve romanticism perhaps came out in the fact that she seemed always to be 'in love' with some man or other. Her idealism and enthusiasm could be seen in her determination to pursue her own career in spite of criticism from even the most progressive Irish women in the 1930s and 1940s. And when she met an Irish former freedom fighter in London, she was very impressionable, certainly enough to be bowled over by him: they married in June 1929, in a Catholic church in Soho. Their first child was born less than nine months later.

The Irish former freedom fighter was Joseph Noel D'Arcy. This surname is surprisingly common in Ireland: it may derive – ironically perhaps, in this case – from a twelfth century Anglo-Norman invader of Ireland. The invasion of 1169 was the very first attempt by the English (actually, the Normans, who had conquered England) to subdue their western near-neighbour. But there is a Gaelic name, O'Dorchaidhe, which could have evolved into D'Arcy over centuries. Or it could originally have been the name of a French Huguenot, fleeing persecution in France.

Joseph D'Arcy was born in Dublin in 1898, and got his first job in the British Civil Service there. He was still only eighteen when the Easter Rising took place against his employers, and he joined the Dublin Brigade of the IRA to fight for Ireland's freedom. Apparently he rarely spoke to his children of his own deeds in this struggle, but he was involved in the well-documented action at the Custom House, a significant turning point in the war. The Irish volunteers in the building were able to make mayhem for a while until finally they were surrounded by British soldiers. They had to escape, and as Joseph D'Arcy reached the street he found himself face-to-face with an armoured car, with a soldier on top aiming his machine gun straight at him. With a piece of admirable quick-thinking, he adopted the pose of the happy-go-lucky Irish rogue, who shrugged his shoulders cheerily at the British invader, gave him a wave, and walked past unharmed. Despite his insouciance, he was later imprisoned in Mountjoy Gaol, though it is not clear how or exactly why he had been arrested, and his incarceration lasted for a compar-atively short period. Nevertheless, only when the Treaty with Britain was signed did Joseph D'Arcy return to a desk in the Department of Agriculture in the now-Irish Free State Civil Service. At the same time he attended evening classes and was diligent enough – and intelligent enough – to obtain his B.A. After 1923, he was posted to London, where he serviced the Free State's agricultural interests in England, and while in London he was also able to study at the London School of Economics. He was to play a significant part later in ending the Trade War with Britain in 1938, and smoothing the path for Irish agricultural products to be imported into the United Kingdom.

Joseph D'Arcy, c.1945.

Though a Civil Servant all his working life, he was also, according to his daughter, an 'archetypical loquacious Dubliner, living convivially beyond his means'.[42] Catholic in the loosest way – he didn't attend mass, there were no holy pictures on the walls of his home – he was, like so many other men, allowed to run up far too much debt 'on the slate' of his favourite public house, which was only repaid at his death through the use of his Civil Service annuity. He loved Dickens, Joyce and Wordsworth, 'gracious living' and Sunday picnics, and in the 1930s he struggled to fulfil an obviously creative mind. After his death, his daughter found the script of a radio documentary which had been broadcast on RTE in 1937, as well as plans for at least two other radio documentaries, and also a few more or less academic papers, which either had been delivered or had been intended to be delivered, on various aspects of Irish life and history.

The Irish Free State of the 1930s did not provide easy solutions for creatively-minded or artistically-inclined people. There was a level of idealism remaining from the years of the struggle for independence, but it had a kind of untouchable Puritanism about it. Independent or innovative thought or action was almost impossible because the Catholic Church wielded such enormous power socially and intellectually. Censorship was pervasive and unremitting. The result was a defensive narrow-mindedness in even the most intelligent of Irishmen, often to the point of bigotry. Moreover, the society was weighted down by continuing very widespread poverty. The poor stayed poor, and sometimes it seemed that the church liked to

29

keep them there in order that the rich could exercise their charity without hindrance.

The monkey on Ireland's shoulder was the division of the country. In January 1922, at the conclusion of the war for Irish independence, Dáil Eireann, the Irish Parliament, had voted narrowly, by 64 votes to 57, to accept Britain's offer of a 26 county free state, with the residue of six north eastern counties remaining in the United Kingdom. A large, militant, idealistic section of the population across all thirty-two counties refused to accept the finality of this vote. They believed that only a thirty-two county free Ireland was worth having; anything less was a betrayal of centuries of struggle. A terrible bloody civil war followed, between those who accepted the Treaty with Britain and those who rejected it; and even when peace was restored, Ireland's wound of Partition continued to fester. The IRA, which did not accept the division of the country, and its political wing, Sinn Féin, under Eamonn de Valera, refused to take part initially in constitutional politics, preferring to continue the armed struggle to free the whole of the country. But in 1926 de Valera broke away to form the Fianna Fáil party, and adopted the position of a constitutional opposition. While the taoiseach (Prime Minister), W.T. Cosgrave, was establishing a system of military tribunals instead of regular courts to try IRA members, de Valera was preparing for elections. They came in 1932, and Cosgrave, to many people's surprise, was defeated. de Valera's Fianna Fáil won 72 Dáil seats to Cosgrave's 57. de Valera took power, and immediately suspended the military tribunals. He also informed the British Government that the Oath of Allegiance to the King was to be abolished. In February 1933 he won a second election, this time gaining 77 seats to Cosgrave's 48, which though still not enough to form a one-party government gave him a position of dominance in Irish politics which he was not to relinquish for a quarter of a century. As the 'synthesis of republicanism and Catholicism',[43] de Valera's strengths and weaknesses were to be indelibly imprinted on the developing free state.

Roman Catholicism dominated every area of social life, as well as the political scene, and was in every sphere a drag on progress and innovation. It made virtually no original intellectual contribution to the country during this period, yet the power of the priest was ubiquitous and unarguable. A good example is recorded by Margaretta D'Arcy. When her somewhat bohemian family went to Carraroe in Connemara for a summer holiday in the late 1930s, their slightly unconventional – though utterly harmless – behaviour (her mother wore shorts, breast-fed her baby, played tennis on a Sunday) provoked the priest to 'have a word' with their landlady, who obediently immediately asked them to leave.

D'Arcy was the third of four girls – Claire, Judith, Margaretta and Rosemary. She was not born in Ireland, but in Whitechapel, in the east end of London, where her Billig relations were so firmly established. The family was actually living in

Hampstead Garden Suburb at the time, from where the father was able to travel to his work at the Irish Department of External Affairs. But soon he was transferred back to Dublin to the Department of Agriculture, and the family returned to Ireland. Here they were able to rent a largish house in its own grounds in Killiney. Killiney is now a desirable, not to say exclusive, suburb of Dublin on the south east edge of the city beyond Blackrock and Dún Laoghaire. Then it was much more rural, the place where George Bernard Shaw had owned a cottage and which boasted a beach which had been a popular resort for Dubliners for two hundred years. Its main attraction for Joseph D'Arcy perhaps was the informal radical liberal circle, centred on progressive intellectuals like the family friends, Louie Bennett and Helen Chenevix, who lived here.

Margaretta D'Arcy however felt herself to be something of a misfit. She was, she noted ruefully, the third child in the family of four, which made for a special dimension of discord. 'Two's company, but three's a crowd', she thought:

> Number One and Number Two stick together, and isolate Number
> Three. Number Three could adhere to Number Four, but that would
> mean that Number Four would be isolated from One and Two: and
> Three and Four together would only become a second-class One-and-
> Two, the one family thus splitting into a dualism of continued power-
> struggle.[44]

The D'Arcys, c.1940: Margaretta, Rosemary, Judith, mother, with Claire kneeling behind.

However, the girls did play together, as this theatrical memory suggests:

> When I was a little girl we had a children's book called *101 Things To Do
> For a Rainy Day*. One of the chapters was headed, 'Let's Do A Play'. My
> mother had just made each of us a new summer-green nightdress with
> short puffed sleeves. So if we Did A Play, it would be an opp-ortunity to
> wear our nightdresses during the day. We put together our story in our
> sitting-room, to present to our mother, a story about four princesses –
> but were they who they thought they were? My eldest sister was the

dramatist, of the Artaud school, with a taste for the sinister. My younger
sister, a toddler, walked off in the middle of the piece and sat on mother's
lap, and no harm was done to the drama.[45]

We are not vouchsafed any more about the play, but the incident is suggestive, not just of D'Arcy attraction to the theatrical, but also of her love of 'playing'. Perhaps indeed this was her first experience of what she came to call 'Loose Theatre'.

There was perhaps something of 'Loose Theatre' in her appreciation of her London Jewish family, with whom she stayed at least twice during her childhood. She loved it especially when her grandparents took her to the Jewish synagogue, where she remembered looking down from the women's gallery onto the heads of the men in the congregation below. She remembered her grandfather, Barnet's prayer shawl too, as well as the plums he bought for her and the porridge her grandmother made which tasted so special.

In 1937, Joseph D'Arcy was transferred to London again, and the D'Arcy family moved back to Dublin, to an upstairs flat in Wilton Place, a dogleg-shaped crescent in a residential area south-east of St Stephen's Green and not far from the port and docks. Its main attraction was its proximity to Trinity College, where Miriam now began to train as a doctor. It was a very different kind of place from Killiney, and not surprisingly the downstairs neighbours complained of the noise made by the young girls who were used to the much wider spaces of the country by Dublin Bay. However, the family did not stay long, moving again to join the father in London, though no sooner had they moved than the Munich crisis occurred, and they scuttled back to Dublin in fear of a Nazi invasion. But the scare of war receded, and the family returned to London – only for them to have to retreat again, this time in greater haste even than before and in effect as refugees, when the Germans invaded Poland and the Second World War really began.

The stress for Europeans, and especially for Jewish people, in the period leading up to the war, was of course exacerbated by its advent. For the D'Arcys, this experience of alienation and despair was intense. Who were they? Part republican Irish in a torn and divided country, part Jewish in the very heyday of anti-Semitic extremism and the search for a Jewish homeland. They were potential victims of the horror of the cruellest war man had yet managed, and for them the trauma was increased because their family was split apart. The father was still based in London – his children only saw him two or three times during the whole of the six-year war. To make matters worse for the four girls, the mother also left for England in 1941, where she not only cared for her husband, but also worked as a research scientist on the application of aviation plastics. No doubt leaving the children in neutral Ireland made rational sense; but the effect on the apparently abandoned children may be imagined.

When the family returned (without the father) to Ireland because of the Munich crisis, they had rented a house with a garden in Greenville Road, Blackrock, south east of Dublin. It was while living here that D'Arcy's formal education began, at Avoca Elementary School, a rare interdenominational establishment founded in 1891 by Cyril and Cerise Parker. They were well known Irish educational pioneers, and the school was famous for its reforms: IQ tests, a Parent Teacher Association, even sex education. This latter, however, did not extend to public masturbation, which D'Arcy, proud of discovering this act for herself, proceeded to practise for the benefit of her classmates and her teacher. Nothing was said at the time, but that afternoon after school the young female teacher appeared at the house in Greenville Road and had words with her mother in a voice muffled behind the closed sitting room door. The import was obvious, the situation dire, and D'Arcy did not again attempt to exhibit her masturbatory prowess in public.

She did, however, get her first taste of theatrical performance here when she was cast as the Mouse in a dramatisation of nursery rhymes. Unfortunately, nerves got the better of her. She developed a stammer which prevented her from saying her lines, and so was recast as the (silent) Bo Peep.

In 1939, the family found accommodation in County Wicklow, just south of Dublin – well out of the way should the Nazis invade Ireland. They rented the lodge of the Glendalough Hotel in one of Ireland's most beautiful valleys on the edge of what is now the Wicklow Mountains National Park. The place is most famous for its significant monastic sites. St Patrick reputedly visited the area, and the hermit St Kevin is supposed to have died here in 617 CE at the age of 120. The remains of his cell can still be seen, along with the ruins, now considerably restored, of the early medieval monastery, which was destroyed by fire in 1214. The place was remote enough for the D'Arcy girls not to go to school at all while they lived here, and their mother's unconventional values of freedom and closeness to untamed nature found full expression. The children ate fresh vegetables and drank fresh milk. They played out, unashamed of being naked. They gathered wild food, read books, and lived free from the constrictions and stigmas of fashion or other people's opinions.

They also acquired a nanny. With both the D'Arcy parents pursuing their independent careers, a young Tipperary woman called Kitty Spain was hired to look after them. Kitty was something of a free spirit herself, elusive, self-possessed but also a fine organiser of children's lives. She was gregarious, too, and several years later, whenever the family moved, it was she who first became acquainted with the neighbours. One such, some years later, was Oliver, footman to the Earl of Powerscourt. Oliver lived in the earl's nearby mansion but had nothing to do when his lordship was away. He had ambitions to be an operatic tenor in the mould of the popular John McCormack, and demonstrated to the D'Arcy children how he prepared his voice. He held a glass in one hand and an egg in the other. He cracked the egg and poured its contents into the glass. Then, adding cream and honey, he tossed off the mixture, presumably to the advantage of his throat, for then he sang to them.

Kitty was more modern, more up-to-date, or perhaps just younger than the D'Arcy children's mother. She understood fashion. When she was going out, she dressed in what seemed to the young D'Arcys genuinely exotic finery. It was not in fact exotic, but rather was typical 'best' for a young Irish girl of the period: several layers of underclothes and petticoats beneath a tight skirt, blouse and hat. She made up her face, too, with lipstick and plenty of sweet-smelling powder. And of course she had a young man, Jimmy Timmons, whom she adored from afar, and whose apparent indifference D'Arcy prayed nightly would melt into a reciprocal ardour. It never did.

It was about now that D'Arcy discovered what she calls, tellingly, 'the joyous illusion of theatre'. The nearest small shop was kept by a Mrs Cohen. Once, when Kitty took the children to the beach, D'Arcy saw this lady,

> strolling along in great style, a two-piece bathing suit, high-heeled
> peekaboo sandals a la Betty Grable, bright red lipstick, hair dyed blonde;
> she was followed adoringly by her tiny lover holding in one hand a
> parasol to protect her from the sun and in the other a brightly coloured
> beach towel. In her great rolls of fat she walked every inch as though she
> were the most desirable golden-haired beauty that ever existed . . .[46]

She seemed both real *and* a figure out of, say, pantomime.

Around this time, too, D'Arcy was taken to see *Peter Pan* at the Gaiety Theatre in Dublin. She did not much enjoy the experience, however, her reaction being strikingly similar to John Arden's: Mr Darling living in his dog kennel seemed too like her own father, in his suit and hat. Besides, the responsibility of keeping Tinkerbell alive by shouting out that she *did* believe in fairies seemed somehow dishonest: though she believed in Tinkerbell, she did not believe in fairies in general. And the responsibility for keeping Tinkerbell alive continued for days after she left the theatre, until she inevitably forgot about it.

In 1941 the Wicklow hills were exchanged for a return to Dublin city, where the family rented a ground floor flat on Pembroke Road, not far from Wilton Place. D'Arcy was sent to Pembroke School, familiarly known as 'Miss Meredith's'. Housed in a fine Georgian mansion, this Catholic girls' day school had been founded in 1929 by Kathleen Meredith, and had rapidly acquired an enviable reputation. Miss Meredith's educational practice seems to have been founded on the notion – unsurprisingly popular with the parents – that happy children learn best. The emphasis in the day-to-day affairs of the school therefore was on the happiness of the children, so that for the young D'Arcy, perhaps, the loss of her Wicklow freedom was not as keenly felt as it might have been. She seems to have thrived here, her main achievement being to learn to read.

However, this near-idyll, too, was to be interrupted. The family moved again, out of Dublin back to County Wicklow – just. Their new house was a rented wooden bungalow with Indian-style verandahs called Garry Ard, situated in the village of Kilmacanoge, just south of Bray. It was almost underneath the famous Great Sugar Loaf Mountain, once sketched by Edward Lear (as was the Round Tower at Glendalough). The move coincided with the careers of their parents taking them away from Dublin for long periods, which also meant yet another change of schools, this time to boarding school.

All four sisters were now sent to the Cabra Girls Convent School in Dublin, run by the Sisters of the Dominican Order. Perhaps this too was a refuge from possible Nazi invaders. The Dominicans, sometimes known as 'The Order of Preachers', or the 'Black Friars' in England, were founded by St Dominic in the thirteenth century, coincidentally within two years of the burning down of the Glendalough Monastery. One of the Dominicans' original aims was to confound the Albigensian heresy of the Cathari of Languedoc, for whom women were equal, if not superior to men. The Dominicans' typical misogyny is further evidenced by the fact that Heinrich Kraemar and Jacob Sprenger, co-authors of *Malleus Maleficorum* (*The Hammer of the Witches*), were also Dominicans. For the nuns the convent was 'enclosed', that is to say they were not allowed to go outside its walls. And everyone, nuns, pupils, all, had to walk unobtrusively, hands clasped, eyes down. Not surprisingly the girl boarders led a very isolated existence, though there were the dregs of old rivalries and attitudes remembered by some of the nuns from decades ago, before they entered the convent. Thus, girls from Celtic backgrounds were set above those from more anglicised families (such as the Norman-originating D'Arcys); and there was a preserved nationalism from the days before 1916, as well as admiration of and firm belief in the power of money.

In spite of this, the nuns emphasized meekness and charity, within a religious practice which was heavy and cloying. D'Arcy loved this, and noticed a certain theatricality in the world of the convent, though she may not have articulated it as such:

> In the May processions, when we followed (the Virgin's) statue around
> the gardens singing 'O Queen of Heaven' and responding to the litany of
> 'Star of the Sea, Mirror of Justice, Seat of Wisdom, Tower of David,
> Tower of Ivory, House of Gold, Morning Star, Ark of the Covenant', my
> whole being was taken up in the worship of her.[47]

The Gregorian chanting in the convent she later described as 'Grotowskian', that is, having the characteristics of Jerzy Grotowski's anti-Stanislavskian ritualistic 'poor theatre'. Imagining and identifying with Christ's suffering, on the other hand, was a Stanislavskian exercise in 'What If'. The settings devised for the girls' spiritual uplift also had a theatrical quality:

> The chapel, magnificent, gold, silver, marble, and fresco on the wall and ceiling round the sanctuary. The altar-cloths and the priests' vestments. The gleaming monstrance, and the canopy over it, the thurible with the smoking incense. The year, divided into the liturgical seasons, a different colour for each one, green, purple, white, gold.[48]

It is reminiscent of John Arden's later assertion that 'the theatrical poet' must be aware of how,

> in the ballads the colours are primary. Black is for death, and for the coalmines. Red is for murder, and for the soldier's coat the collier puts on to escape from his black. Blue is for the sky and for the sea that parts true love. Green fields are speckled with bright flowers. The seasons are clearly defined. White winter, green spring, golden summer, red autumn.[49]

And indeed, some of D'Arcy's intensest moments at Cabra came with her participation in the school plays, big scale productions with hired scenery, make-up, spectacular costumes and lighting effects. One was *Hiawatha*, in which she played a fire-fly in a phosphorescent costume, as well as a dancing daffodil. Another dramatised the story of St Theresa of Lisiex, in which she was an altar-boy carrying a lantern – a part which, however, was taken away from her for talking during a silent period.

Her experiences at Cabra convinced the young D'Arcy that she should try to establish her own order of saints, whose members would give all they had to the poor. Somehow, her move sparked another girl from a wealthy family to go to the nuns and 'sneak' on how she, the wealthy girl, had been excluded from D'Arcy's new order. The nun in question took the accusation (or her parents' wealth) extremely seriously, so that in assembly that evening, D'Arcy was called out and made to lie on the floor, while the other girls, led by the tale-teller, walked over her.

Worse was to happen when she was preparing for confirmation and her certificate of baptism could not be produced. Suddenly the nuns thought they had found a girl who had been attending communion services unbaptised. D'Arcy was pulled out of her class so dramatically, she thought one of her parents must have died. She was brought to a room where her younger sister was also confined (she, too, had no baptismal record), and they were told that they were not to mix with the other children, as if they were somehow diseased or contaminated. They were not to tell anyone they had not been baptised. They would be baptised very soon and very secretly, lest the Catholic hierarchy find out. When one nun, already D'Arcy's enemy, saw D'Arcy entering the library, she cried out: 'Get out! You are filled with the devil!' Soon the baptism occurred, and D'Arcy became at least partially acceptable again. But for her the episode tarnished for ever the lustre of the Catholic church.

36

Her experience of the extreme introversion of the church was in any case becoming more puzzling as she grew older. When she returned home for holidays, her non-Catholic mother would remove her holy pictures and other relics, to her chagrin and even despair. Out of school, the family had friends such as the progressive Protestant women, Louie Bennett and Helen Chenevix, and the socialist Peadar O'Donnell. They were socially and politically far in advance of the Cabra nuns. And when her father, and then her mother, returned to live in Dublin after the war, they brought with them disturbingly free attitudes, including a love of classical music, and interest in plays on the radio.

At last the family were properly re-united. The strains of the previous years were over, though adjustments had naturally to be made. Miriam D'Arcy was never a stereotypical housewife. There were rows, sometimes 'explosive', often about money, and the father's inability to understand the need to pay bills on time – a problem for many government employees, apparently, for whom regular and reliable pensions were waiting. Despite the fact that her mother was increasingly unhappy at this time, the adolescent Margaretta found herself arguing with her more and more forcibly. The difficulties were compounded because Miriam D'Arcy was constrained to take locum jobs in England in order to gain the professional experience necessary for final qualification as a doctor. Then in 1947 Joseph D'Arcy had a heart attack. More changes inevitably followed: the three younger D'Arcy sisters were removed from Cabra and sent to a convent much nearer the family home, Loreto College in Bray, to the south of the city. The Loreto Order was founded in 1822 with the express purpose of educating girls. Though she did not stay at Loreto College long, D'Arcy remembered cycling the four miles to school each morning, and the four miles back at night. She also remembered playing in the school orchestra, and, after seeing a Gilbert and Sullivan opera at the Gaiety Theatre in Dublin, deciding to write her own opera.

Loreto was not to stay long in her life, though, and soon she was transferred to yet another school, this time Alexandra College, then housed on Earlsfort Terrace, immediately to the south of St Stephen's Green in a large building which is now a hotel. Alexandra College was – unlike D'Arcy's previous schools – a Protestant establishment, just to further confuse her young mind. Prestigious and successful, it had been founded in 1866 by a progressive Quaker, Anne Jellicoe, who was a fierce campaigner for the equality of women. The school was to provide middle class girls with a liberal education, equal to anything which boys received. Her ultimate aim was to prepare girls for University entry, and indeed the school did provide Trinity College and other tertiary institutions with their first female students by the turn of the century. Alexandra College had also employed the future revolutionary Irish leader, Padraig Pearse, to teach pupils Irish.

Margaretta D'Arcy found herself playing hockey on Saturday mornings, but her most absorbing activity during her five terms at Alexandra was to research and write about the theatre in Ireland in the eighteenth century. This was her response to a task set to her class to discover and write about any aspect of Dublin. She found out about Dublin's Restoration theatre on Orange Street, known as Smock Alley, where James Quin, Harry Woodward, David Garrick and Peg Woffington had all starred, and Thomas Sheridan, the dramatist's father and no mean actor himself, had been manager. But her essay mostly explored the history of Smock Alley's successor, the Crow Street Theatre, founded in 1758 by Spranger Barry, and Ireland's leading drama house for sixty years. Then, in 1819 the Theatre Royal opened and the Crow Street Theatre was closed. It was demolished in the 1830s. D'Arcy persuaded her father to type up her paper for her before she presented it to her teacher.

D'Arcy's childhood had been rootless, perhaps confusing, her parents often away and adult directions contradictory. Perhaps in reaction it was the theatre in all its facets that began to consume her imagination and energy. She left school in 1950, determined to find a way onto the stage.

Four : The Aspiring Actress

In her later teenage years, Margaretta D'Arcy's life found its focus outside the home. Her father was embedded in the life of Dublin, a city still to an extent coming to terms with its hard-won freedom, for which of course the great majority of its population had struggled. But it was still also pervaded by a domineering Catholicism. Moreover, the city was small enough for the circles of acquaintanceship and endeavour, especially among the intelligentsia, to overlap and interlock. All this fed a curious kind of inward-looking vibrancy, especially in the dissident, intellectual life where Joseph D'Arcy found his place. He was the author of two radio plays which RTE broadcast, and he read not only 'highbrow' literature, but also progressive magazines like *The Bell* and *Envoy*. Meanwhile, D'Arcy's mother spent quite long periods of time in England, where she was working as a locum in order to qualify finally as a doctor. After so many schools and so many different homes, no wonder D'Arcy's world was beyond the home. Perhaps when she came to think of her identity, too many troubling questions arose, especially at a time in Ireland when the very notion of 'Irishness' was under close scrutiny. Was she Jewish? Or Irish? Loyal to the state? Or a rebel? Rooted in the land? Or an emigrée? Perhaps even a refugee? Catholic? Or Protestant? She was angry, ambitious, perplexed, with an attraction to danger and a refusal to accept.

Ireland herself seemed to be undergoing something of an identity crisis, too, at the time. A new radical republican party, called Clann na Poblachta, 'The Family of the Republic', with its roots in the old anti-treaty forces of the civil war, was now formed. It was led by the idealistic and charismatic Sean MacBride, whose father had been executed in 1916 and whose mother was the famous beauty, beloved of W.B.Yeats, Maud Gonne. MacBride himself was a former Chief of Staff of the IRA, and he led the new party to two unexpected but decisive bye-election victories in 1947. Fianna Fáil suddenly seemed tired, dull, a party with no vision, and in the general election of 1948, de Valera, for the first time, was beaten. But not by much, and Clann na Poblachta won only ten seats. Nevertheless, they joined the new governing coalition which was formed under Fine Gael's John Costello. MacBride became Foreign Minister. It seemed the moment for a fresh start, a new Ireland. In fact, despite MacBride's energy and high profile, the new government faltered and failed. The new Irish identity evaporated, and in 1951 the Irish voters ran back to Fianna Fáil. Clann na Poblachta was reduced to two seats (one of them MacBride's), though three others were elected as Independents. Perhaps no change was possible in Ireland after all.

The young Margaretta D'Arcy was one of those who were excited by Clann na Poblachta. It was at about this time that she went with her father to Armagh in the six counties of Northern Ireland, to a kind of conference of people, mostly from the north, who, like the Clann na Poblachta, opposed Partition. The group met regularly, when they read socio-political papers and enjoyed Irish music and dancing. The conference was held 'behind closed doors and lace curtains in a genteel, damp-smelling hotel in the middle of the town', and on the Sunday they visited 'a kind of landed-gentry house' owned by the writer, George Buchanan.[50]

But politics was by no means the driving wheel of D'Arcy's life: it was theatre which excited her. The new government may have been chaotic, but she noted how the private lives of the great actors had been, too – as chaotic as her own seemed to be. To get away from home, she often spent her whole pocket money on a ticket to the Saturday matinée at the Gate Theatre, with its narrow auditorium and narrow-er proscenium. The audience at these matinees rarely numbered more than twenty, but the repertoire of the resident Longford Players was wide-ranging and – to the young D'Arcy – educative. She saw plays by Farquhar, Shaw, Chekhov and some uncontroversial contemporary works. The Longford Players were a traditional stock company: each play was performed in the same style by the same journeyman actors every week. But the young D'Arcy was entranced: it took her imagination to a new level, and she wrote to the company, asking for a job – without success.

In 1948 she joined the amateur Thespian Players at Bray. The Players were themselves a splinter group from another amateur company, and had very few active members. Consequently, in their production of *Frieda* by Roland Millar, D'Arcy was cast as a middle-aged woman. The audience for the performance was poor, but a second performance at the local TB hospital where Dr Noel Browne had worked to eradicate tuberculosis was more rewarding, and D'Arcy was a success. Noel Browne, deputy leader of Clann na Poblachta and Minister of Health in Costello's government, was present, adding a special glamour to the performance. The whole experience, including her own performance, during which she rescued a fellow actor who had forgotten his lines and was floundering, was exciting and satisfying. With perhaps typical impetuosity, D'Arcy decided that she would make the stage her career.

But how could she acquire the necessary training? Nowhere in Ireland seemed to offer her anything which was both competent and affordable. Another girl at Alexandra College was intending to go to London, to join a course which was designed to lead aspiring actors to qualify for admission to the Royal Academy of Dramatic Art (RADA), England's leading actor training school. It was a sort of 'Pre-RADA' establishment. This, D'Arcy eagerly decided, was what she, too, needed. Her parents may have found the idea interesting, even adventurous, but there were practical difficulties. Help came, however, when her aunt Hannah, 'the Angel of Cable Street', offered to pay for her to attend the course and to provide her with accommodation. Dream seemed to be transforming into reality.

But there was one more theatrical adventure left in Dublin for D'Arcy before she departed for England in the autumn of 1950. She and her sister Judith were offered the chance to work as unpaid usherettes for the Ronnie Ibbs Theatre Company during their summer season at Bray. This was a stock company of the most basic type, performing two plays per week, each usually rehearsed a mere three times before it was shown to the public. But each play was a light comedy or simple thriller, and the actors knew precisely how to present them. It was in fact another old-fashioned stock company, less prestigious perhaps than the Longford Players, but of the same type. There was a single basic stage set, with variations, the actors provided their own costumes and the whole season ran like clockwork. D'Arcy, as usherette, was within touching distance of the professional theatre!

Before she left for England, and her next steps towards a career in acting, she needed to obtain the necessary papers. To do this, she had to choose whether she was Irish, as her father was, or English, after her mother. She chose to be a citizen of Ireland. It was a statement with significant consequences for the rest of her life.

London, when she arrived in 1950, was still a city of bomb damage and rationing. But there were exciting or tempting places to go – the docks, for instance, or cafés in the Kings Road, Chelsea, where poets and actors might be found. But whereas the sixteen-year-old was eager to explore and experience whatever London had to offer, her aunt Hannah, acting *in loco parentis*, was considerably less keen. For much of the time, therefore, the young D'Arcy was kept close, which of course meant living as a Jew in Hannah's Jewish household. D'Arcy found it hard to remember which towel should be used to dry which crockery, or to distinguish between Sabbath bread and ordinary bread. This induction into Jewish life did not convert her to Zionism, though her London experience did bring her Catholic faith further into question – the churches she went to seemed so busy, noisy and commercial.

The Pre-RADA training school should have been an antidote to these negative experiences. But it, too, seemed less than satisfactory. It had been established originally by Dame Irene Vanbrugh. A brilliant star of the theatre in the early part of the twentieth century, and the wife of Dion Boucicault Jr, she had been for long involved with the development of RADA, whose new student theatre was to be named the 'Vanbrugh' after her in 1954. Consequently, it was no surprise that she had wanted to establish a sort of preparatory school for the main establishment. Though she died in 1949, her Pre-RADA school had already passed into the charge of the theatre director, Eric Capon. He was an unashamed Marxist, who had in 1943 published a pamphlet called *Actors and Audiences in the Soviet Union*. He thought of himself as a Brechtian before the German master was much known in the west. He organised and directed an open reading of *Mother Courage and Her Children* at the I.C.A. in 1955 even before Joan Littlewood's Theatre Workshop production of that play. And a year later he was to acquire a certain notoriety when he described Peggy Ashcroft's Shen Te in *The Good Woman of Setzuan* at the Royal Court Theatre as a 'Roedean whore' in *Encore* magazine.

Margaretta D'Arcy became a day student at Capon's school, which probably meant that she lost out to some extent compared with those who boarded, but still overall the course disappointed her. The students numbered about forty, and were a wide assortment of hopefuls, mostly women, some of whom went on to significant achievements in the theatre, but many of whom did not. The work consisted largely of traditional British voice classes, and worked-up scenes for presentation to a tutor. What often happened was that each group of students rehearsed a scene from the same Shakespeare play, and then all the scenes were presented one after the other, so that the whole play was in effect presented. Students also, of course, prepared audition speeches for their future progress. The teachers were mostly actors who were currently 'resting', though Capon himself occasionally gave a lecture, in which he would reveal his strongly held views about the necessity for a political theatre. It is difficult to say, however, that this greatly influenced D'Arcy's later engagement with politics and theatre.

D'Arcy probably learned almost as much from her visits to London theatres during her year in London as she did from the Pre-RADA school. Eric Capon suggested to his students worthwhile productions to visit, and D'Arcy lists plays by Shakespeare, Jonson, Molière, Vanbrugh, Garrick, Shaw, Chekhov and Pinero as among those she attended.[51] Her aunt Hannah often went to the theatre with her, including to the Yiddish theatre, and they were sometimes accompanied by her uncle David as well. After a performance of *Hedda Gabler* which they went to, D'Arcy found herself identifying violently with the psychologically-imprisoned spirit of Hedda. And she bought drama texts, too – anything from Shaw's *Saint Joan* to Picasso's *Desire Caught by the Tail*. She became 'extremely excited', she remembered, by the German Expressionist Ernst Toller's still underestimated plays.

At the end of her year at Pre-RADA, Eric Capon told her that he did not think she was ready to move up to RADA, and indeed he implied that D'Arcy had been something of a disappointment to him. She left London rather subdued. But she knew she had a job waiting for her in Dublin, for in the Christmas holidays, when she had been back at home, she had worked backstage for Ronnie Ibbs, and he had offered her a job in the summer. Still backstage, and still unpaid, but it was in the theatre, and the young D'Arcy was happy enough.

She worked hard – twelve hours a day, often – fetching props, standing in for actors, preparing the stage for performances, and so on. The company, which was now known as 'The Irish Players', had been strengthened by the addition of some new actors. But Ibbs himself continued as the 'leading man', the repertoire was still popular, and this year there was the promise of a tour to the USA in the autumn.

There was never a question of D'Arcy being invited to be part of this (she was still simply a volunteer helper), but it was the making of at least some of the company, including Ibbs himself: they were able to stay and forge careers on the other side of the Atlantic, thanks in part to the strong network of Irish actors there.

At the end of the summer, after Ibbs and his Irish Players had departed for America, D'Arcy was at a loose end. Indeed, she was deflated. She stayed too long in bed in the mornings, looked around for inspiration, or interest, and enlarged her circle of acquaintances without ever getting much closer to whatever it was life might be going to offer her. She was on the edge of Dublin's intellectual and theatrical life as it struggled for some kind of freedom in the era of fashionable pessimism and comfortless existentialism. Sartre, Kafka and Joyce were the writers most widely admired, with a few Dublin *cognoscenti* aware of the Paris-based Samuel Beckett. But literature was on the whole cowed, especially by the Catholic Church, whose Lenten Pastoral from as far back as 1930 had pronounced that evil literature was a greater danger to the country than strong drink.

This dictum, with its obvious implications for a severe censorship, was followed with a vengeance – literally – in the field of theatre. Thus, in 1951, the year D'Arcy returned to Ireland from her pre-RADA training, the Belfast Arts Theatre brought Jean-Paul Sartre's *Huis Clos* to the Royal Irish Academy in Dublin. The hosts, while accepting the play, requested that the name of the author be removed from all publicity as well as the programme, since Sartre was a self-confessed atheist, and his name might prove offensive to the Irish people. That same year, a troupe of 'Hawaiian serenaders and hula-hula dancers' were banned after the Catholic Church had made known its objections to 'lightly-clad girls'.[52] Two years later – too late for D'Arcy – Alan Simpson and Carolyn Swift established the tiny *avant-garde* Pike Theatre in Dublin. It was here that the first Irish staging of *Waiting for Godot* took place in 1955, and in 1957, at the Dublin *tostal*, or Festival, it presented the European premiere of Tennessee Williams's *The Rose Tattoo*. Nine days after the play opened, Simpson was warned by the police that it broke the law, and if he did not remove the production from the stage he would be arrested. But the script was available in bookshops, and the play had been approved by the *tostal* committee. However, two days later Simpson was arrested and taken to Bridewell Gaol, where he was charged with allowing a condom to be seen during the course of the performance. It was almost a year before the case came to court, and when it did it was dismissed: Simpson had 'no case to answer'. Despite this, he was not awarded costs, and the Pike Theatre was effectively destroyed.

The fortunes of Ireland's leading dramatist, Sean O'Casey, who was always an influence on the drama of Arden and D'Arcy, was even more egregious. On 28 February 1955 (the year Dublin Municipal Gallery of Modern Art refused the gift of a Henry Moore reclining nude sculpture, by the way), *The Bishop's Bonfire* opened at

43

the Gaiety Theatre. All bookable seats had been sold in advance, and over a thousand people queued for the 400 gallery seats available on the night. Once the performance began, it was clear that an element in the audience was seeking trouble, and disturbances continued throughout. The trouble spread to the streets, where there was rioting in protest against the play's apparent blasphemy. The play is indeed an open protest against the power of the church, though it is not clear that this is the same as blasphemy. And it is the church which O'Casey attacks, not only in lines such as when Father Boheroe declares he is tired of 'all the (Church's) gilded foolishness',[53] but in fact at the very heart of the play in the tragedy of Foorawn's arid life and pointless death.

Worse was to follow for O'Casey. His next play, *The Drums of Father Ned*, which celebrates the free anarchic spirit of 'natural' man, was a centrepiece of the second *tostal*, along with an adaptation of Joyce's *Ulysses*. O'Casey cunningly puts a *tostal* at the very heart of his play, contrasting this with most Irish festivals which seem to celebrate nothing but the dead and the domination of the Church. Here, the central image is of the building of a Roman Catholic church in the Republic of Ireland with timber grown in a Communist country and supplied by a Protestant Belfast businessman! But as the play demonstrates, wood is neither Communist nor Christian, just as music is neither Protestant nor Catholic – a message too far for John Charles McQuaid, the awesome Archbishop of Dublin. He was supposed to open the *tostal* with a votive mass, but in view of the plays to be presented, he refused. The Festival committee tried to withdraw both productions, but without them there could be no *tostal*. The whole event collapsed. And O'Casey instantly banned all productions of his plays in Ireland – an order which was to last for six years.

Some writers of the 1950s, such as the poet, Anthony Cronin, argued the need for an Ireland in which writers would be recognised and encouraged, but Aosdána and its policies were still many years away. It was the power of the Church which continued to dominate literary and cultural life for years after this. Thus J.P.Dunleavy's play, *The Ginger Man*, was withdrawn from the Gaiety Theatre after three performances in 1959, when the author refused to make the cuts demanded by the theatre's under-pressure management. In 1966, thirty-five books, including Edna O'Brien's *The Country Girls*, were banned in Ireland. In the 1970s, when D'Arcy, with Arden, took a play of theirs about travelling people to a pub near Galway, an uncomplimentary reference to the Bishop of Galway led to the landlord immediately halting the performance – which was finished by the company in the garden outside.

Such a situation was not encouraging for the young and idealistic Margaretta D'Arcy, who was eager to discover a progressive artistic *avant-garde*. It was made worse by the fact that she was a woman, for the position of women in this mid-century Ireland was also depressingly unfavourable. The 1937 Constitution forbade divorce or remarriage; it prohibited the import or sale of contraceptives; it even forbade blasphemy. A woman's place, it asserted, was 'in the home', and the Irish Free State was to 'endeavour to ensure that mothers shall not be obliged by economic necessity to engage in labour to the neglect of their duties in the home'. Even champions of women's rights, such as Helena Maloney, Abbey Theatre actress and close colleague of James Connolly and Countess Markiewicz, who fought in the 1916 Easter Rising and later became President of the Irish Congress of Trades Unions, supported this; though the National University Women's Graduate Association did not.

1951 was also the year of the struggles of Noel Browne for a Mother and Child support scheme. Browne, Health Minister in Costello's coalition government, wanted to set up a free (though voluntary) government-supported scheme for pre- and ante-natal care for mothers, together with free medical care for all children under 16 years of age. 'Socialized medicine!' cried his opponents, foreshadowing battles still being fought in the USA in the twenty-first century. The Catholic Church expressed its unremitting opposition to any suggestion that Catholic mothers might be treated in matters gynaecological or infant care by non-Catholic doctors. Led by the formidable and energetic McQuaid, ably seconded by the Bishop of Galway, they announced that the proposal was incompatible with Catholic teaching. Though Browne met the bishops and tried to persuade them to soften their opposition, they remained adamant, and Browne was forced to resign. The taoiseach, John Costello (with the support of the mercurial Sean MacBride) stated that he accepted 'without qualification in all respects the social teaching of the Church as interpreted by the Roman Catholic hierarchy of Ireland'.[54]

In this atmosphere, attitudes to sex can be imagined. Romantic nationalism conjured an image of pure and chaste Irish maidens, in contrast to the *louche* and unrestrained British woman. Catholicism taught that sex indulged in when the object was not the procreation of children was evil, and punishable by the eternal fires of hell. And there was a widespread belief that the famine of the nineteenth century had been caused by overpopulation, so that celibacy was to be greatly encouraged. Sex for its own sake, therefore, was synonymous with damnation, or at least shame, and was very frequently accompanied by violence, abuse and exploitation. It was hidden away, and lied about. Consequently, prostitution was rife, and illegitimate births common. In 1956, when *The Observer* ran a perfectly responsible series on sex, Irish newsagents themselves tried to have its importation banned. The attitude continued: in 1974 the Irish Attorney-General argued that the possession of contraceptives by unmarried women should be made a criminal off-ence; in 1991, the Virgin Megastore in Dublin was prosecuted for selling condoms; even well into the twenty-first century, Irish women may not have an abortion in

Ireland – though in an extraordinary piece of casuistry they may go to England for an abortion.

In this society it was no wonder that D'Arcy's mother's desire to study medicine and become a doctor were frowned on, even by progressive women: she had, after all, four children. In 1937 she had supported the National University Women's Graduate Association in their campaign against the Constitution, and had spoken out at a meeting in favour of state-funded crèches and child care. But she had been shouted down, and abandoned by her self-styled 'feminist' colleagues. Something of her attitude clearly rubbed off on her daughter, Margaretta. When the latter was accepted by the 37 Theatre Club in 1952 as an actress and assistant stage manger, she was notably comfortable with the fact that the company's driving force was a woman, the dynamic Nora Lever.

This was the next step in her attempts to create her own career. She had already made an unsuccessful attempt to become a theatre professional in an interview arranged by her mother with Micheal Macliammoir and his balding, pipe-smoking English partner, Hilton Edwards, but they had witheringly rejected her. Now, her friend Colette Delaney suggested she apply to the recently-formed 37 Theatre Club. She was invited to audition. But her mother knew nothing of the Club, and had had no hand in the audition arrangements to which her daughter had agreed. She was furious, Margaretta was defiant and in the ensuing rumpus, the mother forbade her daughter to attend the audition next day. D'Arcy was so distraught she made a serious effort to commit suicide, swallowing a handful of tablets and waiting for the end. Of course, it never came, and the next morning her mother's rage had burned out. She took D'Arcy to the audition, where she was offered a post as an assistant stage manager. She accepted with alacrity. And no sooner had she started work, than one of the actresses in the current production, *The Man with a Load of Mischief* by Ashley Dukes, left to join the Gate Theatre. D'Arcy stepped into her role: the maid. A professional actress at last (though as yet without a salary)!

37 Theatre Club was a youthful, aspiring theatre, set up in 1950 by Barry Casson, later better known as a film actor, and Nora Lever, who was to head the campaign some years later to save Bernard Shaw's Dublin birthplace from demolition. She seems to have been the real driving force behind the 37 Club, as Ria Mooney was at the Abbey. These strong women of the Irish theatre gave D'Arcy some kind of role model almost without her noticing it. Physically, the 37 Theatre Club occupied a tiny space in an old building in Baggott Street. There was no foyer. The audience walked straight into the auditorium, where they could purchase a ticket, whose price included coffee in the interval. The company produced a range of interesting, often rarely performed plays by writers such as Bjornsterne Bjornson and Clement Dane. Among the company were actors who later acquired high

reputations, including Norman Rodway, one of the Royal Shakespeare Company's brightest stars of the 1960s and 1970s, and Anna Manahan, who played Serafina in the controversial production of *The Rose Tattoo* at the Pike Theatre, and was the original Big Rachel in John Arden's *Live Like Pigs* at the Royal Court Theatre in London in 1958.

Early in 1953 the theatre club moved to larger premises on Lower O'Connell Street, during which time D'Arcy appeared in a production of *She Stoops to Conquer* at Trinity College. Back at the 37 Theatre Club, she earned one Irish pound per week and appeared in some noteworthy productions which the company presented in their new home. The first of these was the Irish première of J.M.Synge's *The Tinker's Wedding*, which was part of the 1953 Dublin *tostal*. Inter-estingly, in view of the controversy which was to engulf later *tostals*, the fierce blasphemy in *The Tinker's Wedding* evoked never a murmur from Archbishop McQuaid or his minions. D'Arcy's memory of Anna Manahan as Sarah Casey in this production, 'astride the cart, defying the priest, refusing to pay the marriage money', was vivid enough to remain with her for over fifty years. A second significant production was *Aisling* by Maurice Meldon, an Irish dramatist who acted under the name of Art O'Phelan, and who was killed in a motor accident in 1958, when he was only thirty-two. *Aisling* was a highly imaginative, almost surrealist dream play, with a large cast, unflinchingly nationalist and using satire and parody to underline its strongly feminist subtext. Sean O'Casey would not have been ashamed of *Aisling*, and though it seems to be largely forgotten now, those who know it would probably agree with Robert Hogan that it is 'without doubt one of the most moving, experimental, and accomplished plays to come out of Ireland'.[55]

Through the 37 Theatre Club, D'Arcy was able at last to participate in the intellectual and artistic life of the Irish capital. She was one of four striking young sisters, daughters of a well-known Dublin personality, who kept them on a very loose rein, and as such she was certainly noticeable. She wore outlandish clothes, went to art exhibitions, and was marginally involved in film making. She struck up a friendship with the writer Aidan Higgins, with whom she would discuss people and relationships intensely and in intimate detail. He it was who introduced her to the work of Samuel Beckett, and through whom she discovered Sam's cousin, John Beckett's *avant-garde* music. She met John Beckett, and his outrageous partner, Vera Slocum, as well as the actress Pamela Scott and her painter partner, Neville Johnson. Other writers and members of the intelligentsia whom she encountered included the poets Patrick Kavanagh, Anthony Cronin and John Montague.

Her excited, if naïve, fascination with the artistic, social and sexual life of Dublin's postwar bohemia came to an abrupt end in the summer of 1953. She had already become faintly disgusted with the insularity and smugness of the small group who frequented the endless parties, and had indeed rejected the advances of

Alan Simpson, founder of the Pike Theatre. When she found herself at another party, feeling emotionally hollowed out, she deliberately put her arm into a candle flame. Perhaps it was some kind of cry for an existence which might chime more closely with the intellectual aspirations which dominated her brain. But she was 'rescued' by a group of medical students at the party. They began to slap her face, saying this was how to bring her out of her state. Gradually their slapping turned into a full scale physical assault They hit and bruised her till she tried to run away, only to be pursued by these now thoroughly roused young men. She tried to throw herself into the sea, was somehow dragged away and discovered herself in hospital being treated for burns to her arms. It was time to leave Ireland behind.

Later she was to feel that she had betrayed Ireland by leaving for England. But at the time she dismissed Dublin as narrow-minded and backward-looking – and on one level at least she was correct. Nevertheless, by her own account she was at this time 'snobbish and immature, believing that anyone who wasn't 100% dedicated to, and starving for their art, was not worth knowing'.[56] She believed that the theatre had the potential to change the world. So when she reached London, and stayed at her mother's flat in Pimlico, she scoured *The Stage* for any opportunity. One advertisement she answered took her for an interview with Stuart Burge, the young Artistic Director of the new repertory company at The Queen's Theatre, Hornchurch. He offered her a post as Assistant Stage Manager with occasional acting roles, at one pound per week.

The Hornchurch venture broke new ground, and D'Arcy was in at its birth. It was the first British repertory theatre financed by a local authority. And Stuart Burge, its first artistic director, was something of a pioneer, who went on to a successful career of well over fifty years in the theatre and television, and who was a material influence on John Arden's career, as we shall see. He had trained before the second world war at the Old Vic Theatre School under Michel Saint-Denis, Glen Byam Shaw and George Devine. 1953 was in fact also the year of the break-up of this partnership of directors and actor trainers, something which Laurence Olivier called 'a great and dire tragedy in the life of our theatre'.[57] Burge himself, small, with a lop-sided grin, respected playwrights, but also managed to achieve a deep *rapport* with his actors. His full time designer at Hornchurch was Jean Love, the 'Master Carpenter' was Harold Brooks, and Anthony Bavage was the theatre's administrator. The theatre itself was a long, narrow converted cinema, without wings or flying space. The bar was converted from the old projection box, and the dressing rooms were tiny. Nevertheless, the so-called 'Queen's Players' attracted an extraordinary number of famous actors on their way up the ladder to success, including Joan Plowright, Timothy West, Nigel Hawthorne, Wilfred Bramble, Anthony Hopkins, Brewster Mason, Bernard Cribbens, Prunella Scales and Glenda Jackson. Not all these, it should be said, acted for Stuart Burge, even though he was responsible for over sixty productions, mostly presented in two-weekly repertory. The plays he presented included everything from Shakespeare through the best contemporary drama (*The Deep Blue Sea* by Terence Rattigan, *The Lady's Not for Burning* by Christopher Fry) to West End farces (*See How They Run* by Philip King) and an annual pantomime, which was the only production which ran for more than two weeks.

Margaretta D'Arcy, c.1953

D'Arcy was the most junior member of the company when it was opened by Sir Ralph Richardson on 21 September 1953. Since she was Irish, she was given the highly original nickname, 'Bog'. As ASM, she (with the rest of the stage crew) was responsible on alternate weekends for dismantling the set for one play after it closed on Saturday evening, and building the next so that it was ready for the actors on Sunday afternoon. They worked overnight. Any changes then needed had to be completed by the Monday afternoon when the next production was dress rehearsed ready for opening on the Monday night. She was also responsible for collecting props by whatever means seemed suitable, on a miniscule budget, as well as any necessary wigs, guns or whatever from specialist London suppliers.

She was also given small parts to act. Older West End actors often tried to make her conform to expected stereotypes both socially – in her dress – and on stage in her acting. She should aim to be the conventional 'ingénue', they thought. In fact, her quirky and original interpretations seemed to appeal to Stuart Burge, who did not accede to the senior actors who asked him to change what she was doing. Thus, she presented Desdemona's servant in *Othello* as a black woman, and she created a vulgar concierge in Noel Coward's *Private Lives* who shuffled along in worn bedroom slippers with a cigarette drooping out of the corner of her mouth.

D'Arcy's special friend at Hornchurch was the actor Christopher Burgess, later seen on television in *Dr Who, Jane Eyre, Sherlock Holmes* and many other programmes. Articulate and knowledgeable, he helped the young D'Arcy not only in making sure she ate properly, but also in introducing her to some of the cultural life she craved, taking her, for example, to rare London productions of Jacobean tragedy, and introducing her to the then-voguish *New Left Review*, where she read Doris Lessing, Lindsay Anderson and other radicals. He also tried to give her a perspective on the work in Hornchurch: it was a job, not a crusade, something to experience and move on, not something which would answer her existentialist *angst*. And as always with theatre, the time came when D'Arcy did indeed need to move on.

For the next two years or more, D'Arcy lived the life of an impoverished, peripatetic, jobbing actress, taking what theatre work she could get, filling in with other ways of earning a subsistence income, and depending on friends for support and companionship. She auditioned for Joan Littlewood at Theatre Workshop's Stratford East theatre, but was unsuccessful. She had more luck with the Hovenden Players at the little Hovenden Theatre Club off St Martin's Lane. This company, under the direction of Valerie Hovenden, whom D'Arcy had met at the Pre-RADA school, was dedicated to reviving forgotten classics. She was reputed to be the only person in England who had directed both parts of George Chapman's *Bussy D'Ambois*. D'Arcy appeared here in at least one part of this, as well as in *The Seraglio* by David Garrick and other plays. She also went on tour with the Hovenden Players' production of the children's play, *A Frog He Would A-Wooing Go*. Other less glamorous jobs, while she was 'resting', included selling programmes at Bertram Mills Circus, posing for a magazine photo shoot and modelling for the well-known and then popular painter, Matthew Smith.

Her mother, meanwhile, was practising as a psychiatrist in south London, since no such positions were available in Dublin. One day she discovered D'Arcy and a young man in her flat. Outraged, she expelled them, and now, too often, D'Arcy's nights were spent either on the floors of sympathetic friends or simply tramping the streets of London. She managed a few more theatre jobs over the ensuing months. She appeared in a touring production of an adaptation of Abraham Merritt's hugely popular fantasy novel, *Creep, Shadow Creep*, in which the human characters are turned into shadows which must obey the slavemaster-magician who transformed them. This production spent weeks in the industrial north, mostly in Lancashire, introducing D'Arcy to a kind of society she had hardly encountered heretofore. Another touring production in which she took part was Albert Husson's

We're No Angels, a comedy which had been popular on Broadway in 1953, and in 1955 was made into a film, starring Peter Ustinov and Humphrey Bogart. She also appeared as an extra in *The Prince and the Showgirl*, which starred Laurence Olivier and Marilyn Monroe, and caused enormous excitement at the time.

Then came the time when she auditioned for George Devine of the English Stage Company, which was just beginning its journey to the heart of radical British theatre. She was accepted into the company, and for her a new life began.

Five : At the Royal Court Theatre

John Arden and Margaretta D'Arcy first met in the autumn of 1955. When Arden had arrived in London late that summer to take up his post in Ronald Ward and Partner's London office, he had lodged in a hostel. But soon a colleague in the office, Tom Austin, invited him to become his flatmate. Arden was glad to accept. Austin was an Irishman from Dublin, a friend of the D'Arcy sisters, who was to go on to run his own successful architect's firm back in Ireland. Now he decided to throw a welcome party for Arden and invited – among others – the young Dublin actress, Margaretta D'Arcy. The two were immediately interested in each other, and D'Arcy invited Arden to the Hovenden Players little theatre off St Martin's Lane, where she was appearing in David Garrick's *The Seraglio*, in which she appeared as an Irishwoman trapped in a Turkish harem. She wore green see-through pantaloons, which neither she nor Arden ever forgot. Apparently, Arden and Tom Austin were the only members of the audience that night: Arden said it was like a private performance for them, and duly enjoyed it. D'Arcy was the first professional actress he had ever met. Afterwards he offered her his King Arthur play to read. She did so, and was duly impressed: it 'excited me hugely', she wrote later. 'The language and the rhythm and the genius leapt out'.[58]

However, the relationship did not progress. D'Arcy went on tour to the north of England. Arden went back to his office, and in the summer of 1956 he was struck down with appendicitis. There were complications and he returned to Barnsley where his mother looked after him. But later, back in London, they did meet again, on a wet afternoon in Charing Cross Road. 'There in front of me I saw a pair of bright wild eyes behind spectacles', D'Arcy recalled. 'The rain dripping off his hat …'[59] She was, by her own confession, an 'idealist' at this time, devoted entirely to the theatre. She was 'uncompromising, and a terrific-looking woman'.[60] He was thin and diffident, with bright brown eyes and an earnest manner. In many ways he was a typical young Yorkshireman, conservative in his personal habits, his clothes, his attitudes. He was not so much against modern culture, as uninterested in it, preferring Elizabethan to twentieth century drama. It was D'Arcy who was to introduce him to Brecht, Strindberg, Brendan Behan and other modern dramatists. But he was also, as D'Arcy had recognised, a genius, a man who could sing a ballad with piercing honesty, and a fine poet. He wrote of her:

> *The Young Woman from Ireland*
> I was walking out
> Upon this rainy day
> A half-blind gay young woman
> Came agreeably in my way

She travelled out of Ireland
Into England to live
To blink for a young Englishman
And her affection to give

'Oh I have had sorrows
I have had grief
So many men's sorrows
As the dew falls on the leaf

So many said they loved me
With words at my ears
Like needles of sharp ivory
They scraped me with their beards

So many said they loved me
And I blinked at them again
But all that they did for me
The wind does for the rain'

We were in Trafalgar Square
Where the rain was blown to hail
Lord Nelson's eye was filled with feathers
From every pigeon's tail

'I can half see you, you young Englishman
And naked shall you stand
Between my white bosom
With your hand in my hand

If you want I can then clothe you
In red and in white
Your eyes in my bedroom
Shall be all I need for light'

Her eyes being weak and watery
She took liberty to use mine
She said, 'Where I could see three tall chimneys
Now I can see nine'

The eyes she borrowed from me
She returned to me once more

And I see a whole great waterscape
I never saw before

So I am rowing out today
On this rainy windy lake
That throws my boat so up and down
I am sure my oars will break.[61]

It was soon clear their mutual attraction focused on the theatre, and they found they shared a dissatisfaction with it. The relationship took root.

The Korean War had come to its inconclusive end in 1954. In April 1955, Winston Churchill resigned as Prime Minister, seemingly letting in new light. His successor, Anthony Eden, immediately held a general election which his Conservative Party won convincingly. Britain settled down to enjoy the fruits of an unprecedented consumer boom, a new affluence which in a very few years brought refrigerators, washing-machines, televisions, even small cars, into the lives of rapidly-growing numbers of people. Less than one per cent of the workforce was unemployed. There were no beggars on the streets. Politically, there was consensus, tranquillity, symbolised by 'Butskellism' – the symbiosis of the two main political parties whose leading economic politicians were 'Rab' Butler for the Tories and Hugh Gaitskell for Labour. When the newly-forming European Coal and Steel Community invited Britain to join in 1955, Harold Macmillan, then Chancellor of the Exchequer and known as something of a Europhile, condescendingly refused: 'The Empire must come first,' he asserted,[62] not wishing to disturb the United Kingdom's ongoing snooze.

The apparent passivity of the British population in the mid-1950s was in a sense echoed – perhaps inevitably – in its contemporaneous intellectual and artistic life, which was frequently seen as passive and dull. Literature was dominated in the middle 1950s by 'The Movement', a loose group of writers who seemed only concerned with the minutiae of existence, formulated with good manners and fastidious care. They included Philip Larkin, Kingsley Amis, Donald Davie and D.J.Enright, and they almost all seemed sadly etiolated emotionally.

As for the theatre, Charles Duff has noted correctly that in the early 1950s 'young intellectuals were looking seriously across the Channel to the post-war Expressionist drama of France, or the Marxist plays of an East Germany struggling out of defeat and ruin',[63] and Kenneth Tynan noted in 1954 that 'nowadays intellectuals go to the cinema' rather than the theatre.[64] Though there were some highly respected talents, especially among directors – Tyrone Guthrie, Michel Saint-Denis, the young Peter Brook – the most prominent dramatists – Charles Morgan, Christopher Fry, Emlyn Williams, Terence Rattigan – seemed to many to suffer from a kind of intellectual 'Butskellism'. Rattigan famously invented 'Aunt Edna', the notoriously middlebrow spectator whom his dramas aimed to please. And – however unjustly – these writers seemed to those who were still at the beginnings of their careers, incapable of smashing through the flummery and obfuscations of contemporary life. There was felt to be a strong need for a new theatre company which might uncover and nourish new playwrights.

And such a company was in the making. At the Taw and Torridge Festival, in Devon, in 1953, Ronald Duncan, a poet and playwright with higher aspirations than his talent probably warranted, the Earl of Harewood, cousin to the new Queen and a suave and ubiquitous motivator well-known across the arts world, an energetic local schoolteacher, James Edward Blaksell, and the composer Benjamin Britten had met to discuss possibilities. They soon involved Oscar Lewenstein, a Communist theatre producer whose career had begun with Glasgow Unity Theatre, and Alfred Esdaile, who had just taken a three year lease on the Kingsway and Royal Court Theatres in London. But it was really only when Neville Blond, a rich diamond-in-the-rough married to a Marks and Spencer heiress, was co-opted to become chairman of the company in 1954 that its affairs began seriously to progress. Helped by the fact that the Arts Council was looking to support building-based, London theatres, and 'new writing', he insisted that a permanent London theatre be found, while Lewenstein enticed George Devine and Tony Richardson to the artistic directorship of the new venture. While Richardson was a fairly inexperienced television director, Devine's experience and credentials were impeccable. Oxford-educated, he had been a professional actor and director at the highest levels who was playing Tesman to Peggy Ashcroft's Hedda in *Hedda Gabler* at the Westminster Theatre when Lewenstein approached him, and he had been a driving force behind the acclaimed Old Vic Theatre School, with Glen Byam Shaw and Michel Saint-Denis, immediately after the war. Moreover, he was to prove a man of courage and character who would stand by his writers – most notably perhaps John Arden – through thick and thin. Now he and Richardson arrived complete with production plans and a budget.

After a false start at the bomb-damaged Kingsway Theatre, the English Stage Company settled at the Royal Court Theatre in Sloane Square. This was a small, somewhat rundown Victorian building. A few steps inside the little foyer took the patron up to the Dress Circle; a few down led to the Stalls. You could hear the underground trains rattle past. And that was not all. Dodgy drains which allowed water into the stalls were matched by a leaky roof, with its inevitable threat to the building's electrical systems. There were no workshops or storage space, the dressing room accommodation was barely adequate, and the small proscenium stage was flanked by tiny wings. There was minimal office space up two flights of stone steps, and the top floor was taken by a night club-cum-restaurant, run by Clement Freud for the bright young things of the day.

This was the theatre whose most significant earlier days had come fifty years before when Harley Granville Barker and J.E.Vedrenne had run it. They had staged not only Barker's work, but new plays by George Bernard Shaw, John Galsworthy, Somerset Maugham and Elizabeth Robins, among others. Barker's agenda was clear: to make naturalistic theatre, the most modern trend on the continent, post-Ibsen, accessible to English playgoers. When the English Stage Company was inaugurated, its desire was also to put 'new writing' on the stage. But it evaded the question – *what* new writing? The successful French theatres of the time were categorised as 'post-Expressionist'; in east Germany, Brecht's drama was a very specific kind of epic. The problem for the Royal Court – and this affected John Arden's work particularly – was that it supported no school, it was wholly eclectic. It ranged indifferently from Brecht to Beckett, from epic theatre to absurdism, and actually found its greatest successes in the old-fashioned naturalistic plays of John Osborne. The 'Royal Court writers' were an extraordinarily large and hetero-geneous group: how could the theatre hope for a strong identity, as Brecht's Berliner Ensemble, or Chekhov's or Gorky's Moscow Art Theatre, or even Granville Barker's Royal Court had had, when they were attempting to launch and support the multifarious and diverse careers of John Osborne, Michael Hastings, Arnold Wesker, Keith Johnstone, Kathleen Sully, Doris Lessing, Christopher Logue, Edward Bond, N.F.Simpson, Ann Jellicoe, Nigel Dennis, Gwyn Thomas, and more, as well as John Arden? A typical British radicalism flourished here, intuitive and inclusive rather than stringent and intellectual. As Derek Paget remarked forty years later, 'Remove John Arden from the "angry decade", and radical forms and practices are con-spicuous by their absence'.[65]

The English Stage Company had obtained start-up grants, very largely from the Arts Council, amounting to almost £10,000 before it had presented a single play. As Richard Findlater pointed out, 'Without that state aid the English Stage Company could have had no hope of enduring'.[66] From the outset, Devine let it be known that he was in search of new playscripts. He asked novelists for scripts. He advertised in *The Stage* – and received seven hundred replies, enclosing scripts, only one of which (*Look Back in Anger*) he accepted. And he and his colleagues contacted other writers they knew of or heard about, asking for new dramas. One of these was John Arden, whom Oscar Lewenstein heard of from Louis Golding, one of the judges in the competition which Arden had won for *The Life of Man*. Lewenstein contacted Arden, and Arden sent him the latest version of his King Arthur play. Lewenstein 'did not think he could do anything about it but was impressed enough to ask him if he had written anything else'.[67] Arden had. According to Lewenstein, he now sent him *The Waters of Babylon*.

Arden's version of this is that at about this time he noticed a competition announced in *The Observer*. It was for a play 'set in the contemporary world', and it was to be judged by Kenneth Tynan. Tom Austin, his flatmate, encouraged him to enter. He suggested that Arden forget about 'those old Celtic heroes' and write about one of their odder colleagues in the office. Austin knew about him, had been to his house, and described to Arden an extraordinary slum with all sorts of strange people crammed into it. To Arden, Austin's energetic description virtually conjured the whole play, at least after he had disguised the characters and sparked their adventures by devising a lottery which was a satire on Macmillan's just-introduced Premium Bond scheme. Perhaps the inspiration for it had actually come on that night when D'Arcy and Arden had sat romantically 'under a mulberry bush in an Earls Court garden, (on) a mild moist night with the smell of the dew on the fallen leaves'.[68] It was here that Arden had promised to write great parts for her, worthy of the new kind of theatre they dreamed of. *The Waters of Babylon* was his first attempt at this, and though it did not win the first prize in *The Observer* competition, it was accepted by the Royal Court for a Sunday evening production.

Then D'Arcy became pregnant. She was touring again with *We're No Angels* when she discovered, and wrote to Arden, who seemed delighted. When she returned to London, however, there was no question that he could live with her: his parents might find out, he explained. This was 1957, after all. But he promised to pay for the baby. Which may have seemed an honourable way out: D'Arcy's Catholicism presumably forbade an abortion. But she was not satisfied. His offer seemed to her mean. Whereupon he offered her marriage. D'Arcy was clearly baffled by this. He was not the kind of man she wanted to marry, despite his genius. She consulted her friends, and one of them, Hector Freeman, promised he would pay for a divorce if she was still dissatisfied after three years.

So on 1 May 1957, Arden and D'Arcy were married at the local Register Office. One month later, on 1 June 1957, they were married again in the Catholic Church, even though D'Arcy was still a fortnight short of her twenty-third birth-day, that being the age a Catholic woman could marry in church. Catholicism was still a force in her world-awareness: she had discovered in England that it was not such a monolith as it seemed sometimes in Ireland. She had become attracted by some of its more radical strands, and by spiritual ecclesiasts like the American Thomas Merton, who was a poet, social activist and Trappist monk, who also had connections with the Dalai Lama and with Japanese Zen.

The two partners were suddenly happy. But there were still family battles to come. D'Arcy had to establish her position with the Yorkshire Ardens – she was from the south of England, after all, or from Ireland, or Jewish. At any rate, she did not fit the expected mould, and they did not know how to cope with her. She refused to be coped with, or cowed, and it is probable there was never much love lost here. D'Arcy's mother posed other difficulties. She offered her flat to the newly-weds, but a few weeks before the baby was due, she expelled them. But then she was kind again. Then cruel again. Just days before the baby was born, with Arden away, D'Arcy borrowed a chamois-leather from her mother. Later that night, her outraged parent arrived at her door, demanding the chamois back. There was a furious altercation, which ended with D'Arcy telling her mother that if she did not leave immediately, she would call the police. The problems exhausted D'Arcy. But, she records, 'from then on I was free of both mothers'.[69]

Meanwhile, 1956 had come and gone. For many, it had seemed a momentous year, perhaps some kind of watershed. Khrushchev's denunciation of Stalin in February had amazed the world. The Soviet invasion of Hungary in October had horrified it. And Britain's adventure in Suez, conducted at the same time as Khrushchev's in Hungary, amazed, horrified and amused it all at once. The world had certainly changed from its postwar lethargy. The theatre, too, seemed to acquire a new life. The English Stage Company opened at the Royal Court Theatre on 2 April with a production of *The Mulberry Bush* by Angus Wilson, directed by George Devine, and followed this a week later with Arthur Miller's *The Crucible*, also directed by George Devine. In May, John Osborne's *Look Back in Anger*, directed by Tony Richardson, opened, and the theatre arrived in the general consciousness. It staged new plays by Ronald Duncan and Nigel Dennis, as well as *The Good Woman of Setzuan* by Bertolt Brecht and *The Country Wife* by William Wycherley before the end of the year. The following year, it staged plays by Samuel Beckett, Jean Giraudoux, Eugène Ionesco and Jean-Paul Sartre, as well as William Faulkner, Aristophanes, and W.B.Yeats and new plays by John Osborne, Carson MacCullers and others.

One of the English Stage Company's happier and more radical innovations was that of the Sunday evening production-without-décor. Before an audience of club members, a new play would be produced to dress rehearsal standard, thus providing playwrights, directors and actors with experience and an opportunity, without the risk or expense of a full-scale production. Authors were paid five pounds for their play, and the actors and directors received two guineas each. The first of these, on 26 May 1957, was *The Correspondence Course* by Charles Rob-inson. John Arden's *The Waters of Babylon* was the fourth to be presented, on 20 October of that year, directed by Graham Evans.

The Waters of Babylon is a rumbustious Elizabethan-style comedy, and indeed Chapman's 1596 play, *The Blind Beggar of Alexandria* suggested how the plot might work. Nevertheless, it is remarkably assured for a beginning playwright. It centres on Sigismanfred Krankiewicz ('Krank'), a Polish immigrant with his eye on the main chance and a past in the Nazi concentration camps – as inmate, we think, till we discover he was a guard – and his manoeuvrings to set up a comfortable way of life for himself. His ambiguous past is matched by his ambiguous present: not only is he a slum landlord who appears to be running a prostitution racket, he is also a respectable architect's assistant and an unashamed flirt. The pace is fast and funny, the cast includes an M.P., an Irish Republican, a Polish anarchist and a black local councillor, and the resolution is no resolution at all as the hero is shot by mistake:

> I said I was not going to die;
> Truth? I'm afraid I think it was a lie.

And the company are left to be organised by the superannuated Yorkshire-born fixer, Charlie Butterthwaite, into singing an absurd song as a non-stop round.

The tale is complex, arresting and amusing. There are reflections on identity, especially but not exclusively Krank's identity, which he changes each morning in a public toilet on his way to work: he slips happily from one suit of clothes, and one name to another. The play is also 'theatrical' to an almost alarming degree, with poetry, rhetorical prose and songs, recognition scenes, last dying confessions and direct address to the theatre audience. It is all a far cry from Osborne-style naturalism. It is a satire on Harold Macmillan's Premium Bond scheme, on the Russian communists Khrushchev and Bulganin, and on political chicanery in general. It also addresses issues of community and housing, racism and social responsibility with its own sort of stiletto. Michael Billington points out that within a year of its performance, vicious race riots did indeed break out in Notting Hill: 'And the xenophobia that was to be a sickening feature of British life for the next decades is unerringly captured by Arden'.[70] Perhaps most innovatively, *The Waters of Babylon* is performative, each character performing their role 'as if on the stage of the Abbey Theatre', as Teresa remarks of Cassidy. And it is this which gives the play its final resonance, and makes it into a tale which sweeps us along with fun, anger and its own desire to please. It is – and was in 1957 – a completely original work, fresh and surprising even today.

It seems it was, however, a little too far ahead of its time. According to John Russell Taylor, 'it was greeted with extreme puzzlement, if not outright hostility'.[71] Mostly, this was because of its method, its breaking the frame of the traditional stage – as Shakespeare, Groucho Marx and others had done, and as S.L.Bethell had meticulously documented. Krank's final speech continues:

> So, only a few minutes to live,
> I must see can I not give
> Some clearer conclusion to this play?

But despite the critics' reservations, George Devine was impressed enough to take an option on Arden's next play. He also offered him an ongoing job reading scripts sent in by hopeful authors at ten shillings per script, and with his young wife's encouragement, he dared to give up his post with Ward and Partners, and seriously try to make a living as a writer. He was anyway, he said, becoming dissatisfied in an office where he did no designing. He had considered post-graduate study, but the

Architecture Association had not been encouraging. It seemed he was almost destined for writing.

Meanwhile, the baby, named Gwalchmei Francis, was born with *spina bifida*. He lived less than two months, dying in November 1957. It was a devastating wound, and one which took years to heal. Arden paid his respects with one of his finest poems:

> To Gwalchmei Francis Arden
> Who put out his head in October,
> Kept it out until November,
> Drew it in then.
> > Please remember:
> He was young enough to take his choice.
> What he did not like he did not have to face.
> We who are older
> Must needs be bolder.
> The pen must crawl:
> The black ink fill the waiting space:
> For tortoise and child alone
> The shell is an honourable home.[72]

In 1958, Arden and D'Arcy committed themselves wholeheartedly, energetically and hopefully to the Royal Court Theatre. Arden was already writing what became the television play, *Soldier, Soldier*, as well as an excellent short comedy for students at Central School, called *When Is A Door Not A Door?* in which workmen mend the door to an office while a chaos of arguments, jealousies and strikes erupts between the people in the office. In their crescendoing frenzies, they go in and out of the door, never noticing the workmen, who in turn never really notice them. It is high farce, and hugely theatrical. Also of course, and centrally, he worked on the commission George Devine had given him, a play for full scale production at the Royal Court. This was to be *Live Like Pigs*.

Arden felt at this juncture that the theatre had truly invited him to be a part of it. He felt his hopes and ambitions were within reaching distance. He was given not only the script-reading job, but also a pass which enabled him to attend rehearsals and see performances of any plays at any time free of charge. And he joined the newly-formed Writers Group. The first meetings of this group were held in a disused shop in Flood Street, Chelsea. The participants sat round in the 'romantic but dirty' setting,[73] writers almost outnumbered by directors – George Devine, Michel Saint-Denis, William Gaskill, Lindsay Anderson and John Dexter were all present at the first meeting, as was Miriam Brickman, the company's casting director. The early meetings, not surprisingly, were somewhat stiff, and the discussion rather aimless. Later, most of the directors dropped out, and the group re-formed, now meeting in the house of one of its members, Anne Piper, where matters loosened up considerably. This was at least partly due to the new venue, which was only a couple of doors from Devine's own home. Situated beside the river just west of Hammersmith Bridge, it was, Arnold Wesker remembered, 'a huge Georgian mansion, cosy and relaxing, full of children, nicely scruffy, both children and mansion'.[74] William Gaskill recalled 'a large room on the first floor which always had a blazing fire and there was fresh coffee and bread and cheese for the hungry writers'.[75] Anne Piper's husband, David, was Director of the National Portrait Gallery, and the house was also well used by leftwing and radical groups for discussions and campaign planning.

With Keith Johnstone ('a large earnest man who chewed huge cooking apples and carried his scripts round in carrier bags'[76]), Gaskill was effectively responsible for reconvening the Writer's Group and indeed running it. He insisted that the group was not established for writers to discuss their ongoing work, but rather it should be seen as an acting forum, in which writers would learn theatre 'by doing it'. How good they were at acting was not the point: Edward Bond, for instance, quiet and serious, acted with intensity and concentration, but not much skill. Arden, on the other hand, was a good actor, especially noted for his brisk headmasters and Army officers. They were exploring what Keith Johnstone, in a letter to *The Times* written with Ann Jellicoe, N.F.Simpson and Harold Pinter asserted was 'a demonstration through images, in which words expressed relationships but were never used for the promotion or discussion of ideas'.[77] Beyond the core group of Arden, Jellicoe, Wesker, Johnstone, Wole Soyinka, David Cregan, Edward Bond and a few others, there were up to twenty more writers (including D'Arcy) who occasionally participated. John Osborne was, according to Anne Jellicoe, 'too grand' for the group;[78] he described the sessions as 'committee wanking'.[79] Actually, the group was, in a sense, self-selecting – warm, aspirant, mutually supportive. Those who were not prepared to subsume their own egos soon found the meetings less than appealing, and left of their own accord.

The group met on Wednesdays (or Saturday afternoons, according to Michel Saint-Denis[80]), and sessions were usually led by a director. Sometimes they simply improvised, either on set themes, or more or less spontaneously, and only occasionally did they actually improvise round a scene from a play currently being written by a member of the group. There were scenes at bus stops – Jellicoe remembered Miriam Brickman as a nun at a bus stop. The improvisation proceeded rather drearily, until she became a drunken nun, which improved matters considerably! They improvised television interviews, or items from the news. Another well-remembered improvisation involved someone stealing a bird's egg and, when accosted by a policeman, concealing the egg in his mouth, and then trying to discuss the problem nonchalantly. Sometimes the improvisations were more focused, and took a particular acting problem, such as the Stanislavskian 'objective', as its subject. Gaskill worked on Brechtian techniques, including the third person narrative, and used *He Who Says Yes* and *He Who Says No* as the basis for a session on questions and statements. George Devine led a set of workshops on the use of the mask, especially memorable as they inspired Arden in his writing of *The Happy Haven.*

The Royal Court thus did take its attempt to build a theatre for writers seriously. Not only Devine himself, but the assistant directors, Gaskill, Dexter, Anderson and Anthony Page, all tried to establish a stable of writers, of whom Arden was one, whose work was developed by the theatre, and who were associated with it. And to an extent they succeeded, even if 'their' writers turned out to be a fairly disparate group. Indeed, the Royal Court tag has hung probably too heavily round Arden's neck for too long. He was always much more than that implied. Nevertheless, it is hard to exaggerate the importance of the start the theatre gave him.

The assistant directors' tiny office upstairs at the Court was the social hub of the place. There may have been no windows or ventilation in this room, but still writers and actors were often to be found there. Conversation flourished, plans were laid, arguments pursued, and people, sometimes in fun, sometimes in des-peration, even wrote on the walls. Here is one such effort, reputedly by Arden:

> There's a cock in father's barnyard
> Who never trod a hen
> And it seems to me my fair young man
> That you are one of them[81]

Several of the writers were employed reading scripts. They were a sort of clearing house for the shelf-loads submitted. The reader was to write a report of no more than two or three sentences, only so much as could be contained on an index card, and it was this which would be read by Devine or one of the assistants. They wanted plays which dealt with contemporary Britain, but too many writers ignored this, and, for example, after the Russians sent the Sputnik into space, Devine predicted a rush of space-based plays. And his prediction proved correct.

The assistant directors, most actively Lindsay Anderson and Anthony Page, were also responsible for setting up the Actors Rehearsal Group, of which D'Arcy was an integral member. After the death of her son, she auditioned for George Devine, presenting speeches from *The Tinker's Wedding* and *Yerma* by Federico Garcia Lorca. The words of Yerma's longing for her child were almost unbearable for D'Arcy who spontaneously burst into tears. Devine and his assistants were not accustomed to such a show, and were truly impressed. She was accepted im-mediately. Here perhaps she would be able to fulfil her idealism:

> I really believed that the theatre's power to open and extend the imag-
> ination would somehow make a concrete change in society, that this

could be achieved through the audience's reflection upon the issues raised in a stage-play and through the catharsis arising from the shock-effects of certain dramatic situations.[82]

The Actors Rehearsal Group would, it was hoped, form the core of a future permanent company. They were paid three pounds per week, and conducted their sessions in a large, rather dilapidated house just off Kings Road in Chelsea. The most important work would be done under the direction of Anthony Page, himself fresh from working with Sanford Meisner in New York. Meisner's technique, like most versions of the American Method, sought imaginative truth in the actor, and often involved the release of deep emotions. But Meisner's special emphasis was based on his belief that truth could best be accessed through *interaction* rather than the simple action itself, and he emphasised that such interaction should be physical as well as dialogic. Page was to concentrate on Meisner's workshop techniques, while movement would be taught by Yat Malmgren, a Swedish actor-trainer working in London. Malmgren's particular approach aimed to synthesise Laban's movement techniques with Jung's concept of character types and the principles of acting developed by Stanislavsky. If this sounds esoteric, it was actually fairly understandable to a trained actor, and Malmgren was renowned as an excellent teacher.

The acting group consisted of six core members. Besides D'Arcy, these were David Andrews, Peter Birrel, David Buck, Tamara Hinchco and Johnny Sekka. Most of these young actors were altruistic and idealistic in their motives, like Tamara Hinchco, who came from boarding school and RADA, and now 'wanted to help poor people'.[83] D'Arcy, who was five years older than Hinchco, helped her to put this vague aspiration into a more acceptable political perspective. Others associated with the group included Harold Pinter, still unknown as a playwright, though clearly a sensitive actor. They started by understudying for the main pro-ductions, and also helped authors whom Devine was encouraging by playreadings of the scripts-in-progress. D'Arcy remembered one such play in which she and Pinter were cast as a married couple locked into a spacecraft. However, the play was so long that they never finished the reading, so that 'for evermore Pinter and I remain suspended in outer space'.[84]

The more serious improvisation work was rooted in Stanislavsky's concept that the actor must never acknowledge the presence of the audience. It was also dedicated to making members of the ensemble bond with each other, using the Meisner techniques to uncover 'emotional truth'. Whole days were devoted to physical explorations of the themes and ideas presented by Page, and the work frequently involved rushing all over the house, fighting, and uninhibited physicality – 'nothing like what we'd learned at RADA', Hinchco commented.[85] According to D'Arcy, the actors often ended 'battered and bruised',[86] but they were totally committed to the group, and trusted Page completely.

D'Arcy experienced a real liberation here, and believed it was a strong factor in enabling her to do much of what she later did. Tamara Hinchco, who became a lifelong friend of both D'Arcy and Arden, remembered her energy, and her laughter: 'We laughed a lot, we used to collapse laughing', she recalled. Every day, D'Arcy wore the same clothes – a black jumper with holes in it, and a red corduroy skirt. 'She looked great,' Hinchco said, though some members of the group wished she would change these clothes occasionally. Nevertheless, her energy and her drive were unmatched. She was 'alive', in the words of her friend.[87] It must be added that the group was also self-important, and perhaps not a little arrogant. Members enjoyed breaking the unwritten but hallowed rules of the theatre, such as that actors do not walk through the foyer, but enter their dressing room area through the Stage Door. Nevertheless, for a short period at this time, the Royal Court Theatre seemed to be the answer to Arden and D'Arcy's shared dream of a new, energising, revolutionary theatre.

On 19 October 1958, the acting group offered something of the fruits of their work. They presented an evening of experimental pieces, including *The Tent* by John McGrath, two short playlets by Frank Hatt, in one of which, *The Lodger*, D'Arcy appeared with Peter Birrel and David Buck, and *Top Deck* by John Arden. In this, D'Arcy played the conductor of a London bus who encounters an African-American serviceman, played by Johnny Sekka. But the performance was not a success. Partly this must be put down to the internal politics of the Royal Court itself, for it had become apparent that Tony Richardson's aims for the English Stage Company were increasingly at odds with those of George Devine. Richardson wanted a theatre in which the director was paramount, and in a position to cast whatever actors he (and it was always 'he') wanted, rather than draw his cast from an ensemble. Devine, of course, wanted a writers' and actors' theatre. Since Devine was absent when the experimental actors' group presented their pieces, it was perhaps in evitable that after it the group broke up, and the idea of the ensemble more or less perished at the Royal Court. Richardson was certainly responsible for the abrupt dismissal of the group, the shock of which was compounded when the evening's performances were attacked by *The Observer's* imperious theatre critic, Kenneth Tynan, and dismissed by many Royal Court insiders.

Two years later two members of the group, David Andrews and Tamara Hinchco, by now married, made *Top Deck* into a short film, with D'Arcy again playing the bus conductor and the American actor, Jimmy Anderson, playing the serviceman. They obtained a grant of £1000 from the British Film Institute, and though the camera they used functioned poorly, and the sound equipment was also inadequate, this was in the end a forceful and unexpected piece of cinema.

Live Like Pigs opened on 30 September, with a promising cast including Anna Manahan, Wilfred Lawson, Robert Shaw, Frances Cuka and Alan Dobey, as well as

Margaretta D'Arcy. But there were soon problems with the production. Devine had promised to direct it himself, but dropped out quite early in rehearsals, handing over to Anthony Page. But Page's Method training made him a particularly unsuit-able substitute. This was perhaps most obvious in his handling of the Ballad Singer, a part partially modelled on the singer in *The Threepenny Opera*, which Arden had seen in the Oscar Lewenstein production. Ewan MacColl had played Brecht's Ballad Singer with an irony which did not mask an incipient threat of violence. In *Live Like Pigs*, however, A.L.Lloyd, MacColl's equal in the 'folk revival', was 'put on the stage between the scenes and quickly taken off again so that no-one was really clear whether he was in the play or out of it'.[88] And finally, the design, by Alan Tagg, was unnecessarily fussy and complicated.

Later productions, including some well into the twenty-first century, have shown how misguided all this was. 'What impresses about *Live Like Pigs* is ... that it survives in performance as a warm-blooded, undogmatic and beautifully-written piece of theatre', one critic wrote of a 1972 revival,[89] and the play has proved to be one of Arden's hardiest. It is more focused than *The Waters of Babylon*, and on one level more intense: if that was Jonson, this is Ford, or the Middleton of *Women Beware Women*. But these parallels only go part of the way to explaining how Arden's play works. As Albert Hunt has persuasively demonstrated, *Live Like Pigs* also falls into the tradition of music hall and pantomime. The scenes often work as developed music hall sketches, and the characters may fruitfully be related to stock types, perhaps from the *commedia dell' arte* – Sailor Sawney is Capitano, Jackson is Dottore, Col Arlecchino. There are set scenes – The Arrival, The Seduction, The Dispute over Territory – which are performative, part of their strength lying in their ability to recall other, similar scenes, their 'intertextuality'.

But the play 'caused much controversy', as Humphrey Carpenter records.[90] Kenneth Tynan, for instance, completely misunderstood it. Tynan's 'double-act' with his wife, Elaine Dundy, was, according to Arden years later, 'one of the wonders of the London theatre in the hothouse 1950s': they would parade together 'through the foyer of the Royal Court Theatre on first nights, like Justinian and Theodora receiving the homage of the Byzantine eunuchs'.[91] Arden, according to Tynan's review, saw 'the world outside as a world of stuffy, small-souled hypocrites, inferior simply *because* they are ordinary'.[92] Nothing, of course, was further from Arden's view. *Punch*'s critic was even sharper:

> No-one in his right mind would go to *Live Like Pigs* for pleasure ... We
> simply wallow in the filth of a bunch of boozy, lecherous, dishonest
> tramps ... (Yet) in spite of its incredibilities (where were the council
> officials, where the other neighbours?) and the maddening sandwiching
> of its many scenes with dreadful doggerel ballads, *Live Like Pigs* is
> powerful. But so is any cartload of manure.[93]

No wonder it only played to 34% of audience capacity, and only lasted for twenty-two performances. However, financially the picture was not as bleak as has sometimes been supposed: the production cost £1778, but it took £1486 at the Box Office, a loss of less than £300.

The ambition, the precision and the strengths of this play have since come to be widely recognized, as suggested above, but its initial reception went a good way to shattering Arden's hopes, and perhaps those of D'Arcy as well. The dream was not so easily realized.

But there was something else about the Royal Court Theatre which left both of them feeling uneasy. What that 'something' was was not easily pinned down. But it may have been instructive that Joan Littlewood, the greatest theatre director of the period (equal only to Peter Brook), hated it. And John Whiting, the playwright, when asked how he would achieve his ambition of writing a theatrical masterpiece, replied: 'By not going to the Royal Court'. There was something incestuous about the people associated with it. They have been likened to a family, and certainly the theatre contained as many jealousies, hatreds and emotional strangulations as any family, fictional or real. Richard Findlater wrote: 'Everyone in that little building knew each other, even if they were at odds. And they were. Almost everyone was involved emotionally in what happened'.[94] Perhaps D'Arcy, an Irish woman at the heart of the British liberal-intellectual establishment was particularly sensitive to this, especially after *Live Like Pigs*. But for her, the arguments, and the competing egos and ambitions, became too much to bear. Her ideals were nowhere near being fulfilled. She became downcast, then genuinely depressed. She even contemplated suicide, and went to the rooftop of the building, thinking to jump. But she thought better of it: why should she be destroyed by all this? It was not for her, this kind of theatre. She operated differently, more creatively. To realize this was a liberation.

For Arden, however, the case was different. From being one of the theatre's greatest hopes, he now became of little significance. Where once everyone in the building had welcomed him, now he was frequently ignored. 'At the Royal Court', he remembered years later, 'if your play wasn't a success, you were dead. People were very nice to you but you felt an embarrassment and psychologically speaking it wasn't very pleasant'.[95] D'Arcy put it slightly differently: 'Whenever the theatre was empty, there was gloom all round, and the playwright in question got the blame'.[96] Arden craved understanding, success, a transfer to the West End perhaps. He received only snide comments, accusations that he was attacking the Welfare State, and a sneering remark from Ronald Duncan, one of the theatre's founders, that *Live Like Pigs* was precisely 'the sort of play the Court should *not* be doing'. Duncan said this volubly at the end of the first performance from a position immediately behind where Arden was sitting. It was surely intended for the young author's ears. It certainly stung.

That *Live Like Pigs* could succeed was manifest a very little time later, when Ann Jellicoe directed it with the students of Central School of Acting, where *When Is A Door Not A Door* had also been well received. But before 1958 had ended, D'Arcy and Arden had left London. Still suffering also from the death of their firstborn, they decamped to a cottage they rented in Peter Tavy, Devonshire, there 'to lick their wounds'. 'If we hadn't moved out of London', D'Arcy said later, 'it would have been the end of John's playwrighting career'.[97]

Six : Towards Collaboration

1959 began with Arden and D'Arcy living in Peter Tavy in Devonshire, and Arden writing a new play, which was to be called *Serjeant Musgrave's Dance*. George Devine had promised to stage it at the Royal Court. He worked flat out, his imagination 'on fire'.[98] A number of factors had helped to light this fire. One was an American film, a western called *The Raid*, which he described in an interview in 1961:

> A group of men – Confederate soldiers in disguise – ride into a north-ern town. Three quarters of the film is taken up with their installation in the town, and the various personal relationships they establish. On the appointed morning, they all turn out in their Confederate uni-forms, hoist a flag in the square, rob a bank, and burn the houses. Finally … the cavalry arrives at the last minute, although in this case they are too late.[99]

The Technicolor of the film contrasted in Arden's mind with the drab tones of *Live Like Pigs*: 'I suddenly wanted to write a play with a visual excitement as well as a verbal one. I visualised the stage full of scarlet uniforms',[100] he recalled. He turned, perhaps more or less subconsciously, to other plays which had dramatised an intrusion into civilian life by one or more soldiers, including his own television play, *Soldier, Soldier*, written before *Live Like Pigs*, though not produced yet. Equally pertinent was John Whiting's *Saint's Day*, which Arden had seen and been impressed by when he was an undergraduate at Cambridge. In this, the action takes place in a village cut off and divided into hostile factions. Three soldiers enter, in order to teach the civilians a lesson. Structurally, *Saint's Day*, like *Serjeant Musgrave's Dance*, includes the death of a major character in the second of its three acts, and there is a dance at the end – though here, a whimsical child's dance, which proceeds while the gallows is erected off stage, not in the audience's view.

Arden's imagination – and his fury – had also been triggered by a notorious incident in Cypress, when a British soldier's wife had been shot by local freedom fighters, and a group of soldiers had run amok, killing five local civilians in revenge. It was a typical incident from the end of Empire. *Serjeant Musgrave's Dance* is deeply concerned with colonialism and its meaning in human and social terms. Britain was, apparently, giving away its Empire to its hitherto subject peoples in a series of controversial acts. For many on the left this was a matter for celebration, and the Movement for Colonial Freedom had been founded in 1954 to speed the process along. The MCF was 'one of the most important post-war British political pressure groups,'[101] according to one historian, which at its height claimed a membership of over three million (though many of these were members of affiliated trade unions). Still, it was in some ways a model for later protest groups, such as the Anti-

Apartheid Movement, various anti-Vietnam (and other) War campaigns and, most significantly, the Campaign for Nuclear Disarmament. It is worth noting that MCF's most reliable outlet for publicising its activities and its views was *Peace News*. This carried a weekly column by Fenner Brockway, Labour MP and founding Chairman and dynamo of the Movement, and frequently printed articles by other prominent members of MCF Arden was to become the paper's chairman in the 1960s.

The Movement had addressed itself to Ghana, which became the first black African state to gain independence from Britain in 1957, as well as to the ongoing struggles of the Mau Mau freedom fighters in Kenya. The turmoil in British Cypress, however, was more difficult. The Cypriot leaders, Georgios Grivas and Archbishop Makarios, were by no means socialists and nor were they pacifists. Should they be supported by the British left? The problem was exacerbated by the incontrovertible evidence of British abuses and atrocities against the local people, such as that behind *Serjeant Musgrave's Dance*.

Perhaps also Arden was motivated by memories of his mother's deep-felt anti-imperialism, and perhaps also of those stories of colonial repression described to him by his colleagues in the Army ten years earlier. The problems of colonialism also informed later struggles which caught up both Arden and D'Arcy. For in no case did an imperial power simply walk away from its former colony, and two decades later, the results of imperialism/colonialism were still depressingly visible. Most obviously, centuries of British imperialism was at least partially the cause of the 'Troubles' in Ireland from 1968 to the end of the century.

The writing of *Serjeant Musgrave's Dance* was just about finished by the summer of 1959, when D'Arcy and Arden's second son, Finn, was born. This time, the baby was healthy and happy. And so were his parents. Around the same time, D'Arcy noticed an advertisement in *The New Statesman* magazine for a Playwright in Residence at the University of Bristol's Drama Department. With her encouragement, Arden applied. He was asked to show the University a play which he was writing. *Serjeant Musgrave's Dance* was the obvious choice. The lecturers in the Department were duly impressed, and Arden was offered the appointment, thus becoming the first Fellow in Playwrighting in an English University.

But Peter Tavy in Devonshire was too far from Bristol. Arden and D'Arcy needed somewhere nearer. They looked in the city, but were unable to find suitable accommodation for a young couple with a small baby at a fair rent. Then they discovered a ground floor flat in an old vicarage in the village of Brent Knoll, near Burnham-on-Sea in Somerset. For Arden, the bus and train service were convenient enough to pursue his residency satisfactorily, and D'Arcy had room and space enough for the infant Finn.

By now – late summer 1959 – the Royal Court was gearing up for the production of *Serjeant Musgrave's Dance*. Lindsay Anderson was to direct, and the cast would include some of Britain's best young actors – Alan Dobey, Frank Finlay, Patsy Byrne, and Ian Bannen. And when it came to the first night, on 22 October, Anderson's production was, according to Michael Billington, 'brilliant', with Bannen giving a 'demonic performance as Musgrave'.[102] But it was, perhaps, ahead of its time. It was not popular, and ran for only twenty-eight performances. The Box Office recorded an average of only 21% of seats sold, and the production lost just over £500.

This was probably partly due to the stony response of the critics. Harold Hobson, in *The Sunday Times*, surpassed himself: 'Another frightful ordeal', he wrote. 'It is time someone reminded our advanced dramatists that the principal function of the theatre is to give pleasure'.[103] Eric Keown of *Punch*, whose comments about *Live Like Pigs* have already been noticed, wrote: 'There might have been some felicities of dialogue or wit to leaven this lump of absurdity, but I failed to detect them'.[104] But the damnation of *Serjeant Musgrave's Dance* was not total. Philip Hope-Wallace in *The Manchester Guardian* was more thoughtful:

> (This) is a long and challenging play. Even now, at curtain-fall, some of
> its import escapes me, but for the best part of three hours it has worked
> on my curiosity and often put that ill-definable theatrical spell on my
> imagination. I think it is something short of a great play. But wild horses
> wouldn't have dragged me from my seat before the end.[105]

Lindsay Anderson stoutly defended the play in public, Sean O'Casey declared it 'far and away the finest play of the present day',[106] and soon student theatres and radical amateur groups across Britain were producing it. In the following decades, the play was performed all over the world, and it was set as an 'A' Level text for schools for many years and by many different examining boards. It was presented successfully on television in 1962, and in 1966 was revived by the Royal Court Theatre, when the production cost £1602 (less than the first production) but took £6771 at the Box Office, a profit of over £5000. Revivals continue into the twenty-first century, when critical opinion is virtually unanimous in echoing recent remarks by Michelene Wandor, who called it 'this extraordinarily powerful play',[107] or Michael Billington, who described it as a 'towering modern classic'.[108] After such a difficult, not to say disastrous, introduction to the world, it is ironic that for years it was *Serjeant Musgrave's Dance* (together with the nativity play, *The Business of Good Government*, discussed below) which kept bread on Arden and D'Arcy's table. Indeed, from their point of view, it may have become too successful – anything else Arden did later disappointed people who should have known better because it was not *Serjeant Musgrave's Dance*.

Our appreciation of *Serjeant Musgrave's Dance* today as 'a towering modern classic' includes an awareness of the furore it originally sparked. The fact was that audiences were simply not ready for the range of dramatic and theatrical strategies which Arden deployed, which are unlike anything which had gone before. Although *Serjeant Musgrave's Dance* is not Arden's (or D'Arcy and Arden's) greatest play, it is the one which shattered the horizon of expectations, and opened the way for the greater work to follow. Arden himself admitted later:

> Musgrave himself is trying to have a meeting of minds with the coal-mining men. He fails, and the reason he fails is not, I think, inherent in the meaning of the play but in the author's incompetence. I just didn't get that relationship developed.[109]

The play eluded the original critics because they had no idea what questions to ask of it. John Osborne's work they could appreciate because it used a naturalist form. The same was largely true of the Royal Court Absurdists, such as N.F.Simpson, who was following a track already beaten by Eugène Ionesco. But Arden was a different case. What questions should be asked of his play to elicit a positive aesthetic response? He was often considered to be a follower of Brecht, and perhaps the clue lay there. But Brecht was not much known in Britain in the late 1950s, and what was known of his ideas was much misunderstood – witness the labelling of Robert Bolt's *A Man for All Seasons* (1960) or Osborne's *Luther* (1961) as 'Brechtian'. And in any case, as John Russell Taylor noted at the time, Arden should by no means be regarded as a *follower* of Brecht:

> Arden paradoxically is at once the most and the least Brechtian of all modern British dramatists: most, because their views on the proper relationship between the audience and what is happening on stage and their means of achieving it are almost identical; least, because one could readily imagine that Arden's plays would have been written in exactly the same way if Brecht had never existed.[110]

Arden's dramaturgy, in some ways similar to Brecht's, actually probably owes it almost nothing. And fifty years since the original production of *Serjeant Musgrave's Dance* have wrought an extraordinary turnaround. What was once a 'lump of absurdity' has become a 'towering masterpiece'. But for Arden, the critics really never caught up. By the time they had come to terms with something of the real Brecht, and found that they could appreciate *Serjeant Musgrave's Dance*, Arden had himself moved on, and the critics were left acclaiming Edward Bond, Howard Brenton, David Edgar and others as Britain's contemporary political makers of epic theatre. By the 1970s and 1980s, Arden had developed a different, idiosyncratic, always original path of his own. He still eluded them.

Serjeant Musgrave's Dance is still worth pausing for because it demonstrates so clearly Arden's conception of poetic drama in the late 1950s. He describes the play on its title page as 'an un-historical parable', that is, it is not 'real' history even though it is historical in its content. Rather than baffle critics, this should have made it easier for them to appreciate that the play is likely to operate between the 'real' world and the play world. Indeed, it emphasizes the distinction between the two, as well as their relationship. History may be seen as a narrative of the past which leads to the present. The point of studying history is to better understand the present. So here we are given a historical narrative – a story set in the past – which aims to illuminate the present. But it may do this the more clearly by not being literally factual.

First, we are invited to enjoy the story as such, its vivid incidents, its slow-burning rhythm. We soon note, however, that the story is poetically conceived. At the very beginning of the play, we notice its language. Sparky and the other redcoats are waiting by a cold canal wharf. Sparky says:

> Brr, oh a cold winter, snow, dark. We wait too long, that's the trouble.
> Once you've started, keep on travelling. No good sitting to wait in the
> middle of it. Only makes the cold night colder.

And he begins to sing an old ballad – 'One day I was drunk, boys, on the Queen's Highway ...' As G.W.Brandt noticed soon after the play was first performed, the language 'is earthy, with a rich north country flavour, but it is not naturalistic for all that. It is a highly charged prose that at times abruptly rises into verse'.[111] Arden himself acknowledged the influence of John Masefield, especially his ballads and his drama, *The Tragedy of Nan*. The poetry in *Serjeant Musgrave's Dance* is equally evident in its imagery and symbolism. There are the colours we see, for instance – the red of the soldiers' uniforms and the Mayor's robe, the colour of blood; black, the colour of coal and of Black Jack Musgrave himself; and the white of the snow and Billy Hicks's bones which dangle before us at the end of the play. In the last song, the 'blood-red rose (that) is withered and gone' is set against the green apple which 'holds a seed will grow In live and lengthy joy'.

This last song, and much else in the play, suggests the world of the ballad, and this world gives further clues to the way this play functions. Consider a typical old ballad:

> As I was walking all alane,
> I heard twa corbies making a mane;
> The tane unto the t'other say,
> 'Where sall we gang and dine to-day?'

> 'In behint yon auld fail dyke,
> I wot there lies a new slain knight;
> And naebody kens that he lies there,
> But his hawk, his hound, and his lady fair.

> 'His hound is to the hunting gane,
> His hawk to fetch the wild-fowl hame,

His lady's ta'en another mate,
So we may mak our dinner sweet.

'Ye'll sit on his white hause-bane,
And I'll pike out his bonny blue een;
Wi ae lock o his gowden hair
We'll theek our nest when it grows bare.

'Mony a one for him makes mane,
But nane sall ken where he is gane;
Oer his white banes, when they are bare,
The wind sall blaw for evermair'.[112]

Here we are presented with a whole story, vivid before our eyes, in five brief stanzas. There is a ritual quality to the ballad: 'his hound, his hawk and his lady fair'. A whole society and its geographical location is painted – bleak, cruel, in black (the corbies) and white (the clean-picked bones) and gold (the knight's hair). And we are left to imagine the jealousy, the murder, the all-consuming lust and more, which fuel the action. But we are not asked to sympathise with any of the characters, we are given no 'moral compass' such as Kenneth Tynan demanded of *Serjeant Musgrave's Dance*. Here is simply the essence of a harsh society, in which perhaps the knight has tried to bind his lady, or to treat her as his chattel, or perhaps she has struck for her freedom, or her illicit lover has committed murder. Each character may be morally wrong, but each needs understanding, for what we see are actions and the consequences of actions. We are not informed of the precise details, we only sense the cruelty, the passion, the darkness of unacknowledged deeds and these shine a ' brilliant light on the workings of the particular society – and by extension, on all societies, including those apparently more civilised than this one.

And that precisely is how *Serjeant Musgrave's Dance* and other Arden and D'Arcy plays, make their impact. In a sense, the play – like the ballad – is artificial. It is a story, which is told with a certain distancing, and a certain irony. This is obtained through the *means* of the story-telling. The ballad author has little chance to deploy many narrative strategies, but for the author of a full length play there is a myriad of devices which can be used. And here Arden deploys verse, poetic prose, song, and so on, like the bards whom Graves identifies in *The White Goddess*: 'It seems that the Welsh minstrels, (and) the Irish poets, recited their traditional romances in prose, breaking into dramatic verse, with harp accompaniment, only at points of emotional stress'.[113] One interrupts the other, and when that happens, the auditor, or spectator, is forced to readjust, refocus. The treatment of the characters in *Serjeant Musgrave's Dance* is similar: they appear at different times like figures from the toy theatre, or toy soldiers, at others like the participants at a military parade, or the actors in a cheap western, or in a dance of death. Each performs whatever role the moment demands, though just occasionally a restless something releases a more complex and demanding reverberation, as when Sparky meets with Annie in the stable, or Musgrave is imprisoned at the last. Each characteristic manifestation contradicts or interrupts what goes before, and the result is to disturb the audience's acceptance, to prevent its sloppy assent to whatever is put before it, to challenge its understanding. And each such inter-ruption sets up resonances between the play world and the real world, and helps to create an audience like that described by S.L.Bethell in the 1940s, one 'critically alert to the play as play, not duped into accepting it as if it were real life'. Only thus, Bethell asserts, can 'the two planes of past history and current affairs … be attended to simultaneously, yet without confusion'.[114] The point of the juxtapositions and the coruscating imaging is to ensure that the audience will respond simultaneously on different levels, enjoying the story while still pondering the implications of the action. This is true of all Arden and D'Arcy's dramatic work.

These and similar points can be made today, but they were not made in 1959 (though Hobson, for instance, did later recant his horrified rejection of the play). At the time, *Serjeant Musgrave's Dance* seemed yet another failure. Arden was depressed. However, this time his depression was interrupted by more cheering news. The play won the Encyclopaedia Britannica Prize, and also, jointly with Arnold Wesker's *Roots*, the prestigious Evening Standard's Best New Play award, in January 1960. Even better, in February the BBC transmitted his earlier play, *Soldier, Soldier*, in a live performance directed by Stuart Burge and starring Margaretta D'Arcy, and this proved an almost complete success.

Soldier, Soldier is described by Arden as a 'low-life comedy'. It dramatizes the story of a soldier or adventurer, perhaps a deserter, who capitalizes on the anxiety of the wife and relations of another soldier, who is missing. He arrives unheralded in a dull northern town. Charming, but also perhaps vicious, the soldier effectively fleeces the relatives, fools the townspeople and seduces the wife, before striding away into the unknown, leaving the townsfolk aghast and amazed.

There are affinities here with *Serjeant Musgrave's Dance*, which was composed later. Like it, *Soldier, Soldier* is a kind of dramatized ballad:

> O Soldier Soldier
> Will ye marry me now
> With a hey and a ho
> And a fife and drum.
> O Lady, Lady,
> How can I marry you
> When I have already
> A wife of my own?

'I enjoyed writing it', Arden said. He regarded it as an experiment in using verse on television: in that respect he did not believe it was completely successful.

But otherwise it fulfilled all his hopes. During the active preparation of the script, he had been able to work closely with Stuart Burge, the former artistic director of the Queen's Theatre, Hornchurch when D'Arcy had worked there. Burge now advised Arden consistently and constructively. Moreover, he encouraged him to attend rehearsals, for which he came to London specially from Somerset. The excellent cast, including Andrew Kerr and Frank Finlay, as well as D'Arcy, understood what they were doing, expressed it through their acting and the result, gratifyingly, was a performance of 'raucous vitality'. J.L.Styan recorded: 'the energy ... the simple opposition of the play's attitudes, and the spirit in which its hero, a virile but theatrical creature of arrogant nonchalance, was conceived, hypnotised the viewer'.[115] This was 'live' television, not a recording, which sadly could never be reproduced today. However, it was rewarded with the Italia Prize for television drama, and perhaps more importantly, it encouraged Arden to write more for television.

At this time, Arden and D'Arcy retained a *pied à terre* in London, as they did for the following two decades and more. Friends remember that they had a certain amount of money, and a very pleasant flat. It included two large rooms and was well provided with contemporary furniture, probably from the then-fashionable Habitat. D'Arcy was comparatively domesticated. She was called Margaretta Arden, was a good cook, very hospitable, and provided large meals for visitors. When two of the actors from the Royal Court's Acting Group, Tamara Hinchco and David Andrews, married, Arden and D'Arcy were the witnesses. They brought baby Finn to the ceremony with them in his buggy, and afterwards returned to the flat. D'Arcy had made a large cake, and she had also bought white wine to cele-brate. Later, she, Arden and Finn tactfully went out for a walk, leaving Hinchco and Andrews alone on their wedding afternoon.

Meanwhile, from the autumn of 1959, Arden was also conscientiously pur-suing his duties as Playwright in Residence at the University of Bristol. He found significant support, and friendship, among the staff of the Drama Department, in-cluding Professor Glynne Wickham, George Brandt and Jocelyn Powell. His duties included attending a weekly graduate seminar, which was usually a lively meeting where budding playwrights or other theatre practitioners could meet him. He also attended a few other lectures, and, of course, he was given space and time for writing.

Among the pieces he wrote was probably his most significant essay to date, 'Telling a True Tale', which was published in *Encore* in May 1960. This short piece almost serves as a manifesto for what he thought he was about. Starting with a brief glimpse of the work of some of his contemporaries – Wesker, Osborne, Pinter and

Arthur Miller – Arden states his own concern: to translate 'the concrete life of today into terms of poetry that shall at the one time both illustrate and set it within the historical and legendary tradition of our culture'. He then outlines that tradition. The 'bedrock', he asserts, 'is the ballad'. It is the ballad which has informed the work of the literary tradition he upholds, those 'who have always built close to the bedrock: Chaucer, Skelton, Shakespeare, Jonson, Defoe, Gay, Burns, Dickens, Hardy, Joyce'. It is a tradition which, he believes, 'will always … reach to the heart of the people', not the false tradition which we now call 'heritage', but one in which 'the English prove to be an extraordinarily passionate people, as violent as they are amorous, and quite astonishingly hostile to good government and order'. In terms of theatre, this requires 'hard edges' in costume, music, movement and so on, it must not be afraid of verse or song, and its themes must be those which traditional culture has always addressed. But Arden warns that this road is hard because its workings are easily misunderstood. For instance, many playgoers will expect to 'form judgments' based on what they believe to be the author's 'social standpoint'. But, he argues, in the ballad 'we are given a fable, and we draw our own conclusions'. The tale 'exists in its own right. If the poet is a true one, then the tale will be true too'.[116]

Besides 'Telling a True Tale', Arden was working on two plays, an adaptation of Goethe's *Götz von Berlichingen* and a new original play, to be called *The Happy Haven*, the idea for which came to him after a nightmare involving some 'wild events' at an old people's home. This became the play which fulfilled the last condition of his Residency. Besides these, the Royal Shakespeare Company, which was only formally established under its ambitious young director, Peter Hall, earlier that year, now offered him a commission for a new play. And the success of *Soldier, Soldier* stimulated him into beginning a new television drama, *Wet Fish*. At last Arden's career seemed to be accelerating as the first experimental practical work on *The Happy Haven* began at Bristol University.

It was experimental because the University Drama Department had stipulated that it should be. It was also to make use of the Department's new studio theatre – a small enough space, but adaptable to Shakespearean, eighteenth century or other configurations. In fact, *The Happy Haven* turned out to be a *commedia dell' arte*-style farce, using masks, an open stage and even a pastiche University lecture. It was presented by a company of students reinforced by professionals from the Bristol Old Vic in the early summer of 1960, and went on to be the fourth Arden play in four years to be produced by the Royal Court Theatre, in London, premiering there September 1960.

The play addresses the problem of old people in the Welfare State. It is ostensibly set in an old people's home where the director, Dr Copperthwaite, is engaged in making an elixir which will rejuvenate his ancient 'patients'. At first they are excited by this prospect, but soon they are persuaded by a dissident among their ranks to reject the whole process, and in the shenanigans which follow, they capture Copperthwaite and inject him with the elixir, so that he becomes a child himself, with a 'round, chubby and childish' face, and sucking a lollipop. It was staged without a proscenium arch, but with two doors at the back of the stage, separated by an alcove with sliding doors, and above the alcove a small balcony. The actors wore grotesque masks, the props were huge and two dimensional and the lights were bright and flat. This meant that the University audience, who arrived eager to enjoy themselves, found a refreshingly unusual atmosphere, quite unlike anything to be found in the typical professional London theatre. The stage was set, almost, for 'pretending', for something 'playful'.

Playfulness is at the heart of *commedia dell' arte*. In *The Happy Haven*, the old people play hopscotch, not because old people really do play hopscotch, but as a reminder, perhaps, of their second childhood. The play also uses a favourite *commedia* trick – the imaginary animal which cannot be seen by the audience, even though the character on stage is 'acting' with it. Dr Copperthwaite is a brilliant scientist bent on discovering the elixir of life, like Ben Jonson's Subtle, though of course Copperthwaite, unlike Subtle, really does believe in his alchemy. For the elixir of life must be taken seriously if it is to be discovered. It was the goal of alchemists through the ages, the potion which would prolong life to infinity. The provenance of this search for eternal rejuvenation across mythologies is notable: in Greece it resided in Medea's cauldron, in Germany in the white stone in Reynard's ring. Copperthwaite is (or would like to be) a reincarnation of the divine king who brings health and prosperity to those in his kingdom, a King Arthur-like figure, who is also a magician, and whose relation to the Fool indicates the 'magical dimension of folly'.[117] It could be said that Copperthwaite brings health through laughter, not to the pretended old people in the play, but to us, the spectators.

By the end of the summer of 1960, preparations for the production of *The Happy Haven* at the Royal Court were beginning. Arden was busy on this and his other projects. D'Arcy was left in Brent Knoll in a cheap, damp ground floor flat with a baby. She was, it appeared, of no significance, a mere appendage to the fast-rising hope of the new radical British theatre. But in fact, when Arden was discovering problems with the realization of *The Happy Haven*, he had turned to her. In particular, he remembered a playlet she had written about two old people playing hopscotch. Delightedly, Arden incorporated this into *The Happy Haven* virtually unchanged. But D'Arcy's contribution went unacknowledged at the time, and the play was made public under the name of Arden alone. To some extent D'Arcy must have accepted this, but perhaps that is illustrative of the times, and her mindset within the times. But this partial collaboration, if not its unacknowledged status, can be seen now as a crucial moment in the Arden-D'Arcy relationship: it was the seed of the future, the first move towards working together.

But that summer and autumn of 1960 saw something of a crisis in their relationship because of the different paths down which convention seemed to be sending them. Arden was content – excited, even – to go where his career was leading him, but D'Arcy was far from happy. All her past – the wild Irish girl, the eager seeker after Dublin culture, the fast-learning professional actress – refused to accept her subordinate status. There was little or no social life in the village of Brent Knoll, no companionship of like minds. She was simply left to herself. She was young, energetic and still intellectually involved with the Catholic church, specifically the burgeoning radical movement inside that church. But she was an Irish woman, alone in a dormant English village. What was she do to while Arden was in Bristol, consorting with leading theatre intellectuals and lively-minded students? She would have liked to attend some of Arden's seminars, but she was not invited.

She was, however, invited to accompany him to the International Universities' Drama Festival, held in the summer of 1960 at the University of Erlangen, in Bavaria in what was then West Germany, an event which made a significant mark on both of them. Accompanied by George Brandt, Lecturer in the Bristol University Drama Department, who interpreted for them, they found themselves plunged into the centre of a series of debates, largely concerning the role of drama in society. It was 1960. The influence of Bertolt Brecht, who had died four years previously, was at its height, especially in West Germany. Now Gunter Grass argued for a drama not 'hidden' in theatres, but one which escaped into society, an idea which probably lit a slow-burning fuse in D'Arcy's brain.

For Arden, the festival was most notable for a one-man performance of the thirteenth century German poem, *Meier Helmbrecht*, which tells the story of the peasant Meier leaving his rural home to join a band of dispossessed knights-turned-outlaws. With them he commits a series of appalling crimes, but he is nevertheless welcomed home like the Prodigal Son. However, at the wedding of his sister to one of his companion robber-knights, the forces of the law surprise the gang, and ghastly punishment follows. The now blind and mutilated Meier is rejected by his father, and is hanged by his fellow-peasants whom he betrayed. The poem's didacticism does not detract from the force and realism of the tale, and in the performance here Arden and D'Arcy noted the intensity of its simple story-telling style and its stripped-down theatricality.

Meanwhile, *The Happy Haven* was coming to the boil in London. William Gaskill, the director, proved helpful with adjusting the text to the proscenium stage, and his rehearsals were creative and dynamic. But when the play opened, it was probably Arden's biggest disaster, at least in commercial terms. It ran for just twenty-one performances, during which it sold a mere 12% of capacity at the Box Office, and it lost the English Stage Company over £1000. The critics were also unkind. Not untypical was Kenneth Tynan, according to whom it was 'an elephantine comedy of humours'.[118] The chairman of the ESC, Neville Blond, voiced his displeasure, but George Devine defended Arden's work with some asperity, calling Arden 'probably the next most important dramatist to Osborne we have produced'. He went on: 'We must support the people we believe in, *especially* if they don't have critical appeal',[119] and he enlisted the novelist, Alan Sillitoe, to defend the play publicly.

It was the use of masks, which derived from George Devine's workshop with the writers' group, which most worried both professional critics and ordinary spectators; indeed, almost every published discussion of this play seems to founder on the use of masks. Admittedly, masks are not usual in British theatre. But Arden had a right to expect at least the professional theatre critics to be aware of theatrical history, and therefore to be able to see how he was using the tradition of *commedia dell' arte*, and perhaps even explain this. Albert Hunt demonstrated a few years later how *The Happy Haven* can become a delight to performers and spectators alike in performance, and his account of the work of his students is well worth considering. Speed, simplicity and fun were the key ingredients, and an absolute rejection of intellectualisation:

> The costumes were anything we could find in the wardrobes of local
> dramatic societies, or in junk shops. The props were huge cardboard cut-
> outs – for example, for the scene in which the liquid turns green, we
> simply had a cut-out two-dimensional card, in the shape of a decanter,
> with the liquid painted brown on one side, green on the other. The
> moment of the greatest discovery in human history became a very
> obvious showman's trick.[120]

D'Arcy, who was perhaps the original of Mrs Phineus, which part she played in Dublin in 1963, attended one or two of Hunt's rehearsals, and explained to the group how they must not play 'being old', but rather play young people *showing* 'being old'. The difference is key. And she also suggested the use of music which transformed the finale in Hunt's production. It is worth noting, too, that the play's continuing relevance was amply demonstrated by the audience's reaction when Arden and D'Arcy revived it, in a community production in Galway in 2009, fifty years after its premiere.

Now, however, in the autumn of 1960, Arden returned to Brent Knoll 'shattered and humiliated'.[121] The professional theatre had failed to nourish him. But D'Arcy had found nourishment. She had began to 'scratch around' the life of the inhabitants, particularly the older women, of Brent Knoll. When she met an old woman while out pushing Finn's pram, she would engage her in conversation, and 'the underside' of rural culture was gradually revealed to her: 'the ancient folklores, the old mother-goddess still breathing her message of randomness, chaos, anarchy, anathema to the military-industrial complex'.[122] By now she was pregnant again, but as the unborn baby grew, so ideas for working with the local community grew, too. Remembering playing during her childhood, she began to wonder about creating something playful here, substituting the neighbours for her sisters. She discussed the idea with the vicar, Rev Gliddon, himself a theatre enthusiast. He encouraged her to make a Christmas nativity play, which would involve local people, and be presented in the local church. This was a small but beautiful old building in the Perpendicular style, with a Norman doorway and fascinating and impressive carved bench ends. After the experience of *Meier Helmbrecht* the simplicity and strength of the church made an instant appeal. So while the vicar, with help from D'Arcy, sweet-talked the locals into committing themselves to the venture, she and Arden created the play.

The Business of Good Government is like an updated medieval mystery play, with the kind of naïveté which even today makes the mystery plays so powerful. But D'Arcy and Arden's play is also informed by contemporary attitudes. This is seen most obviously in the treatment of Herod. For Herod's dilemma is a very real one: in the political boiler house he inhabits, ruling over a fractious kingdom which is dominated by the might, and the suspicions, of the Roman Empire, how is he to deal with the unexpected appearance of three powerful-looking foreign dignitaries, who claim they know of a baby who will be a king when he grows up, just born in Herod's territory? The business of good government requires that this threat to good order be dealt with peremptorily and effectively, and in having all the new-born infants of Judaea slaughtered, he takes the only practicable solution open to him. The play dramatises succinctly, tactfully, the problem order has with anarchy, logic has with illogicality, for what could be less logical, or less susceptible to good order, than the unexpected birth of a Saviour in a stable? For George Brandt, Arden and D'Arcy's Herod was reminiscent of President Truman trying to justify dropping the hydrogen bomb on Hiroshima.

The nervous cast gathered to rehearse in Arden and D'Arcy's flat next to the church. Most of them had never acted before, but they gained confidence as they realized that they were not being asked to emulate Marlon Brando in a smouldering Tennessee Williams' film, that they really had to do no more than stand and speak their lines with clarity and conviction. This they could do, and if they subtly altered some of the written lines to fit their natural speech rhythms, so much the better. The production developed its own kind of fluid staging, which used the church's architecture creatively but unobtrusively: the chancel steps became the main acting area, with the processional entry taking place down the nave, the Angel stationed in the pulpit, and so on. Costumes were largely improvised by the cast, though some came from Bristol University's Drama Department, and they retained a suitable emblematic quality: Herod wore robes and a crown, for instance, and also swung a large sword; the Wise Men (two women and one man – John Arden) wore tunics and fur hats; the womenfolk were dressed in a manner somewhat reminiscent of Breughel's peasants. The lighting was supplied by three flood lamps at full power on the acting area. The organ was used occasionally at set points in the play, but the songs were unaccompanied.

Here was a drama not 'hidden in a theatre', but a part of the community's life. It was hardly what is conventionally considered to be 'theatre,' even amateur theatre, and 'the vicar was so sure it was going to flop he washed his hands of the whole business'.[123] But for D'Arcy and Arden, this was a theatrical situation where their ideas were able to obtain some grip. It was impossible in Brent Knoll church to pretend to illusion. As D'Arcy did most of the directing, and Arden acted, they found a new, and natural, place, as writers, in the production process. What they created, in fact, was a true community theatrical event, in what might today be called a 'site specific' performance: cast, audience, time and place were all as specific as they could be, and the story was one all were glad to share. Moreover, the play, and its unexpected originality, was noticed beyond the village of its performance, due partly at least to the enthusiasm of the staff of Bristol University. There were warm reviews in some of the national newspapers, and West of England television also broadcast a piece on it. The play has lived on, too. It was broadcast on 16 December 1964 with a cast which included Tony Britton, Ralph Truman and Patrick Waddington, and has been probably the most frequently performed play (mostly by amateurs, students and school groups at Christmas) in the whole Arden-D'Arcy canon. A Dutch company made a film of it, *Een Zaek van algemeen belang*, directed by Gerard Rekers, and with Jos Bergman, Wim de Haas and Jerome Reehuis in the caast in 1963, and in 1974 there was a Finnish film, *Herodes ja pyhä yö*, with Kalevi Haapoja as Herod. And today the play is as effective as ever as a shot across the bows of Christmas complacency.

The whole experience developed D'Arcy and Arden's thoughts and ideas about the theatre in significant directions. Its non-professional basis actually made it seem more meaningful. And, equally important, this was their first true collaboration. It was, said Arden, his 'most enjoyable theatrical experience' to date.[124]

Seven : Festivals of Anarchy

Two days after *The Business of Good Government* was over, Arden and D'Arcy's third son, Adam, was born. But like Gwalchmei, their first son who had died, Adam was desperately ill. The new baby's problem was pyloric-stenosis, exactly what D'Arcy herself had suffered from when she was born. He was taken to Taunton Hospital, where he was operated on, at first unsuccessfully, but then successfully. D'Arcy stayed in the hospital with him, increasingly distraught as this experience recalled so vividly that of her first son.

Meanwhile, the purpose of their life in Bristol and Brent Knoll had come to a natural conclusion, and Arden's parents, now living in Knaresborough, urged them to move nearer to them. Arden himself was happy to go to Yorkshire, and his father found a cottage for sale, which was within their means, in the village of Kirkbymoorside on the York moors. Arden visited it, liked it and took it. It required extensive renovation, including a new roof, but still, Arden was a qualified architect and was confident he could oversee what needed to be done. In the meantime, the family would live in rented accommodation in Full Sutton, south of Kirkbymoorside, by the battlefield of Stamford Bridge, near York.

The cottage at Kirkbymoorside proved more of a challenge than Arden had imagined, and in the end the family lived for more than a year in the two furnished rooms in the cold farmhouse in Full Sutton. They also had the use of a scullery as a kitchen. They were more or less forced to eat outdoors, and D'Arcy remembered occasions when she had to sweep snow off the table before breakfast could be set. The house was the property of the farmer's widow, Mrs Husband, who lived in the rest of the house, and its setting was marred by the fact that out of the window could be discerned an American rocket launching site. Mostly the missiles were out of sight, but in times of crisis, the rockets would be animated, their sleek noses pointed towards the invisible Communist enemy over the horizon. It was an alarm-ing reality.

Their time in Full Sutton was not particularly uplifting. D'Arcy spent long hours pushing the pram and walking the children, while Arden was absorbed in his writing. His most interesting new work at this period was done with the BBC. *Death of a Cowboy* was a short experimental work which derived from the American folk song, *The Streets of Laredo*, in which a young cowboy is dying. 'Once in my saddle I used to go dashin'', the song proclaims, but now he has been 'to card playin'' where he 'got shot in the breast' and killed.[125] Arden's play explores this: a wild young cowboy forswears gambling, but will have one last game with his last dollar, provided the cards are turned up by a total stranger. The stranger does not approve of gambling, but since this is the cowboy's last game, he obliges. The young cowboy wins, and demands another game. The stranger refuses, guns are drawn, and the young cowboy is shot dead. The stranger turns out to be the sheriff.

More substantial was *Wet Fish*, transmitted in September 1961. Arden hoped that this would capitalize on the success of *Soldier, Soldier*. Television could perhaps offer an alternative to writing for the live stage where so many of his plays had been so poorly received. Less fanciful than *Soldier, Soldier*, this play concerns an architect's assistant who is building an extension to a client's fish and chip shop, but is constantly hampered, and finally altogether prevented, by all sorts of corruptions and self-interests which surround him in the shape of the other characters, both in the office and outside at the site. The play contains plenty of comic social observation, a way with names which puts Arden firmly in the tradition of Ben Jonson and Charles Dickens (the best is probably Archdeacon Pole-Hatchett), and sometimes it employs characters seen in other Arden plays. Sir Harold Sweetman, later to figure prominently in *The Workhouse Donkey*, makes his first appearance here, while 'Krank', Sigismanfred Krankowicz from *The Waters of Babylon*, makes his last – still sinister, still suspicious, sidling in and out, seducing women, buying up derelict property and running a prostitution racket. There are also a number of gorgeously mad *commedia dell'arte*-style moments, as when

> Workmen are bringing in enormous quantities of their apparatus and
> materials for the building, passing and repassing between the shop and
> the street. Two of them, singing 'When Father Papered the Parlour',
> come through with a number of long planks carried between them. They
> barge through the wet fish area and dump their load down across the
> door leading to the frying department. Doris, dodging about the place,
> trying to keep an eye on things, endeavours to intercept them. Etc.

Anyone who has seen a silent movie which included a 'long plank' will immediately understand the potential for comic mayhem here.

But much of that potential was not realized in production. After the BBC had commissioned *Wet Fish*, Stuart Burge, the director who had made such a success of *Soldier, Soldier*, moved to Granada Television, where by the way he presented the television adaptation of *Serjeant Musgrave's Dance*. *Wet Fish* was handed to Peter Dews, a bluff Yorkshireman who had made his name directing a number of vernacular comedies. Dews was not interested in meeting Arden, who, after *Soldier, Soldier* thought he knew what he wanted, nor was Dews prepared to use the script in anything other than a literal manner. His approach did not include exploration or experimentation with the ideas, which was how the play had been conceived. Moreover, Arden's preferred actors were not cast. One consequence of this was that several roles were misconceived, and the play clearly suffered. The critics were not hostile; indeed John Russell Taylor wrote generously of it, calling it 'rather a ragbag, but a lively one, bursting all over with scenes and strands of good plays which do not quite, in the end, hold together'.[126] But Arden himself was disappointed.

His disappointment stemmed not solely from the finally transmitted production, but perhaps more significantly, from the production process. He had looked for input into the selection of director and cast, as well as involvement in the way rehearsals and filming were conducted. In the event, Dews not only failed to consult him about these matters, he never spoke a word to Arden during the whole of the work. In the Preface to *Soldier, Soldier and Other Plays*, Arden made plain his grievance, and complained that there was 'an easy let-out for a management faced with a difficult author', namely, that the author's approval for any such matters should not be 'unreasonably withheld'.[127] He was learning that theatres and television studios can be autocratic and bloody-minded, but his phraseology gave a dangerous hostage to fortune: was Arden really suggesting he was 'a difficult author'?

Two weeks after the transmission of *Wet Fish*, Arden and D'Arcy were both caught up in political protest, separately, and in new ways. The so-called Cold War had been intensifying since the 1940s. By 1961, the crises were extremely dangerous. In April, the newly-elected and inexperienced President Kennedy authorised the invasion of the Bay of Pigs in Cuba to try to overthrow the Soviet-aligned revolution there, led by Fidel Castro. It was a disaster. Then in August, Soviet Union forces in Germany began to construct a wall across Berlin, physically divid-ing east from west.

The unspoken danger behind these moves had been apparent since the 1945 bombing of Hiroshima: the hydrogen bomb. In April 1957, a British Defence White Paper admitted that there was no real defence against an enemy's nuclear attack. Popular unease grew, and found expression in November 1957, when the ageing socialist novelist and playwright, J.B.Priestley, wrote an impassioned article in the *New Statesman* magazine, protesting against 'nuclear madness,' and asserting that there was 'no decency, no faith, hope nor charity'[128] in the H-Bomb. His article brought a rush of agreement and an instant desire to organise against it. In January 1958, the editor of the *New Statesman* called together various religious, political and cultural figures, who in turn called a public meeting on 17 February 1958 in Central Hall, Westminster. Over 5,000 people attended – a number far in excess of anything which had been foreseen. J.B.Priestley spoke, as did Canon John Collins of St Paul's Cathedral, the philosopher Bertrand Russell, the historian A.J.P.Taylor and others, and the Campaign for Nuclear Disarmament was launched. Arden and D'Arcy both joined.

At Easter, the first annual Aldermaston March took place, and the movement grew so fast that three years later there were at least 100,000 people in Trafalgar Square at the end of the march. But as with so many progressive movements, CND soon found its activists disagreeing among themselves. By 1960 it had become obvious that Canon Collins's position – that CND was a vehicle of protest, and no more – was at odds with that of Bertrand Russell, who advocated a campaign of civil disobedience comparable with that of the suffragettes fifty years before. On 21 October 1960, Russell resigned as President of CND, and the following day he and Rev Michael Scott officially inaugurated the Committee of 100, dedicated to direct action, civil disobedience along the lines of Gandhian non-cooperation, non-aggression and non-retaliation. The first announced supporters included John Arden and Margaretta D'Arcy, along with John Osborne, Arnold Wesker, William Gaskill, Christopher Logue. Hugh McDiarmid, Ewan MacColl, Vanessa Redgrave, Shelagh Delaney and many more. The idea was that an arrest of a prominent person would be newsworthy, whereas the arrest of an ordinary member of the public could pass unnoticed. Therefore one hundred prominent people would be arrested for civil disobedience at an appropriate demonstration, and that immediately a further one hundred prominent people would take their place. When they were arrested, another one hundred would step forward. And so on. It was a classic anarchist policy.

The Committee's first direct action took place on 18 February 1961, to co-incide with the arrival of American Polaris nuclear-armed submarines, to be based in Holy Loch in Scotland. Up to 20,000 people supported the demonstration, and several thousand of them sat or lay down outside the Ministry of Defence in London. After this success their subversion gathered pace. They pioneered a kind of pirate radio station, using a broadcasting unit inside a van to send out their message on the BBC television frequency after it had closed down for the night. The police cautioned them, but this only added fuel to their flame. On 29 April, at a demonstration in defiance of the police, 826 people were arrested, and then processed though the courts ten at a time. It was stated that 422 fines had been handed out in five and a half hours at Bow Street Magistrates Court.

The Committee of 100's greatest demonstration, however, was planned for 17 September. Pre-emptive arrests were made of prominent supporters, especially those who lived in or near London, before the planned date – an action which, of course, increased the numbers at the protest. Thirty-six people, including Bertrand Russell himself, were accused of inciting members of the public to commit a breach of the peace. They were required to promise good behaviour for twelve months, and when they refused, they were sent to gaol until the planned action had passed. On 17 September, the Committee of 100's supporters – including John Arden – arrived at Trafalgar Square to discover it had been cordoned off by the police. Many still infiltrated, and sat on the ground, Gandhi-fashion. Others marched round the square. Gradually, the non-violent intent weakened, there was pushing and pulling, and scuffles broke out. One commentator, by no means a supporter of the anti-nuclear campaign, described how:

Committee of 100 demonstration, 17 September 1961.

arrests began, to an obligato of jeering and bawling from the milling
demonstrators and onlookers. A steady stream of prisoners, some
demonstrators and some not, were herded into vans and carted away ...
After midnight the reason for the summary removal of prominent people
became suddenly and shockingly obvious. Ranked policemen ...
launched a deliberate and vicious attack against the scattered remnants of
the crowd ... Demonstrators, onlookers, passers-by – it made no
difference – were punched, knocked down, kicked.[129]

Approximately 1500 people, including John Arden, were arrested that day, and most
were held overnight in police cells. The following day, several courts were kept busy
sentencing them. Those who pleaded 'Guilty of necessity' to the charge were usually
fined £50 and discharged. Some replied that they did not recognize the right of the
court to pass judgment on their moral stand. The ringleaders were sentenced to
months in prison. Michael Randle, the organiser of the first Aldermaston March,
because of his past record, received eighteen months.

Arden had proceeded to London after the London members of the Committee of 100 had been arrested. Once there, had linked up with William Gaskill,
who had directed *The Happy Haven* at the Royal Court. They went to Trafalgar
Square early in order to be there before the police cordoned it off, and decided to
wait in the National Gallery café. There, however, with a mixture of chagrin and

amusement, they discovered several other supporters, including theatre people, who had had the same idea. Gaskill remembered that Arden, 'who always aped the gypsy in his dress, was for once wearing a suit as a form of disguise. I was wearing a rather camp striped mackintosh. "You look very conspicuous," John said. "So do you," I replied'.[130]

As Margaretta D'Arcy tells it, Arden attended the demonstration, where he sat quietly in Trafalgar Square while the mayhem was proceeding around him. Finally, a theatrical acquaintance, who had been arrested, spotted him from the back of a police van, and called out to him: 'What the fuck are you doing? Get in with us!'[131] Arden in fact had taken literally the Gandhian prescription to avoid confrontation, and to remain simply disobedient. If then the police took action, it would be they who were disturbing the peace. (It should be added that Arden was always and on principle against making any sort of martyr of himself.) On 17 September, having dispatched a telegram to D'Arcy telling her what had happened, he spent the night in a police cell with John Osborne, and was duly fined and sent on his way the next day.

Meanwhile, D'Arcy, unable to be in London, devised her own protest against militarism and the bomb. She bicycled from Mrs Husband's farmhouse to the American base nearby, through the prohibited area, with a letter which she delivered to the commander. It asked him to examine his conscience: was his mind easy with the idea of causing mass devastation and destruction? She bicycled home. Some days later, in the evening after dark, the local policeman called. He had in his possession D'Arcy's letter, which could be interpreted as an incitement to military personnel to desert. He pointed out to her that this was a treasonable offence which carried a penalty of up to twenty years in gaol. He left her to ponder this.

A little later, Mrs Husband suggested that her accommodation was perhaps not suitable for them, perhaps they should seek somewhere more appropriate. Whether this was connected with the policeman's visit was never made explicit. Arden offers an alternative reason in the television film, *John Arden, Playwright*, that the final straw was that the area round the house, composed of beautiful cedar trees – 'the most beautiful cedar trees outside Lebanon' – including a field in which a donkey dwelt, was being redeveloped for houses. The cedar trees were cut down and the donkey killed.

An advertisement which D'Arcy placed in the *New Statesman* was answered by someone with a tiny island on Lough Corrib in the west of Ireland for sale. The price was just affordable. Arden contacted his former London flatmate, Tom Austin, now settled in Dublin, and he negotiated the purchase. The family moved there in the early summer of 1962.

They thus left the Committee of 100 behind. Life on the tiny island on Lough Corrib effectively isolated them. The outside world took on 'an intermittent and illusory quality',[132] and the Cuba Missile Crisis of October 1962 and Harold Macmillan's deal to acquire Polaris submarines from USA that December happened without much immediate effect on them. They lived in a small wooden hut, the only building on the eight-acre island. They kept a small rowing boat in which to reach the mainland, where they stored a pair of bicycles in order to go to the shops in the nearest town, Oughterard. In Arden's story, 'The Fork in the Head' in *Awkward Corners*, an Englishman lives with his Irish partner on just such an island. In the hot weather, insects plague them; on wet nights the rain rattles on the corrugated iron roof, and the roof leaks. The story is not autobiography, but it surely echoes some elements of their island life. When the couple in the story return home after time away, they 'unlock the cabin, collect twigs and dead branches, light a fire on the hearth, cook some sausages and boil a kettle for coffee or tea.' He eats the sausages while his partner 'gather[s] blackberries from the brambles all round the back of the cabin'. They spend hours cleaning up the cabin, checking that rats have not damaged anything.[133] Another perspective is offered by the actor and director, Gavin Richards: 'I first met them in Ireland where I was taken to a lake where a rowing boat came out of the mist and (in) it was John. At that time he was a mighty figure in the theatre so I was pretty awestruck'.[134]

Life on the island was clearly difficult in some respects, and the lack of a meaningful social dimension probably meant that eventually it lost its flavour, especially for D'Arcy. But for a while she found a freedom which was highly attractive. Perhaps it reminded her of her childhood days in Glendalough in the Wicklow mountains. There was no traffic, no telephone, no radio or television, and no electricity. The children were free – 'They knew nothing but the birds and the bees – they were pretty wild', according to their friend, Nancy Coughlan.[135] Arden told them stories at bedtime by candlelight. There was plenty of space to grow vegetables, which formed the basis of the large meals D'Arcy provided. Her fourth son, Jacob, was born now, in Galway Hospital in July 1962. Yet she herself was still rejecting political Ireland. The furore aroused by the anti-nuclear campaign in Britain had failed to engage the Roman Catholic Church, which frowned on the protesters. D'Arcy found herself losing her allegiance, freeing herself from Catholicism, reordering her thinking. She studied topics such as workers control, the new cinema, direct action, children's playgrounds, anarchism and squatting.

Arden's work done on the island included plays, but also a filmscript of the story of Ned Kelly for Karel Reisz, and poetry, including:

> *The Lobster Pot*
> Who can tell how the lobster got
> Into the lobster pot?
> When he went in he did not doubt

There was a passage out.

There was not.

Did he feel himself on this island somewhat like the lobster? In any case, in late 1962 the Kirkbymoorside council contacted them, demanding to know what was going to happen to the cottage Arden had bought? If nothing, why should they (the Council) not pull it down and charge for their services? And in December Joseph D'Arcy, Margaretta's father, died. Next spring they returned to Yorkshire.

Kirkbymoorside was something of a cultural backwater. The economy was based in agriculture, but the people were not rich. Most of them regularly attended one of the five different denominational churches. The village had something over two thousand inhabitants but with the nearest theatre over thirty miles away, and the nearest cinema seven miles distant, their local entertainment – especially since the railway had been closed – hardly extended beyond one of the six pubs in the town. There was also a more or less defunct youth club, and a market which was held once a week. Arden and D'Arcy's cottage was on the outskirts, 'in a funny little collection of houses that ran along by a disused railway and a disused gasworks – very odd houses that were rather squalid-looking outside but highly decorated inside with enormous quantities of vast candlesticks and things'.[136] Nearby more or less itinerant tinkers stayed – 'scum of the earth ... beggars', according to a local schoolteacher.[137]

Nevertheless, to Arden and perhaps to D'Arcy, there was a pervasive atmosphere conducive to their work. He recalled that this vicinity was a centre of Christian culture in the Dark Ages. There were one or two small evocative Saxon churches, and a sense of people being tucked away to avoid notice which he imagined might be a tenuous hangover from the days of Viking raids. For Arden this kind of association spread as far as Whitby, where the ruined Abbey's aura still overshadowed the contemporary fishing village, for all the latter's depressed economic state, its rundown fish and chip shops and scruffy bingo halls.

'You must be mad coming here', one young mother scolded them. 'Kirkby's dead. All it's good for is dying'.[138] To the locals Arden and D'Arcy were clearly eccentric. They had no telephone, no radio and no television. The local Police Force even seemed to find Arden suspicious because of his long hair, and he was questioned more than once. Their lifestyle was unconventional in the extreme. Albert Hunt, not a local and certainly not conventional himself, remembered visiting them, and being 'amazed':

> I was just totally knocked out by Margaretta's way of life ... they lived in
> this council house in Kirkbymoorside, and there was a main road that ran
> from Kirkbymoorside to Pickering. Margaretta and I were sitting
> together, and a man comes down with a little boy – Jacob, I think – very
> small, and this farmer was bringing him and he was stark naked. And the

guy said to Margaretta: "We just found him on the main road, and thought we'd better bring him back", and Margaretta just said to me, "Oh, look at him, isn't he lovely?"'[139]

John Calder, the *avant-garde* publisher, remembered visiting 'on a sunny Saturday morning':

> The small Arden children, cherubic crawlers and toddlers, some able to run, were all naked, playing in the dust near a main road with no fences and fast traffic. I kept picking them up and bringing them back to the cottage but John and Margaretta Arden were unconcerned. They let the children go where they wanted, heedless of the dangers.[140]

But to D'Arcy, who was in the process of rejecting the metropolitan-based culture of the liberal élite, life in the country had one great advantage: it 'meant creating one's own entertainment ... Moving into a village just because the rent was low was a bit arrogant – what had *we* to offer?'[141]

The answer turned out to be an event which has come to be known as 'Kirkbymoorside 63'. The idea for this was D'Arcy's. She was angry that Arden had received virtually all the credit for *The Business of Good Government* (it was even published under his name alone): she saw that she was thought of as merely an appendage to him. Yet she had animated the whole event. Now she decided to use some of the ideas she had developed, partly from her reading, to create a new sort of arts festival. The idea was in the air: Arnold Wesker was at this time organising Centre 42, and Joan Littlewood had imagined a Fun Palace, but both these failed. D'Arcy spent most of the rest of her life pursuing something like what was expressed in both these, what she came later to call 'loose theatre'. The kind of event which she now created in Kirkbymoorside was, if not a start, because *The Business of Good Government* was perhaps her start, at least a conscious setting-forth.

D'Arcy's idea was both more and less ambitious than Wesker's or Littlewood's. It began with simply exploring the community, as she had in Brent Knoll: this was something that neither Wesker nor Littlewood had thought of. Yet it was at the core of what D'Arcy was attempting: famous or progressive poets, playwrights, painters or musicians were welcome to participate, but the key people involved would be the locals. If Kirkbymoorside was to have a festival, it would be Kirkbymoorside's to create and possess first, though after that others were welcome, too. Albert Hunt, theatre director, cultural *animateur* and educator, recalls how he went to a fairground with her at this time, 'and she was looking round at people that she might contact, that she might involve in some way – the sort of things that intellectual people were looking down on in those days – Saturday night dances, that sort of thing'.[142] She obtained a film camera, and began to make a film of the town, which 'seemed to be so cold and dead'. But 'if a film were to be made, the people could hardly fail to be interested, she thought'.[143] Indeed, almost everyone was interested, and Tamara Hinchco remembered that during that summer, 'whenever you went there (Kirkbymoorside), Margaretta always had this camera'. The people were curious, then co-operative; they had a new interest, a new life. Finally, D'Arcy obtained so much material that she divided it into two separate films. The first focuses on Derek, the disillusioned son of a laundry worker, who is utterly depressed by the lack of social or cultural life or indeed any opportunities in the town. The other is a more general record of the community, with a commentary spoken by Arden. According to Hinchco, 'It's a wonderful little film'.[144]

It was from this soil that 'Kirkbymoorside 63' grew. D'Arcy wanted to open up the town, to offer an open-ended, arts-biased event, lasting over weeks, in her own home. It would cost nothing. Anyone who wanted to come could do so – either to create, or to watch others create, or to discuss, argue, suggest, criticise, or simply to be there. The idea was discussed, including with anarchistic and artistic friends in London, and then this mock-heroic advertisement, taking a whole page, was inserted in *Encore*, the radical theatre magazine of the time:

AN APPEAL BY JOHN ARDEN

Living as he does in Kirkbymoorside, a small Yorkshire town … From which the railway has been removed; in which there is neither theatre not cinema: nor indeed much industry (save for a small Glider Factory and a Brickworks): near which the principal Sign of our Times is the alarming, unearthly, impossibly beautiful and probably totally unnecessary Early Warning Station on Fylingdales Moor …

And where the population in general, deprived of their old social entertainments such as

A German Band

A Dancing Bear

An annual Goose-Fair

The arrival of a daily Train at the Railway Station

(all remembered with grave nostalgia by the older

inhabitants)

Resort to no fewer than five distinct sectarian Churches of a Sunday, thereby splitting into excessive fragments a community already sufficiently fragmented by the Cruelty of the Twentieth Century and the Affluence of the South …

JOHN ARDEN

Has conceived the idea of establishing

A FREE PUBLIC ENTERTAINMENT

in his house.

To take place at intervals between the fifteenth of August and the fifteenth of September.

MR ARDEN has been indirectly described by MR WESKER as a
Paralysed Liberal ... If anybody wishes to assist him to overcome this
paralysis, which he is inclined to admit
MR ARDEN is resident in London until the tenth of July at: 9 Kings
Avenue, Bromley, Kent (Tel: RAVensbourne 1991) and thereafter at Mill
Cottage, Kirkby Mills, Kirkbymoorside, York. He would be inordinately
grateful for suggestions or offers of assistance towards the furtherance of
this small project.
No specific form of entertainment is at present envisaged but it is hoped
that in the course of it the forces of Anarchy, Excitement, and Expressive
Energy latent in the most apparently sad persons shall be given release.
- - - - - - - - - -

MR ARDEN also needs a number of helpers to come back with him to
Kirkbymoorside to stay until the fifteenth of September, for whom he will
be prepared to Pay Expenses and Provide Food and Accom-modation.

COME TO KIRKBYMOORSIDE AND HELP ARDEN TO SPEND HIS MONEY LIKE WATER[145]

Baz Kershaw comments on this 'appeal':

The curious strategy of advertising a local and rural event in a national
avant garde theatre journal is nicely matched by the notion of public
anarchy in a domestic setting. In the advertisement Arden mentions
Arnold Wesker, drawing attention to the implicit contrast between the
dotty idea of the home-spun entertainment and the grandiose plans of
Centre 42 ... It (the appeal) warns against solemnity and pretentious-
ness. So if the aims of the experiment appeared faintly ludicrous, then at
least its aesthetic would be good fun.[146]

With a number of expressions of interest from members of the London
intelligentsia, Arden returned to Yorkshire to prepare the festival.

And once it was under way, it was apparent that D'Arcy's filming intervention
in the community had had its effect. Very many local people attended, seventy or
eighty of them almost every night. Ian Watson's account of the event records how at
the beginning of each evening people would wander into the house, help themselves
to cups of tea in the kitchen, and then sit and chat easily while waiting for any
performance. Later they played darts, or watched themselves with amusement in the
community films. They seem to have been remarkably unaffected by the visits at
various times through the month of fifty or more members of the radical
intelligentsia, including Henry Livings, Roger McGough, Brian Patten, John Calder,
Jon Silkin, John Fox and others. Indeed, if anything, the boot was on the other foot:
there is an amusing description of Sir Herbert Read arriving late one evening with

Lady Read and their daughter, and watching nervously from the doorway as the locals, oblivious as to who the newcomer was, merrily performed their piece.

Ian Watson's description begins by setting the tone:

> "We start at 8.30", says John Arden, rushing through the kitchen carrying a chamber pot. It is now 7.50. Upstairs, Adam Arden, aged two, is screaming for his pot, Finn, his elder by two years, sits in his pyjamas on the window sill, looking out, waiting. In another upstairs room, an undergraduate of Durham University is putting on a grotesque make-up. Downstairs the kitchen is full of people; some talking in groups, others standing silent and nervous, all occasionally stuffing sausage pie into their mouths and washing it down with tea.[147]

The evening usually began with one or two more or less formal presentations, though hardly formal by conventional standards. People sat round the living room, while a foreign film or a silent comedy was projected; or a visiting theatre troupe presented their piece, Charles Lewsen's *The Bubonic Plague Show*, for instance, or David Campton's *Little Brother, Little Sister*; or a group of local children performed. There might be music, or a poetry reading, or perhaps simply a discussion and argument. A fire-eater was a permanent fixture, though he performed outside, as was the potter who built a kiln for himself in the garden. There were readings from Brecht, Machiavelli, Sean O'Casey, and others, and one highlight was the plays improvised from newspaper headlines: Arden's Army Sergeant who forced his wife to tickle his feet for hours on end and thereby drove her to the divorce court, was one such well-remembered impromptu. Later in the evening, there was dancing, often to rock and roll music, and the evening ended at two, or even three in the morning – only to be repeated the next night.

Albert Hunt's memory of the event is not untypical:

> The thing they did at Kirkbymoorside was really extraordinary, you know. She (D'Arcy) just went out to various places and took a lot of young people – picked them up, you know, and persuaded them to come round to the house. The Sunday night that I was there, there were a whole gang of young people there, including a rock band and – neither of them liked rock, as far as I know – but there was a rock band. And then the evening ended with someone playing again and again, 'Twist and Shout'. I'd never heard 'Twist and Shout' before, and I drove back with it in my head the whole time ... but I mean, it was just amazing – the way she just accepted people who came and did things, and if what they wanted to do was play rock and roll, well, okay . . .[148]

Implied here is D'Arcy's driving motivation, which the artistic and political élite could never understand: an extreme intolerance of those who were culturally well-fed, self-appointed artistic or theatrical pace-setters or simply smugly complacent about their own work, and – equally – an extreme tolerance, even indulgence, of those who were culturally starved or without the means to express themselves.

The politics, or perhaps the ideology, of Kirkbymoorside 63 was suggested by the posters on the living room walls – propaganda posters from the Communist Party and the Conservative Party, a picture of Queen Victoria and a poster for World Peace, as well as an old-fashioned sign: 'God Bless Our Home'. It suggests Arden was correct when later he wrote of the festival being based on 'broadly libertarian anarchistic artistic views,' adding that 'its politics were implicit rather than overt'.[149] No-one was told to do anything – except, perhaps to 'create'. Or to wash up. At least that was the intention, though Arden found himself doing more organising than he wished to, and later, somewhat tongue in cheek, accused himself of 'neo-Stalinism'.[150]

There was inevitably something subversive about Kirkbymoorside 63. This was neither theatre, nor a party, it was neither a public event nor a private one. It was betwixt and between, 'liminal', beyond categorisation. Openness, lack of dogmatism and leaderlessness were built into it, so that its debates were genuine and its events valid: no artist or *animateur* led them. Being non-judgmental, it was not judged, merely enjoyed. Anarchistic it may have been theoretically, but it seems as though in reality it was closer to Dionysian, a sort of Bakhtinian carnival. It was disruptive, even interventionist – yet with the lightest of hearts and the lightest of touches.

And because it was unstructured, liminal, it was dangerous. Arden noted: 'To fill our house every night with a crowd of complete strangers whose behaviour could never be anticipated and whose potential dissatisfaction with the entertainment must always be allowed for was necessarily hard on the nerves'. He also recorded:

> The police had warned us that we would be broken up by hooligans. In
> fact we never were; but the anxiety was always present. One night, after a
> dance in the town, no less than two hundred men came and stood in the
> garden in a menacing manner. They were not from Kirkby but from
> neighbouring villages; they had been in the boozers all evening till eleven,
> and had then propped up the wall of the dance hall, without dancing, I
> imagine; and then they thought that something was on at the Ardens'.
> When we told them that there was no room, they did not go away. They
> stood and growled, (though) in the end they drifted off.[151]

Perhaps the most important feature of Kirkbymoorside 63 was the way it involved local people. A surprising number became involved creatively, making things, performing, and so on. Plenty more were interested, even eager, spectators. Even those who held aloof were responding in their own way, so that it can be said that the whole community was animated by the festival. There was some disagreement about whether it provided cover for young people to enjoy sex, and though this can never be properly ascertained, if it were so that would surely do honour to old Dionysus! Ordinary people learned that they could generate their own entertainment, even in the depressed conditions then prevailing in the town.

For those professionally engaged in the arts, Kirkbymoorside 63 was both eye-opening and influential. It was one of the first, if not the first, of the sixties alternative happenings, and it was one of the more uncompromising. It pointed a clear way forward and lodged deeply in the creative consciousness of those who participated. For instance, Arden and D'Arcy remembered how Bert Howarth, then twenty-two years old, arrived full of enthusiasm, red-bearded and wearing military-style gaiters. He participated energetically, but probably more significantly he met John and Susan Fox, and the seeds of Welfare State International, the most spectacular performance troupe in twentieth century Britain, were sown. One of Fox's earliest ventures was a somewhat similar village festival in Hawnby in Yorkshire in June 1965. The central performance here was Albert Hunt's production of D'Arcy and Arden's short play, *Ars Longa Vita Brevis*, which was presented on the school playground and then in the village hall, with Arden in attendance. Other events were music hall turns, a film show, a piano recital as well as a barn dance and free supper. The *Northern Echo* called Fox's festival 'spontaneous, interesting and relaxing' and said that it was 'undoubtedly cultural but not really highbrow'. It reported:

> The village entered into the spirit of the event. The burst of enthusiasm
> has broken down old barriers between the whist drive group and the
> cricket and the football group. Suddenly the whole village is united.[152]

The event concluded with a musical entertainment and social, including dancing.

As for Arden and D'Arcy, the progenitors of Kirkbymoorside 63, 'the experience was', Arden wrote later, 'educative and finally rewarding'.[153] This is surely too modest. The themes and urges which found expression here would resurface again and again in their work, providing a root and an invigoration which never seemed to flag, and being a kind of prototype for the form which D'Arcy later called 'Loose Theatre'.

In the immediate aftermath, Arden visited the Edinburgh Festival, where he took part in the international drama conference. He surprised some here by insisting that spectators could never be 'converted' in the theatre, though they could perhaps have budding ideas confirmed. Preaching, he averred, merely alienated. However, virtually anything any participant said was overshadowed at the conference by the notorious 'happening' on the last day. A medley of odd occurrences took place, climaxed by the appearance of an apparently-nude woman (only her top half was visible) on a BBC lighting trolley at the back of the stage. She was apparently a model hired by Joan Littlewood. But the event, which caused something of a stir in the nat-

John Arden speaking at the Edinburgh Festival Drama Conference, 1963.

ional press, seems essentially trivial when put beside Kirkbymoorside's festival of a few weeks before.

Eight : A Playwright without his Breeches

In the mid 1960s, John Arden looked, according to the theatre critic, Harold Hobson, like 'a romantic minor prophet (who had just) come hot foot from Sinai'.[154] When it was suggested that the queen should meet him after a special performance of his play, *Left-Handed Liberty* at the Mermaid Theatre, she was advised to beware: 'He needs a haircut. He's one of those hairy ones'.[155]

Nevertheless his writing was increasingly attracting attention. In 1961 he had won the Trieste Festival Award, and this was followed in 1966 by the Vernon Rich Award. When *Armstrong's Last Goodnight* was produced in Glasgow in 1964, the theatre magazine *Encore* recorded 'the eagerness with which the metropolitan pens swarmed up into derelict Gorbals', and suggested this was 'an indication that anything Arden does is now taken seriously and regarded as important'.[156] Later, the editors called him 'the most fascinating and controversial writer in the country'.[157] And by his own account, he had become 'an established writer':

> I earned a reasonable income from royalties, translation-rights and the like; I was invited to give the occasional lecture to a university or literary society; I did not have my next few plays rejected by the managements to whom I offered them.[158]

This was, perhaps, a good time to be a rising playwright: not only had the new Royal Shakespeare Company come into being with theatres in Stratford-upon-Avon and London in 1960, but the new National Theatre, under Sir Laurence Olivier, had also appeared, with its theatres in London and Chichester on the south coast. Opportunities seemed to be increasing.

And Arden was finding plenty of work. He and Lindsay Anderson, director of *Serjeant Musgrave's Dance* at the Royal Court Theatre, were discussing a film of *Live Like Pigs* with Harry Saltzman, best known for producing the first James Bond movies. He was also scripting *Ned Kelly* for Karel Reisz, a film which was never produced, though a later one on the same subject bore a surprising, not to say suspicious, resemblance to Arden's script. In 1963, Peter Brook mounted a controversial production of *Serjeant Musgrave's Dance* in Paris. Albert Hunt, one of Arden's most articulate supporters, disliked the production intensely, believing it 'simply reversed the meaning of Arden's fable'.[159] J.C.Trewin, on the other hand, praised the production, and described something of the controversy:

> On the day after the major reviews, which had spoken of a hysterical and pretentious bore, only five people appeared, though there had been enthusiasm among the intellectual Left Wing critics. Brook was sure that somewhere there ought to be an audience, so they advertised a trio of free performances and immediately had to face swarming crowds and queues

around the theatre. Police pulled iron grilles across the main doors. The company, stirred by a crowded and swiftly alert audience, had never acted better. It appeared to be a young, well-dressed house; when after the play Arthur Adamov, the Left Wing dramatist, and the film directors, Alain Resnais and Jean-Luc Godard came up on the stage along with Brook and the actors, a debate lasted for two hours, indeed until after the last metro had gone; nobody left his seat.[160]

Arden himself, by the way, was happy enough with Brook's production.[161]

Arden also at this time received commissions from opera companies. In 1965, Sadler's Wells presented his gritty, vernacular version of Sonnleithner's libretto for Beethoven's *Fidelio*, and three years later the Bath Festival presented Arden's version of Gamuz's libretto for Stravinsky's *Soldier's Tale,* a production which was later televised. Also for television, BBC2 commissioned a trilogy of original plays: Arden had no three-parter in his mind at the time, but D'Arcy reminded him of his old obsession with King Arthur. Could not this be the moment to revive that project? It was, but the trilogy was not actually produced until 1972, by which time it had transmuted into a stage play, *The Island of the Mighty.*

Meanwhile, Arden was working out the dramaturgical implications of his Royal Court plays in a series of four extraordinary dramas which currently await rediscovery: one rumbustious comedy (*The Workhouse Donkey*), two historical fictions (*Armstrong's Last Goodnight* and *Ironhand*, adapted from Goethe's *Goetz von Berlichingen*) and one history play (*Left-Handed Liberty*), plays which, according to Ronald Hayman, demonstrate that 'alongside (Arden's) extraordinary sociological sensibility' he was now developing 'an extraordinary historical sense'.[162] But still, too often, the contemporary critics found the work problematic. Thus, the poet, Edwin Morgan, in *Encore*, confessed to 'a feeling of uneasy disappointment' when he saw *Armstrong's Last Goodnight*. Broadening his attack to include Arden's apparent equivocation in several of his earlier plays, too, Morgan soared to his peroration:

> If Arden doesn't know what he thinks about kings and outlaws, or gypsies and householders, or soldiers and colliers, or doctors and old women, he should try to find out. It matters![163]

Arden published a long and spirited reply which included the observation that when a journalist had said to him:

> 'Your plays often deal with violence: but are you ever going to write one which presents a solution, or a means to avoid violence?' I replied that there is no solution, except not to practice violence. I don't think she thought this was a very good answer: but in all humility, it is no worse than the answer given by Christ to similar questions. His method was usually to tell an illustrative anecdote. I believe that this is also the method of the theatre.[164]

In other words, what baffled the critics was Arden's refusal to supply a glib answer to the moral problems which his plays addressed. Such apparent naïveté, however grittily presented, was actually, of course, unusual honesty, and as such it provoked rattled uneasiness – as Arden noted mischievously in a little poem which prefaced the published version of *The Workhouse Donkey*:

Some Critics said:
This Arden baffles us and makes us mad:
His play's uncouth, confused, lax, muddled, bad.
Said Arden:
Why do you accuse me and abuse me
And your polite society refuse me,
Merely because I wear no belt nor braces?
There would be reason for the wry mouths in your faces
And reason for your uncommitted halting speeches
If you would but admit I wore no bloody breeches.[165]

And in an interview in 1963, noting that Brecht's *Galileo* was a great play 'because at the end ... you still don't know where you are', he asserted that

Plays are not public arguments. They are a presentation of life. I think that in a play like *The Workhouse Donkey* the action itself is the argument. And anybody who's following the action with his mind open to it ... sitting there and absorbing the play without preconceptions, should be able to tell exactly what the play's about. And this does not need to be reinforced by verbal argument or by cheap theatrical tricks to make one side appear to be the winner.[166]

The Workhouse Donkey was the first of this series of plays for large, conventional stages. It was originally commissioned by the Royal Court Theatre, and intended for production by Lindsay Anderson at the Belgrade Theatre, Coventry, as part of the festival devised to celebrate the opening of the new Coventry Cathedral. However, it was rejected for this purpose. It was seen as dangerous. One strand of its plot clearly reflected the dismissal of nearby Nottingham's Chief Police Constable Popkess a mere three years earlier. Perhaps worse, another strand, depicting disagreements concerning the commissioning of a new Art Gallery, had echoes of Coventry Labour Party's objections to the re-building of the new Cathedral itself, the subject the production was intended to celebrate. However, a copy of the script reached Sir Laurence Olivier, then plan-ning his new Chichester Festival Theatre's programme, with an eye to the est-ablishment of the National Theatre, and he accepted it for production.

The play opened at Chichester on 8 July 1963. It was directed by Stuart Burge, and boasted a star-studded cast including Dudley Foster, Fay Compton, Frank Finlay, Jeremy Brett, Anthony Nicholls, Robert Stephens, Robert Lang, Derek Jacobi,

Norman Rossington and others. Arden aimed, he said, to 'set on the stage the politics, scandals, sex-life and atmosphere of Barnsley, as I remember shocked Conservative elders talking about it in my youth, and ... to deal with local personalities in a raucous Aristophanic manner'.[167] The play has a long and highly complicated story, which unfolds with extraordinary energy and dramatic originality. It was often described as 'Brechtian' by its earliest reviewers; actually it is considerably less like Bertolt Brecht's plays than it is like a Jacobean citizen comedy by Thomas Middleton or Ben Jonson.

Set in a northern town much like Barnsley, the play opens with the ceremonial laying of the foundation stone for a new Police Headquarters, and introduces the just appointed, clipped and straight-backed Chief Constable, Colonel Feng, to the town. He is greeted by Sir Harold Sweetman's Conservatives, and less effusively by Labour's Alderman Charlie Butterthwaite and his supporters. Feng asserts his political neutrality, but both Conservatives and Labour suggest privately to him that he investigate corruption in their opponents' ranks. Faced not only with intrigue, but also with inefficiency, not least in the ranks of the police itself, and also with the apparently-irresistible charms of the local doctor's daughter (the doctor himself having a notoriously 'shady' area to his practice – he fixes abortions, for instance), Feng begins to find even his rigid adherence to order and precedent melting. Meanwhile Charlie Butterthwaite, pressed by the doctor to repay his gambling debts, robs the Town Hall safe for the money he has not got. The ensuing adventures and misadventures lead to his losing his hitherto-iron grip over his Labour colleagues (he was 'the Napoleon of the North'), even as Feng loses all purchase on his post. Feng retires to London, while Butterthwaite appears at the head of a ragamuffin mob, disrupts the opening ceremony of the new town Art Gallery and is driven off like a marauding beggar.

Stuart Burge's production was able to match Arden's writing – it was bustling, brilliant and *louche*. Especially memorable among the excellent cast was Frank Finlay as Butterthwaite, though Anthony Nicholls's ramrod-backed Feng and Norman Rossington as Blomax are also both also etched on the memory. Chichester's wide open stage enabled the contrasts between the dingy pub back room and the spring-bright sun-bathers' garden to be sharply realized, and the roisterous final scene, with Charlie Butterthwaite leading his plebeian crew on stage, dressed as a kind of tatterdemalion Lord of Misrule, really seemed like a Saturnalia. Javed Malick, in his analysis of this play, suggests that it can be read as depicting Butterthwaite's 'spectacular decline and fall',[168] but in production Butterthwaite's recourse to those at the very bottom of the municipality's social scale suggests at least the possibility of a plebeian renaissance, which the defensive solidarity of the 'high-ups' at the end may not be proof against – they proclaim, 'The old sod's gone for good!' But perhaps one may be forgiven for wondering if this is really so.

The critics gave *The Workhouse Donkey* a mixed, not unfriendly reception. The formidable Harold Hobson decided that 'the reason why Mr Arden's work is rarely appreciated properly at a first hearing is that what Brecht pretended to do, Mr Arden actually does',[169] comparing Arden, infuriatingly enough, with Brecht again, though not to Arden's detriment. Less sympathetically, Alan Brien, in *The Sunday Telegraph*, called it 'a theatrical folly, an enormous rambling warren of dead ends and blank walls without any architectural merit'.[170] Rather more subtly, Geoffrey Carnall, in *Peace News*, taking Butterthwaite's final ungovernability as rage, wondered whether the play was not 'an uncritical glorification of the tantrum, going on the rampage'. Arden answered sardonically that since he was bringing Dionysus onto the stage, 'rampage' was what he wanted.[171] More positive was Charles Marowitz, who said:

It is intelligent ... it is funny ... it is a generous play ... It is meaningfully complex ... Municipal corruption is its amusing façade, but the play winds downward to connect with hard-boned ideas concerning law, justice and developments in social history ... Arden has given us a richness and a fulsomeness, and I, for one, prefer a well-stocked buffet to a predictable round of fish and chips.[172]

The Workhouse Donkey's Bakhtinian qualities can perhaps be more easily detected fifty years after the play was written. They connect with what Arden wrote about Sean O'Casey's plays, when he said that *Cock-a-Doodle-Dandy* worked as 'fertility comedy in roughly the medieval morality or even mummers' play tradition'.[173] Explaining the sometimes lukewarm reception audiences gave the play, he noted it was 'a north-of-England fertility comedy (performed) in Chichester, in 1963, when the Home Counties stuffed shirts were still reeling from the shock of the Profumo scandals'. It was, he opined, 'too near the bone, and yet too far from it'.[174] The last word might go to *The Guardian's* knowledgeable theatre critic, Michael Billington, who in 2003, called *The Workhouse Donkey* simply 'the best play ever written in Britain about municipal corruption'.[175]

In 1960 the Royal Shakespeare Company had given Arden a commission for the play which became *Ironhand*. In a sense, therefore, this play pre-dates *The Workhouse Donkey*, even though it was first produced six months later. *Ironhand* is Arden's adaptation of Goethe's *sturm und drang* tragedy, *Goetz von Berlichingen*, which concerns Goetz, a free spirit in a wild time, who has no interest in developing or improving society, yet retains his own sense of honour and loyalty. The play deals with politics in the raw – betrayals, lust for power, cunning and ambition – and the freedom of the individual in a changing and violent society. Arden 'reconstructed' the antagonist, Weislingen: according to Simon Trussler, 'Goethe's "wet" politician' became in Arden's version 'a statesman whose arguments are reasoned and strong'.[176] Brother Martin in the original now became Martin Luther, giving that part of the action greater coherence and increased moment. And the radical-conservative Goetz, who asserts 'we must follow tradition',[177] takes an anti-bureaucratic stance which makes his struggle clearer and more comprehensible than in Goethe's play. The play thus becomes 'a real conflict between freewill and statesmanship'.[178]

Ironhand is so called because Goetz's right hand is made of iron; but it is designed in such a way that at first glance it appears to be a normal hand in a gauntlet. His anarchic opportunism, somewhat reminiscent of Charlie Butterthwaite's, and certainly like Johnnie Armstrong's in Arden's next play, *Armstrong's Last Goodnight*, cannot be allowed by those in authority to thrive in the 'new' developing Germany of the sixteenth century. But his devil-may-care exuberance can only be caught by trickery. He is gaoled, but escapes, is recaptured and incarcerated again. His nemesis, Weislingen, who now is being poisoned by his wife and her lover, remembers how earlier he had betrayed Goetz, and tears up the death sentence. But it is too late. Goetz dies in gaol. It is left to Maria, Goetz's daughter once beloved of Weislingen, to ask the last, haunting question: 'How can we talk about freedom and justice without accusing ourselves?'

Ironhand was first presented by the Bristol Old Vic on 12 November 1963 in a production by Val May. Its strength was generally admitted: 'the cumulative effect is masterly', wrote *The Times* critic. 'There is not an inch of superfluous rhetoric in the text, and Mr Arden skilfully differentiates between the idioms of the various social groups'.[179] The play was effectively translated to television in April 1965, and was further extended when it was broadcast on BBC radio in November 1966. The excellent reception which a later radio production in 1999 was accorded speaks for the strength of Arden's adaptation.

The third of these four large-scale plays for conventional theatres was *Armstrong's Last Goodnight*. Arden himself has related how he sat in the long grass among the gorse bushes on the island in Lough Corrib and read the ballad of Johnny Armstrong, in a shortened edition of F.J.Child's monumental collection of English and Scottish ballads. 'With the Connemara mountains in the distance and the gray water all around me, it seemed to have a sudden immediacy', he recalled.

> With the poem all alive inside me, I took a bicycle ride into the nearest town, Oughterard, to do the week's shopping. On the way I passed the ruin of Aughnanure Castle ... The castle was in a very similar style of architecture to that of the Border peel-towers. I stopped and walked about in the ruin. I imagined the events of the ballad emanating from there.[180]

Though the events of the play are largely grounded in history, the play is in no sense an accurate chronicle, and has perhaps more in common with the old ballad than it does with historical fact. Johnny Armstrong of Gilnockie was indeed a freebooting reiver of the Scottish borders, a wild ungovernable man (like Goetz von Berlichingen). His raids into Northumberland and Westmoreland had, among other consequences, the effect of checking the predatory territorial ambitions of England. However, Scotland gained little by this, for Armstrong yielded nothing to his nominal sovereign. And the English pressed hard for reparations for losses suffered from Armstrong's raids. In 1530, King James V decided to pacify the lawless border country himself, and journeyed there with a large number of Scottish lords and soldiers. The ballad takes up the story. The king writes a letter of invitation to Armstrong, who dresses himself in his most magnificent finery and with his allies and kinsmen, comes before the king.

> When Johny came before the king,
>> With all his men sae brave to see,
> The king he movit his bonnet to him;
>> He weind he was a king as well as he.

The king calls him traitor, has him arrested and condemns him to death. Armstrong pleads with him, offers him horses, 'ganging mills', soldiers, even the rent from all the Border lands as far as Newcastle. To no avail. Armstrong realizes he has 'asked grace at a graceless face', and blessing his brother and son, he takes his farewell.

> John murdred was at Carlenrigg,
>> And all his gallant companie:
> But Scotlands heart was never sae wae,
>> To see sae mony brave men die.[181]

The ballad itself, as can be seen even from these short extracts, suggests that there is a wider political context to Armstrong's betrayal, to do with English pressure on Scotland. Nevertheless, it was only when he read Conor Cruise O'Brien's account of his mission to the Congo in the early 1960s, *To Katanga and Back*, that Arden realized there was a contemporary story not unlike that of Johnny Armstrong, which could give focus and immediacy to a dramatisation of the old ballad. The Congo, with its wretched history of Belgian exploitation, had achieved independence in 1960 under the leadership of Patrice Lumumba, but soon after this the mineral-rich eastern province of Katanga, under the leadership of Moise Tschombe and with support from USA and Belgium, attempted to break away and form an independent state, rather like Armstrong's dream of an independent Border state in Arden's play. A brutal and bloody civil war followed. In January 1961 Lumumba was kidnapped and murdered, but a peace settlement reasserting the country's indivisibility was only reached in 1963. It was very much in the public consciousness as Arden was writing his play.

The parallel between Armstrong's story and that of the Congolese civil war is, of course, suggestive but actually not very close. Certainly the play is no *drame à clef*, but Stephen Lacey has made the point that it is much richer, and indeed much subtler, than such contemporary historical dramas as John Osborne's *Luther* or Robert Bolt's *A Man for All Seasons* precisely because of the echoes of contemporary political struggles. One of the suggestive dissimilarities was the figure of O'Brien himself, an Irish writer and politician, appointed as the United Nations' representative in the Congo. Arden's programme note for the National Theatre's 1965 production of the play explains how he co-opted this figure into Armstrong's world:

> Tschombe of Katanga was ... not his own man. He was backed by Belgian mining interests and also by foreign governments whose activities at the United Nations bear a certain resemblance to the activities (in the play) of Maxwell and his friends in Edinburgh. The attempt of the U.N. to persuade (and finally to force) him back under the control of the central government brought Dr O'Brien – a man of letters as well as a diplomat – into a society where intrigue (to which he was professionally accustomed) was no less common than violence in its most marked form. Who, for instance, killed Lumumba? Did Dag Hammersjkold's plane fall out of the sky on its own, or was it induced to fall, and, if so, by whom? The fact that a man like O'Brien found himself immediately confronted by such apparently melodramatic questions which urgently required a realistic answer suggested to me the introduction of Sir David Lindsay into the play. The play is dedicated to Dr O'Brien, but Lindsay does not *represent* him, as Gilnockie does not represent Tschombe nor Wamphray Lumumba.[182]

The introduction of Sir David Lindsay is indeed a masterstroke on the part of the playwright. Arden had seen and enjoyed Tyrone Guthrie's production of Lindsay's *Ane Satire of the Thrie Estaitis*. Now his position in the Scotland of James V as an intellectual, a writer and a politically-aware diplomat made it possible for the play to become 'an exercise in diplomacy,' as Arden's subtitle has it. Who should carry the king's letter to Armstrong of Gilnockie? Lindsay, of course. And it is the weaving of Lindsay's careful plot to bring Armstrong to heel, its miscarrying and his eventual betrayal of his own liberal protestations so that he effectively sends Armstrong to his death, which gives the play its special flavour. To use Lindsay thus is, as Arden freely admitted, quite without historical evidence. But it makes for compelling drama, even though it (again) removes any simple handle for the floundering critic to seize on. Armstrong is a conservative anarchist, Lindsay a progressive liar, and between them love and lust, religion and indulgence, truth and expediency are apparently confounded. Moreover, the precise and detailed accuracy of the story's context, as

John Arden, c.1964

Arden presents it – Scotland, 1530 – makes it both specific and, paradoxically, of surprisingly wide application.

The play's ballad style – short vivid scenes, one interrupting another – gives the play a verve and momentum which the first production, at the Glasgow Citizens' Theatre under the direction of Denis Carey on 5 May 1964, managed to convey. Arden himself approved. While acknowledging the production's low budget and the severe lack of rehearsal time, yet he liked the way it seemed to share the Scottish experience the play offers with its Scottish audience. There were problems: for instance, one actor found the Scots language hard to work with, so that two days before the premiere his character was changed to a Frenchman, a disturbance to the play's integrity which was regretted. When the play was taken by the National Theatre, William Gaskill the director invited Arden himself to work with the actors on the language, which he did with conspicuous success. 'He has a marvellous ear', Gaskill noted, 'and speaks the lines better than any actors, attacking them with that peculiar hard, astringent North Country delivery'.[183] Many critics enjoyed this play. Edwin Morgan, for instance, whose problems with it have been noted above, yet called it 'bold, interesting and vigorous',[184] while Tom Milne (like a number of critics) was particularly struck by some of its 'images', contrasting the king emerging from his palace, young but still stately and regal, with Armstrong erupting onto the stage in his shaggy fur pelt. 'Arden's play – language, emotions, situations – is as rich and full-blooded as anything seen on the English stage for years'.[185] Michael

Coveney said simply that *Armstrong's Last Goodnight* was 'probably the best "Scottish play" ever'.[186]

The fourth play in this group was *Left-Handed Liberty*, which was commissioned by the Corporation of the City of London to commemorate the 750th anniversary of the sealing of Magna Carta. As such, it was the only commission Arden ever received to write on a particular subject for a particular occasion. Unsure whether to accept it, he read round the subject and became sufficiently interested to try to make a play, but, because of the very specific and unalterable deadline, found himself in danger of not completing it. D'Arcy's advice helped to save the play, when he was 'tangled in a confusion of baronial and Episcopal minutiae': she 'had the idea that I should use the Papal Legate – until then a very minor character – to pull the whole play together'.[187] She also advised that he 'open the play out' before the end, which resulted in the long monologue from King John near the end of the play. 'But it remained clumsy', he remarked later. 'And my device of Lady de Vesci sitting mute behind him as a sort of human visual-aid was sheer cruelty to the actress'.[188]

As with Gaskill's *Armstrong's Last Goodnight*, Arden was able to sit in rehearsals and work with the director, David William, and the cast, which included Bernard Miles, the Mermaid Theatre's artistic director, Patrick Wymark, Sonia Dresdel, Robert Eddison and others. As a result, he made a number of significant changes to the script, which he believed improved it. However, it still seems somewhat undercooked, too wordy and with not enough typical Arden moments of action or comedy.

The title of the play, *Left-Handed Liberty*, with its possibly denigatory slur on left-wing concepts of freedom, caused some consternation to local Labour councillors, whose feathers Miles eventually managed to smooth. However, he was unable to persuade Arden (strongly backed in this by the republican D'Arcy) to meet the queen when she attended a special performance. He stayed at home, pretending to be working on re-writes for the play, though his parents attended, proud to be there, but disappointed that their son was not.

The play opened on 14 June 1965 at the Mermaid Theatre on Puddle Dock. It showed King John, browbeaten by his mother, in submission to the Pope, delaying and procrastinating but finally signing the charter presented by the barons. Each party doubts the others' good intentions, however, and suspicions turn to quarrels and so into rebellions. The charter is used to justify things it was never meant to justify: it helps no-one. The Scots and the French invade England. John marches his troops towards London, but they are caught by the tide in the Wash, his treasure is lost, and he dies. The play's reception was decidedly lukewarm. *The Times's* comment was not untypical: 'Apart from odd glimpses of wintry comedy and a couple of scenes which show off the King's peremptory tactics, the play resembles an elaborate piece of mechanism impressive in all respects except its failure to work'.[189] Simon Trussler, some months later, appeared to have understood at least what Arden was attempting:

> It was to be expected that Arden, presented with a commission to write a
> play about the origins of democracy ... should have ended up showing us
> the dubious motives of the liberty-mongers and the case to be made for
>
> King John as an effective monarch.[190]

Much can, and indeed has been, written about these four plays. Here, it is enough to note Arden's stringent but supple use of language. It is extraordinarily versatile, often muscular, often vernacular, but shining, exciting, and above all speakable. Tamara Hinchco remembered Arden at this period speaking the lines out loud as he wrote them, whether in his writing room, the bathroom or wherever, and in the television film, *John Arden – Playwright*, we see him doing this and also singing to himself the song he is writing. Consequently, for any actor with energy and intelligence, these scripts seem almost heaven-sent. Prose interrupts verse which interrupts song, but all are crafted and honed for the tongue. Prose mostly conveys the story itself, verse often signals moments of heightened emotion or inward questioning or reflection, and song most frequently crystallizes or illuminates an aspect of the action, and is often not immediately related to the characters on stage, operating perhaps at a more tangential or thematic level. We remember Robert Graves's observation in *The White Goddess*: 'the Welsh minstrels, like the Irish poets, recited their traditional romances in prose, breaking into dramatic verse, with harp accompaniment, only at points of emotional stress'.[191] Here is Weislingen's protest to Adelheid, an example of Arden's use of language, chosen literally at random:

> I have already been foisted off with the old cast clout of the Bishop of
> Bamberg: I will not accept advancement through the Holy Roman
> genitals of a half-elected Habsburg schoolboy.

Arden is equally at home with regional dialect. Mayor Boocock, laying the foundation stone of the new Police Headquarters in *The Workhouse Donkey*, says:

> Fellow townsmen, ladies and gentlemen, er, voters. This afternoon's little
> ceremony is, as you might say, a double one. Clapping as it were two
> birds wi't 'yah billet.

Rhythm, vocabulary and syntax combine to give the unique full-blooded flavour which permeates these plays.

The most notable example of Arden's mastery of language comes in *Armstrong's Last Goodnight*, written as it is entirely in a kind of accessible medieval Scots. As William Gaskill, director of the National Theatre production of this play, commented:

107

It is, apart from anything else, a major work of scholarship for a writer to absorb the writing of a period and then to sit down, and be so steeped in it that he could write a perfectly straightforward play in that language. I don't know any other writer who could have pulled that off.

Gaskill adds:

> Arden is to me a writer a bit like Shakespeare in his approach, in that the writing not only has to convey the communication, the dialogue of characters speaking together, but also has to carry the sense of the social environment, and the texture of people's lives; in addition it has to carry the writer's attitudes and his philosophies about the situation. All that has to be supported by language. Now what I think is marvellous about *Armstrong* is that Arden pulls this off – into the language he pours all the things which a writer doesn't normally bother about. Therefore it appears, and is, in fact, very dense, very rich; anyone will tell you that on a second or third viewing, you get more and more.[192]

The language in *Armstrong's Last Goodnight* is a marvellous, sinewy medium, at least as powerful as Arthur Miller's language in *The Crucible*, and growing out of Arden's reading of Scots literature, tempered by his experiences as a soldier and then a student in Edinburgh. Here is the Lady, speaking to Johnny Armstrong, before their love is consummated:

> When I stand in the full direction of your force
> Ye need nae wife nor carl to stand
> Alsweel beside ye and interpret.
> There is in me ane knowledge, potent, secret,
> That I can set to rin ane sure concourse
> Of bodily and ghaistly strength betwixt the blood
> Of me and of the starkest man alive. My speed
> Hangs twin with yours: and starts ane double flood:
> Will you with me initiate the deed
> And saturatit consequence thereof –
> Crack aff with your great club
> The barrel-hoops of love
> And let it pour
> Like the enchantit quern that boils red-herring broo
> Until it gars upswim the goodman's table and his door
> While all his house and yard and street
> Swill reeken, greasy, het, oer-drownit sax-foot fou –

Language is a vivid way to get 'inside' the world of the play. As Michael Kustow noted of *Left-Handed Liberty*, 'We are sucked into the time, the flavour and perspective of the thirteenth century, effortlessly. Arden puts us right inside the medieval world'.[193] This is something few writers are able to do. Most use history as a backcloth for the exploration of character. With Arden, it is the movement of history itself which is the drama, and the specificity of time and place comprise the warp and weft of the experience he offers. History clarifies and objectifies the dramatist's themes. We enter the world of the past, and are able to view it with understanding, dispassionately but compassionately, and are thereby stimulated to feel the reverberations with today's society. The plays often deal with kings and high politics, the 'news' of the day. But Arden is able also to relate the high politics to the low life, and indeed many of the most striking moments in these plays are those which expose the view 'from below', as in the extraordinary scene in *Left-Handed Liberty* when the three girls sing 'harshly and loudly' the song, 'Good people of London', when the relationship between their world and the world of the Mayor and the power-hungry barons is powerfully, yet implicitly, exposed.

History here is process. Arden shows how things happen, with the implicit suggestion that if you understand how things happen, then you yourself can help to steer them. It is inherently collectivist, for it asserts that society is changeable, whereas the commoner individualist approach pits a hero or heroine against a fixed society and an inevitable fate. This is why the plays reject illusionism or naturalism and assume a historicist and materialist viewpoint. They are within the epic tradition and as such, carnivalesque, celebrating life with all its absurdities, in-justices and problems, while simultaneously criticising those very things.

These public plays of the 1960s established Arden as the most exciting, challenging, significant playwright of his generation. But it was still not clear that there was a place in British theatre for work in this tradition. O'Casey's drama had been largely misunderstood or ignored for the last thirty years of his life; MacColl had had to establish his own company, Theatre Workshop, to produce most of his plays. It was the naturalism of the Royal Court, associated with the plays of Osborne, Wesker and others, which dominated the contemporary stages. John Russell Taylor was one of the more thoughtful critics of the time, but he, like others, found Arden hard to grasp. 'Difficult though Arden's vision may be to accept on first acquaintance,' he wrote, 'and puzzling his way of expressing it, familiarity makes the approach much easier and breeds nothing but respect and admiration. John Arden,' he concluded, 'is one of our few complete originals'.[194] Raymond Williams went further: to him, it had been 'clear for some years that John Arden is the most genuinely innovating of the generation of young English dramatists of the fifties'.[195] For Peter Brook, Arden was like Genet and Beckett, in that he created 'a stage image – a structure of stage behaviour and attitudes whose meanings can be read off continually in different and complementary and contradictory ways'.[196] John Calder called him 'Britain's Brecht'.[197]

Arden himself said he wanted to recreate a 'Dionysian' theatre, which would include both Dionysian comedy, which was uninhibited and rude like pantomime but was also capable of raising serious religious and social issues, and Dionysian tragedy which reflected the sacrificial god, killed each year for the fertility of the land. He wanted a legitimate theatre which was yet able to produce what he had seen in a Dublin pantomime:

> An individual dressed as a gorilla bounded onto the stage and did a lot of knockabout with two comedians, and then came leaping off into the audience in a completely hideous stage gorilla costume, and raced about the audience, plonked himself down into a fat woman's lap and took her hat off, deposited her hat on a bald man, then flung its arms round another bald man and nuzzled him in the face ... and just as you began to wonder how far it was going, the gorilla suddenly bounded back on to the stage, unzipped the costume, and it was an attractive chorus girl in a little dress.[198]

This conflict between the respectable and the disreputable is one of the beating hearts in all Arden's best writing.

By the middle 1960s, Arden's dissatisfaction with his acquired position as 'an established writer' for the conventional theatre, that which boasted not only a new, permanent Royal Shakespeare Company, but also a new National Theatre, was sadly manifest. He wanted something more informal, something more open-ended and spontaneous, like perhaps his experience of *The Business of Good Government*. Simply to write admired plays for subsidised theatres seemed to move him not a step further on the path to the revolutionised theatre he had vowed to make with D'Arcy. But what would fulfil this? He wrote that presenting his plays should be akin to telling his friends stories round the supper table after a pleasant meal, but when he revisited the production of *Armstrong's Last Goodnight* at Chichester, he found the actors 'had no idea what I was doing there'.[199] He felt completely out of place. Not only that, but he was discovering that what Brecht had called the 'theatre apparatus' was likely to undermine the playwright's work before it had even been seen. At the Berliner Ensemble's production of *Mother Courage and Her Children* in 1956, he had been amazed by the care which had obviously been taken over every detail of the production. He realized then that work of this quality was im-possible in the English theatre, for all the vaunted 'revolution' post 1956. He complained that once the script had been 'passed into the hands of a company, the pressures of time and money will combine to ensure that it will be presented in a manner so slapdash and unconsidered, that if it were a ship to be put to sea or a building to be lived in, a prosecution for dangerous negligence would inevitably follow'.[200]

In the Preface to the published text of *The Workhouse Donkey*, Arden proposed a radically different kind of theatre, one where the play might last for 'six or seven or thirteen' hours in a theatre with restaurants, sideshows, amusements and music, and spectators would move between these attractions as they felt inclined. It was a 'casual or "prom-concert" conception',[201] perhaps the alternative theatre which he and D'Arcy had dreamed of in 1956, and which was already emerging tentatively in his collaborative work with Margaretta D'Arcy.

Nine : Alternatives in Politics and Theatre

The middle of the 1960s: Lyndon Johnson had not yet escalated the war in Vietnam, but was concentrating on his 'Great Society', with civil rights legislation and a war on poverty; in Britain, the seemingly youthful Harold Wilson had replaced the faded Old Etonians, Harold Macmillan and Sir Alec Douglas-Home; while in the Soviet Union, Nikita Krushchev had fallen before Leonid Brezhnev, who became the new General Secretary of the Communist Party. Even Ireland apparently had its own new broom when Gaelic sportsman Jack Lynch became taoisech, albeit to many an 'interim taoiseach'.

And Arden and D'Arcy's lifestyle was undergoing change, too. Still living mostly in Kirkbymoorside, but also spending time in the summer on the island on Lough Corrib, their dwellings had a few tables and chairs, and pots and pans, but no carpets on the floor, and no nicely-upholstered easy chairs. Cleaning was an occasional, not a regular, occupation. Mealtimes were irregular, and the food provided was unpredictable. It was certainly not the rather *chic* Habitat-style of their London flat of the 1950s. Albert Hunt, who spent time with them both in Kirkbymoorside and in Ireland, described their mode of living as 'extraordinary'. Going to visit them on the island was, he said, 'quite an adventure'. D'Arcy was responsible for ferrying visitors across the water, and once there, there was no escape unless D'Arcy organised it. He and his students had come to work on drama, but found they were almost 'prisoners! 'I don't mean that in any oppressive sense', Hunt added, but 'once we were there, we were stuck there. I've never felt less independent'.[202]

Margaretta D'Arcy, c.1964

112

The youngest Arden child, Neuss, was born early in 1964. He and his brothers were brought up highly unconventionally, in a manner which implicitly rejected any traditional patterning of the experiences of childhood. It was a largely instinctive means of avoiding the kind of school-regimented system which, for example, a friend of Arden's, who had gone to teach drama in a London comprehensive school, described to him. She was assured by the headteacher that she would have a free hand to develop her work with the pupils in whatever way seemed best to her, and decided to ask them what topic they would like to address. This, it transpired, was 'bullying'. She proposed staging a mock trial which would dramatise the overt or hidden violence in the school, and suggested that teachers and others be invited to participate. Her plan was vetoed:

> Democratic procedures, said the head, were not part of the school's
> system; her project was disruptive and would damage the 'authority of
> the staff'; freedom of speech in the context of secondary education could
> not possibly be permitted.[203]

But the unconventional, apparently freer, upbringing of the Arden children also included, as Finn, the eldest, remembered, the four boys sometimes being locked in a room so that their parents could get on with their writing.[204] Another time, one of them stood on a table in a Galway café and flaunted his genitalia, to the scandal of the local residents! When asked, D'Arcy admitted she had not been a good mother as her children grew up,[205] and it seems that Finn and Adam did a good deal of the parenting of Neuss, the youngest boy. Though they came to realize that they lacked regular education, yet each grew up to be respectable citizens with jobs in the police, the army and the bureaucracy of London Transport.

In 1965, *The Observer* called John Arden 'the most enigmatic figure in the English theatre today', and noted that he was 'totally immune to London's giddy glamour'.[206] Perhaps because of the seeming 'enigma', BBC North chose to make a film about him that year. Entitled *John Arden – Playwright* and filmed in black and white in and around Arden and D'Arcy's Kirkbymoorside home, it is an interesting, at times revealing, portrait despite the somewhat artificial 'staginess' of parts of it, as well as a sort of inbuilt romanticism about 'the writer'. It opens with Arden, a thin young man in a black sweater, taking a sheet of paper, fitting it into his typewriter, and writing. Later, he wanders about Fountains Abbey and there are brief glimpses of Kirkbymoorside itself. Though he seems very much alone, and, we are told, 'arranges his life so he can write', he is in fact, according to the commentator, a 'very friendly person'. He reads his work to D'Arcy, who comments constructively, and both are glimpsed with their children, Arden showing them a history book and discussing how Lord Nelson's body was preserved after the Battle of Trafalgar, D'Arcy painting with them messily and freely on old newspaper, and also blowing bubbles with them – to Jacob's especial delight. One of the more amusing scenes shows the blond-headed four-year-old Adam determinedly removing the interviewer's tie. The interviewer resists as best he can, remarking with forced good humour: 'You're going to win, aren't you? You're going to get it off, aren't you?' And sure enough, despite his father's rather feeble reprimand, he does.

Arden admits in the film that part of him would like to be free to live alone, to read and write as he would like to, with no other responsibilities. But then he needs someone (D'Arcy) to read his work to, to discuss it with, and when he has been alone for any time, he has found himself 'loafing around not doing anything of any value to anybody'. In his life at the time the film was made, his habit was to write in the morning, but to 'pay attention' to the children in the afternoon. It gave his life order. In the film, he appears to be 'between' *Left-handed Liberty* and *The Hero Rises Up*, but he is working on an unnamed television play which, like other projects at the time – a play for Centre 42 to be staged at the Roundhouse, for example, and a war play in collaboration with writers from France (Roland Dubillard), Germany (Peter Weiss) and USA (Paul Foster) – seems to have come to nothing.

D'Arcy comes over in the film as modest and even playful, and indeed Tamara Hinchco remembered her at this time as first and foremost kind and supportive. But she was nobody's fool, as she had demonstrated during rehearsals for the 1963 production of *The Happy Haven* at the Gate Theatre, Dublin, when, finding herself in disagreement with the director, she clouted him across the face – an incident which apparently marked the whole production. 'She was formidable, but she'd always laugh at herself', was how one friend put it.[207]

In the television film, *John Arden – Playwright*, one of the most effective sequences shows D'Arcy rehearsing their play, *Ars Longa, Vita Brevis*, with a group of Girl Guides in Kirkbymoorside. First we see the authors discussing the best approach to the project at home: they decide they should read the speeches which are to be the basis for improvisation aloud to the Guides; they also decide that the few lines of verse can be learned by them. Then, D'Arcy is seen in the local school gym explaining the story, and the character of Mr Miltiades, to the group gathered informally round her. She is gentle and good-humoured – exactly the opposite of the conventional schoolteacher. 'The children in the art class fight with paint-brushes', she says, 'and there's paint everywhere, and all the children are killed!' The Girl Guides giggle, clearly enjoying themselves. She hands out white masks, conventional but forbidding, while Arden distributes weapons. The children put on the masks, look in the mirror. 'Oh, that's lovely', says one, rather breathlessly, wondering. The masks transform the girls into something weird and other. They wear tin hats like crash helmets above their masks, and stamp round the room in their guide uniforms. It is a strange, ugly, compelling moment.

Ars Longa, Vita Brevis is a short play of just a dozen pages in print. In truth, the authors say, 'it is not exactly a play, nor is it anything else in particular'. They suggest it might be called 'a theme for variations'.[208] The first public performance was on 28 January 1964, when it was presented at LAMDA as part of the Royal Shakespeare Company's 'Theatre of Cruelty' season, instigated and directed by Peter Brook. Tom Milne found it 'a corrosively funny, freewheeling examination of the relationship between Art, War and Education'.[209] The 'Theatre of Cruelty' project was Brook's attempt to strike out from the jelly of ubiquitous naturalism, the complacency of the big theatres and the dominant paternalistic culture. The phrase was coined by the French theatre practitioner, Antonin Artaud, whose ideas the season explored. By 'cruelty', Artaud meant intensity, or vividness. In this theatre, text was downgraded, and indeed the performance itself became the text. Text-as-performance may be a comparative commonplace today, but in 1964 the notion was extremely radical. It chimes with Arden and D'Arcy's comments on their dialogue, which, they said, was of two kinds – long, complicated speeches which could be learned, but should probably be thought of as bases for free improvisation; and token speeches which carry the story forward but which were really also to be thought of as starting-points for the actors' elaborations. In addition, they note, there are a few short verse passages, which, they propose, would be best spoken as written.

The story begins at St Uncumber's School: Uncumber was the bearded female patron saint of women who wished to be free from their abusive husbands. Freedom of speech, the authority of the staff and democratic procedures appear here as surely as they did in that comprehensive school where Arden's friend taught. So, too, does bullying. The Headmaster of St Uncumber's, in his Speech Day speech, laments the lack of an Art Teacher. Later, he appoints Mr Miltiades, who is obsessed with preventing the children from becoming sloppy, and so undisciplined. He insists they draw geometric figures, with rulers. When this fails to produce the results he requires, he starts to drill them, turning them into an army who begin re-enacting the bloody Battle of Camlann between King Arthur and the traitorous Sir Mordred. The headmaster intervenes. He suggests Mr Miltiades join the Territorial Army. When Miltiadees gets home, his wife asks what happened at school but before he can explain, the Territorials are heard outside. They are recruiting. Mr Miltiades joins them. He puts on a uniform, and goes on manoeuvres. The soldiers dress themselves up as trees. A shooting party enters the woods, and the Headmaster, one of the party, mistakes Mr Miltiades for a stag and shoots him dead. A subscription is taken up for his widow, who uses the money to buy 'clothes, food, wine, a new house and she enjoys herself in fast cars with innumerable young men'. She meets his funeral:

WIFE : I shed a tear upon his bier
    Because to me he was ever dear.
    But I could not follow him in all his wishes
    I prefer the quick easy swimming of the fishes

Which sport and play
In green water all day
And have not a straight line in the whole of their bodies.

When Arden was approached by Brook for a Theatre of Cruelty piece, he had also received a commission to write a play for children. D'Arcy had reminded him of the case of an Art Teacher who had been shot in a wood while on a Territorial Army exercise. He decided this story could be used for both commissions. But really, the true genesis for *Ars Longa Vita* lies in the cultural world embodied in 'Kirkbymoorside 63'. Part of it came simply from watching children improvising in Kirkbymoorside itself. Albert Hunt suggests that 'one of the germs' of it

> was a box of old clothes (Arden and D'Arcy) got from a local junk yard.
> They put it in a shed outside their cottage at Kirkbymoorside, and a
> group of local children came and dressed up and began to make their
> own plays. They improvised stories – one I saw was a lot like *The Tinker's
> Wedding*. It didn't have the language, of course, but there was a quality of
> fable about it, and it was alive. It was the story of a man who pretends to
> be dead, and who suddenly sits up as his wife is running off with another
> man – his last words in this version were, 'Well, bugger you then'.[210]

(The play by J.M.Synge in Hunt's mind is actually *The Shadow of the Glen*, but this Irish reference is important. And it is worth remarking that D'Arcy and Arden use the *motif* themselves again in *Friday's Hiding* and in *The Ballygombeen Bequest/The Little Gray Home in the West*.)

In fact, sometime shortly after 'Kirkbymoorside 63', a group of girls knocked on the cottage door and demanded to do a play. D'Arcy worked with them, as shown in the television film. Some of the parents objected that *Ars Longa, Vita Brevis* 'wasn't a *real* play, there was no curtain, they made up their lines instead of having to learn them'. They also thought that wearing masks or make-up was unsuitable for 'young females'. But the children who made the play revelled in 'ridiculing the military-industrial complex and overturning all the taboos of family and thrift'. [211] So through their improvisations with D'Arcy the story was created, and Arden then wrote a sort of fantastical dialogue, which rather than simply presenting a conventional dramatic scene, worked to expose the underlying desires and dreams of the characters in highly stylised, or open-ended, form. The story thus proceeds by means of a series of 'turns', or even games, which are on one level to be relished for themselves, but on another are to form component parts of the story. To keep these two elements in balance is no easy task: when Albert Hunt showed his version to Arden, Arden approved of much of what he had done in each scene, but complained that the story line had been lost.

Ars Longa, Vita Brevis, directed by Albert Hunt, 1965

Ars Longa, Vita Brevis is pivotal in the art of John Arden and Margaretta D'Arcy, because not only does it work on several levels simultaneously, as S.L. Bethell had noticed of Shakespeare's drama, it also seems to be presented as almost conventional theatre, yet is something much less formal, more less *expected*, than that. A superficial reading of it suggests that it is a satire on the Art Master, Mr Miltiades, who is an almost caricatured Fascist, apparently, and that we must respond to and support the contrasting spontaneity and freedom of the children and Roxana, Mr Miltiades's wife. Hunt's production, however, suggests something much subtler. In this, the children wore masks with eyeholes and the scene in the art class, which was developed wholly through games and improvisation, never through abstract discussion, 'took on an element of sheer terror', as one audience member described it:

> The art master compels the pupils to perform drill movements which
> they do with impeccable accuracy of movement – all except one; the
> master talks to them, they fail to respond, not even by being openly
> disobedient; he turns away, they surreptitiously change places. All this is
> done with a precision of movement that approximates to dance and has a
> great formal beauty of its own; instinctively one's sympathies are all on
> the side of the class, for spontaneity and against discipline, and yet the art
> master is so pathetic, as he seeks to establish a relationship and fails, that
> one begins to pity him, and the class takes on a fiendish and nightmare
> atmosphere.[212]

The refusal to rely on easy audience responses makes all the work by these authors compellingly rich. Even in an occasional newspaper article about a soldier, whose appearance on television had stirred great revulsion in progressive circles, Arden articulates a more complex attitude than may be expected: 'he seemed to me to be exactly what he wants his men to be like – "hard, lean, mean",' Arden writes, adding:

'But gentlemanly, withal, and remarkably intelligent. Also devilish handsome'.[213] Neither the humour here, nor the irony, cloak the fascination.

Ars Longa, Vita Brevis, according to the authors, belongs to 'schoolboy's mythology ... the lunacy and villainy of teachers, the unpredictability of adult life, and the extraordinary possibilities of military behaviour'.[214] In the extraordinary, dream-like but familiar world of this play, all sorts of values are shown up in the retreating and distorting mirrors of the imagination. The real army is not the Territorial Army. The teacher is as imprisoned in the classroom as the pupils. Militarism and sexual relations are horribly inextricable. I have myself produced this play more than once. The first production used sexual motivations and concentrated on the repressed desires and unexpected forms of release the action contains; but the second made the motivations political, with images of Fascism and anarchy, and the confusion between organisation and disorganisation. It would be difficult to say which was the more powerful. The authors report a production in Yugoslavia which was broadcast into Greece at the time of the colonels' junta. They hoped it helped to topple them! For, as Baz Kershaw has pointed out, this play is not political in the narrow sense, but it is highly subversive, posing an 'implicit radical challenge' despite – or because of – its 'child-like' naïveté. And, he goes on, the nature of the challenge is closely related to the context of the performance,[215] which the above examples help to illustrate. It may be added that Eila Arjoma made a film of this work in Finland, entitled *Taide pitkä, elämä lyhyt*, in 1967, with Toivo Lehto, Mikko Majonlahti and Maria Aro.

D'Arcy and Arden's next joint project was *Friday's Hiding*, which was a deliberate effort to capitalise on the work done on *Ars Longa, Vita Brevis*. They worked on it in the west of Ireland with Albert Hunt's students from Shrewsbury School of Art, who had come to Galway to perform *Ars Longa, Vita Brevis* in Oughterard and elsewhere, and who therefore had some knowledge of the D'Arcy/Arden mode. *Friday's Hiding* was commissioned by the Royal Lyceum Theatre, Edinburgh, to be a play without words, though the version we have does include a very few speeches and one song. It is an exploration, with a captivating and pervasive irony, of certain conservative values, which the play explores rather than endorses. Two farmhands need the wages which the farmer, every Friday, is loath to pay them, though he goes to the bank, and has the money. After a series of comedic episodes when the hands try to obtain what is their due, it seems that one will get more than wages – the farmer's spinster sister for his bride. But it is not to be, though there is whisky and a wedding dress ...

The play, intended for mimed performance, is written in a sort of free-wheeling free verse, designed to stimulate the imaginations of the performers:

John Balfour, hame frae the bank, looks into the yard

118

he sees his two labourers on the watch, he retires.
> The pair of them, weary with waiting, bring out their bread and kebbuck,
> contrive to keep an eye on the gate, but grow careless.

John Balfour throws a stone, it goes over their heads,
hits the wall on yon side of them, they turn toward it – suspicious –
then creep over there and watch, their backs turned towards his entry.
> Which he makes, concealed in a haycock.

> The haycock sneezes.

> They turn at the noise.
> There is nocht but a Haycock.
> Whaur the hell did that come from?
> They look at it – dubious –

A dog barks beyond the house, distracts their attention, they swing around and run over there.

The script, in a 'rather tentative' state, was sent to the Lyceum Theatre, with the aim of eliciting feedback. But they heard nothing. Then early in March 1966, Arden's agent informed them that rehearsals of *Friday's Hiding* were about to commence. Neither D'Arcy nor Arden was invited to attend. The play opened – without them – on 29 March. They were never able to do the exploratory improvisational work they felt the script needed. It was an experiment with no satisfactory outcome, though they did see a production in Arabic in Morocco in 1990 which they enjoyed.

Once again the legitimate theatre had failed them. D'Arcy and Arden turned back to the illegitimate, or alternative, theatre therefore for their next production, a play for children, *The Royal Pardon*. Growing out of bedtime stories told their children, *The Royal Pardon* is a comedy, full of absurd situations and comic contrivances, though there is more than mere foolery here. Ostensibly, the play shows and compares two ways of life. On the one hand are the actors of Mr Croke's company, who represent uninhibited enjoyment, self-centred, flamboyant and out of the ordinary; on the other are the Constable and his officials, who live by the rules, the proper processes. In the inevitable clash these two groups engender is caught the central figure, Luke. He appears to be an Army deserter, but claims to be on his way to London to obtain his discharge in a regular fashion. While the actors tangle with the law, he mends their scenery and becomes their stage manager. His resourcefulness wins them the right to represent English theatre at the forthcoming wedding celebrations of the Prince to the French princess, and pursued by the Constable who is desperate to arrest Luke, they reach the French Court. Here, Luke again saves the day, and the acting company is invited to become players to His

Majesty the King. The Constable is turned to stone, and Luke and the young actress in Mr Croke's troupe leave together, rejecting royal patronage, determining instead to

… entertain the people
Under castle wall and proud church steeple.

It seems a not-so-vague echo of Arden and D'Arcy's promise to each other in the garden in Earl's Court a decade before.

The Royal Pardon was staged by the authors at the newly-established Art Centre in Beaford, Devon, opening on 1 September 1966. They had been invited here by the Centre's director, John Lane, who had first met Arden and D'Arcy at the Kirkbymoorside 63 festival. Beaford, in the heart of rural Devonshire, was the place chosen for an experimental arts venue, set up by Dartington Hall Trust. Though the performance was by all accounts swashbuckling fun, the rehearsal period was somewhat fraught. The authors assembled a rather ill-sorted cast, with some professionals (including Tamara Hinchco and Roger Davenport, who played Luke), some friends, including Frank Challenger from the Shrewsbury Art College group who was involved with D'Arcy at the time, and Mark Wing-Davey, the acting teacher son of a friend, and a group of students from LAMDA, including Maureen Lipman, who all knew each other and spent a good deal of time grumbling at the apparently unprofessional approach of Arden and D'Arcy. Rehearsals, mostly in Muswell Hill, were watched proprietorially by the young Arden children as well as Hinchco's four-year-old. When the company reached Devon, their evenings were sadly unsociable, as the cast split into exclusive cliques and there was no entertainment beyond the centre, where they all slept.

The play was presented in the billiard room of the old house, a pleasant room about thirty feet long and twenty feet across. There was no formal stage, and children in the audience sat on the floor almost among the feet of the actors. The production had all the energy Arden and D'Arcy usually generated and employed their trademark emblematic devices and theatricalities. For example, the actors wore a basic costume of their own clothes to which were added tabards, wigs, hats, and so forth, and the actors in the plays-within-the-play wore masks. Music was a vital part of the show, and Boris and Russell Howarth created a sort of light wood scaffolding upon which they hung drums, cymbals, bells, xylophones, whistles, a banjo, a guitar and more, and blew, banged and plucked them as necessary as the action developed. The musical accompaniment, a feature which Arden and D'Arcy came to rely on increasingly through the next ten or fifteen years, was worked up improvisationally during rehearsals.

This is the most meta-theatrical of Arden and D'Arcy's plays. It asks: what is real? What is theatre? What is play? In my own production with students, the actors appeared at the opening all dressed in black. They put on their costumes over this in full view of the audience. Thus, the spectator saw that Mr Croke was no more – and no less – 'real' than Sir Lancelot, the character he played. Similarly, the props were on display from the first, and the Prince's 'real' sword was as wooden as Croke's 'wooden' one. In the text, Luke's positive actions – winning a partner, learning to act, saving the company, demonstrating the attractions of peace – turns the negative face of law and order (the Constable, originally played by John Arden) to stone. He fulfils himself by learning to play – something Serjeant Musgrave, another apparent deserter, never learned. And just as the Headmaster in *Ars Longa, Vita Brevis* mistook Mr Miltiades for an antlered stag, so here the Constable, disguised as a French gendarme, mistakes the Princess of France for the man he is seeking. The Prince indicates his coronet to show who he and the Princess really are:

> PRINCE : What's this – upon my head?
> *He indicates his coronet.*
> CONSTABLE : Cardboard. You can't fool me. I know a theatrical
> property when I see one. (*The Prince has drawn his sword.*) And don't
> you threaten me with your old wooden sword. I've not reached my
> term of years and experience without learning summat about mas-
> queraders' ways and means. (*The Prince pricks him with the sword.*)
> Ow-hey-up, that's sharp! You've got no right to use a real blade like
> that upon the stage – it's dangerous, you could hurt someone – ow-ow
> … ! (*In struggling with the Prince he knocks the latter's coronet off.*)
> Wait a moment, that was a funny noise to be made by just a bit of
> cardboard …

But actually, of course, the coronet *is* cardboard, the sword *is* wooden. The noise is made by the musicians. The Constable is correct, they *are* theatrical properties. The nature of truth is elusive. And the climax of the play is even more complex, as Luke improvises a drama round the apparently real Constable, who is really chasing him, but is made to play the part of the dramatic villain who is chasing him. It is like a series of reflecting mirrors, each as 'true' – or as 'false' – as the other. But the authors have warned us at the start of the play:

> All is painted, all is cardboard
> Set it up and fly it away
> The truest word is the greatest falsehood,
> Yet all is true and all in play.

The Royal Pardon was presented at the Arts Theatre in London at Christmas 1967, and again at Easter the following year. But it is extraordinary to those who know this remarkable play that it is not a permanent fixture at theatres across the land at, say, Christmas time: it is more fun, more fascinating and better written in every scene than J.M.Barrie's ubiquitous *Peter Pan*.

The Royal Pardon, directed by Robert Leach, 1968

One of *The Royal Pardon's* most lethal levels of meaning lies in its debunking of the idea that only intellectually-respectable drama at prestigious theatres is worthwhile: Luke and Esmeralda are treated with the utmost disdain by Mr Croke, the theatre manager and star, who is happy to be rid of them as he accepts the hefty subsidy the royal household offers. The 1960s saw increasing interventions in the arts through the use of financial subsidies from the Arts Council and from local authorities. This enabled the creation of large, state-funded theatres dominated by their 'Artistic Directors', who were happy to provide drama and theatre of which the liberal progressive establishment approved. The situation echoed the central contradiction in western democracies, in which a *laisser faire* capitalism was some-how supposed to coexist with a Welfare State. John Arden found himself 'profoundly depressed' in 1963 by the idea of the then-new National Theatre being 'another old stodge', and pictured it and the Royal Shakespeare Company dividing up the theatre world as Moscow and New York were dividing up the nations of the world.[216]

So where was the theatre radical to go? If part of *Ars Longa, Vita Brevis's* meaning was realized in the *where* of the performance, and its *when*, and in the *how* of its production, the same would apply to the established theatres, who opened their doors just after the hour of its bourgeois spectators' dinner, and whose actors repeated their well-learned lines. Yet to leave the 'mainstream' behind seemed to mean trying to forge a Centre 42 or a Fun Palace, and those options had failed. The later 'fringe' theatres of the 1970s were equally unable to solve this con-tradiction, accepting generous state subsidies in order to attack the state, and when the subsidies dried up under Mrs Thatcher, most of the companies dissolved, too.

It was a dilemma which faced Arden and D'Arcy, as unattached theatre practitioners, particularly acutely. The conventional theatre, despite Arden's growing stature there, was constantly unsatisfactory and unsatisfying. 'I don't think John (Arden) was ever really heading for a life in the theatre in the way that, say, Osborne was', Michael Hastings remarked,[217] and Arden himself wrote that 'somehow I was never able to feel that I belonged in the modern theatre'.[218] His experiments with D'Arcy in alternative approaches to theatre led him to the conclusion that:

> The idea of a building with a fixed number of seats all facing a fixed stage, where a fixed number of people will watch a fixed performance for a fixed period of time, and then leave all together with fixed ex-pressions (of pleasure or of boredom) on their faces, is not necessarily the only possibility.

He suggested an alternative:

> There is no reason why an entertainment should not include a variety of forms, music, plays, films, readings, recitations, dancing, etc, in front of an audience which may feel itself at liberty to go or come at any time it wishes. There is nothing particularly new about this, it has always happened in music halls or singing pubs or at pierrot shows or punch-and-judy on the beach; but it is perhaps less usually associated with 'serious theatre'. If it comes to that, there is no particular reason why 'serious theatre' should be serious anyway.[219]

It was an idea which related back to Kirkbymoorside and *The Business of Good Government*, and had been voiced in connection with *The Workhouse Donkey*. It was an important statement of alternative possibilities.

Arden also noted that the only difference between professionals and amateurs was that the former were paid: there was no necessary artistic superiority. He and D'Arcy had discovered that work outside the mainstream or conventional could be equally exciting, and personally and artistically as rewarding. And they also inspired others, as Baz Kershaw noted: 'whilst Arden and D'Arcy were not a part of the 1960s counter-culture, their community-based projects did have a direct effect on the younger generation.' He observed that 'in the 1960s virtually single-handedly, they invented prototypes which later became the common currency of the extensive community drama and arts movements of the 1970s and 1980s'.[220] But they were not bureaucrats: they had no wish to set up a theatre company of their own. The problem of the development of alternatives in theatre thus tied in with finding alternatives in politics.

As Arden noted in the Introduction to *Left-Handed Liberty*, the times increasingly needed clear thinking. He was properly radical. He gave the royalties from the 1965 revival of *Serjeant Musgrave's Dance* to Christian Aid's work in South Africa. He joined the 'Who Killed Kennedy?' Committee, along with a host of famous radicals – Bertrand Russell, Caroline Wedgwood Benn, William Empson,

Michael Foot MP, J.B.Priestley, Hugh Trevor-Roper and more; they sponsored a tour of Britain by the American investigative writer, Mark Lane, though the organisation soon petered out. And in 1966 he became chair of *Peace News*, for whom he wrote a regular monthly column until 1969. According to Nigel Fountain, *Peace News* 'stood at the crossroads of mid-1960s culture'. It took a strong leftist line, and commented freely on a wide range of issues. It criticised British politics and the Labour government of Harold Wilson fiercely. It reported on the civil rights movement in USA and gave space to writers such as the radical jazz critic from New York's *Village Voice*, Nat Hentoff. It was interested in ecology, internationalism and the arts in all its forms. 'Under the editorship of Theodore Roszak and Rod Prince, *Peace News* trailed the bulk of the preoccupations for the next half decade',[221] and Arden was at its heart. 'I was a militant war-resister', he said, not without irony, 'perpetrating civil disobedience at every flourish of my coffee-cup'.[222]

In 1966, Arden and D'Arcy sold their Kirkbymoorside cottage, and moved to a house in Cranbourne Road, Muswell Hill. Soon after they moved, one evening there was a knock on the door. It was Arden's agent, Warren Tute. Tute was a slightly slippery individual. He had himself tried to make a career as a playwright, and now he was spending money trying to make his way as an impresario. He once told a newspaper reporter, half amusedly, that 'if you send (Arden) a telegram demanding an urgent reply you can be sure of only one thing – silence'.[223] Nevertheless, Tute had always provided Arden with what money he asked for when he asked, and all had seemed well. Arden's account with him stood at around £10,000 – a considerable sum at the time. But now something had changed. Tite brought ill news. He had lost all the money. All £10,000 (or more) of it. What kind of speculation had consumed their savings was never satisfactorily vouchsafed. The fact was, the money was gone.

Suddenly D'Arcy realized that though all this money was in the name of John Arden, some at least was rightly hers. *The Business of Good Government*, for instance, was proving extremely popular, selling well and bringing in performance fees from groups wishing to present it. She was at least as responsible as he was for its very existence. Yet she had received no financial reward for it at all. Arden had always been somewhat careless about their income, and D'Arcy had never properly questioned him about this. It was clear a new, more equal relationship would have to be built.

It could be asked, why did they stay together? Theirs was the first generation when divorce became relatively easy, and many theatrical and artistic people took full advantage of the fact. They were not even wholly faithful to each other. But somehow their parting never seemed likely. D'Arcy may have been fiery and impulsive, her 'mongrel, Irish background'[224] leading to her natural dissidence and her constant desire to unmask hypocrisy wherever she found it. Arden was much more thoughtful and, in a way, timid. But they were somehow a creative team. Their friend, Tamara Hinchco said: 'He wouldn't have been John Arden without her. They're two very strong individuals in their own right, but they've had a lifelong dialogue together'.[225] This is borne out by other remarks. Thus, D'Arcy records, when they began to rethink the King Arthur material, there was 'much discussion between myself and J.A.'[226] When, late in his life, I asked Arden himself why they had stayed together, his answer was disarming: 'We are partners of the imagination', he said.

By 1966 it was clear that the artistic collaboration itself enriched their personal relationship just as their personal relationship enriched the collaboration. The film, *John Arden – Playwright* shows him reading his work to D'Arcy and asking for her comments, this process was followed throughout their working lives. My impression is that D'Arcy was the more spontaneous of the two, that she would let the ideas roll around her subconscious, and that for her contribution she would go where the wind of inspiration blew her. Arden seemed the more thoughtful, even pedantic, partner, who worked with words – yet whose words were capable of an extraordinary magnificence, which could pin you to the wall like a drunk man on a blowy Saturday night. No twentieth century English writer is more powerful than Arden at his best. They therefore complement one another. Arden told an interviewer in 1991, 'If it hadn't been for living and working with Margaretta and involving myself in her projects … I think I would have become much more desiccated as a writer'.[227] It seems that each presents the other with their work and ideas, and that this process can be competitive, and can expose vulnerabilities. And they each 'spoil' the other's solutions to problems. They may want to take the work in different directions, they struggle, argue, debate and finally find the way to reach something which perhaps they did not know they wanted to reach. Sometimes it must be hard even to remain friendly. But they do. And after each solution, more work lies ahead. They both know that collaborative work is likely to produce better ideas, better solutions, which neither might have found alone. Claudia W.Harris, who spent time with them in 1992, was to write:

> Listening to them all day argue the same points, finish each other's
> sentences, fill in alternately the gaps in plot or approach or idea gives
> some sense of how closely they have become of one mind. Then listening
> to them discuss their differing writing styles, bemoan their ruthless but
> necessary critiques of each other's work, describe their final, careful
> shaping of the whole gives a sense of how thoroughly their working
> methods have become complementary.[228]

This is extremely unusual and exciting. But by 1966 or 1967, for whatever reason, critics had begun to criticise the partnership, and especially D'Arcy's part in it. Those plays by John Arden which companies like the National Theatre had mounted seemed accessible (now that his earlier plays had at last been accepted), whereas something like *Ars Longa, Vita Brevis* was bewildering. Moreover, there was a sort of puzzled disbelief that Arden could prefer the intimacies or chaos or unpredictability of 'community' drama, or improvisation, to plays 'done properly' by conventionally acclaimed national theatre companies. It seemed to many critical minds not used to widening their horizons or seeing beyond their own hutches, that clever John Arden was being led astray by a wild Irish woman. Furthermore, the fact that she was a woman fed into the unrecognised male prejudice of many critics. The fact that the woman was his wife seemed to make matters worse. D'Arcy, who suffered often extraordinarily vituperative abuse and discrimination, described it, only slightly ironically, thus:

> A wife (as opposed to a straight or gay lover) is expected to serve the playwright-spouse as an unwaged, invisible typist or secretary or manager or comforter, while the critic is left free to be the real lover and pursuer and owner of the man-of-talent. If he finds (and it always is a *he*) that his playwright has discovered a different way of making love or is wearing a different kind of nightwear, or prefers the shower to the bath when the critic was hoping tenderly to sponge him down in deep warm water, then at once he is filled with alarm, turning to resentment, turning to sheer vindictiveness.[229]

The number of creative partnerships in the history of drama and theatre is legion, but somehow D'Arcy and Arden always seemed less acceptable than Beaumont and Fletcher or Gilbert and Sullivan, or the Russian revolutionaries, Erdman and Mass, or the *chic* thirties radicals, Auden and Isherwood, or more recently Brenton and Hare or the brothers Mikhail and Vyacheslav Durnenkov.

Yet there was one married couple who bestrode European theatre in the second half of the twentieth century, who had considerably less trouble with critics *as a result of their partnership* than Arden and D'Arcy – the Italian Nobel prize-winner, Dario Fo, and his wife, Franca Rame. They married in 1954, and collaborated from the beginning. Both did their own work, too, of course. In 1968, like D'Arcy and Arden, as we shall see, Fo and Rame's work became much more overtly political and revolutionary, and was frequently censored and sometimes banned. Moreover, they were subjected to physical attack and to arrest and prison for their work and beliefs. The comparison with Arden and D'Arcy is unmistakeable, even down to the work itself, which Stuart Hood described:

> Franca Rame and Dario Fo work within a tradition of improvisation which means the texts of their plays are difficult to 'fix'; they change according to the changing political situation, according to the different audiences. They are like living organisms but within them there is a hard skeletal framework – framework of radical criticism of our society and of relationships within it.[230]

Yet as husband-and-wife they were never attacked. Is it that Italians understand the nature of creativity better than Saxons or Celts? Or that they see marriage as a potentially creative relationship? For whatever reason, Fo and Rame's marriage was taken for granted, while Arden and D'Arcy's was viewed as disastrous. Their partnership may not have threatened the political *status quo*, but it clearly shook something at the root of the British artistic and cultural establishment, and offended a peculiarly British sense of propriety.

In February 1967, Arden accepted an appointment as Visiting Professor in Humanities at New York University for six months. His one *proviso* was that D'Arcy should accompany him, and work with him.

Ten : Cartoons, Archetypes, Slogans, Theatre

When Arden and D'Arcy arrived in USA in February 1967, it was a country at war in Vietnam and in turmoil at home.

From 1955, when the French had been driven out of their colonies in southeast Asia, the Americans had been trying to shore up the area against the encroachment, as they saw it, of Communism, especially Chinese Communism. Gradually their involvement had grown. In March 1965, President Lyndon Johnson enormously expanded the effort by ordering the bombing of the Communist north of Vietnam. This was in response to an incident, actually fabricated by the Americans themselves, when an American warship had been fired on by the North Vietnamese. Though the truth of the American dishonesty only emerged later, it was widely thought at the time to be an extraordinarily flimsy excuse for such massive 'retaliation'.

A week after the bombing commenced, 3,500 US marines were sent to South Vietnam in what amounted to an invasion. By the end of 1965, there were 200,000 US military personnel there. Their presence only served to rouse the Vietnamese people to greater resistance, and by 1967, US 'progress' towards their desired settlement was self-evidently no nearer. In January 1968 the Vietnamese launched their counter-attack, the so-called 'Tet Offensive', and a fearsomely bloody conflict ensued. In US it became increasingly obvious that the generals' and the President's reports to their electorate and the world were grounded in hope not fact – and still young soldiers were being sent to die.

In the face of this, in the spring of 1967, sit-ins, strikes and other forms of dissent, especially on college campuses, accelerated in numbers and in bitterness. In London and across the world, there were big anti-Vietnam War demonstrations. Heavyweight boxing champion, Muhammed Ali refused to join the US forces, and in San Francisco, a 'human be-in' attracted over 30,000 supporters. In March 1967, Martin Luther King led a huge protest in Chicago, and in April protesters temporarily halted business on the New York Stock Exchange. According to Gallup Poll, over half of all Americans opposed the Vietnam War; obviously across the rest of the world, the percentage was considerably higher.

Arden had been invited to New York University's Humanities Faculty by Professor Conor Cruise O'Brien, to whom he had dedicated *Armstrong's Last Goodnight*, to lecture on 'Theatre and Politics'. Arden had visited New York in 1965, when *Live Like Pigs* had been presented here, and in 1966 for *Serjeant Musgrave's Dance*. In 1966 he had also participated in a conference at Long Island University on 'Alienation and Commitment'. But now, in addition to the lectures, he was asked to conduct practical sessions with student writers, directors and actors. He agreed, but only on condition that D'Arcy should also be fully involved in the work. The University agreed she should be.

John Arden and Margaretta D'Arcy, c.1967.

Arden was provided with an office on the fifth floor of an air conditioned sky scraper. He was, apparently, 'slim, logical, articulate and sometimes bearded'.[231] He was still working on the King Arthur play, for which he had received a commission from the BBC, and his fifth floor office was a good place to write. But a number of factors disturbed this apparently-cosy arrangement. One was an attack on him by George Steiner, eminent man of letters, who told D'Arcy he ought to be working on something more contemporary than ancient mythic tales – Vietnam by implication. Another was that at his third seminar, D'Arcy, exasperated by the seeming good manners of academic discussion, launched into a tirade about the war in Vietnam, and the complacency of American society, including student society. Finally, the students themselves, reading Arden's Preface to *The Workhouse Donkey*, challenged him to produce what he there had dreamed of – an all-day theatre event. Arden initially floundered, but he was rescued by D'Arcy, who began to conceive what would become the *War Carnival*.

The idea survived both Arden's reluctance and the strong suggestion from the University authorities that something less ambitious would be more appropriate. Political intrigue in the University grew as the work developed, and there were fears that funding might be threatened. According to Arden, 'it was all very unpleasant. People whom you thought were on your side suddenly turned out not to be there when you wanted them …'[232] D'Arcy found that a kind of McCarthyism still operated, if covertly. Several participants in the work were warned off by what seemed like a sort of Mafia, and the CIA or perhaps the FBI – organisations not

129

easily distinguished by lay people – informed a young Greek student that if he took part he would almost certainly be expelled from the USA, and returned to Greece, which at that time was ruled by a Fascist junta. Despite all this, the Vietnam *War Carnival* became a highly significant event in the creative lives of both D'Arcy and Arden.

For one thing, it was heavily influenced by the vivid and radical theatre culture sprouting in USA at the time, often in response to political events. D'Arcy had been amazed, for example, in an earlier visit to USA, to see an establishment figure like Sammy Davis Jr stop his show and harangue the audience about civil rights after a number of black people had been shot during an anti-discrimination protest. More important were contacts she now made with New York theatre groups, including La Mama, the off-off-Broadway company founded in 1961 by Ellen Stewart, fashion designer and boutique owner, on Lower East Side, Manhattan. La Mama's aim was to give a platform to new writers, and already work by Paul Foster, Lanford Wilson, Sam Shepard, Adrienne Kennedy and others had been staged here. Foster's *Tom Paine* made a particular impact – a fantastic, fast-moving kaleidoscope of images, a little like a jazz riff on the history of late eight-eenth century revolutions. There is, for example, an absurd chess game between France and England with American diplomacy as the board; a battle conspicuously like that in *Ars Longa, Vita Brevis*; and an extraordinary scene of over-eating, when George III and Louis XVI stuff their bellies to bursting – an image used here as effectively as Brecht used the same image in *The Rise and Fall of the City of Mahagonny*.

Stewart cared so much for 'her' playwrights that she literally housed and fed several of them when they were at their lowest ebb. In their early years Stewart's company worked in a tiny space seating no more than twenty-five spectators on the floor, and the plays only ran for a week. Still, her work was marked – and feared – by her self-proclaimed 'betters', and she was harried from one venue to another. With extraordinary courage, however, she persevered: she turned La Mama into a club and quickly gathered several thousand members. Her *alumni* ranged from actors such as Al Pacino, Robert de Niro and Richard Dreyfuss to directors like Robert Wilson and composers like Philip Glass. Her artistic director was Tom O'Horgan, who was much influenced by Viola Spolin's approach to acting through improvisation and games, and he and Stewart trained their actors in non-psychological, movement-based techniques. Recognition of this work came with the performance of *Hair*, the 'tribal love-rock musical' by Gerome Ragni and James Rado, which proved a world-wide commercial hit – though some La Mama members regarded it as a betrayal of their work. Stewart's meeting with D'Arcy and Arden was important for more than artistic reasons. She remembered: 'When John was in New York lecturing I was trying to travel with the troupe in Europe. No one seemed to care about us in America and we certainly couldn't raise any money. But

John would visit and tell us to keep going and he donated his whole fee from his time at NYU. He was more than our mentor, he was our white knight'.[233] When they did come to Europe the following year, they stayed at Arden and D'Arcy's Muswell Hill home when they were in London.

Also in New York on the Lower East Side, were the Bread and Puppet company, founded in 1961 by Peter Schumann with the aim of stirring spectators to political action. Born in Germany, this strongly anti-war artist was a dancer, musician and sculptor, who harnessed the power of puppets, especially huge, fantastical creations which swayed way above spectators' heads, in his radical presentations. After 1968 this company acquired world-wide fame with tours to European cities, but they first appeared in Britain in 1968 at D'Arcy's invitation, and they too stayed at the house in Muswell Hill. 'Everyone (in Britain) was excited by them', she commented, 'but actually the British theatre people weren't ready for that type of theatre'.[234] For now, she persuaded Schumann to contribute huge war-god puppets to the *Carnival* project.

D'Arcy also visited San Francisco, where she made contact with Joseph Chaikin, the radical director and actor, who had worked with La Mama and had founded The Open Theater in 1963; and met the San Francisco Mime Troupe, which had been founded in 1959 by R.G.Davis as a sort of contemporary *commedia dell' arte* company, staging controversial plays in public parks, at least one of which had been banned for obscenity. In this year, 1967, they were creating a modernised version of Goldoni's *The Military Lover* as a satire on the Vietnam war, and touring it to college campuses where Dow Chemical Company, the makers of the napalm being used in Vietnam, were trying to recruit graduates. One of their later shows was *Seize the Time*, an epic history of the Black Panther Party, whom D'Arcy also discovered here. The Black Panthers were militant anti-racists, part of the Black Power movement just coming to public prominence. Founded by Bobby Seale and Huey Newton, with an influential newspaper, *The Black Panther*, edited by Eldridge Cleaver, they articulated a hard-line, quasi-Maoist position from a black perspective, but were also a respected and original voice in the counter-culture of the 1960s and 1970s. They rejected a narrow black nationalism in favour of a more inclusive communism, but their activism never compromised: they were renowned – or notorious – for their armed citizens' patrols which often ostentatiously monitored police activity.

These radical American groups influenced Arden and D'Arcy, not only during the making of the Vietnam *War Carnival*, but throughout all their artistic and political work. The *Carnival* itself was staged in the University's 300-seater theatre on 13 May 1967, the same date as a noisy pro-war demonstration was marching in New York. The *Carnival* was collectively assembled and largely improvised, though it was overseen and shaped by Arden and D'Arcy, with Leonard Shapiro and Omar

Shapli. Shapiro went on to become the director of the radical Shaliko Theatre Company, deriving inspiration from Jerzy Grotowski; their 1968 anti-Vietnam war 'street musical', *Brother, You're Next*, aroused controversy across USA. Omar Shapli, who taught at New York University, also directed a radical company, Section 10, dedicated to improvisational theatre.

The *Carnival* lasted virtually twelve hours and left participants and spectators alike exhausted and perhaps to some degree purged. Arden's own description of the event, written as a pastiche of *Time* magazine, exposes some of its frenzy and fury.[235] It started calmly enough with people being invited to take part in fairground-style games like hoopla, but was interrupted by an apparent quarrel between two participants, one of whom 'killed' the other. Stilt-walking Oriental gods appeared, and Arden himself called for 'peace', which was taken up as a chant by all. The vehemence of the call led to two groups – opposing armies – being formed, and while film of American troops, intercut with film of Nazi armies, was shown, the main 'game' was begun, to the accompaniment of ritualistic drum beats. Participants were segregated into two armies (not unlike what happened in the classroom of *Ars Longa, Vita Brevis*), the members of each army having its distinctive red or green mark painted on their foreheads. The armies circled each other until Shapli blew a whistle, and chose a participant from each army as antagonists in some form of contest. Sometimes this was cerebral, the opponents being asked to make up a rhyming poem, the first to fail to find a rhyme being the loser; sometimes it was more physical, such as an obstacle race of some kind. The loser of each game was condemned to death, or not, according to the traditional thumbs up or thumbs down sign, and the execution was carried out in mime.

This 'game' was then intercut with scenes from a nightmarish soap opera, more or less improvised by the participants. There were twenty-four episodes, performed by masked actors, which allegorised American involvement in southeast Asia though the story of Grandma. After the accidental dropping of a nuclear bomb on an isolated American farm, the farm family begins to glow in the dark. Anxious to hush up what has happened, President Johnson invites Grandma to be his Vice-Presidential running mate. They win the election, and she becomes Vice-President. Her grandson, having been drafted to fight in Vietnam, takes the Administration to court, however, and the war is declared unconstitutional. Consequently Grandma impeaches Johnson for violating the constitution, and takes over the Presidency herself. She revises the war declaration so that it is now constitutional, and her daughter Jezebel, 'a soldier's whore' in Saigon, south Vietnam, begins to drop bombs instead of babies from her womb. Meanwhile, her son invokes the gods of war to confront Grandma, who, as President, represents the nation. In the final confrontation, they kill each other, and the towering war gods emerge from their puppet paraphernalia to show they are merely human, and therefore need not be obeyed.

This grotesque fable was constantly interrupted by a variety of interludes, including the huge puppets stalking about the theatre. A black gospel choir sang, there were Jewish folk songs and revolutionary songs from a Hungarian student, Paul Neuberg. Two young women, wearing nothing but flags, performed a sort of striptease, revealing bodies painted red, white and blue. As the day proceeded, the participants became increasingly frantic, almost carried away by the relentless intensity. Suddenly Arden declared himself a CIA agent, who was testing the participants' dissent. The event was out of control, he said. He would now bring it to an end. He had all the lights put out. The excitement shrivelled, the people became nonplussed, deflated. Then Arden himself calmly unpinned the American flag ('old glory') and desecrated it by walking on it. 'He said it was better to burn a flag ... than to burn flesh',[236] as the Americans were doing with their napalm in Vietnam. A slide of a burned Vietnamese child was projected, and the final appeal from Arden to people not to join the war, and not to pay taxes which financed it, brought the *Carnival* to a close.

The Vietnam *War Carnival* was a one-off, experimental event. On one level, it tried to appropriate the spectacle of society before Guy Debord's work had become generally known (*La société de spectacle* was published in 1967). As a statement against the war, it was as effective as could be expected, through its passion and the way it demonstrated alternative ways of interacting, especially in the games. It was mostly unscripted, certainly under-rehearsed and moved through its various scenes and sequences without much overall rhythm. But it brought participants and spectators into a warmer fellowship, and Arden admitted it was 'a remarkable fulfilment of exactly the kind of aspiration I had given voice to in the *Donkey's* preface'.[237] Part of its importance was that it exemplified how the *form* of a presentation was as important as its *content* in conveying meaning. It could be argued that the content of the *War Carnival* was simplistic or muddled, but as a freewheeling extravaganza, comic, surprising and open-ended, it *embodied* its alternatives. Could this only be achieved through an improvised, provisional sort of show, such as the *Carnival*? And if so, where did that leave the writer? These were problems still to be confronted. For now, Arden moved after D'Arcy along a path which was leaving pacifism as such behind, and becoming increasingly sympathetic to some kind of revolutionary communism.

Their position was not unlike that of the European Situationists, who were largely behind the 1968 Paris *événements*, though it must be stressed that neither Arden nor D'Arcy ever overtly identified with them. Nevertheless, this somewehat disparate group theorised advanced capitalism as 'spectacle', which depended on the deceptive and mind-numbing images pumped out by television and advert-ising;

133

and the consequent fetishisation of commodities. They attempted to bring this communistic political critique into a dialectical relationship with an *avant garde* artistic sensibility from which would emerge a new revolutionised world. 'Since everything is part of the spectacle, however, resistance can only take the form of targeting the spectacle with its own products by perverting, displacing, disfiguring and redefining them in such a way that the ideology of the spectacle is both revealed and challenged'.[238] And since art, and theatre, are part of the spectacle, the Situationists renounced them in favour of *situations* which could be seen as highly politicised happenings. It was perhaps unsurprising that theatre was particularly problematic for them, because the *situation* is really a kind of theatre beyond the theatre – just what the New York *War Carnival* had been.

Arden and D'Arcy left New York in June 1967, just at the start of America's 'long hot summer' of race riots and disturbances. Back in Britain there was an Angry Arts Week, a protest of arts workers against the Vietnam war, which they joined. The main event of the week, organised by Neil Hornick, was a large gathering of London literary and theatre people at the Roundhouse in Chalk Farm to protest at the British government's 'complicity' in America's war. There was a performance of a show called *The Gang Bang Show*, written by Peter Buckman, Eric Idle and others, in which the writers and performers waived their fees. And there was a television debate, chaired by Kenneth Allsopp, in which Kingsley Amis and Robert Pitman defended the British Government against Arnold Wesker, Annie Ross and John Arden. Amis threw Wesker, Ross and Arden off balance by asking where the money the Angry Arts Week was collecting would go, to which they were unable to supply an answer. The week was not a success.

Society was becoming more polarised, and political protest more violent. Arden himself began to feel that the situation in Britain and America was 'even more shakey than it appears', and found himself asking: 'Are we on the verge of a revolution?'[239] In October – the same month that Che Guevara was killed in the Bolivian jungle – there had been an attempt to occupy the Greek Embassy in London six months after a Fascist *coup* in that country, with the result that three protesters had received twelve month gaol sentences. Recognising that the occupation had been a 'muddle', he argued in December the need for clear thinking on the left. But the momentous year of 1968 was to overtake these ruminations.

In January 1968, Alexander Dubcek assumed power in the Soviet satellite state of Czechoslovakia, and instituted a programme for decentralisation and democratisation which came to be known as the 'Prague Spring'. The continuing escalation of the war in Vietnam provoked more bitter student sit-ins in USA, as well as other protests, including hunger strikes, and in Britain, too, students found a new militancy. In December, as Arden was discussing the need for clear thinking, the first students sit-ins were happening in London colleges. Their demand for an end to the war was conjoined to calls for much greater democracy in their academic institutions. Their cry was taken up early in 1968 by students of Aston University in Birmingham, and the Universities of Edinburgh and Leicester. There were protests and sit-ins in other colleges and universities through the spring and a febrile political atmosphere, such as Arden had foreseen, developed: three cabinet ministers were physically assaulted at different times, dockers went on strike in the ports, the prominent Conservative M.P., Enoch Powell, deliberately stirred the fires of race hatred in the midlands, and the anti-Vietnam War demonstrations only got larger and more virulent. In May, notable protests included Essex University students' rebellion and 'sleep-ins' at Hornsey College of Art. Beyond Britain, the whole of Europe and the USA seemed ablaze with revolutionary fervour, especially after the assassination of Martin Luther King in April, and of Robert Kennedy early in June. King's murder set off rioting, arson and mayhem in over one hundred American cities. In Paris, in May, striking students demanded top-to-bottom reform of their universities, and began a month-long protest with sit-ins and sleep-ins, and furious political debates, supported by a general strike by the French trade unions. Only President de Gaulle's implicit threat of armed force held a new French Revolution at bay. Moreover, those involved were developing a new and wider political consciousness, their concerns now embracing civil rights, feminism, anti-apartheid activities and more.

The relationship of culture and the arts to these '*événements*' was most clearly demonstrated in Paris, where some Situationists deliberately tried to bring them together. Intellectual figures such as Jean-Paul Sartre, theatrical luminaries like Jean-Louis Barrault and all sorts of hitherto scarcely known writers and thinkers like Hélène Cixous and Guy Debord became passionately involved. As for Britain, Peter Ansorge noted that it was 'impossible to deny ... a link between the most publicized political events of 1968 and the creation ... of the new "alternative" circuit of arts labs, cellar theatres and environmental venues'.[240] D'Arcy and Arden were among the first to experiment with these new venues in a series of productions in this year, the first of them in and around Unity Theatre in a collaboration with the Cartoon Archetypal Slogan Theatre (CAST). D'Arcy had seen a performance of CAST's play, *John D.Muggins Is Dead*, and had found their rapid-fire style and strong sequences of images somewhat reminiscent of the radical companies she had seen in USA. They shared a platform at a Vietnam Solidarity Campaign rally in a hall on Tottenham Court Road in late 1967, when Arden read a poem by Allen Ginsberg, and CAST performed *John D.Muggins Is Dead* so that when CAST advertised in *Peace News* for rehearsal premises, D'Arcy and Arden were happy to offer them a room in their house in Muswell Hill. This offer was not taken up, but later, at a party Arden and D'Arcy hosted for La Mama troupe, who were now in Europe, they and Roland Muldoon, CAST's director, agreed to work together at a hall in Notting Hill.

135

Here 'we began some improvisations on the takeover of a café by gangsters, *à la* Kray-Richardson ... This was to be an environmental play set in a practicable café, and directed towards the local community'.[241] However, the venture fell through, and the project was seemingly shelved.

Still seeking alternative theatrical outlets, Arden and D'Arcy had some involvement now with Camden's Pentametre Theatre, run by Leonie Scott-Matthews. But before anything took flight here, CAST returned to their lives, offering something perhaps closer to what they sought. CAST had been formed originally by Roland Muldoon and Claire Burnley, who had fallen out with the Communist Party's Unity Theatre, partly because they were radical practitioners with a *penchant* for improvisation, but also because they were supporters of the Trotskyist International Socialist group. The IS were heavily involved with the Vietnam Solidarity Campaign at the time, and were largely the creation of the anti-Zionist Jewish revolutionary, Tony Cliff (pen name for Yigael Gluckstein), whose analysis of the USSR as a bureaucratic state capitalist regime was totally at odds with the Communist Party's line. Despite – or perhaps because of – this, Muldoon and Burnley appeared to continue to harbour ambitions to take over Unity. CAST called itself a 'rock 'n' roll' theatre, anti-realist, presentational ('we don't talk to each other, we only talk to the audience') which performed in pubs and folk clubs, but not in theatres. They relied on physical characterisation, broad humour and cartoon-style editing, and their shows were noted for their breakneck pace as well as their perhaps-unsophisticated ideological content. But they were sharp, integrated and coherent, and Muldoon himself was a manic comedian, wild, political, physically outrageous and fast-talking. 'He is the Left's court jester', wrote Sandy Craig, 'poking fun at their leaders, undercutting their pretensions and loosening the straps on the puritanical straight-jacket which the Left is prone to impose on its members' behaviour'.[242]

Muldoon invented the character of Muggins, a sort of working class Everyman whose dilemmas and difficulties formed the core of a series of shows. The first was *John D.Muggins Is Dead*, a twenty minute anti-Vietnam War piece which impressed D'Arcy. Other productions included *The Trials of Horatio Muggins*, which tackled obfuscatory socialist theorising, and *Muggins Awakening*, 'a frenetic La Mama-ish montage about the Third World, American commercialism and imperialism, and violence everywhere'.[243] It was this character who was to be at the centre of the show Arden and D'Arcy were to create with CAST in what Itzin later called 'one of the classic, legendary events in political theatre in 1968',[244] and what Kershaw referred to as 'a seminal and far-reaching project'.[245]

It probably did not feel much like that to the participants at the time. Muldoon recorded the trepidation he felt at entering the house of John Arden, 'the great playwright' of whom even his mother had heard, though he was clearly taken aback by the fact that the house in Muswell Hill had 'no carpet on the floor and you had to draw up a house-brick to sit down'.[246] Arden proposed writing a play for CAST, and though this did not appeal to all members of the company, Muldoon himself accepted. Unity Theatre was available, but quite soon, so that things would have to move fast if the production were to be ready in time. Arden drafted the script of *Harold Muggins Is a Martyr*, after consultation with D'Arcy, in what was to be their first attempt at an overtly socialist drama. She meanwhile contacted John Fox at Bradford College of Art, and explored the Camden area and its people, before what would become, according to Baz Kershaw, 'a series of almost epic encounters between three generations of political radicals committed to subversive cultural action',[247] the old guard Communists of Unity Theatre itself, Arden, D'Arcy and their ex-anarchist revolutionaries, and Roland Muldoon and the International Socialists of the rock 'n' roll generation.

Harold Muggins Is a Martyr, a 'Gala/Festival/Play/Celebration/Hit', was a fairly simple allegory. Harold, standing for Harold Wilson, was yet still an Everyman figure. He was a petit bourgeois who ran a seedy café, whose sidelines include selling pornography, running prostitutes and receiving stolen goods. Moreover, encouraged by the greedy desires of his traditionally nagging wife, he wrung whatever he could out of his downtrodden employees. The setup was, of course, a metaphor for Britain. When an ultra-modern supermarket (the European Common Market) opened nearby, the Muggins' café was doomed, and it was taken over by Grumblegut, a businessman, and Jakey Jasper, his sidekick, on behalf of Mr Big, or the USA. They reorganised the place: paint, ladders, shopfitters and more lead to a new name – 'The Subliminal Experience' – and piped music and fruit machines. The revamped café attracts customers, but they fight, the employees leave and Grumblegut now wants protection money. His solution to the new crisis is to introduce a striptease act. Further mayhem ensues between the locals and Grumblegut and his crew till only Grumblegut and Muggins himself are left standing.

The script itself was originally not much more than a draft, something like that of *Ars Longa, Vita Brevis*, the basis for improvisation, with at its heart a series of stimulating dialectical oppositions: the refusal to condemn set alongside the virulence of the satire; didacticism as opposed to irony; the pantomime style and the epic context; the inanimate slides Arden and D'Arcy intended contrasting with the live actors; and so on. Arden and D'Arcy's aim was for a final version to be realised through rehearsal and experiment with the cast. Arden told a journalist, 'I want to make clear this play is not by me alone … it wasn't just one person or two, sitting down in a room with an idea and making a play out of it'.[248] The final result, he explained, would depend at least as much on the actors' input.

But the cast was a distinctly mixed group, with Arden and D'Arcy themselves as Mr and Mrs Muggins, Roland Muldoon as Buzzard the solicitor, and two other members of CAST, some amateurs and a few professionals. The slides which CAST were to provide never materialised, and it was soon apparent that Muldoon's struggle with Unity, his desire to take it over like Grumblegut's take-over of Harold Muggins's café, was preventing him from committing wholeheartedly to the improvisational rehearsal process. When he tried to stake his claim to the theatre by running up a red flag on the building, the Unity Management Committee forced him to take it down again. Besides, there was desperately little time available, as the group only managed to rehearse three evenings per week. And the ideological discrepancies began to appear: CAST were self-proclaimed Marxist internationalists; D'Arcy was working with specific groups of local people, mostly children; the managers of Unity were not very interested in her localism, though they were seeking a new role in new times. It was all disastrously muddled.

It seems that despite the fact that Roland Muldoon was nominally in charge of the project, most of the work was actually done by D'Arcy and Arden. John Fox brought a number of his Bradford Art College students to London to create props and scenery, and to construct the 'environment' D'Arcy was keen to build: a stage in the forecourt, with dummy fruit machines in the yard making a sort of caricatured amusement arcade ('to the delight of a largish proportion of the neighbourhood kids'[249]) and a giant cutout ketchup bottle, spewing painted tomato sauce, fixed above the entrance to the theatre. 'What goes on outside the building will be just as important as the stage itself', Arden is quoted as saying.[250] The forecourt stage was the domain of Peter Bowles, the Royal Court Theatre's original Dr Copperthwaite in *The Happy Haven*, who wore – and flourished – a white panama hat; there were costumed carnival parades through the streets of Camden Town; and street 'happenings' aimed to draw in an audience.

> On the garden walls of Mornington Street a line of children balance and
> shout. In the front yard of the little Unity Theatre, the play-wright's wife,
> in a fancy wig, banged a drum; the playwright's children sang giggling
> parodies of TV adverts and the playwright himself, in false moustache
> and seedy silk hat, barked at you to roll up.[251]

D'Arcy hoped to involve people from the local high rise flats, and indeed there was at least one meeting on local issues in the theatre itself. But it seems comparatively few locals attended the show, most of the audiences consisting either of curious theatregoers or activists from counter-culture groups.

A further controversy surrounded the striptease in the show. None of CAST's members were prepared to do this for fear of prosecution by the still-in-place Lord Chamberlain. Arden contacted his favourite professional actress, Tamara Hinchco, and she agreed to do it. Albert Hunt describes how in the play, when the striptease is mooted, Muggins becomes excited and asks to see the act. She strips, 'beautifully but coldly, showing him, and the audience, an attractive body. But when she's completely naked, Muggins simply says, disappointed, "Is that all?"[252] Hinchco remembered it as interesting because it had to be performed 'deadpan'.[253] Unity, true to the puritanical communism of its founding fathers, tried to have the scene cut. Muldoon suggested it be made into something zany, 'light bulbs going up and down on her tits'.[254] But Arden and D'Arcy resisted both these. To Unity's management, they said without this scene the play would not proceed. Similarly, they rejected Muldoon's attempt to make a joke of it. They were intent on examining the sexual exploitation of women. The strip was performed 'deadpan', that is, without salaciousness or eroticism, not only through the actress's performance, but also through the use of a classic Brechtian 'alienation' technique: the audience watched an on-stage watcher, Muggins himself, so that the spectator's response was filtered through his reaction. Since his reaction was the mildly dis-illusioned, 'Is that all?' the whole episode lost its potential *frisson* and the usual purpose of a striptease simply evaporated. To Hunt, it seemed that 'Arden succeeds in this scene in doing what he tried to do in the night-club scene in *The Workhouse Donkey* – in making us both aware of the beauty of the girl's body, and of the pointlessness and frustration of commercialized sex'.[255] However, it was over this scene that communication between D'Arcy and Arden on the one hand and Muldoon and CAST on the other broke down completely.

The play opened on 14 June 1968, unfortunately coinciding with a tube train drivers' strike. It was not a happy omen. The audience was divided between those expecting a twenty-minute CAST rock 'n' roll experience, and those expecting an intellectually challenging Arden play. It was neither. Parts of it were appreciated, including D'Arcy's amusing character based on Barbara Cartland, but Muldoon's natural indiscipline did not help, and to some the play seemed intolerably long. At the end, however, there was always a discussion, chaired by one of the actors, in which spectators and performers joined in often passionate debate, arguing some-times for well over an hour. The play was child-like, perhaps, but never childish, and Simon Trussler compared it with Tudor morality plays, and specifically to Skelton's *Magnificence*. The local children loved the decorated theatre, and at the end of the run there was a special Sunday afternoon improvised version for them, as part of a celebratory party: 'Roland dropped his lighting-plot and tableaux, we dropped the written script, and the result was a fast-moving, funny panto'.[256] The press reception was decidedly mixed. Ronald Bryden, in *The Observer*, called it 'surely the stupidest play ever written by an intelligent writer', adding that 'Arden has contrived a British equivalent of Brecht's *Arturo Ui*',[257] an extraordinary comment considering that the Berliner Ensemble's brilliant extrovert and intel-ligent *Arturo Ui* had been seen in London less than three years previously. It probably lacked the deft touch of Brecht's play, but still Simon Trussler saw it as 'a howl of laughter, occasionally anguished, against the plastic society and its echelons', and found a 'sense of ambiguity (which) underlines and leavens the political directness'.[258] Trussler's later description gives a vivid idea of the play's effect:

> Set-pieces in Arden's highly personal rhyme-patterns – Muggins himself in self-pitying soliloquy or the gangster boss Mr Big on his role in society – merged into episodes of writhing caricature, softened into downbeat scenes of domestic crisis, or escalated into full-scale punch-ups. The combination of Arden's sense of linguistic discipline with CAST's tortuous, harsh-tempered physical expertise was irresistible.[259]

Arden himself thought it was, perhaps 'no great shakes' in itself,[260] though later he said he had found it 'funny' and 'naughty',[261] and maintained 'we got a lot out of the ... project'.[262]

The production raised issues of import concerning the nature of artistic collaboration, as well as problems of the relations between, on the one hand, politics and society and, on the other, theatre and art. In this regard, it seemed to provide a kind of meeting-point for several strands of left-wing cultural and artistic thought. Audiences were provoked, they argued and debated points raised in a way which exposed the shallowness of so many dismissive and self-satisfied reviewers. There were practical results, too: the Agitprop Information Service of the late 1960s and early 1970s, for example, was established as a direct result of the production of *Harold Muggins Is a Martyr*. But the mix of people was unfortunate. It seems that Muldoon was too much in awe of Arden, and too much afraid of D'Arcy, who would not bow to his authoritarian paternalism, for him to be able to contribute fully. His apparent desire to take control of Unity Theatre was not helpful, either. But CAST said 'Never again' to working with D'Arcy and Arden, and that refusal reinforced their reputation for awkwardness

Three days after the opening of *Harold Muggins*, Arden's 'autobiographical' play, *The True History of Squire Jonathan and His Unfortunate Treasure* opened at lunchtime at the Ambience Theatre Club. This was part of the American Ed Berman's extraordinary Inter-Action group, which was responsible for an unparalleled range of community and cultural interventions, with some emphasis on theatre work: Dogg's Troupe theatre company, which toured local housing estates, a Fun Art Bus, and TOC (The Other Theatre) all combined theatre with role play, games and more. Berman also ran the Almost Free Theatre and the Ambience Theatre Club in deliberate opposition to the self-regarding, self-styled 'mainstream' London theatre, and notably gave space to Women's Theatre, Gay Sweatshop and others. Inter-Action, like Oval House, had joined the Roundhouse in Camden Town as an alternative venue for theatrical experiment, giving opportunities to minority voices and the byways of theatrical experiment, in 1967. They were followed in 1968 by the Drury Lane Arts Lab, and Charles Marowitz's Open Space, at the very beginning of what came to be known in the 1970s as 'the Fringe'. It is worth noticing that Arden and D'Arcy were among the earliest – and most influential – participants in this movement.

The True History of Squire Jonathan and His Unfortunate Treasure was originally written in 1963, but was unable to find a producer (it was even submitted for inclusion in *Oh! Calcutta!* but was rejected as being too literary) until Ed Berman accepted it. The play is a transmogrified memory from Arden's days as a student in Edinburgh. It tells the story of Squire Jonathan, who lives in a round stone tower, beset by 'dark men', forests and bogs, and hoards a treasure of gold and jewels in a massive chest. When a large blonde woman tumbles off her horse nearby, he inveigles her into the tower. Here he undresses her, and adorns her with some of his finest jewels. But she flings these off and leaps out of the window to the waiting dark men below. The play is perhaps a fantastical riff on sexual possessiveness and sexual freedom, and as such, excellent fun. Its irony is evident in the unexpected juxtapositioning of almost overblown language with very earthy action. Once again nudity features in the play: this and *Harold Muggins Is a Martyr* were probably the first plays which had shown naked women *moving* in front of an audience in the history of British theatre. According to Arden, it was 'like the type of bawdy caricature that Rowlandson in the eighteenth century was doing', and he also compared it with 'a grotesque drawing by Hieronymus Bosch'.[263]

What did the play mean? Harold Hobson, doyen of theatre critics at the time, found an extraordinary political interpretation which he expounded in *The Sunday Times*: 'Effete Imperialist powers, England and America, with spurious offers of foreign aid, strip the distressed damsel, but in the end have to surrender her to the virile black races'.[264] More likely, the treasure is Jonathan's talent as a writer, which is initially attractive, even seductive, to the blonde woman, but in fact it is the treasure of a man stuck in his tower, cut off from the world. Beyond his tower where he dare not venture, are unpredictable dark men, bogs and forests, which threaten the self-contained, uncommitted writer and his precious talent. If the play has a message, it may be that the time had arrived (in 1963 or 1968?) for Arden to 'get his hands dirty'.

The third Arden/D'Arcy play to be premiered in 1968 was also the best. Shakespearean in scope, in the subtlety and boldness of its structure and in its linguistic brilliance, *The Hero Rises Up* opened at the Roundhouse on 6 November in a production directed by the authors. At the outset the project was anything but Shakespearean. In 1965, Arden's then agent, Warren Tute, had suggested Arden should write the book for a musical show about Lord Nelson which he was setting up with Richard Pilbrow, a stage lighting designer turned impresario. The projected venue for the show was Broadway. With D'Arcy also included, they went to New York where they were wined and dined, and introduced to the composer, Jerry Bock and his lyricist, Sheldon Harnick, who, with Joseph Stein who was responsible for the book, had created the 'smash hit', *Fiddler on the Roof*. They were 'professionals to the last semi-quaver, (who knew) the requirements of the musical form in a way British composers rarely do',[265] and Arden and D'Arcy were now being asked to fill Stein's role. The temptation was obvious: who would not have wanted to work with some of America's slickest talents? Whether they could ever have worked with someone else's lyrics is frankly doubtful, but for two or three years they did more than toy with the idea. Interestingly, we see Arden discussing the project in the television film, *John Arden – Playwright*. It was only when he and D'Arcy saw Paul Foster's *Tom Paine*, performed by La Mama Theatre, that they realized this was not something they wished to pursue, and though there were legal complications in withdrawing from the contract, including agreeing to stage their own play about Nelson in only two countries in the world, leaving the rest of the globe to the Bock-Hamick musical, they did extricate themselves, in order to rework the material into a format more to their liking.

There were other straws in the wind. In 1966, Terence Rattigan's *Nelson: a Portrait in Miniature* was presented on television (it grew into the stage play *A Bequest to the Nation*, premiered in 1970). Considerably less bland than might have been expected, especially as the project had apparently been suggested to Rattigan by the Duke of Edinburgh, this drama relies entirely on dramatic naturalism. The limits of the form are obvious and contrast starkly with Arden and D'Arcy's play which not only gives us a far wider picture of its subject than Rattigan is able to achieve, it in fact demonstrates how a modern history play might be conceived. This is why it is Shakespearean. Few single plays in English have dramatised history so successfully as this one since the Elizabethan and Jacobean period. Certainly it makes Shaw's *Saint Joan* seem parochial, as well as linguistically flat, and Eliot's *Murder in the Cathedral* mannered. And, as Peacock pointed out, it 'was to be followed during the 1970s by an upsurge in the production of politically orientated historical drama'.[266]

The Hero Rises Up has probably not received its due because of the circumstances surrounding its first performance. Michael Kustow, director of the Institute for Contemporary Art, had been present at the same party where D'Arcy and Arden had agreed to work with CAST. With his eye on the main chance, and noting their apparent availability, Kustow was quick to suggest they be part of his evolving ICA as well, despite the ICA's almost total lack of experience in theatre production. Nevertheless, the ICA took the Roundhouse and prepared to mount *The Hero Rises Up*.

Bourgeois forms of cultural production are inevitably bound up with bourgeois ideology: they bourgeoisify the art produced. For *The Hero Rises Up*, Arden and D'Arcy demanded complete control of the production process in order that their play should not be bourgeoisified. The ICA agreed to this, but found it increasingly difficult to maintain their agreement. The difficulties began with minor differences over matters such as the composition and distribution of publicity material, and culminated in Arden and D'Arcy throwing the doors of the Roundhouse open to all comers on the first night, and refusing to charge for entrance. At each stage of their work they had found the ICA management timorous, unhelpful and finally intransigent, though it may be remembered that Arden had characterised himself as 'difficult' in the Preface to *Soldier, Soldier and Other Plays*. Whoever was to blame, on the first night the critics arrived to see what appeared to be a free-for-all in the foyer, which effectively denied them their usual privileged access to the best seats in the bourgeois theatre. No wonder they despaired of the event they were there to report. Arden described how

> as the audience assembled we stood in the foyer liked a pair of vexed
> Picts, committing what in my childhood was the prime social crime of
> the lower middle class suburb where I lived – we were 'Brawling on the
> Doorstep' with the managerial representatives. Bewildered English
> persons, arriving to see the play, stood as Hengist and Horsa must once
> have stood at the ruined gates of decayed Londinium, touchingly
> enquiring – 'Can you please tell me – who is in charge here?' When we
> said we were the authors, they did not regard that as an answer to their
> question.[267]

The continuing course of the row was difficult to follow, but, according to D'Arcy, 'various people were trying to bump us off.'[268] Exactly how this was to be accomplished was not disclosed.

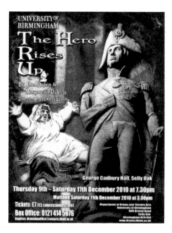

The Hero Rises Up

The play itself still awaits a definitive production. Its premise is close to what Arden wrote in an article in *The Sunday Times* a few months later: 'The British public prefers to do without wars and to make love wherever it can. The top brass

143

cannot do without wars and has nothing to do with love'. The play dramatises this paradox, or set of interlocking paradoxes. Admiral Lord Nelson is the war-time hero who, according to Arden, 'was all wounds and human weakness', whereas his beloved Lady Hamilton

> was the eternal barmaid/tart/stripper-with-a-heart-of-gold, and between
> them they seem to have added up to all that was worth fighting for by the
> ordinary English in the England which they knew. Not everyone could
> hope to possess Nelson's courage, but his big, fat doxy – or someone
> rather like her – was more or less attainable down every street in the
> slums.[269]

The play begins with Nelson, Lady Hamilton and Nisbet, Nelson's step-son (or perhaps their ghosts), arguing about what happened during their lives: they agree to show it. The play proper then commences in Naples where Nelson met Lady Hamilton while cruelly subjugating rebels trying to bring liberty, fraternity and equality to that city. They return to London, where Nelson is acclaimed and he separates from his wife. There follows the Battle of Copenhagen, Nelson and Lady Hamilton setting up home in Merton, with her husband a third party to their new home, and finally the Battle of Trafalgar, with Nelson's ascent to heaven – or perhaps merely to the top of his priapic pillar at the north end of Whitehall.

The authors claimed they wanted to present the audience 'with an experience akin to that of running up in a crowded wet street on Saturday night against a drunken red-nosed man with a hump on his back dancing in a puddle, his arms around a pair of bright-eyed laughing girls, his mouth full of inexplicable loud noises'.[270] The meaning or symbolism of such an encounter might be elusive, but there was something not easily to be forgotten about it. In pursuit of this, the staging at the Roundhouse was stylized and surely closer to a production of the popular comedians, Morecambe and Wise, than to one by, say, Terence Rattigan. The authors deliberately brought children to watch rehearsals, and they used the Havering Youth Theatre's members as 'extras'. On stage they employed half-masks, songs spoken against the music, projected captions, puppet-like movement and direct address to the audience in order to make the play into something almost like a fairground performance of Nelson's time. Albert Hunt notes as 'one of the delights' of the show 'Boris Howarth's home-made, mathematically programmed music, which included a violin with one string, and a steam-organ'.[271] But the psychedelic lighting was inappropriate (though Trussler noted how 'most of the kids' had 'spent the interval raving' about it[272]), some spectators could hardly see much of the action, and the production only lasted for four performances. Arden himself spoke the 'Necromantic Prologue' (which today seems curiously dated), and one spectator remembered for many years one of the battles, when the playwright, wearing a long overcoat, suddenly came on stage. He shouted over the noise of battle, and a manic steam organ, and divided the audience with his hands saying: 'This half are the French; this half are the British. Now everyone on stage, and let's have a battle'. And that's what we had. But the French 'won' which was not supposed to happen. For a time there was confusion, before the play got back on track.[273]

Clearly, here, Arden was trying to recreate what had been so stirring in the New York *War Carnival* (and perhaps in *Ars Longa, Vita Brevis*) – seeking a somewhat similar free form, but now in support of a written play. Was it a success? At this date, it is impossible to judge. But it was another step on the journey Arden and D'Arcy were taking towards an utterly different form of theatre for the times.

Eleven : Looking and Seeing

While Arden and D'Arcy were creating *The Hero Rises Up* at the Roundhouse in London, the fateful year of 1968 exploded its remaining political Molotov cocktails. In August the Soviet Union invaded Czechoslovakia and smashed the 'Prague Spring' movement. The same month in USA, the Democratic Party convention to choose a presidential candidate was held in Chicago. It was disrupted by five days of fierce anti-Vietnam War demonstrations, and police, the National Guard and even the US Army was used to suppress protesters with astonishing violence. In Africa, the festering problems of racism in Rhodesia and South Africa were compounded by the increasing horrors of the Nigerian civil war: Biafra, the oil-rich south eastern province of Nigeria, had seceded in May 1967. Civil war ensued. By the autumn of 1968 the Nigerian government forces had blockaded Biafra, causing enormous suffering, even mass starvation, in what seemed to many to amount to genocide. And in October, there was the massacre by the Mexican government of students and protesters just before the Mexico Olympics opened.

For Arden and D'Arcy, more fateful, even if they hardly realized it at the time, was probably the October civil rights march in Derry in the six counties of Northern Ireland. The Civil Rights Association there had been established early in 1967. Based on the American civil rights movement, its aim was to fight for the rights of the oppressed Catholic minority. Its first march, in spring 1968, had passed off comparatively peacefully, but now the hardline Ulster Unionist Home Affairs Minister, William Craig, insisted that the Civil Rights Association was a front for the IRA and he banned the march in Derry. When the demonstrators ignored this, and continued with their protest, the Royal Ulster Constabulary was despatched to smash it. In the ensuing violence, which was caught on camera and seen on television screens round the world, the brazen despotism of the ruling Unionists was made fearfully apparent. It was the start of the 'Troubles'.

All these events inevitably impacted on the thoughts, and indeed the lives, of Arden and D'Arcy. The year ended with a large demonstration against the illegal racists who had seized power in Rhodesia. This had been preceded four days earlier by an 'occupation' of Rhodesia House by a group of writers. Arden described it:

> We got in at 10.30am by pretending to be *bona fide* visitors, we got put
> out, firmly but 'correctly' by the constabulary, at 3pm: and in the
> meantime we had sat around and stood around and not noticeably
> obstructed the operation of the building. The flag remained illegally
> flying on its pole, such business as had to be transacted at the counter was
> transacted by the staff (they were crowded by us into a corner, but they
> were ladies and could hardly be ejected) and some posters were put up in
> the windows announcing that the building was now in the hands of the

'people of Zimbabwe' – which, except for one cheerful African who arrived at lunchtime, simply was not true.[274]

Describing this protest as 'quiet and polite and small in numbers', he found himself wondering what would be a 'really workable, politically-valuable mode of civil disobedience', and failing to find an answer.

A month or so later, in early 1969, Arden arrived by train at Holyhead, intending to cross by the ferry to Ireland. By his own admission he was tired, dishevelled, carrying a bulging briefcase and a suitcase tied round with string because the handle was broken. He was stopped in the station by an officer from Scotland Yard's Special Branch. He was 'a blond, sneering, cold-eyed young man with a carefully-trimmed fringe-beard'[275] and he questioned Arden for nearly half an hour;

> I said
> My name was Arden and I was a writer –
> His gloomy face did not become much brighter.
> Indeed I was most closely interrogated:
> What were my politics, for whom had I voted,
> Had I ever been arrested, had I ever been convicted?[276]

Was this evidence of a stealthily encroaching police state? Perhaps not, but the policies of western governments seemed especially designed to affront progressive intellectuals: it was discovered, for instance, that the C.I.A. was infiltrating academic and apparently-intellectual or non-aligned journals and other org-anisations. The simple liberal-progressive outlook became more and more difficult to defend. A new radical political atmosphere which encouraged commitment and activism was emerging. In these circumstances, was the pacifism which Arden especially had heretofore espoused and which had led him to accept the position of Chairman of *Peace News*, actually adequate? Or indeed viable? D'Arcy, always ahead of Arden in political matters, was moving with the times. Was it honest for Arden to remain in this apparent no-man's-land, neither disengaged from political struggle, nor yet fully committed?

Such vexatious questions are at the root of the radio play which he wrote at this time, and which was broadcast a year later, on BBC Radio 3 on 27 March 1970. *The Bagman, or The Impromptu of Muswell Hill* is a dream, or a series of dreams within dreams, in which he asks himself: 'who was I, where was I,/What was I for?' The play's protagonist, one 'John Arden', leaves home looking to buy an evening newspaper. Unable to find one, he sits down in the park, and falls asleep. He dreams he meets a gipsy woman who sells him a large canvas bag, hinting that it may contain 'an elegant soft young woman'. Driven out of the park, he finds himself on a moor, peopled with starving waifs, lost and threatened. He is rescued and brought to a city, whose coarse inhabitants are enthralled by fatuous and self-serving politicians, one of whom draws 'John' before them and teases him, like the schoolmaster at Arden's Barnsley elementary school:

> Professor Inkspot tell us now
> Why you walk like a pregnant sow
> Why your nose does root and dig
> Into the earth like a grunting pig
> Tell us tell us tell us quick
> Or else he'll whack you with his stick

In fear of the crowd, 'John' produces the contents from his sack – little people who resemble, dream-like, characters from Arden's plays – a red-coated soldier, a policeman, a hideous Old Woman, and many more. In an interview at the time, he remarked: 'My idea of the theatre is always based on the Victorian toy theatre. A small box in which you have your little figures that move backwards and forwards. And you've got somehow to tell your whole story with a dozen of these in bright colours'.[277] This is precisely what he does here. To great applause, the little figures enact a play which 'mirrors' their life, which turns out to be something like the class war. No-one understands the show, but still 'John' finds himself patted and petted, and he and his bag are spirited away by the rulers: for them, in private, the little people present 'nothing but extraordinary variations of erotic postures and intrigues, couplings and triplings and quadruplings, men and women together, men and men, women and women, women and men and women …' His 'drama' pleases his new masters, he is coddled and sent a young woman to keep him company. But she turns out to be a revolutionary, and she takes him to her comrades, who urge him:

> Your burden is no good to us
> Throw it down – take up a weapon –

But 'John' replies:

> This *is* my weapon!
> You have your spears and knives;
> I have these images of your proud lives.

But his little people are unable to perform for the rebels. They surge back into their bag. There is a great noise of fighting, and Arden finds himself back in Muswell Hill, where he meets again the old gipsy woman, who says:

> You did not find what you expected
> What you found you did not use
> What you saw you did not look at
> What you looked at you would not choose!

'So I pushed past her and went home', 'John' says. He wanted to help the revolutionaries, but his talent (writing) was of no use to them. He concludes, perhaps rather wanly: 'All I can do is look at what I see'.

This play belongs to a respected tradition of ironic, self-examining dreams by playwrights such as Molière in *The Versailles Impromptu*, and more recently by the

French-Rumanian playwright, Eugène Ionesco, whose 1956 play, *Improvisation, or The Shepherd's Chameleon*, opens with 'Ionesco' asleep at his table. He is visited by Bartholomeus, a scholar, who asks about his next play, for which he says he has found a theatre, 'with a scientific director and a young company of scientific actors who want to launch out with *you*'.[278] A second knock on the door admits a second scholar, also called Bartholomeus, who asks about his next play. And a third, also Bartholomeus, who also asks about his next play. They discuss and dismantle 'Ionesco's' work, dressing and undressing him, and hanging labels about his neck. Finally his maid bursts in, frees him from this nightmare, and he begins to harangue the Bartholomeuses as they harangued him. The play asks, What is drama for? What is its relation to its audience?

The dream is also a device favoured by English writers from as long ago as Langland, whose Piers Plowman dreamed of 'a fair field full of folk'. Near the beginning of *The Bouge of Court* by John Skelton, the poet falls asleep and dreams of a ship. He pushes aboard and so sails into the dream. Even more pertinently, in *The Garland of Laurel*, which was a potent inspiration behind Arden's later radio play, *Garland for a Hoar Head*, Skelton lies down, resting on the stump of an old oak tree, falls asleep and dreams he is interrogated as to the value of his poetry. He has to justify himself and his writing, much as Arden has to in *The Bagman* and Ionesco must in *Improvisation*. These works are laced with bitterness as well as irony. *The Bagman* seems to suggest that 'John' could allow himself to be swallowed by his patrons, as 'Ionesco' is in *Improvisation*, or he can abandon his writing and *fight* for freedom and justice for the many. He sits on the fence and observes. The implication – that theatre cannot be a weapon in the fight, however, is implicitly contradicted in the play's action: if theatre was without power, the wealthy rulers would not need to emasculate it, would not bother to coddle its practitioners with subsidy and apparent respect for the writers' intellects. The real question is how should writers *use* their talent? What is the play's relation to its audience?

When *The Bagman* was broadcast, in a production by Martin Esslin, then head of BBC drama, it was widely admired. Peter Porter in the *New Statesman* called it 'a complete triumph ... that mystical thing, pure radio'. He added that it was 'a shining piece of ingenuity as well'.[279] Part of the success was due to Alan Dobey's performance as 'John Arden', given, according to Frances Gray, 'with a wicked imitation of Arden's own Yorkshire vowels'.[280] It seems odd, as others have remarked, that Martin Esslin's view was that it marked Arden's farewell to political commitment, when in fact of course it signalled precisely the opposite. Admitting in his Introduction to the published text that 'it does reflect fairly enough the state of my mind in the spring of 1969', he goes on to assert that actually he soon came to realize that 'the attitude of the central character at the end of the story is reprehensible, cowardly and not to be imitated'.[281] By now he had come to think of himself as Marxist, even if his Marxism came more from Brecht than from reading *The Critique of Political Economy*.[282]

The writing of the play itself no doubt helped to crystallize certain inconsistencies in his position, recognition of which helped to determine him to resign as Chairman of *Peace News*. This almost symbolic rejection of his earlier liberal humanism was also provoked by events in Ireland, where he and D'Arcy still retained their home on the island in Lough Corrib. D'Arcy had taken the island while simultaneously and deliberately keeping her eyes tight shut to any political or social happenings in the country. Ireland had rejected her at the very outset of her adulthood, and she was clear that she wanted no part now in the country's public life. But events themselves were overtaking such determination. First, there was a good deal of persecution of travelling people by the local council in Galway, and Arden and D'Arcy found themselves actively involved in their defence. Then, the Northern Ireland Civil Rights Association's actions were causing world-wide headlines. And now Galway itself was beginning to stir with troubles of its own. For the previous decade, the typical west of Ireland small farms had become increasingly uneconomic, and were being slowly swallowed, one by one, by developers from outside – either from the cities of Ireland herself, or from overseas. The first stirrings of opposition were seen when in August 1967, the US-owned fishing boat, *Mary Catherine*, was destroyed in Rossaveal, ten miles west of Galway City. The IRA claimed responsibility for the act, which was done as a protest against the 'exploitation by foreign interests' of Ireland's natural resources.[283] In June 1969, the IRA was campaigning to the east of Galway city, demanding that an estate near Ardrahan be divided among local smallholders rather than going to developers. They destroyed property on the Mannin Estate in support of their demands. And in Oughterard, on Arden and D'Arcy's Lough Corrib doorstep, they became involved in the struggle of the local Land League.

This was a group of small farmers who were fighting the plans of an alliance of businessmen and developers to build a golf course as part of a drive to increase tourism in the area, when the farmers, long-established locals, had not enough land themselves. The Land League believed the site should have been made available for agriculture. Their leader, Tom Joyce, compared the situation to that of the land clearances a century earlier, which explained his use of the term Land League, and his determination to resist. The further D'Arcy explored this situation, the worse it became: she saw 'rat-infested schools and damp cottages without electricity or running water' and heard about 'the dirty tricks employed by business people to acquire land'.[284] She and Arden summoned practical help by activating their London contacts. They invited members of the Camden Poster Workshop to their island on Lough Corrib to make posters for the campaign. The posters were painted on a table in the open air and hung up to dry on lines strung between the trees. And she began to make a film, *The Unfulfilled Dream*, following techniques developed by Cinema Action, a collective of film makers in London established in 1968. The members of the collective, Ann Guedes, Gustav (Shlacke) Lamche and Eduardo Guedes, saw film-making as political activism, and were noted for the way they co-operated with their usually exploited or oppressed subjects. Their films thus attacked constructively (if such is possible) groups of exploiters or oppressors. One notable example of their work, especially perhaps for Margaretta D'Arcy, was their 1971 film, *People of Ireland!*, which depicted the establishment of Free Derry in Northern Ireland, and suggested this should be seen as a step in the direction of a workers' republic across the whole of the island of Ireland. *The Unfulfilled Dream* had something of Cinema Action's approach, and became extremely popular in the Galway area, where it was still capable of drawing enthusiastic audiences years later.

The land question dominated the politics of western Ireland, and Galway specifically. The agitation had taken the attention of Satish Kumar, a well-known international peace campaigner and Gandhi follower. Kumar had been born in south India into a Jain family. Jain's reverence for life is notorious, and may be illustrated by the fact that Kumar's mother always carried a small broom with which she swept the ground in front of her to be sure that she trod on no beetles, ants or other insects. At the age of nine, Satish had become a monk. At eighteen he had discovered Gandhi, and accepted his teaching that it was necessary to have an 'outer journey' – that is, an involvement with human affairs – as well as an 'inner journey'. He thereupon left his monastery and followed Vinoba Bhave, an ascetic Gandhian whose life was dedicated to walking through India, persuading landowners to give part of their land to the poor. For three years Satish walked with Bhave, time which convinced him 'that you can bring non-violent ways of changing our society, changing our thinking and changing our heart, even in issues like land distribution'.[285] For five more years, Kumar lived in Bhave's ashram, until, inspired by Bertrand Russell's peace activities, he decided to 'walk' for peace. With one friend, but completely without money, staying wherever he was offered food and accommodation, he visited the major capitals of the Cold War, to try to convince them of the overriding imperative for international peace. It was an extraordinary achievement. He walked, first, to the grave of Mahatma Gandhi, then through Pakistan, Afghanistan, Iran and on into the Soviet Union. It was the time of the Cuba missile crisis, but still he was received in the Kremlin by Khrushchev himself. The walk continued through Poland, divided Germany, Belgium and into France, where he stopped in Paris. Then he crossed the channel to England and London. From there he sailed across the Atlantic, walked through New York, Philadelphia and on to Washington. It was just a month after the assassination of President Kennedy, but President Johnson welcomed him to the White House. He ended his journey after more than 8,000 miles, at the grave of President Kennedy in Arlington Cemetery.

Now Satish Kumar was in the west of Ireland, and D'Arcy invited him to the island on Lough Corrib. The upshot of their meeting was an invitation from Kumar to a Sarvodaya conference in Delhi marking the centenary of Gandhi's birth in 1869. Sarvodaya was Vinoba Bhave's Gandhi-inspired movement dedicated to the promotion of self-determination and equality for all strata of society, what might perhaps be called 'in-depth democracy'. D'Arcy was extremely enthusiastic and determined to go, believing she could learn ways forward which could be useful in the west of Ireland land agitation struggle. Arden was considerably less enthusiastic. He was approaching forty years old, about which he had some qualms,[286] and was immersed in re-casting the King Arthur material for the Welsh National Theatre, who had taken up the project after the BBC had dropped their commission. Their son, Finn, suggested that his father might even have feigned illness to avoid the trip.[287] However, there was some suggestion that they might write a play about Gandhi after the visit, or even a cycle of plays about revolutionaries – Jesus Christ, Queen Lakshmi of Jhansi, William Longbeard, Rosa Luxemburg, and, as a sort of pendant, the brave little tailor of folklore. And the traditional Indian theatre promised the possibility of a model for future epic dramas: *The Non-Stop Connolly Show* was already in their minds.

They drove all the way to Delhi – or rather, D'Arcy drove, since Arden had never learned. They stopped at camp sites on the way across Europe and Asia. They would arrive at a camp site in the early afternoon, and pitch their tent. While the boys played, Arden stayed in the tent, typing his new version of *The Island of the Mighty*. Though he was unaware at the time, he was in fact developing hepatitis, and this seemed to show in what he was writing: 'I've never written anything so bad', he later recalled.[288] The family would go to bed early each evening, and set off again at two or three o'clock the next morning: the children, still sleeping, would be lifted into the car and D'Arcy would set off for the next stop. They travelled through Turkey, Iran, Afghanistan, then down the Khyber Pass into Pakistan, through Peshawar, Islamabad, the Punjab, and so to Delhi. The drive took so long, however, that they had missed the Sarvodaya conference.

They stayed in a YMCA hostel in New Delhi. Arden was continuing with his work on *The Island of the Mighty*, getting up at 5.0am to work outside on their balcony in the cool of the early morning. He had always spoken aloud his lines, testing the speakability as well as the effect of what he wrote. Now local people gathered, sitting nearby to listen to him 'shouting his rhythms'.[289] The family also acquired a reputation for eating soup for their main meal. Then the 'virulent attack of hepatitis' struck Arden.[290] It was diagnosed at first as malaria, and the treatment for that made the hepatitis worse. He was in fact near death by the time the illness was recognised for what it was, and D'Arcy had begun to worry about how she might cope without him, and indeed what she should do with his body if he did die. However, he recovered and though he was very weak and extremely thin for a while, they were able to continue with their exploration of India.

They visited communities founded on Gandhian principles, and met friends of Satish Kumar, as well as other intellectuals, academics, artists and political activists of various sorts with whom they discussed the concrete social and political implications of Gandhi's ideas. The most significant Gandhian they met was J.P. Narayan, a prominent veteran of India's independence struggle, and now a leading opponent of the Prime Minister, Indira Gandhi. He was a significant figure in the Sarvodayan movement, and had in fact given up his own quite extensive lands to the landless poor. Becoming disillusioned himself with the movement's apparent lack of success, he was now calling for a peaceful 'total revolution' in India as perhaps the only way to halt the progress of Maoist ideas and rebellion.

They arrived in Calcutta, where Maoism was riding high, the city was racked with strife and the Communist vote was increasing rapidly. They met members of the revolutionary Naxalites, whose extreme prescriptions seemed almost the only ideas which were truly grappling with the appalling conditions of life for the very poor, and the endless corruption which pervaded every aspect of their lives:

> At one place we stopped by a dam, and we got the interpreter to ask some
> of the people who were sitting around if they were better off with the
> extended cultivation and increased yields. And everybody smiled, and the
> translators said ... 'They say that the *landowners* are, indeed, better off.
> For them, it is the same'.[291]

Just outside Calcutta, they visited a 'model steel factory': 'It was a good factory, large, well-run, good wages. And there was a village for the workers, a model village ... It was impressive, hopeful'. But coming away from the factory, somehow D'Arcy lost the correct road. In the heat and humidity of Bengal they drove rather hopelessly, seeking the way until they came to 'an unbelievable, mile-wide oily swamp'. The swamp itself was extraordinary, unlike anything they had seen before.

> But plunging about on this Mars were pitchy creatures, naked and
> shining, staggering under slippery loads. This, it seems, was the offal
> from the model factory and these people, who simply did not count at all,
> had come in from starvation in the country originally to look for work.
> The bosses of these people were of course sub-contractors ... Nothing to
> do with the factory. The factory had no responsibility at all.[292]

So where was the Gandhian paradise? Perhaps the Mahatma's prescriptions were as wrong as those Arden had originally been given for his hepatitis?

Meanwhile, they were exploring the theatrical culture of Bengal and north-east India. They discovered the Jatra drama, a folk theatre form which had become professional during the period of British rule in India, when it had partially ad-opted a western proscenium arch style of presentation. Nevertheless, even today, Jatra is often performed on outdoor open stages with little or no scenery. The epics presented usually open with a musical overture, which may last anything up to an hour, before the play itself begins. This may continue for a further four or five hours, and is highly flamboyant and colourful, even melodramatic. Musicians sit on stage throughout, and play continuously, and the drama consists of flourishes of oration, mixed with plenty of songs and plenty of dances. It also includes the fascinating figure of Vivek, a sort of moralising commentator or narrator, who may propose alternatives to the characters, and sometimes voices their thoughts for the benefit of the spectators.

D'Arcy describes in *Loose Theatre* another theatre they encountered in Bihar:

> a touring … company playing the sacred epic *Ramayana* (in Hindi) in a
> fitup proscenium in the market-place of a village … Most of the action
> was mime and dance, with a vigorous verse narration delivered from the
> corner of the stage, accompanied by drums and an electronic keyboard.
> The rhythm of the verse was exactly the trochaic metre of *Hiawatha*.[293]

Arden described in a famous essay the Chhau dancers they saw in the Purulian countryside in Bengal.[294] They drove over open fields in the dark to reach the village, a huddle of little huts with thatched roofs, where the performance was to take place. This happened in a widening of the main street, with the elders seated at the front, the young men standing and the women and children crowded onto precariously slung and balanced charpoys on three sides of the acting area. Arden himself, still not wholly recovered from hepatitis, felt dizzy and was welcomed to a seat beside the village elders, where young men offered him cups of *chai* and beedi cigarettes. Under hanging kerosene lamps, and to the accompaniment of typically Indian relentless drumming, the drama began with the appearance of elephant-headed Ganesha:

> he is a small boy wearing a suit of black jacket and trousers, all spangled
> with sequins and embroidery; bare feet, bells around his ankles, and a
> huge mask entirely covering his head and shoulders. A cheekily tilted
> trunk about eighteen inches long. A crown of coloured beadwork
> nodding above his white brow. He walked into the arena very slowly,
> pacing like a toy soldier. There was nothing human about him at all. He
> was – to an audience prepared by deep belief and the music of the drums
> – an incarnate deity who was gracing their village by his presence.

Ganesha was followed by a series of other weird, masked characters as the drama unfolded, until Kali, the great goddess of motherhood and destruction, appeared in a black jumper, miniskirt and a necklace of skulls, who wrought havoc and mayhem among the rest.

The performance – a story or stories probably from *The Mahabharata* – went on and on. Arden fell asleep at one point. 'At intervals I half-woke and saw through bleary eyes the same continuous stamping up and down of proud spangled giants, waving their spears and threatening each other with their arrows'. He notes that this was really a revival, encouraged and to some extent engineered by an enthusiastic academic, of an ancient tradition which had fallen into decay. But still it had an authenticity which the official competition of Chhau dancers he witnessed later did not possess. He was troubled by the poverty of the performers, whose accoutrements, masks and stage weapons were surely extremely expensive. Any subsidies the troupes received, he assumed, came from the local landlords in whose interests the old ways were retained. The 'old ways', after all, included landlordism. But Arden wondered whether with only a small amount of ingenuity the performances could not be tweaked in such a way as to become a vehicle for quite opposite and revolutionary ends. It was a thought which bore magnificent fruit in the two huge Arden/D'Arcy, D'Arcy/Arden epics to come – *The Island of the Mighty* and *The Non-Stop Connolly Show*.

For now the revolutionary situation as D'Arcy and Arden felt it absorbed their energies. D'Arcy drove across north India, often well off the usual tourist tracks – not that tourism was much developed then. 'Somebody would tell us, don't take that road; there are bandits', Arden recalled. 'Another would warn, be careful if you go through such and such a district, because the police chief is totally out of control there, and making things very difficult for motorists'.[295] They drove towards Assam in the far north east of India, beyond what was then East Pakistan, though only a year or two later, in 1971, it became Bangladesh. It was night. The border guards slept. They passed on into Assam. Here everyone seemed to be on the move, the province was seething with discontent, riddled with sectarian, or caste-based, or regional, or tribal hostilities and struggles. Some groups wanted independence, others merely autonomy. The poor were fighting the very poor. But the landlords were making hay: while the people were divided, they could rule unchallenged. They maintained their own private armies, who asserted their masters' will by burning down selected huts where people lived, hacking off limbs or simply murdering those deemed oppositional.

The whole cauldron was further heated by the presence of China, a threatening power to the north east, who had only a very few years earlier, marched into this part of India, though they had stopped of their own accord and, having made their point, retreated in good order. The reason foreigners were not supposed to be in Assam was because of the Chinese invasion. For most Indians, the invasion had been a violation of their still-new national sovereignty.

> But in Assam you discovered a totally different view. Our guide told us
> quite cheerfully that when the Chinese came in, the principal effect for
> the populations of the parts of Assam that they occupied was that they

paid for everything that they ate. This policy contrasted favourably with
that of the Indian army who'd been there before.[296]

It was in this far north-eastern region that the Naxalites were operating. They
were a pseudo-Maoist grouping not unlike the Black Panthers in USA. They had
split from the Communist Party of India in 1967 and initiated a violent uprising in
Bengal with the aim of seizing land and redistributing it to the landless peasants.
They were to become the Communist Party (Marxist-Leninist), and though losing
their base in the north-east they were to continue to harry and harass successive
Indian governments in east and central India well into the twenty-first century. In
1970 they appeared to be a grouping of mostly landless peasants supported by some
urban intellectuals who fought for the poorest of the poor, those who were in thrall,
body and soul, to their landlords for whole lifetimes of labour and servitude. Their
policy was to kill the landlords, their goons and the oppressing usurers, often
sticking the heads of these enemies on posts like medieval tyrants. In light of this
ongoing political warfare, the Gandhian Sarvodaya suddenly seemed not only
unviable, but perhaps even irrelevant. Something more brutal was needed: a
Naxalite-style revolution?

Crossing into Assam without waking the border guards and obtaining the
appropriate stamp in their passports – a requirement of which D'Arcy and Arden
knew nothing – had been a mistake. While in Assam, they visited Majuli Island, site
of Vaishnavite satras, or monasteries, where much of the worship is centred around
dance and stylized acting of scenes from the *Bhagavad Gita*. The all-male
establishment was puzzled by D'Arcy's presence: could she, as a female, be admitted?
She was allowed in, but her and Arden's investigations of the place were cut short
when they received a telegram asking them to report to the police in the provincial
capital, Shillong. They left the island quickly, stopping only at Kaziranga National
Park, where they took the elephant trek to see the Park's famous one-horned
rhinoceroses.

At Shillong, they were arrested for illegally entering Assam. They spent hours
in the police station, trying to explain their situation, to little effect. For one thing, all
the policemen seemed to speak different languages, and if English was their
common tongue, it was often English of a highly idiosyncratic kind. They were
despatched to the District Gaol, D'Arcy to the women's gaol, Arden, with the four
boys, to the men's. The women's gaol was also the local asylum so that D'Arcy and
the other prisoners shared their space with the mentally sick and deranged.
Moreover, the gaols contained an extraordinary range of peoples. There were, for
example, snake-worshippers, who believed in sacrificing their womenfolk to snakes,
and, opposed to them, the matrilineal Khasis, whose women dressed somewhat like
Irish peasants in plaid shawls, and whose effete-looking young men wore clothes
more like Harlem pimps – broad-brimmed trilby hats and suits like zoot suits.

Typically, D'Arcy refused any special treatment she might have been accorded as a foreigner or a white person, but accepted the same foul conditions which the Indian women prisoners had to suffer. Also typically, when she was asked about the conditions, 'I lammed into them, and told them, "It's absolutely disgraceful what's happening in this gaol ..."'[297] The men's gaol was somewhat less primitive. Unlike in the women's, there were political prisoners here, some of whom had been behind these bars for years, and had small hope of progressing their cases to the courts. Arden found them educated and intelligent, and learned from them.

They should have been in the charge of the Bengali Governor of the prison, but he was away, apparently on holiday, and his relief was from Madras, a man apparently looking for rewards, or at least praise, for his diligence. However, it seems his ambition outstripped his efficiency, and he had become something of a butt for the satire of the locals. Initially, he mistook Arden and D'Arcy for Germans, and when it was discovered they were British, and that he was imprisoning British children, he was pilloried in the press. At this point the governess of the women's gaol, who it transpired was the Assam Governor's daughter, protested to D'Arcy that she was not professionally a gaoler, she was in fact a botanist, a career she wanted to pursue, especially as her mother was extremely upset about what was happening to the Arden children!

The local British Consul proved utterly unhelpful to their plight. Arden asked the Assamese authorities to phone him, which they did, explaining that they were holding John Arden, 'the famous British playwright', and his family, and asking what the Consul might want to do in the case. The Consul replied that he knew nothing about it, and had never heard of John Arden. (There were books by Arden in the British Council Library, but the Consul had obviously not noticed them.) Meanwhile, Arden's belongings had been searched, and his books had been found dangerous – confirming again that perhaps his earlier belief that his 'little people' were of no genuine significance was less than fair. Especially, a work by Lenin was taken exception to – though Lenin's head actually appeared on a current Indian postage stamp. D'Arcy devised a strategy to get the children out. Arden was to plead guilty, when he would be released with the boys; if that failed, she would go on hunger strike. She gave notice that in twenty-four hours her hunger strike would begin.

As she hoped, Arden's trial was brought on almost immediately. It was held before a female judge, and the main accusation appeared to be that he and D'Arcy had disparaged, or attempted to undermine, the Indian Constitution. A box of papers and books which had been found in Arden's lodging or car were produced, including the work by Lenin, and the police officer gave the necessary evidence. The landlady where they rented several rooms, a rather elderly Assamese woman named

John Arden and Margaretta D'Arcy in India, 1970, with their sons: Jacob, Adam, Neuss, Finn

Mrs Dishi, contrived to muddy the court's waters because she testified that she could not remember anything the defendant had said particularly; all she knew about the family was that they ate foreign food. The order of events is not quite clear. It appears that Arden was now let out of gaol with the children without the court ever reaching a verdict. Two weeks later D'Arcy, who had insisted on defending herself rather than accept a defence lawyer, and who asserted that – as a citizen of a formerly-colonised nation herself – she certainly had not disparaged the Indian Constitution, was also released. The outcome also seems to have been influenced, however, by the fact that the international artist, Feliks Topolski, had contacted the Indian Prime Minister, Indira Gandhi, asking her why John Arden, the famous writer, was in gaol; and that Mrs Gandhi had at least nudged the process forward. At any rate, their passports were now stamped, but this time to say that they had been deported from Assam, and they were escorted out of the province by the Army, accompanied by smiles and farewell waves from the Governor himself. There was a minor earthquake taking place at the time, and D'Arcy, after her hunger strike, was now vomiting as she drove. But the Assam adventure was at last over.

Their friends in Delhi were glad to see them, and were merely amused by their adventure – or misadventure. The Arden family, however, understood how lucky they had been when they learned of one Irish woman who had spent four years in an

Indian gaol, and another who had been taken into the gaol after she had had a mental breakdown while backpacking through Bihar. As with the women's gaol in Shillong, it seemed that there was nowhere more appropriate than the gaol for this woman in her distress and only after representations from the Irish Embassy was she driven to Delhi where she was simply left outside the Embassy rather like an ill-delivered parcel.

The Arden family had time now to recuperate. Finn remembered singing with a Christian group outside Mrs Gandhi's residence in the capital, and it seems that Arden resumed the lessons in history and English he had been giving the four children earlier in the trip. But still, the time in India was undoubtedly extremely difficult for the four boys. 'Going to India was awful,' one told Tamara Hinchco, 'we were really frightened',[298] and when they were in gaol, they thought they would never get home again. In fact, they were convinced they would die.

Meanwhile, it was discovered that D'Arcy's passport was by now out of date. This, too, had presumably been a reason for the Assamese to view her with suspicion.

They returned to Britain by the same road they had travelled to India. At the border, a notably jolly Sikh official asked them whether they had enjoyed their time in his country. Arden assured him he had. The Sikh official noted the stamp from Assam in the passports: 'Have you *really* enjoyed your stay?' he asked. When Arden repeated that, yes, he had really enjoyed it, the jolly man smiled, handed back the passports, saying, 'Well, if you *really* enjoyed it – very good'.[299]

In Afghanistan they stopped to meet some political contact whose name they had been given. Afghanistan was enduring its own political turmoil at the time, and they discovered that – somewhat like Assam – there were Communists, Leninists and other groupings on the left, and a general urge towards some more democratic political system. The Arden contacts welcomed them, and fed them, and promised to show their prize gardens to them. But suddenly some political crisis arose, their hosts went into a huddle and Arden and D'Arcy were quickly dispatched on their way. It seems the disturbance was something to do with political developments, and they noted sardonically that not long after the King of Afghanistan was deposed.

This was not the last political experience on their way home. In Bulgaria they applied to the relevant authorities for permission to visit a working socialist co-operative. The place they visited – no name is recorded – greatly impressed them both. According to D'Arcy, 'everything was properly organised'. This meant effectively that the land was cultivated on a co-operative basis, and that the transport system was integrated so that it worked to support the development of agriculture. The experience impressed them: was not something of this kind exactly what was needed in the west of Ireland?

They reached home, now 'fully-fledged revolutionaries'.[300]

Twelve : An Activist Theatre

If Arden and D'Arcy returned from India 'fully-fledged revolutionaries', there was a question as to how – or whether – this would translate into theatre work. The question had an added urgency because in England the social and political changes noticed before they left were now accelerating. Erstwhile radicals had become bomb-makers: after the 'flower power' of the 1960s, the 1970s discovered Mao Zedong's thought: 'political power grows out of the barrel of a gun'. Among the intelligentsia, political action was taking over from cultural or artistic action: merely asserting your left-wing credentials was no longer enough.

On 17 August 1969, a lodger at their house in Muswell Hill had firebombed the Ulster Office in London. The act was partly intended as retribution for the ongoing victimisation of ordinary non-Protestant people in the six counties of Northern Ireland, but no-one had been hurt, and its chief effect seems to have been to stimulate argument about the tactics of opposition, with Arden holding that such action was pointless, but D'Arcy deriding his 'bourgeois liberalism'. By 1970, when they returned from India, bomb-making and indeed bombing the defenders of the *status quo*, had become considerably more serious.

In May 1970, Wembley Conservative Association was firebombed. In June, Brixton Conservative Association was firebombed. In September the home of the Conservative Attorney-General, Sir Peter Rawlinson, was bombed, and that same month more Conservative Association headquarters were bombed, including in Wimbledon and Hampstead. Meanwhile, Paddington Police Station had been firebombed in May, and in July not only an Army Recruiting Office was attacked, but so was the home of the Commissioner of Metropolitan Police, Sir John Waldron. That summer, the British General Election had resulted in a surprise win for the Conservatives, whose leader, Edward Heath, was installed as Prime Minister, and who seemed to many on the left to have immediately instituted a new phase in the class war. On 8 December 1970, there was a huge demonstration in London against the new government's Industrial Relations Bill; on the same day, the Department of Employment and Productivity was bombed. On 12 January 1971, a month later, there was another large rally and demonstration, and on that day, the home of the Minister for Employment, Robert Carr, was bombed.

The bombings were said to be the work of the Angry Brigade, a rather shadowy left anarchist group, several of whose members were prosecuted in a notorious case in 1972 which ended with four men receiving prison sentences of up to ten years. Influenced by Guy Debord and *les événements* in Paris in 1968, the Angry Brigade's members seem mostly to have been University-educated: they mixed disaffection with libertarianism, and their Marxism had more than a tinge of Trotskyism.

Though more significant than other similar British groups, they were nowhere near as dangerous as their European counterparts, the Red Army Faction in Germany or the Red Brigades in Italy. But still their activities caused something close to panic in the British Establishment, even if their bombs were actually rather small, and their purpose was perhaps less a call to violent revolution than a means of exposing the system, a way to make the Tory Government look silly. But it may have been significant that the police pursuit of them intensified dramatically after the Government introduced Internment in the six counties of Northern Ireland in 1971.

That was in the future. But it was to a group of Angry Brigade members or sympathisers to whom Arden and D'Arcy had let their Muswell Hill house while they were in India. When they returned they discovered that the basement of the house had been transformed into a sort of bomb factory. The bombs were soon got rid of, but Ian Purdie, one of those who had been renting the house, was arrested a few months later in March 1971and charged with a number of bombings. He was kept in Brixton Prison as an 'A' category prisoner, refused bail by Mr Justice Stevenson (of whom we shall hear more later) but when his case ended in December 1971, he was acquitted of all charges.

Muswell Hill was something of a melting pot at the time, home to various left-winger activists, anarchists, political dropouts and different sorts of artists. It was racially mixed, too: there were Irish people, from Dublin, Tipperary, and Belfast, Greek Cypriots, Israelis, people from the Indian subcontinent and Turks. The children mixed fairly freely, though on one occasion the young Ardens, with others, were found to have 'raided' some gardens. D'Arcy took them to apologise, and thus struck up a friendship with her Indian neighbours. Such was always D'Arcy's way: she would talk to people, genuinely interested in their concerns, and she would draw them out till she felt she understood these.

Another person whom D'Arcy befriended was Jo Liebowitz, a big red-haired woman, the mother of children the same age as the young Ardens. When free school milk was stopped by the then Education Secretary, Margaret Thatcher (who thereby earned herself the immortal nickname, 'the milk snatcher'), Jo Liebowitz backed D'Arcy's notion of a street theatre protest against the cut. They placed a postcard in the local newsagent's window, appealing for help with the project, and several mothers volunteered. D'Arcy persuaded Albert Hunt to come to Muswell Hill with some of his students from Bradford, and the street play, *Little Red Riding Hood and Granny Wolf*, was created. Red Riding Hood's free school milk was snatched and gobbled up by granny wolf. The venture may not have succeeded in forcing political change, but it was successful socially and artistically. A nucleus of enthusiasts formed, and they decided to mount another, more general attack on the Conservative Government's cuts. This was *My Old Man's a Tory*, and it was played alongside a big march and demonstration, with boldly artistic posters – STOP THE

CUTS! – and a grand car cavalcade. It was rough agitprop theatre, deriving originally from the Russian Revolution. It was largely composed of short sharp scenes, improvised by the actors, and suffused with plenty of broad humour. It employed a good deal of direct address to the audience, and was fast-moving and emblematic. This was the writer as activist, the new Arden/D'Arcy after their Indian experiences.

A third play which attempted to intervene actively in the political process was *Rudi Dutschke Must Stay* presented by Writers Against Repression. Rudi Dutschke was Germany's most substantial student leader in the turmoil of 1968. Born in Communist East Germany, he had escaped to the west the day before the Berlin Wall was begun in August 1961. His political ideas owed something to Gramsci, and he believed that revolution in the west should go hand-in-hand with liberation in the third world. In April 1968, a would-be assassin had shot him in the head, inflicting terrible brain damage which ultimately killed him at the age of thirty-nine. He had come to England in 1969, seeking to recover his health, but in 1971 the Heath Government expelled him as an 'undesirable alien' engaged in 'subversive activities'. He was staying at the Ardens' Muswell Hill home at the time, and a furious, well-supported but ultimately unavailing campaign was mounted on his behalf, a campaign of which this play was a part. And besides the play, Arden wrote a poem which succinctly summarised the situation:

'I think, therefore I am',
Descartes, in prison, said.
Surrounded by stone walls
He was alone with his own head.
Rudi, being free,
In a mobile free society,
Had a wound in *his* head:
But he was not alone:
His walls were made of paper
Not of stone.

He thinks, therefore they followed him about.
He thinks, therefore he scarcely dared go out.
He thinks, therefore they damn well threw him out.

The biggest political and theatrical undertaking which Arden and D'Arcy were involved with in London at this time was *Two Hundred Years of Labour History*, which was staged at the Alexandra Palace in February 1971 by the Socialist Labour League. Before they went to India, Arden and D'Arcy had been to a number of SLL meetings, which had been organised by their accountant, a Marxist by the name of Michael Henshaw. He also worked for a number of other theatre professionals, and was himself a member of the League. He had held a series of 'At Homes', political discussion meetings with prominent members, notably the leader, Gerry Healy, whose analysis of the position of the theatre worker convinced Arden and D'Arcy. He argued that writers and actors, who typically imagine they are 'free' of the kind of constraints which bind ordinary working people, are objectively in the same exploited position, and should learn to operate like them through, for instance, trade unions. In other words, writers, actors and similar 'artists', were workers before they were anything else. It was a lesson they took with them into the dispute with the Royal Shakespeare Company in 1972.

The League was targeting members of the theatrical professions at this time, and they decided to mount a series of political plays, beginning with the epic of working class history at the Alexandra Palace. These were days of hope, when 'you could actually do things', as one involved actor remembered.[301] The driving forces behind the project were Roy Battersby, a prominent television director, and Roger Smith, one of the moving spirits behind the Wednesday Play, both committed Socialist Labour League members. Beyond Battersby and Smith were the actors, Corin and Vanessa Redgrave and Frances de la Tour, and writers, including Colin Welland, David Mercer and Jim Allen, as well as Ken Loach and Tony Garnett. Those on the fringes of the group included actors Judi Dench, Helen Mirren, Eleanor Bron, Glenda Jackson, Roy Kinnear, Dudley Moore and others, writers Adrian Mitchell and Christopher Logue, and musicians Larry Adler and Annie Ross. *Two Hundred Years of Labour History* was to be collectively written, and Tamara Hinchco was asked to bring Arden and D'Arcy into the team.

Arden's own relationship with the Socialist Labour League had become a little uneasy. He had been asked to speak about his experiences in India to Henshaw's discussion group, and what he said provoked Gerry Healy into a tirade which accused Arden of 'bourgeois idealism' and similar grievous mistakes, leaving him thoroughly chastened. Nevertheless, he and D'Arcy attended planning meetings for *Two Hundred Years of Labour History*, and Arden suggested structuring the show round a number of episodes to be played in more or less pantomime style, which would illustrate the growth of working class political consciousness, and the changing tactics in the ruling class's eternal struggle to hold what they had. The drama would centre on a single central character, who would be called 'Idle Jack', after the downtrodden but good-hearted serving-man in traditional British pantomime. In each scene, he would struggle, be mocked as 'idle' and useless, but he would always win out in the end. Arden even wrote a few scenes which were 'very good stuff' according to Tamara Hinchco.[302] But his whole notion was rejected: the Socialist Labour League could not be seen presenting the British working man as 'idle'! At a script meeting, Roy Battersby, never the most democratic director, was holding forth at some length, when D'Arcy stood up and interrupted (not protocol in such situations), thereby detonating a furious row which was remembered for many years. Battersby learned the hard way that D'Arcy was never to be bludgeoned into acquiescence, or even silence. In the end, though Arden still contrib.uted, it was only on the condition that his work would not be altered in any way. What survived was a scene loosely based on the story of *The Emperor's New Clothes* between Mr Hook and Mr Crook – 'the biggest criminals in the whole of history's book'. Arden found the production, in the end, 'a good show, with some very funny stuff in it',[303] and said later that the development of *The Non-Stop Connolly Show* 'owed an enormous amount to our experience of this production'. [304] And in the final scene, in front of approximately three thousand spectators, D'Arcy as well as their children participated as part of a vast crowd, waving red flags at the packed auditorium. But the production marked the end of D'Arcy and Arden's involvement with the Socialist Labour League. Partly this was simply because they left to live permanently in Ireland later that year, but it was also true that selling the party's newspaper on street corners (which members were expected to do) and accepting the 'line' laid down by Gerry Healy, would never have held D'Arcy or Arden's attention for long.

In any case, they were now in the process of moving permanently to Ireland. The two eldest boys had been placed in a boarding school there, and there was the incentive that writers paid no tax in the Republic. Their income was considerably less than what it had been. They acquired an attractive traditional whitewashed

Cottage in Corandulla belonging to John Arden and Margaretta D'Arcy

cottage in the village of Corrandulla, a few miles north of Galway city, and from 1971 this became their home, with the house in Muswell Hill merely providing a convenient *pied à terre* when they needed to be in London. And, perhaps still influenced by Gerry Healy, they joined the Society of Irish Playwrights, the nearest thing to a trade union for dramatists in the British Isles. There was no counterpart in England.

Before leaving for India, they had been involved in County Galway, in fighting against the victimization of travelling people, and supporting the local Land League. Now, with the beginnings of the fight for civil rights in the six counties of the north, the Official IRA's commitment to a 32-county socialist republic, and the arrival of the British Army on Irish soil, D'Arcy 'determined psychologically to commit myself to the cause of a free Ireland'.[305] Her resolve inevitably brought problems: were she and Arden, the Englishman who had once been a member of the British Army himself, on opposite sides in the desperate struggle that was now unfolding? For them as newly-fledged revolutionaries, clear analysis and understanding was urgent, which was one reason why, after their experiences with the Socialist Labour League in London, they now joined Official Sinn Fein.

This party was in the midst of a life-and-death struggle for the soul of Ireland, a struggle in which D'Arcy and Arden's *The Non-Stop Connolly Show* was soon to play a passionate part. The uprising in the northern counties which began in 1968 was viewed by socialists as part of an international upsurge in revolutionary action, and connected not only with *les événements* in Paris, the Prague Spring and other European drives for liberation, but also with what was happening in Vietnam, among the Latin American rural guerrillas, with the armed resistance in Rhodesia and other African countries, and with the formation of the Palestine Liberation Organisation. Northern Ireland was, it was argued, Britain's last colony, a fragment of the island to which they had no plausible right. But the way forward for Irish Republicans was not always clear, especially in the face of the near civil war which had broken out in the six counties. It was also argued that since the 1921 Treaty had been coerced, it had no force in international law. In January 1969, the Royal Ulster Constabulary, a virtually wholly Protestant and Unionist force, had entered the Bogside in Derry, batoning people in the streets and even breaking into homes and attacking those within. Months of riots, bloodshed, street fighting and police brutality followed. By the end of the summer, over three thousand people had been driven out of their homes in Belfast alone, and over ten thousand British troops were on the streets of the city. Who was to defend the beleaguered Catholic and nationalist people?

The simple answer was, Sinn Fein and the IRA. But the situation was not simple. Ever since the publication in 1961 of C.Desmond Greaves's eye-opening biography of James Connolly, republicanism had been moving to the left. In 1965, the IRA set up its own Department of Political Education, and by 1967 they were defending evicted tenants in Dublin, campaigning against strike-breakers and proclaiming their aim as the establishment of a 'Democratic Socialist Republic'. A series of articles appeared in their newspaper, *The United Irishman*, under the title 'Who Owns Ireland?' attacking banks, multinational corporations and land-grabbers. In 1968 Eoghan Harris, a Sinn Fein sympathiser and television producer, directed a documentary for Irish state television, *The Testimony of James Connolly*, which presented the hero of the Easter Rising, not as some kind of twilit romantic, but as a hard-headed socialist republican. To many in the party all this pointed to a more mature and productive way forward. Other, more traditional members, however, wanted to stick to the old purposes, to re-unite Ireland by military means.

In December 1969, the IRA held an extraordinary convention in Boyle in County Roscommon. A majority of members voted to develop the new socialist lines of policy associated with Sean Garland, Cathal Goulding and Seamus Costello. In consequence, the minority, led by Seán MacStíofáin and Seán Ó Brádaigh, left to set up an alternative IRA The new grouping came to be called the 'Provisional' IRA, taking their name from the Provisional Government proclaimed in 1916 by Pearse and Connolly, while Goulding's group became the 'Official' IRA. The Provisional IRA saw their primary task being to defend the Catholic and nationalist people against both the British Army and the Protestant paramilitary groups which were springing up – ostensibly in response to the growth of the IRA. Theirs was almost a recipe for civil war.

However, in the south, where Arden and D'Arcy were settling, the Official IRA were pursuing less violent ends. In May 1971, Sean Garland wrote an article for the *United Irishman*, stating that the party was working towards a revolution which would mean 'the change of state power from one class to another', and that the Officials 'at this point in history' had a 'socialist character'. Their immediate aim was to achieve 'national liberation', but the ultimate goal was 'political power for the working class'.[306] To this end, they marched against the Vietnam War, they infiltrated the trade unions and they campaigned against joining the European Common Market. Official IRA members in the north were still capable of tarring and feathering a young woman for 'fraternizing' with the British, but in the south members were much more likely to agree with Máirín de Burca, Official Sinn Féin's Vice President: 'The days were gone that I could get very exercised about the North except in terms of social attitudes and social problems'.[307] This was clearly seen in their pro-active countryside campaigns against the activities of both 'new rich' Dublin politicians and absentee aristocratic Anglo-Irish landlords. Thus they de-manded public ownership of Ireland's fisheries and mounted 'fish-ins' in private waters around the country. In May 1970, they entered the Duke of Devonshire's castle at Lismore, County Waterford, and hauled up the Plough and the Stars, and two months later they occupied Slane Castle in County Meath.

It is clear that with much of this, John Arden and Margaretta D'Arcy were in agreement. Moreover, unlike many people, they were aware of the connections between these problems in the Republic and what was happening in the north. In July 1971, D'Arcy was in Belfast at the time of the Orange marches, and noted how the British troops protected these hugely provocative demonstrations: the troops were drinking, shouting insults and making obscene gestures, especially at any women going about their business. At about the same time, a doctor friend of Arden's was in a block of flats tending terrified housewives when drunken British soldiers burst in, shooting anywhere and smashing furniture. Arden noted that the 'group of right-wing fixers' who were in the Fianna Fail government in the Republic, including Neil Blaney, Charles Haughey and Kevin Boland, were in practice supporting Provisional IRA, with whom they shared an ideal vision of a 'clerico-gombeen Emerald Isle … fed by syrupy mythology'. He asserted that

> There will come no revolution for the workers (Protestant or Catholic) of
> Northern Ireland until the workers in Britain and the workers in
> Southern Ireland all realize how they have been had: by Faulkner, and
> Heath, and Lynch, and all their associates',[308]

– that is, the three Prime Ministers of Northern Ireland, the United Kingdom and the Republic of Ireland. Worse than this, while a friend of theirs from Dublin was in Galway staying with them, his friend, a young socialist republican, in his flat back in Dublin, was tortured and murdered: when he was found, he was hanging by his thumbs. His assassin was never discovered.

Arden and D'Arcy supported the Official Sinn Fein land campaigns in Galway, including that against the golf course mentioned above, as well as against land speculators ('Green Orangemen' Arden called them[309]) who were destroying the livelihoods of local farmers. The campaign, indeed, had its violent moments – bulldozers blown up, shots fired – partly at least to draw the attention of the media and politicians to what was going on. In this climate, there were a number of evictions of smallholders. D'Arcy collected material on several of these, as well as lawyers' letters, and they contributed towards her next campaigning film, *The Galway Rent and Rate Strike*, made at this time. Pam Gems saw one of the letters,

> a lawyer-vetted piece of liver-flavoured catsmeat, full of references to the
> Irishman's sense of honour, keeping an honest bargain and not being
> taken in by troublemakers. The letter is full of barely disguised contempt
> and you can drive a coach and horses through the argument.[310]

For D'Arcy, a kind of breaking-point was reached with the case of Mrs Fahey from Oughterard, whose family had lived in their cottage for a century and a half, and who was now threatened with eviction. Her absentee British landlord, a retired naval Commander named Burges, was attempting to take advantage of 'a minor quibble in (British-made) law',[311] as Arden described it. Mrs Fahey appealed against the eviction order, claiming that her husband had been ill and under the influence of drink when he had signed the 'agreement', and a campaign, in which D'Arcy in particular played a part, was launched to support her. The local 'Green Orangemen', of course, backed the eviction. The dispute became violent, with people being attacked, meetings broken up and supporters being blacklisted by local employers.

D'Arcy later claimed it was this campaign which taught her about practical resistance to authority: how to get a press statement into the newspaper, how to distribute leaflets, how to organise a public meeting. Mrs Fahey lent her a large box of legal documents and other papers detailing the dealings over many years between Commander Burges and her family. As D'Arcy scrutinized the contents of the box, she began to realize that here was the skeleton of a play, perhaps an 'epistolary play'.[312] 'We decided that we should write it and use it as a weapon in the agitation', Arden wrote later. 'If enough feeling could be aroused, not only locally but nationally, then perhaps the retired naval officer would agree to proceed no further with his threatened eviction'.[313] This was a new activist's theatre, a considerable development from the writer-as-observer evident in *The Bagman* and more mature than the creator of the Muswell Hill street theatre..

The writing of the play was also perhaps spurred by a prospective commission from Charles Marowitz, the American proprietor of the Open Space in London, who was seeking a play about the 'Troubles' in Northern Ireland. In the event, he found what D'Arcy and Arden wrote 'too local' and rejected it amid some rancour between the parties. Consequently, the first public reading of *The Ballygombeen Bequest* which used elements of Mrs Fahey's story in its plot, took place in Galway as part of the campaign on her behalf. It happened 'in a house in the Connemara countryside where bailiffs were imminently expected to evict the family'.[314] Another reading was held in Galway at the University Theatre Festival, and this also was dedicated to Mrs Fahey's campaign.

The Theatre Festival itself, held in March 1972, had its own drama. Arden had been invited to be the adjudicator, but his adjudications deliberately did not discuss the productions in the usual aesthetic terms – the style of the presentation, the stage design, the costumes, or the actors' performances. Instead, he concentrated on the politics, implicit or explicit in the piece presented. This was, D'Arcy later recalled, 'not to the liking of the traditional minded element' in Galway's intellectual circles. They booed, and thereby 'startled' him, and then set on foot a move to have him removed from his position, though this move failed. However, 'the resultant controversy spilled over, causing political and social division to become very apparent between the competing groups',[315] and it continued to fester in some 'liberal' students' memories, who could neither forget nor forgive Arden's 'Stalinist/Marxist frame of mind', for decades: for example, nearly forty years later one who had been a student then, and was now a journalist, dragged Arden's political stance into an article in *The Irish Times* about another controversy altogether.[316]

Yet politics and controversy were in some senses inherent in the plays presented, and especially in that year of heightened political tensions on so many fronts. Jim Sheridan presented a version of *Oedipus* in the style of the Living Theatre, with spectators having to come through an army checkpoint to get in; Galway University presented *Butley* by Simon Gray, about unmentionable topics such as divorce and abortion; Stranmillis gave Bertolt Brecht's *The Exception and the Rule* in a sadly anodyne production even though one of their lecturers was currently interned in the north; University College, Dublin, clearly imagined they would win the competition with a production by Michael Bogdanov of Aeschylus's *The Persians*; but Arden actually named the production by St Mary's and St Joseph's Colleges of Education in the Falls Road, Belfast, the winners with their version of Sheridan's *The School for Scandal*, which 'carried a whiff of the Civil Rights movement with it',[317] even though they were handicapped by the loss of their scenery and at least some of their costumes on the way to Galway.

And it was the Dramatic Societies of St Joseph's and St Mary's Colleges which presented the first performance proper of *The Ballygombeen Bequest* on May Day 1972. D'Arcy and Arden attended the first performance, staying in a republican house in Belfast which was defended by street barricades. While there, 'Arden nearly got shot in a Crown forces/IRA gun battle outside the Busy Bee supermarket'.[318] And during the performance, the spectators could hear firing in the street, where a deadly gun battle was developing between Provisional IRA volunteers and British soldiers. During rehearsals, the students had in fact been harassed by the Army, stopped in the street, their scripts inspected and themselves mocked.

> At the end of the play – heated arguments – and accusations –
> recriminations – we were stone-age Socialists – we were sectarians, why
> weren't we playing to the Loyalists? Why was the play set in the 26
> counties and not the 6 counties? ...– what right have you from the Free
> State to come and batten on our agony? The Northern arena with all its
> pain, anger, energy and contradictions laid bare for us to experience.[319]

The Ballygombeen Bequest is, according to one critic, 'a stunning political drama, as good as the best of Arden and (let me stick my neck out) an equal to most of Brecht'.[320] Chambers and Prior suggest that 'if *Serjeant Musgrave's Dance* is a ballad, then *The Ballygombeen Bequest* is a political song'.[321] Because of a libel suit, discussed below, it had to be withdrawn and was rewritten as *The Little Gray Home in the West*, a more considered play which D'Arcy and Arden preferred. The main differences are that the Narrator's part in the earlier version is now given to the ghost of Padraig, a much more satisfying dramatic device, and certain political significances, such as the parallel between the way Seamus is duped by his British landlord and the way Michael Collins was tricked into signing the Treaty of 1923, are strengthened. Minor changes in dialogue or action also go to tightening the play which may be considered one of the most powerful political dramas of the twentieth century.

The play opens in 1945, with the war over and a Labour Government in power in the United Kingdom. The newly-demobbed Baker-Fortescue sets up a business exporting and importing 'intimate novelties', and discovers he has inherited a little property in the west of Ireland. He does not wish to live there, but he could let it as a holiday cottage. The problem is the O'Leary family, who have lived in a ramshackle hut on the land, without paying rent, since time immemorial. To minimize trouble to himself, however, Baker-Fortescue decides to let them stay: they will add 'local colour' to the place, and they can act as unpaid caretakers-cum-general factotums. The arrangement is not very satisfactory, and in 1959 he tricks Seamus O'Leary into signing a paper which gives him full rights on the property until he dies, when all the O'Learys' rights will expire. The old man signs. When he dies, Baker-Fortescue begins the process of evicting the family.

Padraig, Seamus's son, returns from Manchester, where he has been a building worker and trade union activist, and decides to fight the eviction. He is a republican socialist, and is able to broaden the fight so that it becomes one not only between the Irish and the British, but also between the exploiter and the exploited. Consequently, the local Irish middle class find him as much of a difficulty as does the British landlord: their intrigues, political and commercial, and involving in-formers, intelligence agents and more, lead to Padraig being tricked into taking some ponies across the border into Northern Ireland to sell. Once in Northern Ireland, Padraig is betrayed to the British as an IRA arms smuggler. He is captured, tortured and murdered, his body tarred and feathered and dumped beside a lonely road. The last scene takes place at the solemn wake for Padraig. Unexpectedly, he sits up on his bier and begins to sing. Baker-Fortescue arrives distraught: his holiday cottage and the O'Leary's shack have been blown up. Hagan, the double-dealing local entrepreneur, is actually responsible, but he hints that the culprits were the IRA. Hagan now offers to take the land off Baker-Fortescue's hands – it will be worth virtually nothing now the IRA have marked it, he assures Baker-Fortescue, who is clearly out of his depth by now. He tries to haggle, and the argument turns into an absurd custard pie fight, with the corpse, Padraig, getting the better of both.

The terror, the tragedy, transform into hilarious farce. It is a brilliant ending, supremely successful because of what has gone before: that is, popular theatre at its best. D'Arcy and Arden employ with dazzling vitality direct address to the audience, cartoon caricature, traditional Irish music, humour, intensified realism, short scenes, a jagged rhythm, and vivid emblematic images. The two houses, Baker-Fortescue's holiday chalet and the O'Learys' 'tintawndub' symbolise and encapsulate the class struggle. The play not only shows how the murky business of politics, the fixing, the treachery, the contempt for human life, happens, it also succeeds in relating the specifics of the Oughterard case of tenant eviction to the problems of colonialism, economics and world revolution.

Much of the energy generated by the play, and especially the ending, derives from the use of popular melodrama forms. A comparison with Dion Boucicault's *The Shaughraun* illustrates the point. Boucicault's play, tells the story of a Fenian who has been transported to Australia but now returns to Ireland illegally.

Boucicault's main concern is with the double love plot and with sensational effects, but D'Arcy and Arden use the play's structure and concerns extensively. Ffolliott's estate is to be sold, but the family want to retain it; Corry Kinchela, the squireen, like D'Arcy and Arden's Hagan, is apparently everybody's friend, who double crosses them all for his own purposes; Claire, Robert Ffolliott's sister, becomes entangled romantically with Molineau, the British agent who is actually a soldier, just as Padraig's sister Siobhan becomes entangled with the British agent, Limegrave (a romance, however, without Boucicault's happy ending); and Padraig's arrest is paralleled by the British soldiers' arrest of Robert Ffolliott in the house of Father Dolan.

Other similarities could be cited, but the most powerful is between the final scene in *The Little Gray Home in the West* and the pivotal central scene in *The Shaughraun*. In the former, Padraig is dead, but sits up on his bier, a ghost, who instigates the custard pie fight between Hagan and Baker-Fortescue. In *The Shaughraun*, Conn is presumed dead, shot by the police agents: during his wake, Conn sits up, has a swig of the nearest whisky bottle, lies down again, and so on. This is, of course, based on an old Irish joke, known as 'Finnegan's Wake', when the corpse wakes at his own funeral. J.M.Synge also develops his own variation in *The Shadow of the Glen*.

But whereas in Synge's play, as in Boucicault's, the seeming corpse is not really dead, D'Arcy and Arden's Padraig is: he has been killed in a particularly brutal scene, and it is his ghost which awakes to haunt Hagan and Baker-Fortescue. Unreal, highly theatrical, it is nevertheless deeply unsettling after the real horrors of the torture scene. Set next to that scene, it shows the nature of the oppositions: that is, Padraig is the *real* opposition to Baker-Fortescue and Hagan, so that he is *really* tortured and murdered by their agents. But Hagan and Baker-Fortescue, though they may haggle over the price of a piece of land, and though one is Irish and the other British, are not *really* enemies. Their capitalistic interests are the same, their opposition to one another a mere custard pie fight.

Despite Arden's intial reluctance to be involved with this play, *The Ballygombeen Bequest*, later *The Little Gray Home in the West*, turned out to be one of the most successful collaborations between the authors. While Arden was an almost scholarly writer who wanted to be actively involved in the community about and for whom he was writing, D'Arcy was a social and political activist who wanted to put her particular theatre talents – writing, acting, directing – to specified political and social ends. This division of labour is, of course, considerably less than the whole truth. Gavin Richards, who directed the 7:84 production of the play remembered them working on it on the island in Lough Corrib: 'John and Margaretta would argue about the history, then about the politics and then whether it should be in rhyme and eventually, somehow, a whole section would emerge. They really were hacking at the coalface of theatre'.[322] D'Arcy wrote later, perhaps ironically, of their collaboration:

> When I want a clear story
> Arden always complicates it
> By putting in too much.
> Like yesterday –
> A simple joke in a short scene:
> One philosopher has taken five years to
> Develop an argument,
> The other has
> Five hours
> Before they are both eaten by lions.
> But Arden
> Has to put in how
> Long they've lived,
> Who they are,
> I say I say
> Old boy,
> A shouting match –
> All to show that
> Arden can write.[323]

In this play, it seems the urgency of the case, the 'five hours', brought them together, and D'Arcy's 'clear story' was what showed that 'Arden can write'. Nevertheless, this became the first play in which D'Arcy's name had preceded Arden's on its title page, indicating that this was her creation, with which he had collaborated.

. The first professional performance of *The Ballygombeen Bequest* took place on 30 August 1972 and was given by 7:84 Theatre Company at Old St Paul's Church Hall in Edinburgh. Directed by Gavin Richards, it was the sensation of that year's Festival Fringe. The programme included a seven-page elucidation of the case of Mrs Fahey in Oughterard, and added the name, address and telephone number of Commander Burges. Before each performance, a member of the cast would explain that what followed had nothing to do with Commander Burges in Sussex: his telephone number was given in case any member of the audience wished to contact him. 'Good theatre can sometimes provide a safety net for a bourgeois audience', Richards maintained. 'We wanted to puncture that by telling them that this is a piece of theatre by a great artist about something that is going on at this very moment'.[324] It was, as Arden remarked later, 'sailing far too close to the wind',[325] and there were soon moves to undermine play and production.

7:84 embarked on a nationwide tour, including two stints at the Bush Theatre, in London, in tandem with an adaptation by John McGrath, 7:84's director, of the early Arden play, now renamed *Serjeant Musgrave Dances On*. This version re-set the play in 1972, and aimed to strengthen the link between imperialism and class conflict. The action now took place in a Yorkshire village, riven by the bitter miner's strike which had taken place that spring. Musgrave and his men return from Northern Ireland, and the events of Bloody Sunday. The miners' strike and the 'Troubles' of Northern Ireland were thus seen as part of the same problem. In the climax scene of Musgrave's 'dance', the names of the people killed on Bloody Sunday in Derry were read out.

Through the autumn of 1972, these two plays made an enormous impact on their audiences, and it was hardly a surprise when enemies of their ideas gathered to stop them. The first distant thunder came with letters to the Arts Council. One was from General Sir Harry Tuzo, Officer Commanding in Northern Ireland at the time, who was responsible for sending 30,000 troops into Republican west Belfast and Derry, to seize back 'control' from local people. Though he had not seen the play, he took it upon himself to query whether it was 'in any way justifiable to devote public funds' to a play 'of this kind'.[326] Another letter, from a different writer, complained bitterly about the violence presented during the torture scene, and questioned how the Arts Council could justify 'such a thoroughly sick and evil display'.[327]

At the same time, Arden and D'Arcy were engaging in a fierce dispute with the Royal Shakespeare Company, described in the next chapter of this book, and there were references in the newspapers especially to D'Arcy, linking her with Official Sinn Fein, whose distinction from the Provisionals was unlikely to be apparent to many English people at the time. Then came a lawyer's letter addressed to 7:84. It informed them that an action for slander was to be taken against Arden and D'Arcy because of what they had written in *The Ballygombeen Bequest*, and that if the presentation of this play was not halted immediately, the action would be widened to include the company as well. 7:84 felt they had no choice but to close the production. As D'Arcy noted later, 'English law cracked down' on an Irish play.[328] It appeared that the crux of the suit was Commander Burges's objection to the way Holliday-Cheype (who becomes Baker-Fortescue in the later re-written version of the play) hoodwinked Seamus O'Leary into signing the agreement by getting him drunk. It was the use of drink to which he objected. Disinterested or vindictive, the threatening letter effectively silenced Arden and D'Arcy.

In Arden's novel, *Jack Juggler and the Emperor's Whore*, written twenty years after these events, the playwright, Fidelio Carver, who has certain experiences similar to those of the author himself, writes a play in 1971 about the Irish situation, *Poison-Voices*. This is presented by a politically-motivated left-wing touring 'fringe' theatre company, but it is stopped by a libel action. 'We were slammed in our midriff', Carver says, of this. The stage backdrop in this fictional production consists of blown-up newspaper articles and pictures, notably of one right-wing critic, who is responsible for the writ. The author in the novel continues:

He was, in legal terms, identified; and everything else about him in the play, *true or untrue*, therefore contributed to the defamation ... If I'd given the man in the play a wooden leg, it would not have abolished the identification; it would only have strengthened it by indicating malice and implying allegorically that the real Barney Brewster was incapable of walking straight. Such is the law ... it provides a substitute for official censorship where political dissent is to be quashed and no protest aroused.[329]

The character in the novel decides to fight the writ. 'Fair comment', he asserts. But his lawyer counsels caution: 'This play of yours is too friendly to at least one of the IRAs, the Marxist one, alas; this is *not* the right season of history for that sort of sympathy. A British jury will eat you alive'.[330] The theatre company, on the other hand, does not receive a writ: Fidelio Carver, in the novel, supposes that suing a whole company might bring too much odium on the plaintiff, and after all the play has been stopped.

All this is very close to what actually occurred, though in fact 7:84 was punished, too. John McGrath was summoned to the Arts Council's Piccadilly headquarters and roundly ticked off. The Council also removed the revenue funding grant from the company and substituted project-by-project grants. 7:84 dissolved itself and reformed as 7:84 (Scotland) and 7:84 (England), but still it was three years before the revenue grant was restored. As for the authors of the play, the case against them remained pending.

Yet the final memory of this play, which has never received the revival its enormous merits deserve, is of one in which the authors 'use the theatre like a chess board: all the moves are simple, but the strategy behind them reveals the mind of a grandmaster'. This review went on to compliment Roger Sloman's 'clear-cut performance as the gruesome Holliday-Cheype'. It was, the reviewer said, 'an object lesson in acting that presents character in social and political, rather than psychological terms'. He also commended the 'vicious menace' of Gavin Richards's Hagan, and concluded that '*The Ballygombeen Bequest* is more than a play about Ireland; it conjures up a nightmare image of capitalism friendless, tottering and ultimately without hope or help, that will linger in my mind for months'.[331]

When Robert Brustein saw the play 'before a predominantly Irish audience in Shepherd's Bush, it was received with the fervour of an Agincourt harangue'.[332] And Nick Redgrave saw the final performance at the Bush Theatre when 'there were a lot of Dublin and Kerrymen in there. The reaction that night I'll never forget. They were just crying and shouting. Incredible'.[333]

Thirteen : A Mighty Bust-Up

On 5 December 1972, the 7:84 Theatre Company received the letter informing them of the legal action being taken against D'Arcy and Arden, and warning them to remove the production of *The Ballygombeen Bequest* from the stage forthwith. The same day, Arden and D'Arcy's play, *The Island of the Mighty*, opened at the Royal Shakespeare Company's London theatre, the Aldwych in The Strand. The conjunction may not have been accidental.

The Island of the Mighty remains one of the most fascinating and provocative works in the Arden/D'Arcy, D'Arcy/Arden *oeuvre*. The title uses an ancient Welsh name for Britain, and it draws its subject matter from the Arthurian cycle, also known as 'the Matter of Britain'. That the final form of Arden and D'Arcy's play is the product of one of their most constructive collaborations is ironic, because Arden had been working on his own on this material from before the time he met D'Arcy. Perhaps this slow growth helps to explain the final play's tantalizing resonance. King Arthur in one form or another had already found his way into a number of these authors' earlier works: Mr Miltiades in *Ars Longa, Vita Brevis* had made his pupils enact the Battle of Camlann; Mr Croke's company in *The Royal Pardon* had tried to present their version of the ancient British myth, only to fall ill and cede their stage to Luke, the stage hand, who with the company's *soubrette* improvised their own *King Arthur II* play; in *Left-Handed Liberty*, the Marshal tries to warn King John of danger by referring to the meeting between Arthur and Mordred before the Battle of Camlann; and so on. It is almost as if they had been engrossing this theme continuously for years.

It should be noted, too, that Arden was not alone in his interest in King Arthur at this time. Through the 1960s, there was something of a revival of interest, perhaps sprung by the publication in 1958 of T.H.White's immensely popular, *The Once and Future King*. In 1960 in USA, the musical *Camelot* by A.J.Lerner and Frederick Loewe opened on Broadway, and became a smash hit on both sides of the Atlantic, as well as a top-selling film, and it was followed by Disney's popular 1963 film, *The Sword in the Stone*. Such works helped to create the comparison between President Kennedy's White House and the Arthurian Camelot, and the comparison was not weakened by Kennedy's unexpected assassination. More subtly, and more generally, however, the 1960s were a time of release from old constrictions: people seemed to be seeking not only new directions, but also, in a sense, new roots. The myth and story of King Arthur was Britain's oldest and most profound, and it held perhaps a glimpse of a different, if elusive social identity.

The Island of the Mighty consists of three plays. The first, 'Two Wild Young Noblemen', concerns Balin and Balan, brothers who have lost their lands. They appear to Arthur who, backed by his official poet, Merlin, is trying to contain the political and military crises which beset post-Roman Britain. Balin agrees to join Arthur, but Balan refuses to be so tied down and leaves for the Pictish lands in south-west Scotland. At Arthur's court, Balan kills the Pictish ambassador, is expelled, and flees to Arthur's enemy, Pellam. But here he is embroiled in further mayhem, and sails for Ireland. However, his ship is blown off course, he lands in the country of the Picts, where he meets the Pictish leader. They fight ritualistically, and both are killed: only then do they recognise each other as brothers. Meanwhile a massive force of English has invaded Britain; Arthur requires all the support he can muster.

Part Two, 'Oh, the Cruel Winter', opens with Aneurin being rejected by the College of Bards. He is from Gododdin, a place approximating to today's Lothian. Gododdin's king seeks the prestige of a Chief Poet, while his perhaps-disreputable sister, Gwenhwyvar, enjoys Aneurin's scurrilous and subversive ballads. Arthur has dug up Bran's magic skull and nailed it to his standard. He prepares now to defend Britain, while Medraut, his lieutenant and supposedly his nephew, goes to recruit more cavalrymen. Gododdin proposes an alliance, to be cemented by marrying his sister to Medraut, but Arthur steps in and takes her for himself. In the upheavals which follow, the poor are seen being cruelly dispossessed, Aneurin's poetry is acclaimed by the people, and Gwenhwyvar, having left Arthur, seems to become a reincarnation of Branwen, Bran's sister. The people are drunk on hope for a new age, as Medraut, with Branwen's mark on his forehead, and his followers, face Arthur. Arthur admits he fathered Medraut with his sister. In the ensuing battle, Medraut and Arthur are both killed, Gwenhwyvar is stolen by an Englishman, and Merlin, realizing his own impotence, runs mad.

The final part, 'A Handful of Watercress', tracks Merlin's madness. He is followed by Aneurin, who tries to help him, and Bedwyr, Arthur's inheritor, who wants to restore the Arthurian *status quo*, as the English invaders continue to advance. Merlin struggles to regain his sanity. When Taliesin challenges him, he stabs him, then finds a kind of crazy companionship with Morgan, Arthur's half sister – she and he crazily leap about the stage ('Leap out of my clothes, leap out of my life'). Aneurin enters an alliance with Gwenddydd, formerly Merlin's wife and Gwenhwyvar's companion; and Bedwyr, deserted by his companions, becomes a wandering priest. A cowman's wife leaves milk out for mad Merlin, who sings:

> I am welcome at last for the man that I am,
> And neither for craft nor art!

The cowman sees his wife with this naked leaping singing man, and in a fit of jealousy murders him. Bedwyr curses him, and avouches Merlin died 'at peace with God'. But Aneurin sings of a different kind of resurrection when the ordinary people will take hold of the whole world.

Even so brief a summary of the stories of the plays suggests Arden and D'Arcy's approach. From his earliest interest in 'the Matter of Britain', Arden had rejected the Victorian confections of Tennyson and the Pre-Raphaelites as too close to a justification for Empire, as well as too fey an embodiment. Their 'Gothic intensity' was, perhaps not surprisingly, 'rather distasteful' to the young Arden.[334] His first acceptable sources were Malory, whose work he had encountered 'in the school library on a wet Sunday afternoon in ... 1945',[335] and Geoffrey of Monmouth, in his twelfth century *History of the Kings of Britain*. But these were supplemented, or infiltrated, over the years by earlier, less accessible sources, often Welsh, such as *Y Gododdin* and *The Mabinogion*. *Y Gododdin*, written somewhere between the seventh and ninth centuries, is attributed to the shadowy poet, Aneurin, the popular poet who is rejected by the College of Bards in 'Oh, the Cruel Winter'; it is a lament for heroes who died defending Britain from the Saxons. One of these heroes is Arthur, in what is perhaps the earliest reference to him. There are also several Welsh poems attributed to Taliesin, another of the poets in the Arden/ D'Arcy play, which mention Arthur. Some of the most interesting poems in *The Book of Taliesin*, however, deal with the kingdom of Rheged on the Scottish-English border, the region where *The Island of the Mighty* is set. *The Mabinogion* itself, of course, also includes a number of references to Arthur, and also to his closest supporters, Cei (Kay), who does not figure in *The Island of the Mighty*, and Bedwyr (Bedivere), who does. *The Mabinogion* tells the tale of King Bran the Blessed, who allies Britain with Ireland by marrying his sister Branwen to the Irish king. When Branwen is mistreated by her husband, her British relatives mount an invasion of Ireland to rescue her. The result is a disaster, and only seven men (one of them Taliesin) survive the battle. Branwen is dead, and Bran mortally wounded. Bran tells the survivors to cut off his head and bring it home to Britain, which they do, and for many years the head continues to speak with them. Finally it falls silent, but not before it has instructed them to bury it under the Tower of London: as long as it is there, no would-be invaders can succeed in conquering Britain. Later stories tell of how Arthur excavated the head for his own protection, which story Arden and D'Arcy also employ.

Another ancient tale which they use is the Irish legend of Crazy Sweeney, who provides the model for Merlin's madness in 'A Handful of Watercress'. Sweeney was the king of Ulster who tried to prevent the establishment of Christianity in his realm by attacking the missionary, Ronan Finn, as he built his first church. Finn cursed Sweeney with madness, and the king ran away, leaping like a wounded bird. Fearing human contact, he ran, naked and hungry, into the wild woods for seven years, until a relative of his found him, and tried to coax him back to sanity. But Sweeney was distracted by an old woman who lived in a nearby mill. She challenged him to leap higher than she did, and again he lapsed into bird-like madness. Later, when he was

177

feeble and old, he was taken in by a holy man, and fed and clothed. He was given a poor woman as a carer, but the woman's husband grew jealous and killed Sweeney with his spear.

Geoffrey of Monmouth's *History of the Kings of Britain*, more legend and folk story than fact-based history, is probably the first attempt to give a coherent narrative to the disparate Arthurian material. In it Arthur appears as part warrior-hero and part magical primitive figure from the Other World. He flourishes, apparently, in post-Roman Britain, and defeats the invading Saxons, as well as the Picts and the Scots. He thus manages to unite the kingdom under his own rule. Monmouth's Arthur's wife is Guinevere, and his teasing adviser is the wizard Merlin. In this version, he invades Europe and challenges the Roman Empire, whose forces he defeats. But before he can march on Rome, he learns that Mordred, his nephew and regent left behind, has stolen both his queen and his throne. He returns to Britain, faces Mordred at Camlann, and though his army is victorious, he himself is killed. It is this version of the death of Arthur (without the invasion of Europe) which is the main source for Arthur's death in 'Oh, the Cruel Winter'.

Geoffrey of Monmouth's is a more rugged, more problematic work than Malory's, which attempts to synthesise Geoffrey's work with the (usually French) later romance tales of Arthur and his knights of the Round Table, in which the king himself becomes a rather benign regal president at the centre of his court at Camelot. The story's focus is on the knights themselves. The real drama here is dominated by courtly love stories – Tristram and Yseult, Geraint and Enid, above all, Lancelot and Guinevere – and the quest for the Holy Grail, with its own heroes, Percival and Galahad. In different versions each of these two is supposed to have healed the Fisher King, who in the French Romances is the guardian of the Holy Grail. This character has been wounded in the leg or groin, so that he walks with a debilitating limp (as Arthur does in Arden and D'Arcy's play), but more important-ly his impotence has caused the land's fertility to dry up: it is a waste land, until the chosen knight appears to heal him. He thus seems to merge with King Pellam in Malory's story of Balin, the Knight with two Swords. In this tale, Balin wounds Pellam with a stroke from the holy lance, thereby causing blight to fall on the land and devastation on the people. Balin is the central character in Arden and D'Arcy's 'Two Wild Young Noblemen', and by implication his wounding of King Pellam in that play, the first of the trilogy, causes the 'cruel winter' of the second play.

The Fisher King's significance was first explored by Sir J.G.Frazer in his influential late nineteenth century work, *The Golden Bough*. Frazer's theory of mythology and religion focuses on a solar god who dies at the end of every year, is mystically united with the goddess of earth, and so revives, or is reincarnated, in spring. This is mimicked in the ritual, common in many religions, cults and cultures, of the periodic sacrifice of the king, his killing by a younger rival, who then takes his place. But in time, this new king is killed by a new rival. The ritual killings ensure the continued fertility of the land. There are several more or less specific references to this in *The Island of the Mighty*, but the most explicit is in the scenes with the matriarchal Wild Cat Picts, especially when Balan faces the limping Sacred King, defeats him in battle, and wins the hand of the princess.

There is a huge and deep well of mythology here, perhaps arising from an intuitive response to Robert Graves's concept of the patriarchal overthrow of a more imaginative, less dogmatic matriarchy, which Arden and D'Arcy tap into. But it is modified through the historical investigations of scholars such as R.G.Collingwood and R.S.Loomis. Collingwood and Myres' history of fifth century Britain revealed a country which was still a 'Roman island' decades after the legions had deserted.[336] The break-up of the old system was piecemeal, but the standard was always 'Roman'. Kingdoms were fluid, tribes warred on one another. More or less skilful or powerful leaders, such as Vortigern or Ambrosius, might arise to hold the state together for a time against external incursions from the continent and internal centrifugal dissent. Notable among the internal dissidents were furious groups of dispossessed or very poor peasants, for whom, Collingwood notes, invaders from Germany or the Low Countries were often less the enemy than the local warlord's tax-collector.

In this shifting, disintegrating social landscape Collingwood and Myres discern the shadowy figure of Arthur. Son of a Romanized, well-to-do family, he emerges as 'Dux Bellorum', the leader of wars. He was not a king, Collingwood thinks, but he led a troop of cavalry to fight wherever they seemed to be needed. Collingwood suggests these fifth century mail-clad horsemen were the reality behind Arthur's 'knights' and it is cavalrymen in *The Island of the Mighty* whom Medraut goes to recruit. Collingwood further conjectures that the site of the last battle, Camlann, fought between Arthur and Medraut, is near Birdoswald on Hadrian's Wall, not far from the evocatively-named modern village of Arthuret, and it is here, rather than in the expected south and west, that Arden and D'Arcy set their story. Collingwood states:

> Arthur, I have suggested, was the last of the Romans: the last to
> understand Roman ideas and use them for the good of the British people.
> The heritage of Rome lived on in many shapes; but of the men who
> created that heritage Arthur was the last, and the story of Roman Britain
> ends with him.[337]

This suggestive historical and geographical locating of Arthur gave Arden and D'Arcy a concrete setting for their plays, and this was extended by more detailed studies of the way the 'Matter of Britain' had developed over the centuries after that described by Collingwood and Myres. Just one example is Loomis's 1963 study, which, for example, explores the figure of Merlin, the central character in *The Island of the Mighty*, in which he is Arthur's court poet. Loomis's Merlin, or Myrddin, was a bard

> who took part in the battle of Arderydd (which was actually fought in
> Carlisle in 573), and when his lord, King Gwenddolan, was killed, lost his
> reason. Hunted by the victor, Rhydderch, a historic king of Dumbarton,
> Myrddin has taken refuge in the wood of Celydon in the Scottish
> Lowlands, enduring the rigours of winter with snow reaching to his hips
> and icicles in his hair, his only companion a pig. In another poem he
> utters prophesies in response to the questions of his sister Gwenddydd.
> Still another consists of a dialogue between Myrddin and his chief of
> bards, Taliesin.[338]

('Arderydd' is the old name for Arthuret.) This recalls Robert Graves's description in *The White Goddess* of the 'guild of Welsh minstrels' who, in the Celtic tradition, were sacrosanct, priests and judges, as well as poets: 'When two armies engaged in battle, the poets of both sides would withdraw together to a hill and there judiciously discuss the fighting', Graves asserts.[339] These bards are in contradistinction to the 'gleemen', or popular poets, who cannot be admitted to the guild. 'Oh, the Cruel Winter' opens with the College of Bards, of which Taliesin and Merlin are members, rejecting the popular poet, Aneurin. The place of the poet or writer in any communal or national polity is, perhaps, the most urgent, and most urgently-felt, question in the whole *Island of the Mighty* trilogy. Official bard or subversive gleeman?

The Island of the Mighty gives us three named poets, as well as a number of others, each of whom relates to his community differently. Merlin is a kind of liberal-humanist intellectual, who accepts the political set-up managed by Arthur, and though he claims potency and clear-sightedness, and we adopt his viewpoint easily, he is also smug and even conceited. As Arden wondered in *The Bagman*, we might wonder now: is this position tenable? Is not poetry (art, playwrighting) subversive by its nature? It is instructive that Merlin is unable to formulate an honest poetic response to Camlann, or the death of Arthur, but goes mad and becomes a bird (the bird as symbol of freedom) or a green man in the woods. Merlin stripped bare, like King Lear, finally relates to the peasantry in the person of the cowman's wife. Politics, in the shape of Bedwyr, cannot catch him. He becomes himself: does this mean he must die? 'The pitiful animal degradation of the artist who has once sold his soul', John Peters wrote of the final scene, when he saw *The Island of the Mighty*, 'is one of the starkest and most original passages in modern drama'.[340]

This Merlin is to be compared with Taliesin and Aneurin. Taliesin is the official Bard, the poet laureate, certain of his morality, jealous of his position. He curses Merlin, but Merlin kills him, in order to liberate poetry and art from officialdom. Aneurin, on the other hand, is a thoroughly subversive poet, as shown by his illicit relationship with Gwenhwyvar. He is certainly truer than the other two poets to his calling, and he asserts at the end that those who are now downtrodden will in the end rise up. The implication, never spelled out as clearly as this, is that true poets are naturally allied with the poor, for both poet and poor man try to create something new, something better than what has gone before, or at least each tries to illuminate alternatives.

In considering these matters, Arden had had in mind for many years David Jones's poetic evocation of the First World War, *In Parenthesis*, first published in 1937. In this epic work, the trenches create a landscape like the Waste Land (Part 4 of this book is entitled 'King Pellam's Land'), and the soldier-author compares himself to a bard singing of the Battle of Camlann. The references to the Matter of Britain are done with extreme delicacy and allusiveness, but Jones is also capable of bringing the apparently obscure down to earth, as when he quotes the Welsh rugby song, *Sospan Fach* alongside the 'half-remembered saying, "To Gwenhwyvar the pot, to Arthur the pan"'.[341] All this was an example to Arden of how the sometimes esoteric material of the Matter of Britain might be brought to bear on the flaring problems of the twentieth century, though Jones's extreme modernist allusiveness was unlikely to help much in the creation of what was intended to be a popular play.

Arden and D'Arcy needed something more responsive, something more resonant for a contemporary audience. This became D'Arcy's special contribution to the work. She was able to relate the post-Roman British turmoil, described by Collingwood, to what she had seen in post-independent India, especially in the cauldron of Assam. Here land, and the need for land, was at the heart of the struggles, as the search for land was what had motivated the British tribes, and the invading Saxons, fifteen hundred years earlier. The many-sided strife in Assam involved indigenous warlords and foreign invaders, rapacious landlords and the very poor (inconceivably poor to western eyes), who fought oppression for their very survival. Any central authority was far away, psychologically as well as physically, and the people often preferred the invading Chinese to the oppressors who laid claim to the governance of their district or province. Explaining later how India had affected the play, Arden remarked that it was 'about land hunger (and) the ordinary people who live their daily lives through these massive upheavals ... how they are affected while playing no conscious part whatsoever in these violent changes in their lives and history'.[342]

The India experienced by Arden and D'Arcy was, of course, like many post-colonial societies. Examples may be quoted as disparate as the Congo of President Mobutu, who called himself 'the all-powerful warrior who leaves fire in his wake'; the Algeria of the socialistic dictator, Ben Bella, who was overthrown in a military coup by his own minister, Houari Boumedienne, who then took Ben Bella's policies to their logical oppressive conclusions; or, more recently, Robert Mugabe, the freedom-fighter-turned-despot of Zimbabwe. To D'Arcy, Arthur was a figure not dissimilar to these, a tyrant, perhaps, amassing power to himself while asserting, and perhaps believing, that what he did was for the good of the people. This Arthur is certainly a more ambiguous figure than he is in most later interpretations of the ancient sources.

And nearer home, Ireland herself had not long lost her imperial masters, and indeed six of her counties remained in British hands: this also provided clear parallels with Arthur's post-Roman Britain. The Provisional IRA was at war with Official IRA and both were fighting not only various Ulster loyalist paramilitary groups (who were often also shooting each other), but also the British Army, who themselves were fighting a rearguard action on behalf of the colonial power. The Irish pressure cooker was further stirred by the 'group of right-wing fixers' and 'Green Orangemen' with greedy fingers in many a murky pie who held power in the Republic itself. And it is crucial to read all this, too, into this trilogy of plays 'on a traditional British theme'.

India had also revealed to Arden and D'Arcy a viable form of extended, popular epic dramas, performed by the Chhau dancers and the Jatra theatre troupes. *The Island of the Mighty* sparkles with devices and images traceable to this source – rituals, dances, masks, music, clowning, spectacular costumes and more. Partly this is to do with how to present character as action function – Medraut as clown, Aneurin as the sort of singer you might encounter in the pub, Balin as a conventional 'angry man', and so on. But partly it is to do with the rapidity of performance, the endless music and drumming, the vibrant, noisy, relaxed enjoyment by the audience of what is going on. Of course there are other influences at work in the dramaturgy here – the dynamism of New York's La Mama Theatre, for instance, the 'crudity' of Cartoon Archetypal Slogan Theatre's 'rock and roll' performances, and much from street theatre and agitprop. But the dominant influence on this extraordinarily fluid and original drama is the Indian folk theatre.

Moreover, it should be remembered that the trilogy had been twenty years in the making. According to Arden, the first version, completed in 1953, failed to reconcile his political theme, at this point concerning rival British generals squabbling and thereby ceding advantage to the Saxon invaders, with the 'Gravesian theme' of the survival of old religious and cultural practices. He tried to bridge the gap by inventing a troupe of itinerant actors, but felt dubious about the effect. Subsequently, he became acquainted with some of Brecht's drama, and read *In Parenthesis*. He also saw the British Empire staggering towards collapse, and noted similarities between this and the crumbling of the Roman Empire in the fifth century. He reworked the Arthurian play, replacing the itinerant actors with two poets, Taliesin, who was presented as Arthur's official poet, and Merlin, an outsider, a 'gleeman' in Graves's term. He also 'introduced a tribe of Picts, votaries of a Kali-like goddess, whose totem was the Wild Cat'. He sent the new version to George Devine at the Royal Court Theatre in 1955, but received no reply. A few years later he discovered the reader's report: 'boring historical play written in phoney verse'.[343]

There the dramatisation of any Arthurian material rested until 1966, when the BBC, seeking original work for their new BBC2 channel, offered Arden a three-play commission. D'Arcy urged him to resurrect the Arthur plays, and Arden began once again to rework the material, this time for television. He dropped Sir Lancelot, and structured the three plays around the story of Balin and Balan from Malory, the death of Arthur from Geoffrey of Monmouth, and the madness of Merlin from the legend of Crazy Sweeney. He also drew material from *The Mabinogion*, and created a substructure around the three contrasting poets, Taliesin, now attached to a lesser leader than Arthur, Aneurin, who became what Merlin had been, and Merlin as the liberal-humanist artist-intellectual. The core of the final version had emerged. Arden was not dissatisfied, and asked for Stuart Burge to direct the three plays. However, by now, 1969, the BBC's expansive policies and generous finances had shrunk, and the request for Stuart Burge was irrelevant: the commission was withdrawn. But the Welsh National Theatre were interested, and Arden agreed to rewrite the scripts once again, eliminating the televisual naturalism and the atmospheric locations, and 'theatricalising' the complete trilogy. This was what he was attempting to do when he and D'Arcy and their children drove to India. In India he fell ill. D'Arcy realized the new script was ineffective, and at this point Arden, still suffering the effects of hepatitis, asked her to help. She certainly enlivened the plays, sharpening the contemporary concerns and making them more sociologically precise. Thus, the treatment of the Picts was strengthened when she realized that 'the *essential* element in their life must have been their fishing and farming', and that their rituals were intended to further these economic interests.[344] The Pictish scenes, in D'Arcy's hands, lost much of their picturesque theatricality and became harsher, more embedded in the social life of their particular community. It was mostly D'Arcy, too, who steered the dramatic form towards the Indian epic theatre, notably its use of strong and vivid story-telling, its sequences of sung narrative, and its emphasis on music and dance. The Welsh National Theatre, however, failed to secure a building in which this trilogy could be produced, so Arden and D'Arcy's agent, Margaret Ramsay, offered it to the Royal Shakespeare Company.

Ronald Bryden, play adviser to the company, was enthusiastic, and the directorate of the RSC debated whether to accept it. They agreed that if it could made into a single evening's play, using perhaps 65% of the original script, they could present it. This meant that the first two plays would have to be amalgamated, and the third play would be reduced to little more than a coda. Even this reduction would make a work lasting over three hours in performance. Bryden visited Arden and D'Arcy in Ireland to put this to them. Arden in particular wanted the play staged, and he and D'Arcy agreed to cut the script and allow the production, stipulating, however, that it should use a presentational – that is, non-naturalistic – style, both in terms of acting and design. As far as the latter was concerned, they urged the use of backcloths. They also obtained a contract which would see them paid for work on the script during the eight-week rehearsal period, though no provision was made in the contract in the case of a disagreement with the play's director or the company's management.

In October 1972, work on the production began. The director was David Jones, then responsible for running the RSC's London base at the Aldwych Theatre. His background was in the BBC, and he had joined the RSC in 1964. In 1969 he had become the company's Aldwych Theatre director, and though he had directed John Whiting's *Saints Day* and Sean O'Casey's *The Silver Tassie*, he had become best known for the detailed realism of his productions of plays by David Mercer and Maxim Gorky. In hindsight it is possible to say that he was probably not the wisest choice for this project. During the first five weeks of rehearsals, Arden was present, while D'Arcy remained in Ireland. Design sketches and unorchestrated music scores were agreed, and Arden proceeded with the cuts and re-writes necessitated by the length of the script and the decision to present a truncated version in a single evening. As Arden said, 'I want this play on. It's a piece of work, and it needs doing'.[345] For David Jones, the first weeks of rehearsal was a 'very creative' period, but Arden was more anxious: Pam Gems, who met him at this time, reported him 'mumbling something about getting on all right with David Jones', but being 'edgy about the large permanent company (and) the necessity for some degree of rigidity and fixed forward planning'.[346] She described him as 'a spare, light man, young in the face ... immediately remarkable for a wild head of coke-coloured hair'. She went on:

> He is sharp, and prudently careful, and his voice is very strong and
> resonant, and he is much better-looking than the whey-faced pictures he
> sees fit to have printed on the backs of his books. He does look dreamy,
> partly the glasses. Now and then, when he sharpens up, the direct gaze,
> because of the magnification of the glasses, becomes a glare ... I get this
> look from time to time, and together with the hair it makes him seem
> slightly mutated ... something crested, night-flying.[347]

After the first week or two of rehearsals, Arden seemed reasonably satisfied, but later he became more apprehensive, less certain of what was happening. He looked forward to D'Arcy's arrival for the first run-through at the start of week six: 'she'll see exactly where it's wrong,' he said, adding, however, ominously: 'I bet we won't be able to change it'. Nevertheless at somewhere near the half way stage of rehearsals, he thought it was 'all right so far. As far as I can see, and that's no distance at all.

Nothing's there yet'.[348] During the fifth week of rehearsals Jones wished to work privately with the actors, feeling that the author's presence would inhibit the close work he wished to do. Accordingly, Arden departed for Ireland, returning with D'Arcy for the first run-through.

Pam Gems also described D'Arcy at this time. She was 'thin, so thin, with dark hair,' she wrote, and continued:

> Big mouth, multipara face, and teeth in the Irish style – one missing at
> the side. Her eyes, which are light and very bright, look frightened …
> frightened? … and she sits back in her seat and talks down into her lap so
> that I can't hear what she says … And then she smiles and her face
> changes so completely it's almost creepy. She looks about twenty, the eyes
> are full and clear, like a child, her face comes alive.[349]

The run-through, her introduction to the production, shocked both her and Arden. After their private work with the director, the actors were playing 'strangely',[350] with Emrys James's Merlin, for instance, 'inserting bits that suggested (Merlin) was a magician',[351] precisely what Arden had tried to avoid by making him a politically-engaged poet. The 'presentational' style had been completely subsumed by a pseudo-Stanislavskian naturalism. To both Arden and D'Arcy this inevitably meant that the meaning of the play was distorted, or was at least slipping away. Moreover, at well over four hours, the play was still far too long. D'Arcy also objected to the music, which was not fulfilling the function of music in the Indian epics, as she saw it. The sets, too, were wrong. For Arden, the dilemma was cruel: 'It's all very well, but I've been here from the beginning, how can I complain? … First it was too early for changes, now if we don't speak up it's going to be too late'.[352] D'Arcy argued that they might as well not be there if they were not going to make their views known. Arden was still arguing that the play must be done, even if the production hardly matched their intentions.

In the evening after the run-through, Arden and D'Arcy met with David Jones. They explained that the production seemed to them to be drastically distorting the meaning of the play, that its anti-imperialist stance was being directly undermined. Jones disagreed. And the cuts he asked for, and the costumes he wanted, indicated to Arden and D'Arcy that he had not properly understood their work. But how could he, having spent his professional life largely in television and the naturalistic theatre of the establishment? He had no experience of Indian folk theatre, and probably knew little about agitprop street theatre or the work of troupes like CAST or La Mama. There was no meeting of minds, so that his suggestions for reshaping the play were completely at odds with the authors'. Arden and D'Arcy then requested a meeting of the whole company to discuss these problems, and to 'get the play back on the rails'.[353] Jones equivocated. Obviously feeling insecure, he refused to discuss his 'interpretation' and opined that the criticisms Arden and D'Arcy had made were so 'universal' that a meeting with the actors would not be fruitful, and indeed might merely demoralise them. As Arden later pointed out, he did not consider the other possibility: that such a meeting might lift their morale. At any rate, the meeting between authors and director broke up that evening inconclusively, with Arden and D'Arcy wondering what to do if the management behaved as 'imperialists', and refused a meeting, or indeed if the company itself declined to listen.

Next day David Jones called the actors together, explained the authors' demand for a meeting (as he understood it), and asked them to vote on whether to meet with Arden and D'Arcy while he left the room. He failed to explain, probably because he did not fully comprehend this, that the authors had in fact requested a meeting which would include the *entire* company of those involved in the work, including technical staff, ushers, Box Office staff and others. The actors were divided, but a majority voted against holding such a meeting. Meanwhile, Arden had contacted Margaret Ramsay, his agent, to ask her to press for the meeting; now she returned to him and D'Arcy to say the request had been refused. Some actors did in fact try to meet with Arden and D'Arcy informally, but when they did, most failed to recognize the authors' standpoint, and indeed complained that Arden and D'Arcy had become abusive.

So Arden and D'Arcy went on strike. The value of the lessons derived from the experience of radio (*The Life of Man*) and television (*Wet Fish*) that the author needed to be present at *all* rehearsals was demonstrated once again, and with a vengeance. As members of the Society of Irish Playwrights (there was no comparable body in the United Kingdom), they were clear that they were not walking out of the production, but were withdrawing their labour because the management had made their conditions of work unacceptable. In other words, they held that the Royal Shakespeare Company had broken their contract. To Arden and D'Arcy, the RSC, in receipt of a large government subsidy, was simply showing itself to be another example of an organisation operating within the Heath Government's unjust Industrial Relations Act. To the press, the dispute was a godsend. *The Sun* put it on its front page, *The Times* printed a picture of Arden standing outside the Aldwych Theatre with a placard proclaiming: 'PLAYWRIGHTS ARE WORKERS BEFORE THEY ARE ARTISTS' and the same paper printed an extraordinary rant by Bernard Levin, admitting that Arden was 'honest' in repudiating a production of his play *before* the critics had had a chance to savage it, but attacking him for 'parrot-headedness'.[354] Was this the 'difficult author' of *Wet Fish*? Some, including certain respected theatre professionals, blamed the dispute entirely on Margaretta D'Arcy, suggesting there had been no problems before she attended rehearsals, though significantly the actor and director Gavin Richards called the attacks on her 'disgusting'.[355] It was notable, too, that the Royal Shakespeare Company throughout the dispute tried to prise the two authors apart, except when David Jones let it be known somewhat disingenuously that he had accepted both their 'resignations' from the production. The implicit suggestion in most of the company's public pronouncements was that D'Arcy was a disruptive political agitator, rather than a serious playwright.[356]

Arden and D'Arcy felt they were fighting not only on their own behalf, but for 'playwrights in general, and, by extension, for actors in general whom we knew to be only too often as unhappy as we were with the bureaucracy of big subsidised managements'. They had been careful to obtain the support of the Society of Irish Playwrights (though the RSC announced that SIP had been 'misinformed' about the action), and they picketed the theatre up to thirteen hours each day, being joined at various times by other sympathetic professionals. Some of the company's actors engaged with them outside, but the majority avoided contact, as did the designers and musicians. David Jones avoided them, too, though Ronald Bryden and Trevor Nunn, the RSC's Artistic Director, offered to talk with them inside the building. Arden and D'Arcy responded that anything that needed saying could be said on the pavement, whereupon Nunn and Bryden withdrew their offer. The theatre technicians consulted their union about crossing the picket line, but Equity, to which the technicians union (ironically, like SIP) was affiliated, informed them that the strike was not official so they should feel free cross the picket line. In fact, Equity never consulted SIP.

Consequently, while D'Arcy and Arden were 'huddled with (their) placards outside the stage door', the previews were proceeding inside the theatre. 'It was a very awkward corner in that back alley off Drury Lane', Arden was to remember. 'All sorts of people, theatrical and other, came to support and sustain us, but others came to revile, and the wind ... was extremely cold'.[357] At one of the previews some members of the audience called for Arden and D'Arcy to be admitted to explain their case. They were brought in from the pavement, and appeared on the stage, only for large numbers of the audience to vociferously hoot and jeer them. According to one account, they (the authors) 'climbed on the stage to pull down the scenery'.[358] Arden certainly tried to speak, but his voice was drowned out. He asked whether they wanted him to leave. It seemed that most of them did. Trying to make himself heard above the baying and the boos, he desperately shouted, 'All right, I shall never write for you again'. It was deplorable, a moment of utter disgrace for the British theatre. Even David Jones described it as 'deeply shaming for all concerned'.[359] It was also a defining moment for Arden and D'Arcy, and perhaps also for the British theatre.

On the day of the opening of the play at the Aldwych Theatre, a letter from Arden and D'Arcy appeared in *The Guardian*. They pointed out that, *pace* certain statements from the company, they did not 'disapprove of the entire production'. Their dispute, which the management had wanted hushed up, had become public, they pointed out, because it was a trade dispute, not a mere artistic disagreement. In response to the authors' demand for the anti-imperialist stance of the play to be strengthened, they noted, Trevor Nunn had simply wondered 'whether the RSC could allow itself to become a platform for political propaganda'. Arden and D'Arcy pointed out that the whole affair was inevitably political, and that the company was simply being shown up as 'the dupe of the Establishment'.[360]

On the same day, *The Times* published a letter from Trevor Nunn and David Jones, in which they asserted their case, including that it was only after the arrival of D'Arcy that the problems had arisen, and that 'the Ardens'' demand for a meeting of the whole company had been rejected 'by an overwhelming majority'. They asserted that the RSC was 'a basically left-wing organisation' and justified this by referring to a number of plays which they had staged written by left-wing writers (without noticing that the plays they staged had nothing to do with whether the organisation staging them was left-wing). They ended by saying that they had invited John Arden 'to give his views from the stage after the performance'.[361] D'Arcy was not invited, apparently. One comic consequence of this letter was the resignation by Angus Maude, the Conservative M.P. for Stratford-upon-Avon, from the theatre's board. He said the comment about the theatre being 'a basically left-wing organisation' was a 'remarkable piece of effrontery' and 'wholly improper'.[362] A leading article in *The Guardian* two days later called Nunn 'naïve' if he thought people went to see plays by left-wing authors (Brecht and Gorky were mentioned) because they were 'polemicists first and dramatists second'. The reverse, it said, was the case.[363]

Meanwhile Arden and D'Arcy replied to Nunn and Jones's letter in *The Times*, pointing out that a meeting of 'the whole company' had not even included the writers, and could therefore hardly be called 'democratic', that theirs was a trade union dispute, which the company (despite being 'a left-wing organisation') failed to recognise, and that they, the authors, had not actually been invited to speak after the first performance of the play. Ronald Bryden then wrote to say that he had spoken to their agent to ask them to speak after the performance, to which in a further letter Arden and D'Arcy replied that a telephone call from the company's play adviser to the author's agent 'tentatively suggesting some class of "talks about talks" ... cannot possibly be construed as a regular formal invitation from the artistic directors of the RSC'.[364] And once they had discovered that the director had cut the play text himself, Arden and D'Arcy went home to Ireland. The play opened without them. They never saw it.

Most of the reviews were lukewarm, though Irving Wardle in *The Times* was aware that the play offered more than was easily comprehended at a single viewing. Michael Billington described it in *The Guardian* as 'unwieldy, inchoate and exasperating'.[365] What he and most spectators forgot, or perhaps never knew, was that *The Island of the Mighty* is a trilogy, and the four hours of the RSC's performance gave an often false impression of the authors' work. In full production, the three plays last a little over two hours each, perhaps six and a half hours in all, in three discrete parts. There was also the matter of the 'presentational style' which the production had betrayed. Albert Hunt understood this. He had written in *Flourish*, the RSC's newspaper, that this play 'demands to be seen as a variety show';[366] in the event, he found the production 'dreadful, desperately dull'.[367]

As noted above, *The Island of the Mighty* derives its style from La Mama's elegant fury, from CAST's rock 'n' roll theatre, and most importantly from traditional Indian drama and dance. It also draws on Debord's idea of society as a spectacle. English theatre practitioners had simply no idea about most of this, no notion of the implications for the theatre. The RSC's usual style, which easily slipped into the clunky and ponderous, was no match for Arden's witty integrity or D'Arcy's more serpent-like urgency. Their theatre experience was far wider and deeper than that of most British playwrights or directors, whose work was – by Arden and D'Arcy's standards – extremely parochial. But it is also true that Arden and D'Arcy found it hard to convey to David Jones and the RSC players what they wanted; as hard as Jones and his actors found it to comprehend what Bengali Jatra theatre or the ideas of a French intellectual like Guy Debord (if indeed they had ever heard of Debord) had to do with a play about King Arthur. They probably did know *Hair*; but again, what had that to do with the drama of Britain's mythic once-and-future king?

One outcome of this extraordinary debacle was the formation of the Theatre Writers Union. The rights of the playwright were strongly advocated in another letter to *The Times* from John O'Donovan, chairman of the Society of Irish Playwrights, who while not defending each and every action of Arden and D'Arcy in their dispute with the RSC, pointed out that

> a play in rehearsal at the RSC is now pretty much in the position of a
> prisoner in Pentonville. It can be visited by its father only by permission
> of the authorities and the father can speak only by consent of, and in the
> presence of, the chief warder. We have seen what happens when the
> father alleges ill-treatment of the prisoner. The official disclaimers of the
> warders have an amusingly familiar ring.[368]

He urged that an English equivalent to the Society of Irish Playwrights was 'clearly overdue'. On 7 December, two days after *The Island of the Mighty* opened, a letter signed by thirteen of the country's most prominent playwrights had in fact been published in *The Times*, urging 'other writers to join with us in the creation of … an organisation within the trade union movement for the playwright'.[369] The Theatre Writers Union was formed as a trade union for playwrights soon after, and over a period of years improved considerably the conditions of work for the playwright in

Britain's theatres. In 1997 the TWU merged with the Writers Guild of Great Britain, which has continued this work into the twenty-first century.

But the problem which the story of *The Island of the Mighty* and the Royal Shakespeare Company so dramatically exemplified is still not solved. The system remains that the Artistic Director of a major company actually has supreme legislative, financial and managerial, as well as artistic, control. In practice, the author's script, once handed over, is controlled by others. It is still true, as Arden pointed out in *The Guardian* in the midst of the contention, that the director has 'a position of quite undue importance'.[370] This blazing controversy was for him perhaps the inevitable climax for a difficulty he had seen years earlier. In the Preface to his 1966 collection, *Soldier, Soldier and Other Plays*, for example, he had written that 'when a play involves anything new in terms of style of writing, or staging, only the author knows exactly what is wanted'.[371] Now he noted, fairly enough, that 'the danger is that the content is subordinated to the skill with which it is presented',[372] arguing that the director should try to realize the play, not create his own meanings. Later he wondered whether the solution might not be to contract the author as co-director, as happened in the USA.[373]

The final upshot of the struggle with the Royal Shakespeare Company was that Arden and D'Arcy left the British theatre for ever. It is true that they knew – and said – that *The Island of the Mighty* was the last of the series of plays designed for 'a well-appointed theatre with a cast of highly professional actors',[374] which extended back through *Armstrong's Last Goodnight* and *Serjeant Musgrave's Dance*. They knew that they had found themselves as artists with a new focus and new subject matter. They were to be subversive gleemen, no longer official bards. Nevertheless, the loss was staggering. The British theatre, which so often boasted smugly of its pre-eminence in the world, could not in fact support its most significant talents. Peter Brook had had to move to Paris for his work to flourish. Joan Littlewood had effectively been driven out of the theatre altogether. Now Arden and D'Arcy, the most abundantly gifted and provocative writer(s) of their generation, disappeared too.

Fourteen : Ireland Once Again

The 1970s were the years when Arden and D'Arcy's collaboration was probably at its strongest. While *The Ballygombeen Bequest* and *The Island of the Mighty* were pursuing their controversial courses in England, other projects showed the collaboration in equally versatile and interesting lights. *Keep Those People Moving* was a two-part dramatisation of the nativity story broadcast by the BBC on 24 November and 1 December 1972, at the height of the Royal Shakespeare Company furore. Aimed at young children, each part lasted only twenty minutes, and focussed mainly on Herod and the Romans, rather as *The Business of Good Government* had. Taking inspiration from Ewan MacColl's ballad of the travelling people, the 'Moving On Song', it focuses on the rulers' typical thought: if the people are made to keep moving, they will have no time to rebel.

Equally interesting was the film, *Portrait of a Rebel*, devoted to Sean O'Casey, which they scripted. Directed by Eoghan Harris, this was broadcast by the Irish national broadcaster, RTE. It was part-financed by Official Sinn Fein, of which Harris was a member. RTE was at this time regarded by some in the Irish Establishment as a nest of left-wing subversion, with the more radical programme makers being known collectively as 'the brood of Harris'. RTE employees were in fact not allowed to be members of a political party, but those who joined Official Sinn Fein were issued with membership cards clandestinely, and were responsible directly to Harris's close comrade, Eamon Smullen, newly-appointed director of the party's 'Republican Industrial Develop-ment Division', and also the Official IRA commander in Dublin. Harris was a longstanding socialist republican from Cork, and had previously directed the influential programme, *The Testimony of James Connolly*, for RTE in 1968. At this time he was a trade union activist and prominent campaigner against Irish entry into the European Union, and was later to confront Conor Cruise O'Brien when the latter, as the Government minister responsible, moved to ban so-called 'terrorists' from radio and television. Harris described himself in the early 1970s as a 'Stalinist', a term of some significance in Arden and D'Arcy's approaching quarrel with Official Sinn Fein; his later political career, after his Marxism faded and died, was highly unpredictable, and included time as a member of the Irish Senate.

D'Arcy and Arden's way continued controversial and politically-charged.

Harris's 'Stalinism' in the early 1970s indicated the development of Official Sinn Fein's policies and priorities. The party was increasingly devoting its time and resources to urban industrial problems – Harris himself was very active with Smullen in the Republican Industrial Development Division. This often came at the expense of their commitments to rural Ireland, and in the summer of 1972, during the public discussion after a performance of *The Ballygombeen Bequest* at University College, Dublin, D'Arcy attacked the party for this abandonment of the farming communities, and also for its maintenance of an illegal army, the Official IRA. This scandalous fact was supposed to be kept secret while the party developed its new political image. But D'Arcy accused the OIRA commanding officer in Galway of supplying gelignite to a local contractor in the dispute over Mrs Fahey's eviction from her bungalow. Those who know *The Little Gray Home in the West* will recognise the incident. But her comments were reported to the party's leadership, D'Arcy's expulsion was demanded and, several weeks later, effected. She was expelled. Whereupon Arden resigned his membership. According to Hanley and Millar,

> his resignation letter included a stinging condemnation of the University College Galway Republican Club over their 'cowardly' failure to support an elderly Oughterard woman who faced eviction. It concluded: 'I would not wish any further to impede you in your political careers … You have good work yet to do, talking big and keeping quiet: and there are many masters of your craft already seated in the Dáil ready and willing to instruct your apprentice legislators when, in due course, they creep into Leinster House'.[375]

Nevertheless, Official Sinn Fein, with its developing Marxist-Leninist ideology and its shadowy military wing behind it, undoubtedly scared those in power, both in Dublin and in London. The establishments' emphasis on 'terrorism' and their unwillingness to debate indicated this clearly enough. But the party had not reached the sophistication of, say, Frantz Fanon's analysis, especially in his classic *The Wretched of the Earth*, where his position is much closer to that adopted by D'Arcy and Arden in this quarrel. Fanon accepts that colonialism must be ended by violence, but in the Republic of Ireland that stage of liberation had been partially achieved. Fanon suggested that 'liberation' must be led by the peasants and outcasts – in Ireland, that is, the rural communities which D'Arcy had been speaking about. The reason for this, according to Fanon, was that colonialism – and, by implication, the kind of neo-colonialism which it could be said Ireland was suffering from at this time – was ultimately a matter of class. Fanon then goes on to argue that liberated colonies must discover new social and political structures, rather than simply adopt those of the colonisers, as seemed to have happened in Ireland. Post-colonial bourgeois political leaders were little less than copies of the original colonial masters, and were therefore incapable of moving towards the new kind of society needed.

The Little Gray Home in the West opens with Padraig's explication:

> Between England and Ireland to this day is so great quarrel,
> To introduce it in a play I know well is to keel the barrel
> Of old dried blood and new wet blood

And steaming pitch and shit and rancorous deep complaint
And altogether such a poisonous flood
As sure would make a cannibal Cyclops faint
For very stink of it; and yet I have no choice.

The biographer of John Arden and Margaretta D'Arcy similarly has no choice but to delve into the murky history of the Irish 'Troubles' of the 1970s and beyond if their lives and work are to make sense to the reader.

In 1972, the 'Troubles' were responsible for 467 violent deaths on the island of Ireland, as well as for 3148 people injured.[376] In this situation, Official Sinn Fein, to which Arden and D'Arcy belonged for most of the year, struggled to discover a distinctive political identity. There were fierce battles in the north between the opposing IRA groupings, with the Provos chanting their anti-Official slogan, 'Better dead than red!' But in the gaol on Crumlin Road, prisoners from both IRAs were actually co-operating to fight for political status. Here, members from both groups went on hunger strike – the first hunger strike in the series in Northern Ireland which was to reach its climax nine years later. Partly in response to this, Official Sinn Fein in the south launched a new campaign, 'Saoirse', for prisoners' rights. Also at least partly in response, William Whitelaw, the British Government's Minister for Northern Ireland, abolished the devolved Stormont Assembly, and imposed direct rule from Westminster.

Official Sinn Fein was by now riven with fierce debate about its own future. This was the classic debate among socialists throughout history, and one which Arden and D'Arcy dramatised most vividly in *The Non-Stop Connolly Show*: reform or revolution? It was sometimes articulated by Official Sinn Fein members as a debate between 'stageism' and 'Castroism' (after the Cuban revolutionary leader, Fidel Castro) or even 'Stalinism' against 'Leninism'. In December 1972, at the party's 'Ard Fheis', or national conference, it seemed that the Castroists, or Leninists, had won the argument, but it was to rumble on among the membership for some time yet. When in October 1973, the party declared publicly that it was a Marxist party, run on Leninist principles, by no means all its members were happy.

The Irish General Election of February 1973 saw Jack Lynch's Fianna Fail party defeated by a coalition led by Liam Cosgrave. For the first time, Official Sinn Fein put up candidates in this election, though none were elected. In the north, a referendum on the future of the six counties was held, but the nationalist part of the population abstained *en masse*. William Whitelaw and Edward Heath then rejected the idea of all power being invested in a single (Unionist) party which governed in the interests of its own section of the population and proposed a kind of power-sharing arrangement. In December, at a conference in Sunningdale, they installed a power-sharing government with 'an Irish dimension' in the six counties. Some Unionists joined with Alliance and SDLP members to try to make the proposition workable. But in February 1974, the Conservatives lost power in a British General Election to Harold Wilson's Labour Party. Three months after that, on 15 May, the Unionist Ulster Workers Council called a general strike against power sharing. It was deliberate defiance, which the British Army failed to tackle. Loyalist bombs were exploded in Dublin and Monaghan on 17 May, killing 33 people, while the strike was solid, crippling essential services in the six counties. On 26 May the power-sharing government collapsed. Direct rule was resumed from London. The IRA bombing campaign, which had hardly halted (the Home Secretary, Reginald Maudling, had been injured by a letter bomb on 2 February), now resumed with new vigour, and there were attacks in Guildford, Woolwich and Birmingham, where twenty-one people were killed. Some people asked who was actually responsible for these: it was even hinted that the British government might have found bombs on their home patch helpful in their efforts to pass a Prevention of Terrorism Act. Certainly the perpetrators of the Birmingham bombing have never been found.

Meanwhile, the debate within Official Sinn Fein was far from over. On 21 February, several high ranking members, including Seamus Costello, vice-president of the party, were expelled from OIRA, and suspended from the political party. In June, Costello stood in local elections as an Independent Sinn Fein candidate, and won a seat, topping the poll in his constituency of Bray. Dissent, plots and counter-plots were bubbling at all levels of the party, and in December 1974 it officially split, Costello taking a good proportion of the members with him into a new Irish Republican Socialist Party, an anti-Soviet left wing grouping, who soon had, like the Sinn Fein parties, its own armed wing, later named the 'Irish National Liberation Army' (INLA). At the same time, tensions in the prisons were in no way resolved, especially in Long Kesh in the six counties, where over a thousand republican and loyalist prisoners were held. In October this came to a head, when the Provisional IRA prisoners burned their living huts down. Helicopters flew overhead, spraying CS gas, as soldiers entered the compound and engaged in hand-to-hand fighting with the prisoners. Many injuries resulted, for which scant medical help was offered.

Arden and D'Arcy's position while all this was unfolding answered well to Frantz Fanon's view of the role of the intellectual in post-colonial society. For Fanon, the intellectual held an important place in the developing of necessary new cultural identities, especially if he or she could maintain a supra-national con-sciousness. At first, Arden and D'Arcy found themselves in 'a state of creative isolation',[377] partly because of *The Ballygombeen Bequest* libel case, partly because of the furore over *The Island of the Mighty* at the Royal Shakespeare Theatre, and finally, of course, because of the 'Stalinisation' of Official Sinn Fein, and their expulsion from it.

But their position also contained elements of liberation. Arden noted that up to now he had been living a sort of double life as a writer, creating mainstream dramas for professional theatres, but also joining with D'Arcy in her independent, alternative projects. The problem had come to a head with *The Island of the Mighty*, which at the time he thought was

> the worst thing that had ever happened to me; then I came to see it quite
> simply as one more dip into the (rejuvenating) fountain – only this time
> the water had been scarifyingly hot and some of the people on the far
> bank did not seem to know who I was when I got out.[378]

By rejecting the mainstream theatre, by choosing to be an outsider, Arden – and D'Arcy – were able to please themselves in their creative work, and to retain their integrity which had been so threatened by the events of 1972. They had space and time, in other words, to concentrate on the biggest project they had ever conceived, the work which was to become *The Non-Stop Connolly Show*.

It is perhaps ironic that just at this time, Arden's work was becoming increasingly appreciated. Among others, there were significant studies by John Russell Brown (1972), Simon Trussler (1973), Glenda Leeming (1974) and Albert Hunt (1974), and in 1973 he was awarded the John Whiting Prize. His case remained something of a puzzle, however. Though he had first become known as a Royal Court dramatist, his work was not like that of John Osborne or Arnold Wesker, both strongly naturalist writers focussed on the problems of the individual. Around 1960 the wave of naturalist drama had ceded precedence, at least for many apparently-discriminating critics, to what was called 'the theatre of the absurd', especially the work of Samuel Beckett, Harold Pinter and Eugene Ionesco. But neither naturalism nor the theatre of the absurd could contain Arden or Arden-and-D'Arcy. And in the 1970s, when the kind of socially-conscious, politically-motivated drama which Arden and D'Arcy had pioneered through the 1960s was becoming accepted, they were cast out of the theatre (or they cast themselves out), and the critics hailed other writers – John McGrath, Howard Brenton, David Hare, David Edgar – for works which were like Arden and D'Arcy's perhaps, though they seemed to many to lack both the dramaturgical daring and the command of poetic but speakable English which Arden and D'Arcy possessed. The latter, however, fell through a sort of crack in the history of the drama of this period.

In the spring of 1973, Arden and D'Arcy were invited to become jointly Regents Lecturer at the University of California, Davis, for one term. They were asked to create, and perhaps present, the American section of the James Connolly play they were making. They were given an office, though it had no windows, and an electric typewriter, which Arden found almost impossible to use.[379] They were also given a group of students, who were to help with the research on Connolly's trade unionism and politics, as well as with the playmaking. The students called themselves the 'Stage Left International Circus Collective', or SLICK, and set to work. However, Arden and D'Arcy expected them to work for at least six hours per day, five or six days per week, for the whole ten-week period, and not unsurprisingly, it was not long before some at least began to wilt. Arden and D'Arcy themselves had discovered that next door to the house where they were living was a woman who was a representative for the University Workers Association, and knowledgeable about U.S. labour history. They found themselves spending more and more time exploring current labour problems, going to meetings of the fruit pickers union, uncovering the struggles within the coalminers union, and so on. In Reagan's California, trade unionism was under severe pressure, and even the campus-workers union was struggling to survive. At one meeting they were staggered to hear a woman whose arm had been severed in the course of her work, speak movingly of the kindness of her employer who had visited her in hospital and given her a box of chocolates. The work on James Connolly was progressing in very unexpected directions.

The University was apprised of Arden and D'Arcy's increasing involvement in ongoing struggles. Their project had never been widely approved of, and the support of those in charge of it began to wither away. They were already uneasy at the presence of these two 'radicals' because of what had happened at the Royal Shakespeare Theatre with *The Island of the Mighty*; now they held a social event to which they invited the students, but 'forgot' to ask Arden and D'Arcy. Some students found themselves unable to attend rehearsals; others, resenting the heavy workload and feeling in any case thoroughly uneasy with the left-wing politics which were emerging in the work, withdrew altogether. Perhaps Arden and D'Arcy were being paranoid in their suspicions of all this, but other occurrences were even more disturbing: 'A young woman from a different department was always present at the meetings of our group, writing everything down in a notebook, in furtherance of some vaguely-defined 'thesis' of her own: she took care never to contribute to the discussions she so assiduously attended'.[380] Arden and D'Arcy expelled her from the group, but were informed by the faculty that this was beyond their powers. Matters reached a head when Arden and D'Arcy were summoned to a meeting with the relevant faculty members. They were told that they were not fulfilling their contract, and that consequently they were in danger of not receiving their fee. Arden argued that they were doing work which was similar, if not exactly the same, as that which they had been contracted for. They wished to continue, he said, and if the authorities would permit it, they would create a show which, while perhaps not being 'James Connolly in America', would be like it, and would certainly be worth seeing. He also noted that there seemed to be very little room for left wing politics in USA, to which a severe faculty member, with a strong East European accent, replied ominously: 'I think I know where you are coming from'.[381]

In the upshot, they were allowed to present their show, though not in the main theatre on the campus. It consisted of nearly eight hours of more or less improvised scenes, interspersed with songs, films and the like, somewhat reminiscent of the Vietnam *War Carnival* of 1967. The subject now, however, was the history of labour in America. It was structured round the endlessly recurring confrontations between Henry Dubbs, the archetypical worker, and his boss, who was named Grabitall. The characters had originated in a strip cartoon published in the newspaper of the Socialist Party of America in the early years of the twentieth century. Dubbs was somewhat like the Idle Jack figure Arden had dreamed up for *Two Hundred Years of Labour History* two years earlier – a 'little man' not in a union, naïve, reactionary and gullible. Grabitall, by contrast, was greedy, unfeeling, and appeared sometimes as a boss figure, but sometimes also as an Army General, or indeed as President Nixon. The authors' experiments with masks for actors continued in this show – Dubbs, for instance, though played by different actors, always appeared in the same mask, as did Grabitall no matter what *persona* he was presenting. D'Arcy showed her film about the campus as a place of work, 'an overt recruiting plea for the campus-workers' union' as part of the performance too. Though this final presentation was virtually wholly ignored by the Faculty which was employing the authors, their absence only allowed the participants greater freedom. And at least the three months in America had provided Arden and D'Arcy with everything they needed – including atmosphere, procedures, form-ulae, as well as factual material – to complete the American sequence in the play about Connolly.

Back in Ireland, they had sold their island on Lough Corrib, partly as a prudent measure in the face of Commander Burges's libel action. They moved permanently to the cottage in Corrandulla, and immediately became embroiled in a new struggle. The village was a far-flung scatter of houses round a main road and bordered by a bog, and any cultural or political life in the village seemed to be well in the grip of the parish priest. He was 'an ancient conservative misogynist Greek-classic-loving' man[382] who controlled the community hall by virtue of its position on church land, but who refused permission to almost anyone who wanted to use it for community – or other – purposes. Yet its erection had been paid for by the villagers. 'Some of them were very, very angry and saw the priest's action as a form of robbery'.[383] Having heard something of Arden and D'Arcy's involvement with plays and films, the local people approached them with a view to changing this situation. It was probably D'Arcy who responded most positively to this: Albert Hunt explained the Arden-D'Arcy relationship by saying that 'she would always push John into doing all sorts of things outside of writing plays. I don't mean he did them unwillingly, I mean that if he hadn't had Margaretta he'd probably have been a reclusive writer surrounded by books'.[384] Pam Gems suggested after meeting him that Arden 'could easily be a farmer ... I think to myself he's probably a lively lover though you'd likely have to set fire to the hearth rug to get his head out of a book'. Gems also noted

D'Arcy's smile: 'She looks about twenty, the eyes are full and clear, like a child, her face comes alive'.[385]

Margaretta D'Arcy, c.1974

D'Arcy volunteered their bungalow 'in the spirit of what is traditionally known as a Ceilidh house, or Rambling-house, a place of informal festivity'.[386] The villagers accepted, and it became rather like the cottage at Kirkbymoorside, though the events were even less formal than that, and more local. Few if any of the village people had television at that time, so offering the house as a meeting place for conversation and activities was of a cultural significance hard to comprehend clearly today. The Arden-D'Arcy house was opened at least once a week, and the group, which had no official membership, called themselves 'Corrandulla Arts and Entertainment'. They showed films (including D'Arcy's pre-India film, *The Unfulfilled Dream*), held play-readings and music sessions, and even made their own super-8 movie, a long, loose documentary about the village itself, directed by D'Arcy. She knew that such filming helped the community, because it helped individuals to understand each other. Since she did not edit what was filmed, it avoided being judgmental, and everyone involved enjoyed it because it showed the living community as it was. The qualities in Arden and D'Arcy which were isolated by their friend Tamara Hinchco were those they needed here. She said: 'What I absolutely love about both of them is – they never condescend – *never!* They are as interested in somebody from nowhere (*sic*), and I'd never met that … It's very rare'.[387]

Guests to Corrandulla Arts and Entertainment included Bob Quinn, the film director, playwrights like David Rudkin and Michael Hastings, and campaigners like Frank Crummy and Nell McCafferty. Crummy was an officer of the Irish Society for the Prevention of Cruelty to Children, but he also campaigned on issues such as family planning and contraception, and had in fact been prosecuted for advocating such ideas. He brought a film and some contraceptives to Corrandulla! Nell McCafferty was a radical feminist who discussed lesbianism, but in such a way that the local farming women felt perfectly comfortable. They accepted that this was the sort of thing discussed in the house of Arden and D'Arcy.

Eamon Smullen was another visitor. He was a legendary IRA man, convicted of shooting and badly wounding an informer as long ago as 1943. Sent to Portlaoise gaol, he refused to wear prison clothes and dressed only in blankets. He had worked on the building sites of London, been gaoled in England and saw himself as a pro-Soviet Communist. He had only been released from gaol in England in February 1973, but he was now the Official IRA commander in Dublin. He brought with him a play he had written, *The Terrorists*, concerning an Irish rebellion against British rule in the early nineteenth century, and this was read by the group. He was keen to establish a left-wing theatre in Ireland which could tour to Fidel Castro's Cuba, and he and D'Arcy and Arden discussed making a play about the Ralahine Co-operative set up in the west of Ireland in the early 1830s. This was probably the germination of *Vandaleur's Folly*. Smullen was to be even more important to Arden and D'Arcy when they were seeking to present *The Non-Stop Connolly Show* in Dublin in 1975. His strong backing helped with both the venue and the financing of the project.

Probably the most telling piece of theatre which Corrandulla Arts and Entertainment created, however, was *The Devil and the Parish Pump* which used a cast of five (Arden, D'Arcy, two school students and a local smallholder), and dramatised problems connected with the piping of water to the village, most of which was still reliant at this time on hand pumps. The improvised play managed to transform an 'arid local dispute into a kind of epic folklore struggle',[388] and depicted the devil arriving in Corrandulla and setting one community against another over the pumping of water. The action moves into a dream and manages to refer to all sorts of episodes in Irish history, before the antagonists reach a kind of understanding. It only lasted twenty minutes, but it contained a wild variety of styles and scenes, and even included a short film excerpt, all of which surprised and delighted the local people who packed into the whitewashed bungalow to watch it.

Meanwhile, partly as a result of the popularity of the Arts and Entertainment provided in Arden and D'Arcy's cottage, the campaign to open the community hall was reaching a climax. A meeting was called, and a committee formed in defiance of the parish priest. But by the next day, he had found legal grounds to dissolve the committee, and now he set up his own committee. Suddenly the community hall began to become available – though not to a group of children with whom D'Arcy was working. Her request for space was totally ignored. But when this priest was replaced by a younger man who was an active amateur actor, the problem for the village seemed to be over. True, 'those without money or influence were left on one side', and after elections to the community council, 'if someone was elected who was not acceptable to the ruling junta, the voting papers were conveniently lost',[389] but at least now, thanks in no small measure to Margaretta D'Arcy, the hall was very much open.

Her own conclusions, however, were not all happy. She felt the struggle had demonstrated in little the way tyrannies control and cannibalise popular protest movements, in order that they can continue in power. But her belief in the arts as an agent to energise people, to give them confidence and extend their imaginative sympathy, had also been demonstrated. And Arden and D'Arcy had both shown also the possibility of realizing Fanon's notion of the intellectual's ability and responsibility to push for new cultural and social structures. Without them the village's life would have taken a different, and less constructive, shape.

Fifteen : Non-Stop

In 1975, D'Arcy and Arden presented their most original, most extraordinary work – *The Non-Stop Connolly Show*, a monumental historical epic about James Connolly, the Irish socialist republican leader who with Padraig Pearse had led the 1916 Easter Rising. As *Faust* is to Goethe's life and work, or *The Ring* is to Wagner's, so *The Non-Stop Connolly Show* is to D'Arcy and Arden's. It is the drama which ultimately defines both of them as artists.

The Non-Stop Connolly Show is a cycle of six plays. The first two are each of one act, while the remaining four plays are full length. The cycle opens with Connolly as a young boy among his fellow Irish people in Edinburgh, his birthplace. He seeks useful work, but finding none, enlists as a soldier. He is sent to Ireland, where he encounters both Irish nationalism and socialism. He deserts and, with his new wife, returns to Scotland. Here he becomes engaged in socialist political struggle, but not with any great success. He moves again to Ireland where his world widens: his republicanism brings him into contact with the people of the Irish literary renaissance and their nationalism, while through his socialism he encounters Keir Hardie, Rosa Luxemburg and others. However, he feels he is making little headway with Irish Republican Socialism, and emigrates to the United States. Here he joins the International Workers of the World (the 'Wobblies'), supports the socialist candidate for the Presidency, but again becomes entangled in ideological controversy. He returns again to Ireland, and now becomes a central figure in the 'Great Lockout' and the ensuing General Strike. When the failure of British Labour to support this ensures its collapse, he forms the Irish Citizen Army amid intensifying threats of violence in Ireland and across the world. In the final play, the First World War provides Ireland with the possibility of striking for her own freedom. Joining with Pearse and the IRB, Connolly brings the Citizen Army into the Easter Rising. The Rising fails, and Connolly is shot. But 'this was not history. It has not passed'.

This is a huge epic work lasting nearly twelve hours if presented straight through. First of all, it should be seen as the latest addition to the long tradition of Irish drama which has dominated the British stage, and particularly the nationalist drama of Boucicault (*The Shaughraun, Arragh-na-Pogue*), Yeats and Lady Gregory (*Cathleen ni Houlihan*), Sean O'Casey (the Dublin trilogy) and Brendan Behan (*The Hostage*). But equally, *The Non-Stop Connolly Show* taps into the tradition of day-long epic dramas like the Hindu dramatisations of *The Mahabharata*, and also the western medieval mystery cycles. The ultimate justification for these is that they find and define a communal, social identity, and from that they are able to assert a communal destiny. Thus the English mystery plays define an English identity, which is bound up with Christianity, and from that they affirm the ordinary English person's God-given destiny. As the medieval mind conceived it, this meant relating the past as far back as the Creation to the present, and then on to the Day of Judgment in the far distant future. Identity thus becomes destiny. *The Non-Stop Connolly Show* attempts to do something similar for twentieth century Irish identity and destiny, but it does this not through illuminating the workings of a dominant religion, but by tracing in detail the changing fortunes and continuing struggles of the dominant ideas of the time – republicanism and socialism. And it does this through the story of a poor boy, James Connolly, who grew into a mature revolutionary. As he finds his identity, so he discovers his destiny. And because he is poor, and his community is one which is exploited as a colony, his social perspective – and therefore the play's perspective – is 'from below'. This is crucial in the working out of the theme.

The cycle plunges swiftly into action. Within a few minutes of the opening, we have met James's 'Uncle MacBride' in hiding from the British, and he himself is working for the anti-Fenian Irishman, O'Toole. Soon he is a soldier in Ireland, the House of Commons has been shown passing the Coercion Act, and Ireland is being wracked by the Land League struggle, Parnell's campaigns and the murders of Cavendish and Burke. All this is presented through a combination of song, direct address to the audience, rhymed and unrhymed verse, and conversational dialogue, to say nothing of various theatrical effects from pastiche melodrama to soldier-style square-bashing. The picture of Ireland presented to the young James Connolly is a collage of evictions, murder, repression and desperation, which Connolly struggles to make sense of. He listens and learns, he hears crude nationalist and then crude socialist preachers, he meets a Protestant woman with whom he falls in love. His brain is seething with the ideas that have forced themselves on him. He deserts and returns to Scotland.

But this whirlwind of dramatic action has also introduced a conscious learning process, which takes its impetus from Connolly's own experience of life. He may have viewed things 'from below', but he was by no means unsophisticated and, informed by Connolly's own dynamic philosophy, the play takes care to articulate how his views develop coherence. It sees, as Connolly did, the nationalist struggle as developing out of a combination of the old Gaelic concept of 'nationhood' and the downtrodden Catholic consciousness of solidarity which was a response to the Protestant Ascendancy. But Connolly noticed that something had changed at the very roots of society since the end of the Ascendancy nearly a hundred years before, and that this change had not been taken account of by the nineteenth century Fenians, which was why the latter's attempts at rebellion had always ended in failure. The intervening Industrial Revolution had created quite new and hugely powerful social relationships which had to be integrated into any thinking about the struggle for national freedom.

This recognition brought Connolly into touch with a much wider, more dynamic set of philosophical and political ideas than any of his nationalist predecessors (or contemporaries, for that matter); it also brings this play into the wider mainstream of twentieth century thought. For Connolly, what the industrial revolution meant was that Home Rule was actually a chimera which took no account of world economic realities. The republicanism which he came to advocate was one which depended on the working class throwing off its shackles and finding its own forms of social, economic and political organisation. Thus Connolly comes to suggest that national independence without economic independence is worthless, that nationalism means nothing without socialism. Consequently he comes to link the two struggles, political and industrial, in a wholly new way, and makes progress in one sphere relate to progress in the other. And the addition of socialism to the already strong tradition of nationalism in Irish drama gives the play itself unexpected resonance which is also wholly new. The play, in fact, matches its subject.

Connolly's analysis of Ireland's problems owed more than a little to Karl Marx, and D'Arcy and Arden go on to use a Marxian methodology to dramatise Connolly's struggles. Marx's historical analysis seems to apply to capitalist society, but it also provides writers with a means to create historical drama capable of functioning as the medieval mystery cycles functioned. Marx's identification of the class struggle as the motivating factor of history enables the playwright to locate the play in it, just as the medieval playmakers had located theirs in the Biblical struggle between good and evil. The story of James Connolly is directly fuelled by the struggle between Capital and Labour, and this, as the authors have pointed out, acquires the dimensions of a mythical framework, especially as it works out in dramatic practice:

> The essential Conflict of the fable, which ostensibly was that between
> Capital and Labour, seemed often lost in the tributary struggle between
> opposed factions of the latter: and that this struggle in itself could time
> and again be summarised as the fight between Revolution and Reform –
> an archetypal *agon* for the drama, comparable to such emblematic battles
> as *Carnival v. Lent, Sacred v. Profane Love, Idleness v. Industry,* et cetera.
> *Capital v. Labour* is the overall context for the secondary conflicts, and
> becomes the war between *Evil and Good* or *Darkness and Light* or *Winter
> and Summer.*[390]

It is important to notice that Marxism, though a theory of history, is not simply about the past, or even just about how the past relates to the present, it is about the relationship between the past, the present and the future. Hence the description on the title page: 'a dramatic cycle of continuous struggle', which leads to the final line of the six plays: 'This was not history: it has not passed'.

If the Marxian orientation of *The Non-Stop Connolly Show* is evident in the treatment of the class whose identity it seeks to celebrate, the working class, and particularly the Irish working class, it also greatly informs the devices the authors employ, which are almost always derived from working class or traditional Irish forms of entertainment. This has caused difficulties for some critics and even theatre professionals, for whom the merry, inconsistent, spectacular techniques of D'Arcy and Arden are viewed with suspicion and perhaps distaste. This approach has been noted with regard to other plays by these authors, but *The Non-Stop Connolly Show* uses them with an exuberance unmatched even in their own collected works. There is melodrama, music hall-style interludes and gags, and pantomime tricks. In the American section, there is American vaudeville, as in the dazzling Presidential election scene when Eugene Debs's campaign 'Red Special' chugs round the theatre to an uproarious version of 'Casey Jones', and a finale which should equal that of any Busby Berkeley spectacular as it 'glorifies' the Yankee dollar triumphant. The election to Edinburgh City Council uses techniques borrowed directly from agitprop, and when the mill girls are in dispute with their boss, there is a non-sectarian brass band. Factory work is mimed as on a carnival float and Connolly's search for a job in Ireland becomes a sort of *danse macabre*. The use of Rumour in the final play recalls popular Elizabethan theatre, as does what is perhaps the most striking scene of all, when Connolly is trying to decide whether to throw in his lot with Pearse and the IRB.

This unashamed theatricality, consisting of brief, self-contained units of action which each present a specific content in a specific style deriving from popular entertainment, gives the picture 'from below' its quality of truth. Equally effective is the visual side of the show. There is from the beginning the striking use of a few suggestive backcloths, based, the authors say, 'on the formal emblematic tradition of trade union banners ... in bright colours with no attempt at impressionism or naturalistic representation'.[391] These are also like pantomime backcloths. Flags and banners play an important role – Union Jacks and Irish tricolours, the green flag of Erin, the red flag of labour. When the ethnic groups race to build American capitalism, their flags surmount their achievements; and when the Oppressed Nations and the Controlling Nations confront one another, their flags display their aggressive intents. The unfolding of the Plough and the Stars is a ceremonial moment, as is the unfurling of Connolly's banner, 'We serve neither King nor Kaiser, but Ireland'.

Visually notable, too, is the use of masks and life-size puppets, derived almost certainly from the authors' contact with the New York-based Bread and Puppet Theatre, and their leader, Peter Schumann. *The Irish Times'* reviewer noted, 'The Unacceptable Face of Capitalism is just that: a nasty masked demon putting his spoke in at every turn'.[392] More Schumann-like, perhaps, is Archduke Ferdinand, 'a gloriously uniformed dummy' and the War Demon:

> a tall figure like an oriental battle-god, all covered with spikes, flags, bits
> of armour and weapons. He has a small drum at his waist, which he
> rattles with his fist or knuckles at intervals. He is attended by two
> SUBSIDIARY DEMONS – similarly attired, but of normal human
> stature. They have castanets or small cymbals attached to their spiked
> fingers.

The Oppressed Nations are represented by a Ragged Woman

> all dressed in strips of green, with one eye closed over with a green patch
> and the opposite half of her face dead white ... Such of her body as can be
> seen under her rags is all bloody.

She is taller than the average person 'by several feet', and is confronted by the equally gross Controlling Nations, and this trio is completed by a third giant grotesque representing the Neutral Nations. Thus, spectators are led into 'multiple seeing', as S.L.Bethell puts it: we marvel at the larger-than-life puppet as a puppet, at the same time as we understand his part in the story, and simultaneously comprehend his symbolic meaning within the design of the whole play.

Finally the use of music and song throughout also connects with the way popular culture, particularly Irish popular culture, has treated certain themes and experiences, and thus further reinforces the view 'from below'. A diverse selection of Irish popular songs is used – 'The Peeler and the Goat', 'A Nation Once Again', 'No Irish Need Apply', 'The Sash My Father Wore', and so on – as well as labour songs like 'The Internationale', 'The Red Flag' (used with considerable irony at the end of Part Five), and the rousing American song, 'If the Boss Gets in the Way We're Gonna Roll it Over Him'. Music hall numbers, popular chants and rhymes, and folk songs and ballads, altered where necessary, are used to make specific points. Thus, 'Oh Dear, What Can the Matter Be' acquires new words in the struggle for free speech in Dundee, and the timid British TUC leaders find 'Labour's Burning' when Jim Larkin fires the enthusiasm of his rank and file: they try to 'pour on water'. The narrative is sometimes forwarded by new versions of traditional songs, such as the pedlar's song when Connolly becomes a pedlar, and other songs provide background or necessary information, like the sung description of Connolly's birth and childhood.

All this breaks every convention academia has identified as being compatible with 'serious drama'. And the use of language, similarly, breaks just about every convention that has tyrannised playwrighting for decades. Is it more than convention, or literary decorum, which insists that a verse play must be all in verse, or that a realist play's dialogue must all be in one mode? In D'Arcy and Arden's drama there is none of this timidity in making the transition from one kind of language to another, but rather the boldness and effrontery of the best Eliz-abethans. Verse changes to prose when it needs to, without self-consciousness, rhyme changes to free verse when that is more appropriate. Oratory stands starkly beside conversation, concrete descriptive writing beside abstract theorising. What D'Arcy and Arden create linguistically is an extraordinarily flexible and responsive tool, at its best perhaps (as Shakespeare is at his best) in 'public' language of various sorts, but still capable of coping convincingly with more commonplace matters, as in the scene of sleepy irritation between husband and wife or their humorous attempts to write a newspaper article.

All these devices shape and control the meaning of the play; indeed the 'from below' view of history can only be satisfactorily disclosed by the use of 'from below' devices. They are juxtaposed apparently arbitrarily like the turns of a music hall or circus, but actually they are unobtrusively, carefully marshalled to create a montage from which the themes can emerge in concrete form. This is what the great Soviet film maker, Sergei Eisenstein, called 'an action construction':

> Instead of a static 'reflection' of an event with all possibilities for activity
> within the limits of the event's logical action, we advance to a new plane –
> free montage of arbitrarily selected, independent ... attractions all from
> the stand of establishing certain final thematic effects.[393]

This, according to Eisenstein, is 'the only means by which it is possible to make the final ideological conclusion perceptible' – that is, here, conveying the authors' idea of Ireland's attainable destiny, and their cry for liberty and democracy.

In the end, *The Non-Stop Connolly Show* is about the struggle to claim that future which Connolly foresaw. And it is about the inevitability of struggle. One of its strengths is that it acknowledges that the struggle is complex, and fraught with difficulties and dangers. The freedom it reaches out for embraces colonial and political liberty, democratic control over the institutions of society and above all, freedom from economic want. 'It's like reading Shakespeare', Noëlle O'Hanlon, a participant in later presentations of the *Show,* suggested. 'Every time you read it, you get more out of it'.[394] And indeed in English drama perhaps only Shakespeare's great historical epic, which shows the connections between the city of London and the Gloucestershire countryside, the royal court and a tavern in Eastcheap, can match *The Non-Stop Connolly Show* in breadth of vision and technical virtuosity in handling a mass of intricate and involved material. By use of a montage technique and a lower class viewpoint, it is able, as Shakespeare was, to incorporate myth-ological elements and folk material, while using history as both parable and inspiration with reference to contemporary social and political realities. As such, again like Shakespeare's historical epic, *The Non-Stop Connolly Show* is able to function in a manner akin to that of the medieval mystery play – it enables us to reclaim our heritage, to affirm our identity, and even to understand a little more of our destiny.

The project which culminated in this extraordinary masterpiece had begun with that idea for a play about Gandhi as a means of contributing to the land struggle in the west of Ireland in 1969. But the Gandhian movement seemed to be failing in India, so that the idea had modified into a series of plays about historical and revolutionary characters to explore the wider themes of social justice, political action and the use of history. It was decided to start this with a play about James Connolly, which could be mounted by a company which the authors would form, and tour Ireland. If it was successful, a second play could be added. And so on. But conversations with theatre people, and especially with the director Robert Walker, later Artistic Director of the Theatre Royal, Lincoln, and the Half Moon Theatre in London, who visited Galway at this time, changed this. His enthusiasm for long theatrical epics as well as political theatre spurred Arden and D'Arcy finally to commit to a long epic drama about Connolly, rather than just a single play. Meanwhile Arden had received a commission from Martin Esslin, Head of BBC radio drama, for a play of 60 or 90 minutes on any subject of his own choosing. He proposed Connolly as his subject. But 'the very idea of such a play was rejected out of hand. It might, said Mr Esslin's shamefaced letter, "inflame passions" in the North of Ireland'.[395] (As if passions were not already inflamed in those six counties!) He was soon to let it be known, too, slyly, through informal contact with Arden's agent, that a collaboration with D'Arcy would not be acceptable, either.

Yet collaboration was absolutely at the heart of the creation of *The Non-Stop Connoly Show*. The authors made charts together, illustrating what they termed 'parallel' happenings in Connolly's life in politics and its geography, tacking them on the walls of their workroom. The wall charts deliberately covered too much ground, so that episodes and arguments could be selected according to dramatic needs rather than academic inclusiveness. The process seems usually to have followed a pattern whereby the two authors would discuss the material exhaustively, and how best to make it dramatic. Though often the ideas were D'Arcy's, it was usually Arden who did the actual writing. D'Arcy saw Connolly as a version of 'the little tailor' of folklore – 'no one takes (him) seriously, but (he) waddles through the forest of giants, resourceful and cunning, and eventually succeeds in winning the hand of the princess'.[396] Tamara Hinchco's description of their creative process is worth quoting:

> They talk about what they're going to write. He writes and then she goes over it, and says, 'No, you can't have that, no, you've got to do this, this is no good'. And he'll say, 'Oh, okay, yes ...' and they're puffing on their cigs.[397]

The Non-Stop Connolly Show was as close to being finished as could be at the end of 1974. Now it was a matter of staging it.

The production which happened on Easter Saturday and Sunday 1975 was primarily enabled by Eamon Smullen of the Official Sinn Fein Party, which considerably subsidised the project, and Des Geraghty, a senior official with the Irish Transport and General Workers Union with a love of folk music and poetry. They were the enablers, without whom there would have been no money for the work, no rehearsal space and nowhere to perform. As it was, the production was rehearsed for its early weeks in Official Sinn Fein's headquarters at 31 Gardiner Place in north Dublin, where the costumes and props continued to be stored even after the company moved to Liberty Hall for the final period of rehearsal. And Liberty Hall, Connolly's base in Dublin when he was organising the 1913 strike and the Citizen Army, was the venue, appropriately enough, for the first performance of the cycle. Smullen and Geraghty both watched rehearsals and commented on what they saw, and were on hand when there were problems of organisation to be dealt with. Notably, neither of their organisations made any attempt to interfere with the production or censure or modify the scripts. Others who supported the venture included Eoghan Harris, the film director and OSF member, Michael Mullen, the General-Secretary of ITGWU, and Cathal Goulding, Chief of Staff of the Official IRA.

Those artistically involved included Robert Walker, the theatre director who had urged D'Arcy and Arden to complete the plays, who had just finished directing *The Rocky Horror Show* in London, and who now became part of the *Connolly* directing team. The other director was Jim Sheridan, who had worked not only at the Belfast Lyric Theatre and the Abbey Theatre in Dublin, but also at the Royal Court and the ICA in London, and who was to go on to found the radical Project Theatre Company, for whom he both directed and wrote. These two, with Arden and D'Arcy themselves, were charged with coordinating the production, rather than directing it. In an attempt to avoid the tyrannical structures of companies like the RSC, this was to be a co-operative production. Sheridan and Walker, by all accounts, did extraordinarily well in this ambiguous position, especially since Arden and D'Arcy themselves became increasingly demanding as the rehearsal period proceeded. Democracy in theatrical production is not easy to achieve. Tensions and anger were not avoided here, and when one or other of the directors did cut through disagreements or arguments, it was probably to the final pro-duction's benefit.

The part of Connolly was played by Terence McGinity, a professional actor whose experience ranged from a one-man show about Edgar Allan Poe to the Stanley Kubrick film, *The Adventures of Barry Lyndon*. At the beginning of rehearsals, Finn Arden was to have played Connolly as a boy, and he was eager to do this, but he was unable to get enough time off school, and when McGinity arrived a few weeks into the rehearsal period, it seemed best to give the whole part to him, though it should be added that when the play toured in Ireland after the Liberty Hall first performances, the part of young Connolly was played by Neuss Arden. The Union boss who was Connolly's antagonist in America was played by Barrie Houghton, who was, according to Kane Archer, 'brilliant': 'utterly disciplined and compelling'.[398] Jerry O'Leary played Larkin. He was a young Official Sinn Fein member, who related more perhaps to rock music and football, but who contributed significantly. Others in the cast of twenty-five included Sandra Rudkin, wife of the playwright David Rudkin, the Galway-born writer, Des Hogan, whose first novel, *The Ikon-Makers* was about to be published, and another writer, Pascal Finnan. A few professional actors, including Vincent McCabe, best known for his portrayal of Beckett characters, and Garret Keogh were joined by Don Foley, a stalwart of the Dublin amateur theatre, a number of Fringe theatre actors, students and young workers, as well as members of the Irish Workers Cultural Centre. These were mostly musicians, who now wanted to act, though they were only able to rehearse in the evenings. D'Arcy and Arden's sons also took part, as well as members of na Fianna Éireann, a nationwide young people's club for children approximately nine to thirteen years old. The music and the stage and costume designs were in the hands of Boris and Margaret Howarth, who had worked with Arden and D'Arcy several times since Kirkbymoorside 63, and were now seconded from Welfare State International.

Rehearsals for the first weeks took place in two rooms in 31 Gardiner Place. They started at 10 in the morning and went on till ten at night. They were long and tiring, and some members of the original group dropped out during the twelve weeks. Things were not helped by a shortage of scripts, by the fact that many of the amateurs could only rehearse at specific times, usually evenings, and by Arden and D'Arcy constantly feeling the need to rewrite episodes, scenes or speeches. There was much recasting, too, and scenes were organised and then re-organised. Arden himself gave a good idea of the process in an interview later that year:

> I find it very difficult to define precisely the type of artistic experience
> that this production was. It is something that combined elements of
> authoritarian direction from the author, plus a great deal of much looser,
> democratic joining in by all members of the cast. Everybody, for example,
> was expected to help in the donkey work of making costumes and props,
> and to play some sort of musical instrument during the show. Everybody
> was somehow involved in all the departments which are normally split
> up.[399]

The first performance of *The Non-Stop Connolly Show* began at noon on Easter Saturday, 29 March 1975, and the performance rolled on till about 2.0pm the following day. Before the opening, in a typical D'Arcy flourish, members of the cast, carrying banners and some of the huge puppets which were to feature in the show, paraded up O'Connell Street to the Post Office to the loud beating of a drum. D'Arcy wanted the show to be somewhat akin to 'a giant pop festival for the Left'.[400]

The Conference Hall at Liberty Hall seated up to 500 spectators; its wide, shallow stage was reduced by raised platforms at either end, and actors also appeared in the auditorium itself. Paddy Marsh, who attended and was a notably unsympathetic spectator, his later report being suffused with personal animosity, noted that 'the actors moved freely from one area to another, and at best this provided for a feeling of spontaneity and close contact between the audience and actors, at worst a feeling of confusion'.[401] There was a small screen at the back of the stage, which itself was hung with banners.

During the long performance, there were intervals between the parts of the cycle when coffee and sandwiches, and even full meals, were available, dispensed by volunteers from the ITGWU's Catering Branch to spectators and actors alike. The plays were interrupted by the Hall's regular Saturday night bingo session, and the sections of the *The Connlly Show* were also interspersed with other shows – two of Eisenstein's films, *Battleship Potemkin* and *The Strike*, short plays performed by Red Ladder Theatre from England and Dublin's Puny Little Theatre, songs from the Workers' Cultural Group, and so on. Even more than the *War Carnival* in New York in 1967, this event fulfilled the dream of a 'six or seven or thirteen hours (performance)':[402] as Des Geraghty put it, 'people can wander in and out, the way you do in *fleadheanna*'.[403] 'It was okay for people to walk out', Margaretta D'Arcy said. 'We can fill them in – it's stress-free'.[404] Nevertheless, Des Geraghty recorded 'the consternation of the conservative doorman … seeing the arrival of an audience carrying sleeping bags'![405]

As for the production, it was perhaps dominated by extravagant colour, movement and comedy. Des Hogan, the novelist who participated in the show, wrote later of it being

> lit with colour, masks, flashes of crazy cartoon wit: would one forget Queen Victoria's Jubilee procession, for instance? Or a very arch looking doll who resembled Pope Pius XII being carried across the stage earnestly pursued by a goonish W.B.Yeats and a Maud Gonne who was much his senior?[406]

And even Paddy Marsh conceded that Boris and Margaret Howarth had

> miraculously transformed cardboard boxes, bits of scrap wood, and old clothes into life-size puppets, series of masks, costumes and props, which were highly effective.[407]

Kane Archer concurred: 'Perhaps the unifying, essential element is to be found in Maggie Howarth's splendid, grotesque, obliquely beautiful masks'.[408]

In such an extravaganza, only Connolly was made to resemble his historical original visually, and that only to an extent. Some purist spectators were repelled by actors with scripts in their hands, not understanding the conventions of the production: it was not that it was not professional, but that it was spontaneous, partial, and not streamlined like a Broadway musical. It asked spectators to use their imaginations, and most did. Thus, D'Arcy's frequent presence in the auditorium and Arden's drum-banging to punctuate the scenes left *The Guardian* critic furious: 'It certainly wasn't theatre', she fumed.[409] But it was fun.

The audience never quite filled the number of seats in the hall, but plenty of people attended even if the numbers were, not surprisingly, much lower in the small hours of Easter Sunday morning than on the Saturday afternoon. Those who came included some middle-class intellectuals, teachers and the like, as well as students, theatre people and politically active leftists. But the advertising had concentrated on trade union and political papers, rather than the general press, and the most illuminating article before the performances had appeared on the industrial page of *The Irish Times*. Probably thanks to this, the majority of the spectators were working class Dubliners, who seem to have understood perfectly easily the conventions of the performance, such as when an actor's part is finished,

> he simply drops out of character, walks upstage and in full view picks up
> his next props, or changes costume. We pay him no attention. Or a body
> lies onstage at the end of a scene. How to get it off? Simply by having
> another actor drop out of character, touch the body and have it turn into
> an actor again so that it may walk off on its own.[410]

Eamon Smullen noted:

> It is a measure of Margaretta D'Arcy and John Arden's high artistic
> achievement that an audience, by no means entirely made up of the
> committed, was moved to stand and cheer one play after another. To use
> material from the dull side of life, from the patient, uninspiring dull side
> of everyday revolutionary grind, and to make of it a number of plays
> which could hold an audience for a remarkable length of time, must be
> an achievement seldom equalled in the theatre.[411]

Jeananne Crawley, not a particularly sympathetic observer, also remarked in *The Irish Times* on the standing ovation at the end, and added: 'As an event, it worked'.[412]

The cycle was presented, one play per evening, the following week at Liberty Hall, and then parts of it were shown in different locations in Dublin, including at the two Universities and in Ballymun Community Centre. There were requests from a number of other groups and individuals in Dublin for further per-formances, but it was impossible to accede to these because the company was booked to perform in Belfast. Here, Liam MacMillan of the Belfast Republican Clubs (affiliated to Official Sinn Fein) organised for five of the plays to be presented in Queen's University, and different sections to other Catholic groups. No Protestant group would accept the show, despite its obviously non-sectarian stance, and indeed at Queen's University, no sooner were posters put up than they were torn down again. Perhaps the most positive outcome from the performances in the strife-riven North were highlighted by Margaretta D'Arcy:

> Because of the political situation – internecine assassinations within the
> Republican movement, to say nothing of the bombings, the British Army,
> and the Loyalist killers – some of our actors cried off at the last moment
> before travelling into the 6 counties. So we had to ask for members of the
> audience to read scripts and fill the gap. From then on, all the rules of
> regular theatre were out-of-the-window and Loose Theatre was the only
> way forward.[413]

One of those who joined the cast here was Martin Lynch, and through his experience working with *The Non-Stop Connolly Show*, he began to write his own plays about what was happening in Ireland. The company went on to Downpatrick and Newry. A few days after they left Belfast, Liam MacMillan was shot dead in the street. The last performances of this production of *The Non-Stop Connolly Show* took place in Galway; further performances had been arranged for Cork and Limerick, but a strike prevented the company from travelling, and they had to be cancelled.

This may have been the end of this production of the play, but new productions were created the following year in London and New York. In London, Ed Berman, a naturalised American who ran the Almost Free Theatre and had presented Arden's *The True History of Squire Jonathan and His Unfortunate Treasure*, was seeking a means of celebrating the bi-centenary of American independence. Was Part Four of *The Non-Stop Connolly Show*, telling of Connolly in America, suitable? The conversation led to Berman's acceptance of the whole cycle to be presented at lunchtimes in fourteen one-hour episodes. Beginning symbolically enough on May Day, the complete cycle was presented as staged readings twice over the next month under the direction of the authors. There was a core group of six paid actors, with extra parts being 'read in' by members of the audience dragooned onto the stage for the purpose. In fact, these extra readers were often actors who had heard about the presentations and were excited by it. The shows received good audiences, consisting more of the public than 'theatre people'; some spectators returned over and over until they had taken in the whole huge cycle. Catherine Itzin conjured up the atmosphere :

> The audience sit bunched informally together on chairs in the centre of
> the Almost Free. The 'theatre' takes place in spaces and on platforms
> around them, against a backdrop of colourful cartoon murals, of gloating
> top-hatted British imperialism king-konging it over the wretched Irish

workers ... Heavy-going historical drama? Definitely not. The show is shaped like a popular folk ballad.[414]

It is clear from all of the above that this cycle of plays comprises a remarkable work, but it has largely inhibited the professional theatre. This seems to spring either from its length, or from its politics. Length in the theatre is too often viewed with a conventionalised rigidity, deriving from the Elizabethans' need to finish the play before dark fell in the winter on their open air theatres, or more recently from the Victorian middle class playgoers' need to dine before they could go out to the theatre. In this age of television serials which continue for weeks, this legacy of our ancestors should no longer hold sway. In any case, parts of *The Non-Stop Connolly Show* can be performed independently, as the authors have abundantly shown over decades of presenting sequences from it. Part One, for instance, could be regarded as a self-contained 'Lehrstuck' (as Brecht called his short 'learning plays'); Part Four – Connolly in America – is a wonderful, spectacular self-contained evening full of razzamatazz. I produced the whole cycle at the University of Birmingham in 1981: it lasted almost exactly eleven hours with no cuts and short intervals between the parts. I used nine different actors in the role of Connolly, and the audience came and went as the authors suggest. The programme contained a full synopsis, and we used a blackboard to show exactly which point in the play had been reached.

As for the problem of the politics in this play, a good production of any historical play ought to produce argument among its spectators. This is not something to be afraid of. Even an unsympathetic critic admits as much: Kate Archer, writing in *Plays and Players* after the first production, remarked, 'For all its *longueurs*, drum-thumping, didacticism and preaching to the converted, this did work, and most effectively'.[415] Furthermore, the plays always offer much, even to those who find the politics problematic. How many people accept the medieval Catholic church's view which is expressed so strongly in the medieval mystery cycles? Yet these plays afford immense satisfaction and interest today. Do all the spectators at Stratford-upon-Avon accept Shakespeare's pro-Tudor view of history, or his love of kingly kings? For Arden and D'Arcy to explore the political contentions of Ireland in the twentieth century was actually extremely brave. As Gavin Richards remarked:

> If you take on historical developments happening in front of you then it is almost inevitable that you will get into conflict. They (Arden and D'Arcy) were in the forefront of theatre work and their influence has been immense. John is a genius writer, but that wasn't the main issue ... His ability to create good drama and to write well was secondary to the material and the courage that was required to deal with the material'.[416]

And the Irish actor Stephen Rea said: 'The fact that he took up the cause of Ireland was wonderful and very important to us when the English theatre really wasn't interested'.[417]

Critics who have engaged with *The Non-Stop Connolly Show* have been virtually unanimous in its praise. Thus, Chambers and Prior wrote:

> Who else in the contemporary theatre but Arden and D'Arcy could have
> held together such diverse strands under the spinning weight of their
> centrifugal tendencies? *The Non-Stop Connolly Show* has fair claim to
> being one of the finest pieces of postwar drama in the English language. It
> is a disgrace that none of the big English companies has even tried to
> present it.[418]

Julian Hilton called the cycle 'perhaps the single most impressive achievement of the British theatre in the seventies',[419] while for Albert Hunt, too, it provided 'the major theatrical development in Britain in the 1970s'.[420]

And for the authors? Nearly thirty years after that landmark production at Dublin's Liberty Hall, Arden recorded that 'it is still probably the work I am most proud of and happiest with',[421] while D'Arcy wrote in the mid-1980s: 'our vows that we had made so many years before had now come to fruition. We made theatre that satisfied and excited us'.[422]

Sixteen : Pinpricks and Follies

The Non-Stop Connolly Show was probably the final embodiment of the dream which D'Arcy and Arden had shared since that fateful evening in the Earl's Court garden twenty years before. The rest of their lives was spent expanding the concept beyond the confines of the theatre as such, finding new means, new avenues down which to take their work and, in a sense, theatricalising life. And if Arden had up till now seemed perhaps the leader in their search, as their concerns spread outwards, it appeared that the lead was more and more taken by D'Arcy. It was, however, Arden who was most prominent in their next noticeable project.

Less than three months after the first performance of *The Non-Stop Connolly Show*, the film *Caoineadh Airt Uí Laoire* (*Lament for Art O'Leary*) was premiered in Dublin. It was directed by Bob Quinn, and had John Arden in a leading role. Quinn was a Connemara-based film maker dedicated to the Irish language, a trail-blazing and untameable talent making mostly Gaelic films for television. His success may be gauged by the fact that he was appointed a member of the RTE Authority in 1995; and his integrity by the fact that four years later he resigned and lifted the lid on some of the goings-on in RTE in his book, *Maverick*.

Lament for Art O'Leary was based on a famous and moving eighteenth century lament, written by Eileen, widow of the eponymous hero. The film received some financial backing from Official Sinn Fein and employed some members of the Corandulla Arts and Entertainment group, including Margaretta D'Arcy, as extras.

The film nails its colours to the mast at the outset with a quotation from James Connolly: 'Fortunately the Irish character has proven too difficult to press into respectable foreign moulds'.[423] It goes on to examine this proposition by creating, as it were, a film within a film. An English film director (played by a heavily-bespectacled and mane-haired John Arden) has obtained money to make a film in the Irish language based on the eighteenth century *Lament for Art O'Leary*. The opening scenes show his amateur cast gathering for a rehearsal. The director, irascible, something of a bully, shows a scene or two which have already been shot. His tetchiness increases to anger as the local 'actors', most notably the player of O'Leary (Seán Bán Breathnach), become less and less responsive to his direction, and to the discipline he is trying to impose upon them. Finally, there is a con-frontation between the director and the leading actor. The director is thrown to the floor. The actors celebrate with a ceilidh at the local pub. Intercut with this 'story' are scenes from the life of O'Leary, a cocky young squireen who has returned home after fighting in European wars. He marries his beloved Eileen and they have a child, but he runs foul of his English landlord, the local sheriff, Mr Morris (also played by John Arden, this time without spectacles but with a Yorkshire accent). When

O'Leary's horse outpaces Morris's in a race, the latter (as was his right under the British laws of the time) orders O'Leary to sell the animal to him for a paltry five pounds. O'Leary knocks Morris down. In a fury, Morris orders up the redcoats, who stalk O'Leary and shoot him dead. In an emotional finale, an old woman gathering firewood covers O'Leary's body with her shawl, while the horse returns home riderless. Eileen clutches the reins: they are stained with blood. It carries her to the body. Then we see the coffin carried in a small sombre procession silhouetted against the wind-slashed sea.

John Arden in Lament for Art O'Leary, 1975

Through its use of montage, and sophisticated cross-cutting (for example, from the confrontation between the director and the actor to the fight between Morris and O'Leary), the film becomes a lament for Irish culture and Irish values. 'After all', the English director insists at one point, 'it's just a play with no real relevance to what's going on today'. The director's voice over the action (for instance, during the horse race, we hear him bawling, 'Read your scripts, damn you!') constantly reminds us that we are watching a film, and this is reinforced by the way characters in eighteenth century dress mingle with people of today. The film thus shares with the Irish plays of D'Arcy and Arden both a non-real method and an urgent intent. The leading Irish film critic, Kevin Rockett, noted:

> Its self-reflective and multi-layered unfolding of the narrative outline draws attention to the film's construction and thereby invites the audience to participate in uncovering its meaning. Film is used in the theatrical space, actors in the present comment on their eighteenth-century costumed appearance and the inter-changeability of actors between the present and the past all lead to a questioning of historical truth.[424]

The film was used by Official Sinn Fein to promote cultural engagement across the whole of Ireland:

As darkness fell in Belfast on Wednesday 29 October 1975 ... in the Cypress Street Club Des O'Hagan was setting up a projector for the showing of *Caoineadh Airt Uí Laoire*, to be introduced by Eamon Smullen. In McKenna's Bar in the Markets, Robbie Elliman and two comrades were among the regulars enjoying a pint. Suddenly one of the group, Jim Mullen, saw three masked men burst in through the front door. One of the gunmen shouted 'Freeze.' He had an Armalite. He ... was aiming at Robbie Elliman's chest. He fired six or seven shots and then the three men ran out. I was lying on the floor and I told the barmaid to call an ambulance. I knew Robbie was dead.[425]

Hanley and Millar go on to describe the Provo onslaught against Official Sinn Fein which took place that evening all across Belfast. It was the signal for a brutal struggle between the two groups which racked the six counties and which, despite two or three apparent 'truces', lasted until well into 1976.

Indeed it seemed that politics in general were being destabilised in the north. Unionism was splitting into more and less hard-line groupings; on the left, the moderates were crystallising in the SDLP (Social Democratic and Labour Party) and those further to the left into People's Democracy; while republicanism was split between the Provisionals (Sinn Fein and IRA), the Officials (to which Arden and D'Arcy had belonged in the south), and the Irish Republican Socialist Party (IRSP) each with its own paramilitary volunteers. All these groups were in conflict with each other: internecine violence, sectarian violence and the violence of despair brought terrifying numbers of killings, which also spilled into England. On 27 November 1975, Ross McWhirter, a right wing pro-Unionist journalist and compiler of *The Guinness Book of Records*, was shot dead at his home in Enfield, and ten days later, four IRA men held two Londoners hostage for five days in their flat in Balcombe Street. In July 1976 the British ambassador to the Republic, Christopher Ewart-Biggs, was assassinated in Dublin by Provisional IRA.

Some of this passed Arden by, for later in 1975 he went as Writer in Residence to the University of New England in Armidale, Australia. For reasons connected with *The Ballygoimbeen Bequest* libel case, he had rejected the opportunity to be Creative Writing Fellow at the University of Leicester at the time, but this seemed far enough away to be acceptable. During his time in New South Wales, he wrote the essay, 'Playwrights and Play-Writers', making an important distinction between the genuine skills of the playwright ('wright' being the old word for 'maker'), and those journeymen dramatists who simply write plays. The distinction is important, and perhaps more so now when the dramatic author is often referred to as a 'playwrite'. Arden points out that where the 'play-writer' needs a director to make his creation effective on the stage, the 'playwright' uses all the tools of the theatre to create something which the director meddles with at his peril. Did Shakespeare need a director? Did Moliere? The essay, which was delivered as a lecture not only at Armidale but also at Sydney University, is heavy with unvoiced references to the *Island of the Mighty* debacle. Arden also gave a public lecture on Shakespeare, which was well received, and joined with other members of the academic staff to act in an enjoyable production of Chekhov's *The Wedding*. Importantly, too, he began work on what would turn into the radio play, *Pearl*.

Meanwhile, the unresolved libel suit was still hanging over Arden and D'Arcy. Commander Burges seemed intent on claiming maximum damages from them in court, apparently happy to bankrupt them. They were called to make sworn affidavits about the case more than once. They rented a property in Galway city to reduce what could be claimed from them if they lost the case, and moved there. Another new beginning. D'Arcy introduced herself by filming people there, as she had in Kirkbymoorside and Corandulla. She soon had many hours of unedited film, which came to be called *The Hidden Valley* by the locals. As before, the film was never critical of the community, rather it observed the people, attempting to show what was happening, exposing simply something living. Seeing themselves on film often excited those who were filmed and enhanced their appreciation of their own neighbours. And though she never showed it publicly, D'Arcy offered those in the film a copy of either all eleven hours she had recorded or of the sequences in which they themselves appeared.

It was about this time, too, that D'Arcy became pregnant for the seventh time. The baby girl, she wrote, 'died inside me. I felt I couldn't cope'.[426] She wrote a poem about it:

> *Dead Foetus*
> The pain seeps as through a filter
> into the sponges of hope.
> Even though the bands were to be removed
> it is not the bands holding her together,
> the inner one curled tight
> not chewing her thumb.
> She is unaware
> the placenta has shrunk.
> Dried skin and bones
> like a shaven rat:
> only the teeth yellowish
> grin through the
> wizened face.[427]

These were not easy times emotionally for D'Arcy or Arden. Commissions dried up. She was suspected of being a Provisional IRA member. Nor was it easy financially, and D'Arcy was soon to take a job cleaning local government offices in Galway in order to make ends meet.

However, two lecturers from Galway University, Des Johnson and Pat Sheeran, who had stepped in to read parts in *The Non-Stop Connolly Show* when it was presented with a much-reduced cast in Galway in 1975, proposed to extend their participation in active drama. Arden and D'Arcy joined them and a few other lecturers to set up a one-evening-per-week workshop, when they played drama games and improvised, their work often based on ideas from Viola Spolin's well-known book, *Improvisation for the Theater*. From this grew the Galway Theatre Workshop, which answered to some degree Arden's desire for communality, and whose first session was held on 26 February 1976.

The early meetings of the Galway Theatre Workshop coincided with a strike at a local factory manufacturing fork-lift trucks, where a shop steward had been sacked. D'Arcy had made a short film in support of the striking workers, which was shown in the autumn of 1975. The workers at the Crown Control factory were members of the same union as many of the University staff, but when the factory workers asked the University members for some show of solidarity they were met with a fairly dusty answer. The Theatre Workshop had improvised around this subject since it seemed a suitable subject for a communally-created drama. *Sean O'Scrudu* was the result. It questions what a university is for, and how it should relate to the society which pays for it. It begins with an academic lecture interrupted by improvised historical interludes on the life and death of Socrates, the prosecution of Galileo, and so on, until in 1908 the British Government establishes Belfast University and the National University of Ireland. Is the purpose of these institutions free enquiry, or do they exist to serve the interests of the colonial state? Meanwhile we see Sean O'Scrudu, a bright lad who attends Uni-versity, joins a union 'riddled with dubious goings-on',[428] and is confronted with an industrial dispute. What should he do? He feels sorry for the strikers, but 'we do have to understand both sides of the question'.[429] His confusion becomes a virtue in his mind, and despite his membership of the union, he finds himself rejecting the philosophy and role of trade unionism in capitalist society. The play was an 'exercise in the academic "disputatory" style, taken to the point of verbal knockabout',[430] but its target audience, academics at Galway University College, were not much amused.

That might have been that, but later in 1976 two people, Marie and Noel Murray, were sentenced to death for shooting an off-duty policeman. Protests were immediate, but in the prevailing political climate, hardly tolerated. D'Arcy, however, noticed Miriam Daly, 'an Irish historian from Queen's University, Belfast, (who) stood outside the Dublin General Post Office and denounced the sentence ... I had never heard a woman be so passionate and ferocious. She urged us into action'.[431]

She and Arden advertised in the local paper for anyone who would be willing to participate in a rough theatre piece opposing the death penalty. About half a dozen people responded. First this new group wrote a letter of protest, then they began trying to put together a play for street performance. But disagreements about the application of the material – whether it was to concentrate on the principle of capital punishment or the particular case of Marie and Noel Murray – caused a split in the group, and their problems were exacerbated by a 'ferocious editorial'[432] in *The Connacht Sentinel*, attacking their integrity. Nevertheless, by November 1976 they had created *The Hunting of the Mongrel Fox*, a powerful and passionate play, and surprisingly formal in construction considering the informal context. It includes quotations which illustrate the church's teaching on the sanctity of life, the judicial position and the voters' responsibility, an exploration of political positions, and the doubts of the people compared with the certainty of the government. The second half of the play dramatises Mary's dream of the hounds of the establishment hunting their victim, whose head is bloodily severed. There are some notably theatrical effects, including the judge's silencing of the press by placing bags over the heads of the newspaper editors, and the presentation of the International Monetary Fund as a circus animal trainer and the Irish government as a performing dog. The scenario also offers scope for improvised embellishments for different performances. Miriam Daly and her husband, John Daly, came to Galway to see a performance of the play, which was put on specially for them in D'Arcy and Arden's house in St Bridget's Place Lower; and Daly then invited the group to Belfast to perform it. Did the play have any lasting effect? It is worth noticing that Marie and Noel Murray were reprieved.

Immediately after *The Hunting of the Mongrel Fox*, the controversy over housing gipsies and travelling people in Galway recurred, and the Theatre Workshop decided to explore this, too. As we have seen, Arden and D'Arcy had become involved in these matters before they went to India, and of course Arden's second performed play, *Live Like Pigs*, centred on the problem of sedentary and travelling people living side by side. In 1968 in Galway, students had marched for the rights of travellers, and they had been confronted by groups of council house tenants determined to prevent travellers gaining access to public housing. In 1970, a Mrs Furey had been found squatting in a condemned building with six children, having been on the housing 'list' for more than ten years. When the council attempted to re-house her, over three hundred people on the estate objected: bloodshed was threatened if the proposal to accommodate Mrs Furey were not stopped. In 1974, a Labour councillor in Mayo had proposed compulsory sterilisation for all travelling people, followed by their deportation to the Aran Islands. It was an ugly situation, and Arden, D'Arcy, Pat Sheeran and others had considerable courage in facing it.

No Room at the Inn was presented, topically enough, at Christmas, 1976. The position of travellers in Galway, and the council's negative attitude, is made clear in a series of scenes. Then, in a dream, a rich Arab arrives in Galway. The councillors think he is an oil sheikh, and rush to please him. He wants a child 'born under the stars'. They think he wants to *buy* a child, so bring him a traveller's child, whom he 'experiences'. When he is gone, they find his box, from which emerges a genie. The genie takes them back through history to seventeenth century Galway and the horrors of the Protestant Ascendancy, when the Irish were the victims of cruel and bigoted discrimination. The councillors awake, and sweep the travellers under the carpet – literally. Calling this work 'an unabashedly confrontational piece', Mary Burke argued that '*No Room at the Inn* collapsed the walls between stage and public space, performance and politics'.[433] She goes on to note that heretofore plays about travellers had always been presented in the cosy confines of a theatre – Arden and D'Arcy had dared to take the subject onto the streets. Moreover, apart from Ewan MacColl's radio ballad, *The Travelling People*, it was hard to think of another drama in which authentic travellers' voices were heard. Again according to Mary Burke, after this, the travelling community gained confidence, won some respect and their spokesperson was even able to gain elected political office in Galway. Nevertheless the show was not always received happily: at least one landlord stopped the performance in his pub when he understood the political content.

In the spring of 1977, Galway Theatre Workshop presented a fourth piece of 'immediate rough theatre', *Mary's Name*. Beginning by examining the pressures on women to change their names when they get married, the montage of scenes broadened out to look more generally at the status of women in the Republic of Ireland. Several of the scenes relied more on mime than words. But the single performance in Galway for the University Branch of the Workers Union caused much controversy and consternation, especially among the male lecturers, and led directly to the foundation of a women's group there. After that, with a grant of £75 from the Irish Arts Council, the play was taken to Belfast, as had been *The Hunting of Mongrel Fox*.

A final piece of guerrilla theatre from the Theatre Workshop took place when the Taoiseach, Liam Cosgrave, visited Galway on 2 June during the general election campaign. Warned that any demonstration would not be met with sympathy, D'Arcy and her two companions on the day, Eva Doherty and James Raftery, put pillow-cases over their heads so that they vaguely resembled Ku Klux Klan members, and joined the crowds awaiting the Taoiseach. When his party appeared on stage, the three 'actors' moved to the front of the audience, where they were again warned not to interrupt. However, when Cosgrave began speaking, they started to sing. Immediately they were arrested and whisked off to the police station. Unfortunately for the police, however, there were people in the crowd who did not appreciate this, and led by a lawyer who told the police they were being ridiculous, the demonstrators demanded the captives' immediate release. After two hours, the police, asserting that the 'prisoners' had been held 'for their own protection',[434] let them go. To general amazement, Cosgrave's Fine Gael went on to lose the election and Jack Lynch became Taoiseach of a Fianna Fail government. Could Galway Theatre Workshop's intervention have changed the course of Irish history?

In all Galway Theatre Workshop's work, D'Arcy was the visible leader, directing the plays and driving the group forward. She was not dogmatic with members of the group, but nor was she easy to convince of alternatives. Noëlle O'Hanlon recalled how 'she knew so much, and she'd worked out her own position so clearly, that you'd really have to argue your case if you wanted something to be changed'. Even with Arden she rarely compromised. 'John would say we should do something, and Margaretta would tell him to shut up. But she was the one leading it, John was more in the background'. This is not to say that Arden's contribution was negligible. On the contrary, O'Hanlon also said: 'His contribution was more hidden … I think more happens within the couple rather than publicly. You see what she does and what she contributes, but I'm wondering what would she have done without John?'[435]

These street plays of Galway's Theatre Workshop initially recall the Russian revolutionary agitprop dramas of the Blue Blouses and others, but they were less professional, more provisional than them, and the political situation within which they were operating was much different. But they are excellent examples of what D'Arcy was to call 'Loose Theatre', and as such they deserve more than the almost total critical silence with which they have been greeted beyond the city boundaries of Galway, even though Methuen published them in *Arden and D'Arcy: Plays One* in 1991. One of the few who has mentioned them is John McGrath, director of the 7:84 Theatre Company, who commented perceptively:

> An intelligent and tradition-conscious writer like John Arden, in his early
> plays, was bringing fragments of an older popular tradition into the
> framework of bourgeois plays – the ballads of *Musgrave*, the songs and
> the language of *Live Like Pigs*, were fitted into a bourgeois theatre form,
> and presented to a (very small) audience of cosmopolitan culture-
> purveyors. But as time went by, Arden – now working with D'Arcy –
> began to turn over the form as well: *The Ballygombeen Bequest* being the
> finest example, though their 'Muggins' play with CAST, and I believe
> some of their street theatre, broke the formal barriers as well.[436]

Later that year, Arden and D'Arcy went to London where their trial for libel was to be heard. While they were away, certain insidious political pressures were brought to bear on those who had been active in Galway Theatre Workshop. Members left the area. When D'Arcy tried to re-start it in 1978, no-one was willing to join.

222

In London, the libel suit was settled, but not without some wrangling. It had been almost five years since *The Ballygombeen Bequest* had been halted: 'it was murderous', Arden said,[437] and the playwright Fidelio Carver in his novel *Jack Juggler and the Emperor's Whore*, who is similarly stung, speaks of how the years have made his reputation 'fester like a cat's corpse in a cesspit', quoting Charles Dickens: 'the protracted and wearing anxiety and expense of the law in its most oppressive form, its torture from hour to hour, its weary days and sleepless nights ...'[438]

The first hearing was on 17 October 1977 before the notorious judge, Melford Stevenson, who had refused bail to Ian Purdie when he had been accused of fire-bombing in 1970. His character may be judged from the fact that he had once remarked that the person before him was only accused of 'a pretty anaemic sort of rape' because he had once been the victim's boy friend; and he called the 1967 Sexual Offences Act 'a bugger's charter'. He was in fact not a particularly good lawyer: he had unsuccessfully defended Ruth Ellis, the last woman to be hanged in England, and had equally unsuccessfully prosecuted the infamous John Bodkin Adams, and been heavily criticised in each case. Arden and D'Arcy were represented by Emlyn Hooson, the Liberal M.P. for Montgomeryshire, who had represented Ian Brady, the 'Moors murderer', fifteen years earlier, and Commander Burges's barrister was Leon Brittan, a Conservative M.P. later to be Home Secretary and a European Commissioner.

Commander Burges claimed that the landlord presented in *The Ballygombeen Bequest*, who got his tenant drunk in order to cheat him out of his rights, could be identified with himself. Arden and D'Arcy maintained that within the context of the play, which would be demonstrated to the court by a long series of eminent Irish scholars and commentators as witnesses, this amounted to 'fair comment'. Judge Stevenson was not minded to admit such a defence. He 'threw up his hands and played, as he so often did, to the gallery: "Do we really have to dredge over acres and acres of soggy Irish bog, in the hope of picking up the odd Irishman here and there?"'[439] It was bad enough, he thought, that the members of the jury had to read the play, which he described as 'this turgid piece of prose'. Further exchanges were recorded by Catherine Itzin, who was in court:

> When the defence replied: 'Milord, these are famous British playwrights,'
> the Judge said: 'I've never heard of them. I have no pretensions to being
> called a man of culture!' He didn't think 'we'd do a disservice to the
> theatre if this case were never heard of again.[440]

'Mr Leon Brittan, counsel for Mr Burges, asked for the Ardens' defence of fair comment on a matter of public interest to be struck out', according to *The Times*,

223

and 'after legal argument between Mr Brittan and Mr Emlyn Hooson, QC, Mr Justice Melford Stevenson agreed to Mr Hooson's request for an adjournment'.[441]

Hooson suggested to Arden and D'Arcy that some character references from the theatrical profession would be useful. Accordingly, Arden sought support from old theatre colleagues but found when called upon like this, 'they all ran like scalded cats ... But John Osborne responded straightaway and said immediately that he would give evidence. It was a very kind gesture', Arden added, 'because I hardly knew him',[442] though he had spent the night of 17 September 1961 in gaol with him. Hooson was further able to show that 7:84 Theatre Company also bore a share of the responsibility. By the time the hearing was resumed on 1 December, a settlement had been agreed: Arden and D'Arcy still denied libel, but they did apologise to Commander Burges and they did agree to make changes to the play. They pleaded impecuniousness, but the damages they had to pay were still several thousand pounds. The fact that *The Little Gray Home in the West* is probably a better play that *The Ballygombeen Bequest* is about the only positive outcome to a hugely depressing affair, one which left Arden and D'Arcy considerably impoverished.

By the time of the libel trial, Arden's collection of essays, provocatively entitled *To Present the Pretence*, had been published. The book's contents were mostly reprints of work from periodicals, from *Peace News* to *History Workshop*. They were divided into four sections: 'Ancient Principles', a series of shortish essays on dramatic writers (and one filmmaker) whose work Arden admired – Sean O'Casey, Ben Jonson, Brecht, Lorca; 'The Matter of Vietnam', describing the Vietnam *War Carnival* and discussing other related matters; 'The Matter of Ireland', including long essays on the Chhau dancers from Purulia and *The Non-Stop Connolly Show*; and 'The Matter of Britain', describing *The Island of the Mighty* imbroglio as well as reprinting the lecture 'Playwrights and Play-Writers' delivered in Australia. It is an impressive and thought-provoking collection, which Redmond O'Hanlon called 'a fascinating work which chronicles the itinerary of a man who took the risk of opening himself and his art to the great forces of contemporary history'.[443] It should be read in conjunction with Arden's comments, also published in 1977, by James Vinson in *Contemporary Dramatists*. Here Arden argues that the gap between the playwright and the working theatre is too wide:

> Figures such as the Director and the Scenic Designer, whose relevance to good dramatic writing is at best marginal, have increased their power and influence in no small measure during the past few years: and they stand ominously between playwright and actors, inhibiting proper communication.[444]

He called on playwrights to conjoin in an active combination 'to secure conditions-of-work and artistic control over the products of their imagination', and also to combine with the actors, and thus become absorbed into the theatre as 'co-workers'. But he added that he was 'aware that these requirements go against all current trends'.[445]

Nevertheless, Arden and D'Arcy threw themselves into helping to create a Theatre Writers Group, which became the Theatre Writers Union, affiliated to the TUC. D'Arcy's diary records some of the struggles, and conjures well the atmosphere of the time:

> *Fri 6 Jan 1978*
>
> Went to delegate meeting at Pam Gems'. David Lan, Linda, George, Greg, J.A., Barbara Creagh, Pam Gems, Caryl Churchill & hubby came along to discuss legality of the blacking of TWU by TUC. Have to be careful to avoid libel. Greg had recommendations for next general meeting on 22nd. Rules of procedure, said my motion on Ireland & David Edgar's motions were illegal because of wording. Linda thought the interim agreement was illegal because only 7-and-a-half was on it. We left. It was later found out that she had been reading the wrong motion which had been rejected by the assembly.

> *Floating diary entry, 10 or 11 Jan 1978*
>
> Went to negotiating committee at Jeremy's. Edgar wants us to make concessions on RSC & Nat. Theatre contracts. I think it is v. dangerous and rather similar to wage agreements whereby better-paid workers have to level off with lower-paid workers instead of the other way round.

She adds in 2004: 'One of our main demands was for playwrights to control their own work and their rewrites; David Edgar rejected that out of hand. George thought that conceding anything in the beginning was bad; we should stand up solid. The negotiations dragged on'.[446]

If D'Arcy and Arden were becoming out of step with their playwrighting colleagues, how much more was that true of their relationship with the mainstream British theatre. D'Arcy noted laconically: 'The gap between us and the theatre was widening',[447] partly because, as Arden said,

> The Aldwych (the Royal Shakespeare Company's London theatre) and the National and the Royal Court are supposedly in competition, but if you get a bad name in one, it spreads. And they do more or less control the market for work of a certain type ... large-scale work'.[448]

D'Arcy added that this then 'also determines what plays are being sold abroad',[449] so that she and Arden were in a particularly unpleasant double bind. 'The management structure is ... an alienating and alienated hierarchy', Arden concluded.[450] To Julian Hilton, this appeared as a potential strength. 'It may be', he reflected,

> that one source of Arden's inventiveness lies the fact that, through his longstanding conflict with the theatre establishment, he has had to improvise and has never been able to rely on efficient professional staging to cover any deficiencies in his conceptions.[451]

But the fact was that the market for Arden and D'Arcy was contracting rapidly. Perhaps D'Arcy's Irish nationality (and Arden's calling Ireland 'home') did not help. She compared the solidarity of French writers during the Algerian war of independence both with one another and with the colonial people fighting the French imperialists, to the fear and ignorance of British writers over the Irish situation. The support D'Arcy and Arden gave at this time to London groups working to have British troops in Ireland withdrawn did not endear them to their colleagues, either. If to objective observers like Colin Chambers and Mike Prior, the treatment of Arden and D'Arcy's work indicated 'a basic deficiency in the structure of British theatre',[452] it did not halt their gradual exclusion.

These were extremely difficult days for Arden and D'Arcy. No theatre was prepared to give them a commission, and though Arden might have obtained something for himself, it would be on the strict condition, made clear by Martin Esslin, that D'Arcy was in no way involved. Financially, they were in an increasingly precarious position, even after D'Arcy accepted the cleaning job to bring in enough to enable them to eat. Almost worse was the inevitable stress the situation caused them.

Almost the only haven they could find for theatre work was Ed Berman's Almost Free Theatre, where *Squire Jonathan* and *The Non-Stop Connolly Show* had already been produced. Now D'Arcy staged her *A Pinprick of History* there. This play begins as a sort of conference set a hundred years into the future, when people come to celebrate their revolutions. Only Britain has not had a revolution, and an expresssionistic montage of episodes – read snippets, drumming, chanting of slogans – leads, after some interesting consultation with the audience, into a sequence about Irish history. Ireland's problems are seen as being compounded by, first, the incompetence of the British trades unions, second, the vacillations and pusillanimity of British artists and writers, and finally, backward elements of the Irish bourgeoisie. But Galway Theatre Workshop had intervened! The Spirit of Ireland was seen, first held back by a police cordon, then pursued by the Irish constitutional political parties. Then came the election race which was interrupted by D'Arcy and her colleagues with pillow-cases over their heads! The result was the winning of a seat by an independent socialist, which caused panic in 'establishment' circles, and silence from 'progressive' British playwrights. After considerable dramatic action, the audience was asked:

1. Should Britain leave Ireland?
2. How can they secure open access to information to enable them to answer question no. 1?
3. How can they secure themselves from the malefactions of the British legal system if they come up against it in their search for the answer to question no. 2?[453]

This summary does scant justice to an extraordinary work of theatre, a *tour de force* unlike almost anything seen at this time, though with echoes of (among other things) early Soviet drama, German Expressionism of the 1920s, the Workers Theatre Movement of the 1930s, and even fragments of the Theatre of the Absurd. It was disturbing, provocative, spectacular, but also topical, so that sadly it could probably never be revived. Even then, 'if you didn't know your politics, you wouldn't know what was happening in the play', as D'Arcy admitted.[454] *A Pinprick of History* attacked the British leftist intelligentsia for collusion with what was happening in Ireland, including the militarism, and the torture, murder and oppression of Irish people. But because it was witty, fast-paced and anarchistic, few intellectuals grasped its import. For D'Arcy this was a further cause for disillusion.

Events in Ireland were leading inexorably towards another crisis. Official Sinn Fein, the party still supported by D'Arcy and Arden, continued to pursue its dynamic cultural policy, supporting the Dublin Arts Project's exhibitions and theatre productions (including Eamon Smullen's 'Brecht-influenced plays expounding SFWP ideology'[455]) as well as its own publishing house, Repsol. By now it was generally referred to as 'The Workers Party' (hence SFWP above). But the real focus was moving now towards the prisons. Britain had withdrawn 'special category' (i.e. political) status from those convicted of terrorist offences in 1976, and by 1978 some three hundred republican prisoners were 'on the blanket', that is, while political status was denied, they refused to wear prison uniform or conform to prison regulations. In January 1978, at the European Court in Strasberg, Britain was found guilty of 'degrading and inhuman treatment' of prisoners in the Maze prison, now extended with the building of eight new 'H Blocks'. The 'blanket' protest turned into a 'dirty' protest: prisoners refused to 'slop out', and soon they began to daub their cell walls with excrement. The protests were taking place in the women's gaol in Armagh, too.

In this climate, no-one in Britain seemed willing to confront the situation by staging plays about it. Arden and D'Arcy approached Stuart Burge and the Half Moon Theatre, both of whom, apparently showing interest, actually prevaricated. D'Arcy 'felt ready to implode with spontaneous combustion'.[456] She became pregnant again, and decided to abort the baby. She wrote in her diary in February 1978:

Should I state now that I have very little interest in the theatre? But what am I going to do, am I really redundant? Middle-aged, no skills, no wonder I am always getting pregnant.[457]

Arden, too, 'came under terrible stress',[458] since as a writer he felt compelled to write about his experiences, yet if he wrote with D'Arcy (as he wanted to), nobody in British theatre would consider his work. They thought about writing individually, and *A Pinprick of History* was D'Arcy's alone, as well as some works she created with Finola Keogh and others for presentation at the Irish Club in Islington – the letters of Countess Markiewicz and Eva Gore-Booth, and a documentary, *West of Ireland Women Speak*.

Meanwhile, Arden had also created a play without D'Arcy's collaboration, his radio drama, *Pearl*, which was broadcast by the BBC on 3 July 1978. It was directed by Alfred Bradley, who 'told a few little lies to his BBC bosses about the play's subject' in order to make sure it was broadcast.[459] This was because the play dealt with Irish problems, which the BBC still seemed not to know how to deal with. It was, after all, less than ten years since Martin Esslin had cut the Irish passages from the broadcast version of *The Hero Rises Up*. *Pearl*, set in England in approximately 1640, concerns an attempt to link the forces of the Irish Catholic leader 'over the water', the clan chief O'Neill, with the Scots Presbyterians who are in revolt against the royal domination of the appointment of church officials and also with the Parliamentarians and Puritans who were to go on to fight the Civil War against Charles I. Such an attempt probably never happened. But, Arden contends, it might have happened if British progressives of the time had been prepared to support the Irish, rather as if British trade unionists had been prepared to support Connolly and Larkin in 1913. As it was – Cromwell happened.

This 'alternative' history is told with all Arden's typical virtuosity, his subtle use of the medium of radio, his deployment of hard, crisp language, theatrical in the best sense, and his use of names in the *dramatis personae* (Gideon Grip, the Puritan, Mother Bumroll the bawd, Lord Grimscar the nobleman, and Pearl herself, the enigmatic central figure). Most interestingly, perhaps, Arden's subplot, or second plot, dovetails with his first plot through his other obsession, the theatre itself. The play deals with the state of the theatres in the mid-seventeenth century, and their potential power. (If they were not powerful, why should the Puritans have closed them in 1642?) *Pearl* begins with a performance of Shakespeare's *Julius Caesar*, which of course depicts the assassination of a tyrant. Now Backhouse, the Yorkshire playwright, and Pearl, the wild Irishwoman (half native American, too) plan to produce a play with the backing of Lord Grimscar which has an immediate concrete purpose as a political intervention (as D'Arcy and Arden's Irish plays did). Their play will attempt both to 'advance the urgent purposes' of the Parliamentary cause, and to 'immediately reverse (the Puritans') whole attitude to the English theatre'.

The plot thus revolves on one level round what can or cannot be achieved by an activist theatre.

There is an interesting comparison to be made between Backhouse and Pearl and Arden himself and D'Arcy. Tish Dace noted that 'The Irish actor/ playwright/social activist Pearl, betrayed and cast out to die, could serve as a metaphor for D'Arcy's treatment', and goes on to quote Jon Wike: 'the root of Margaretta (<Latin *margarita*, <Greek *margaron*) means "pearl"'.[460] But beyond this, there is the proposed revolution on the seventeenth century stage, that women should play the female roles; and this is not simply a *fait accompli*, it is argued through, and Backhouse's sexism is ironically exposed. As important is the debate about popularising the theatre, which goes much further than the perhaps pious hopes voiced at the end of *The Royal Pardon*, partly because it comes out of further, more furious, experience. The problem is stated by Backhouse:

> If this stage is from now on capable of holding only the attention of the
> court-harlots and their embroidered stallions, then Jonson and
> Shakespeare, Christopher Marlowe and all the rest of 'em might just as
> well have spent their lives emptying nightsoil into t'village-midden. We
> spoke once to the whole people. But these days we have rejected the
> homespun jackets, the square-toed shoes, and the forthright word of the
> godly tradesman. And by God they've rejected us.

This is answered by Pearl's description of the contemporary *continental* popular theatre:

> We were thieves, Mr Backhouse, and harlots, and coney-catchers, with
> lewd comedies, antique morality plays, incompetent juggling, we put
> forward our legs in scarlet stockings and pranced around with the
> castanets. We were everything Jack Barnabus is not.

(Barnabus is 'the best actoir in England'.) But at the end of *Pearl*, when the project has fallen flat on its face, Pearl herself states the bald historical fact:

> Every theatre throughout the land was closed down by Act of Parliament:
> and from that day to this the word of the Common People of England,
> most powerful in the strength of the Lord, had little or nothing to do with
> the word of their tragic poets or the high genius of their actors. You
> might say that this did small hurt to the body and bones, but deeper,
> within the soul . . .

Perhaps, indeed, the English theatre has never recovered from this; certainly it is from this date that 'high' art and popular art begin to diverge, the dramatic 'bard' is sundered from the theatrical 'gleeman'.

After these two individually-composed works, there was to be one more D'Arcy-and-Arden stage play, *Vandaleur's Folly*, though this was by no means the last collaboration. Their eldest son, Finn, was old enough now to observe the collaboration in action. He recalled how 'collaboration involves plenty of arguments –

Margaretta's mind tends to go off in all directions, she has too many ideas. John disciplines her ideas'.[461] Arden himself suggested the difference was that whereas he tended to work from a story, which would, as it were, throw up a subject, D'Arcy found a subject which needed dramatising, and then sought a story with which achieve this. How this worked for *Vandaleur's Folly* is not clear, but the origins of the project are traceable to Eamon Smullen's visit to Corandulla in the early 1970s, and discussions with him about future drama which would answer some of the cultural concerns of left-wing and progressive politics in Ireland at the time. In a sense, *Vandaleur's Folly* was conceived for Official Sinn Fein, the Workers Party. It aimed to encourage those campaigning for British troops to leave Ireland, and to draw attention to the H Block prison protests. D'Arcy summarised her longer term aim in two sentences:

> Where the reform of injustice is prevented by political manoeuvring, the
> people themselves must take measures against their exploiters. If they
> cannot do this democratically, then they must do it through force of
> arms.[462]

Vandaleur's Folly concerns the establishment of an experimental co-operative in Ralahine, south west Ireland, in 1831. This is the period of theatrical melodrama, and like *The Little Gray Home in the West*, *Vandaleur's Folly* is constructed – at least on the surface – as pastiche melodrama. The opening scenes are set on the sea shore in murky darkness, there are smugglers, and a murder, seemingly straight from Boucicault's *The Colleen Bawn*, or some such work. Later we encounter secret societies and the slave trade, as in another Boucicault melodrama, *The Octoroon*. However, these dastardly proceedings are set against the open, above-board socialism of those who are setting up the co-operative:

> What need of terrorism, what need of these states of emergency, what
> need of the Orange Order or even of Dan O'Connell within a common-
> wealth so harmonious ...!

There is also a concern with new machinery, a classic subject for pro-Luddite melodramas like *The Factory Lad*, dating from 1832; but again there is a difference. On the co-operative, the machine is a useful and welcome aid to work, not a threat. More obviously melodramatic is some of the violence depicted – the hunt at the start of Act Two, when Baker-Fortescue and his cronies chase a local peasant girl and he who catches her may enjoy her; the duel scene, which ends with Baker-Fortescue's trousers falling down; and the conclusion, in which Baker-Fortescue rapes Roxana, his friend Wilberforce is shot by the hunchback, Roisin, and Baker-Fortescue himself is forced to commit suicide. But there is a dimension beyond the merely spectacular in this play, which raises a series of inter-connected issues which we are invited to consider. One of these is feminism, which this play takes up more potently than any other by D'Arcy and Arden, and what might be regarded as its opposite, male sexual predatoriness. The relations of Ireland and England are also raised, but now in the contexts of colonialism and also racialism.

The whole story of *Vandaleur's Folly* is set within a few short scenes involving William Thomson, a pioneer revolutionary socialist of the period, and his consort, the radical feminist, Anna Wheeler, who provide a frame, a point of reference, for the spectator. Whether all these different strands make the play difficult to digest is a question which may be considered. As far back as 1966, Arden acknowledged his 'principal fault as a writer', which was 'to get so interested in bright ideas that occur to me while I am working on a story that I forget what the play is supposed to be about',[463] and there may be something of that here.

Nevertheless it is a dramatically exciting work. Sadly, given the hostility of the British theatre to D'Arcy and Arden, the question was what to do with it. Just at this time they were approached by John McGrath of 7:84 company, suggesting that now the libel action had been settled, his company might mount *The Little Gray Home in the West*. According to McGrath, D'Arcy and Arden were

> sort of willing but extremely hostile and aggressive towards the company and said, 'The company have got to agree to doing anything that we say and any changes at any time that we dictate. And we are going to direct it'.

However, this production of *The Little Gray Home in the West* failed to materialise, and D'Arcy and Arden, in a further meeting with John McGrath, suggested:

> 'Why don't you do our new play which is about Ralahine on condition that we direct it'. We had a meeting of the policy group and I put forward the proposition that the Ardens might make a mess of it, they might make a triumph of it. Either way they deserved the right to do it because of all the work they've done in the past. We had tremendous respect for them. We said, we place the company entirely in their hands for the period of that production. That was the proposal and that was agreed by the policy group and that was in fact how it went ahead.[464]

According to Margaretta D'Arcy, the production was 'a peace offering' from John McGrath[465] after the disaster of *The Ballygombeen Bequest*.

It was not, however, without problems. Even casting was difficult. Most of the 7:84 regulars, socialist actors with some experience, were unavailable, and Arden and D'Arcy were forced to recruit 'ordinary' actors, who were often deterred by the content of *Vandaleur's Folly*, or whose agents were unco-operative. 'You would think you had a cast', D'Arcy reported, 'and then mysteriously next day a phone call would come saying this or that actor had had to drop out for all sorts of plausible reasons'.[466] Eventually a company was formed.

But before rehearsals began, the authors went to Greece where they attended a production of *Serjeant Musgrave's Dance* in Thessalonika and also a writers' conference under the auspices of the Greek Writers Union. During this conference, a German actress complained to Arden that there were no good roles for women in *The Workhouse Donkey*, nor indeed in any of Arden's plays; and when they examined this further, they noticed that actually there were no roles of power for women in Greek or Shakespearean tragedies either, that women were effectively excluded in all theatres from creating roles of authority or dominance. It sparked one of D'Arcy most radical notions, which later she insisted on for many of her own plays: that women should play men's parts. Actors already played characters of different ages, or skin colour, or sexual orientation: why, then, should they not play roles of the opposite gender?

They also noticed that the conference's organisers, still perhaps loyal to the recently-ousted Fascist junta in Greece, had deliberately excluded gay writers. While Arden returned to London to begin work on *Vandaleur's Folly*, D'Arcy stayed on to give her paper, but now she changed its content. She made a declaration protesting against the exclusion of homosexual writers. There was something of a furore: Greek newspapers picked it up, and D'Arcy herself was thanked by several Greeks. Interestingly, at the end of the conference, participants were invited to stay for two extra days and visit the ancient Minoan sites. At the end of this trip, the coach left to return to Athens without D'Arcy. Had she been abandoned in revenge for her speech to the conference? She took risks with return transport, insisting on being collected by the tour operators.

Meanwhile the production of *Vandaleur's Folly* was proving controversial. The actors found difficulty with lines and actions which could be construed as 'political'. 'The lead actor, having been told that he was giving aid and comfort to the IRA, spoke all the lines but simply withdrew himself from the character'.[467] He was not the only actor to do so. Furthermore, it had been agreed that the décor for the production should include posters and blown-up press cuttings relevant to the 1978 situation in Northern Ireland and that leaflets should be handed out to spectators as they entered the auditorium. But as soon as the production was touring, and D'Arcy and Arden were no longer part of the group, their work having been completed, these 'provocative aspects' were dropped. When the tour reached Belfast, D'Arcy hoped to make up for this by distributing leaflets herself, but members of the Students Union tried to prevent her. In the theatre, the actors disowned her. It was, however, 'a healthy experience for me':

> Professional actors ... go into the state-subsidised theatre primarily to
> earn their living and make a career, not to put themselves on the line
> against the military-industrial complex.[468]

The play itself could not easily be judged from this unsatisfactory tour. Some audiences obviously found it an old-fashioned melodrama with much of its relevance deliberately removed, and a style which in any case was more complex than are most plays. On the other hand, in Galway, the authors' 'home' city, five hundred people filled the auditorium while another two hundred were turned away.

Performances of *Vandaleur's Folly* were scheduled to take place at Queen's University as part of the annual Belfast Festival, where D'Arcy was also booked to lecture on 'Theatre in an Age of Reform', a lecture which is reprinted in *Awkward Corners*. By now she was feeling particularly depressed, partly because of the apparent censoring by the actors of the overtly political elements of her play, partly by the gathering storm in the H Block prisons (the first big march and demonstration in support of the prisoners had just been banned), partly also because two pictures had been removed from the exhibition, 'Art for Society' at the Ulster Museum, supposedly part of the Festival. She attended a poetry reading at the Ulster Museum where Paul Muldoon and Michael Longley read. It seemed to her that they were avoiding the terrible truth about Northern Ireland at a time of maximum horror, that the authorities were being permitted to censor whatever displeased them:

> I leant against the wall, took out a red marker and wrote H Block … My
> marker squeaked; heads turned round; they registered – and they opened
> their mouths and yelled.[469]

It was a kind of loose theatre. D'Arcy continued drawing a frame round what she had written, when the museum attendants grabbed her, dragged her down the stairs and handed her over to the Royal Ulster Constabulary. She resisted their manhandling, but a 'steely-eyed' RUC man threw her into the Black Maria, and she was remanded in custody in Armagh Gaol.

Arden arrived from London the next morning, having consulted a lawyer. The charges to be brought against D'Arcy were serious: three assaults, breach of the peace, incitement to riot and defacing a public monument. Arden delivered her lecture. The performance went ahead. But there was no statement from the University or the Festival as to what had happened to the now-disappeared author of *Vandaleur's Folly*. The actors pretended not to know where she was. They returned to Britain without contacting her. Nor did John McGrath himself write to her.

It was the end of Arden and D'Arcy's active careers in the theatre. The hassles, the difficulties, the personalities, the cowardice had got the better of two elemental forces in British and Irish theatre. As Chambers and Prior noted: 'Their departure is a monumental loss to British drama'.[470]

Seventeen : Unperson – New Person

After her arrest at the Ulster Museum in Belfast, D'Arcy was taken to the local police station for twenty-four hours, before being moved to Armagh Women's Prison to await her trial. Accepted as a Republican prisoner, she refused to co-operate with the authorities or the doctor. After three weeks her case was heard. Though she tried to broaden the hearing out to consider the problem for the artist in a time of repression, this tactic was not successful. She was found guilty and fined £10 on each count. An unknown supporter paid the fine. She was free.

Vandaleur's Folly continued its tour, and D'Arcy returned to London. But she had left possessions in Armagh, and in the new year she returned to collect them. On her way, she arrived by train from London at Stranraer at 5.30 in the morning. She joined the line for security checking, but when she reached the head of the queue, the woman official seemed to know who she was. She consulted a paper, then consulted with a colleague. She took D'Arcy into a small empty windowless room with only a television monitor screwed high up into the wall for decoration. After a few questions, she was told she was to be taken to the Police Station. She was driven there by police car. When she arrived, she saw no-one. She was left alone in the interrogation room for five hours:

> Stare out of the window, get closer to the radiator, three cigarettes left, one match, lean on the radiator. Footsteps, whispering, keys jangling, make no noise. A head pops in – a head goes out.[471]

Sometime before lunch, for no apparent reason, she was allowed to go. She had missed the boat, of course, but there were no charges against her.

In February, D'Arcy was in Armagh, where she was invited to join a protest by Women Against Imperialism planned for International Women's Day, 8 March. Women Against Imperialism was a small group, some of them relatives of Republican prisoners, others who were active feminists based in Belfast's Queen's University. She accepted the invitation, and on the day about fifty women were present at the protest. One of those was the republican socialist, Miriam Daly, who had galvanised Galway Theatre Workshop's *The Hunting of the Mongrel Fox*. The women gathered outside the gaol and began a raucous rendition of an Irish Republican song which called forth an echoing song from the prisoners within the walls. The group gathered close to the entrance to the gaol and were posing for pictures when jeeps of the Royal Ulster Constabulary screeched round the corner, pulled up sharply and the armed and flak-jacketed policemen began grabbing the woman and hurling them into the jeeps. Within minutes the jeeps were hurtling away to the police station, with their captives on board.

At the station, the women were lined up against a wall, and one by one were paraded in front of the doctor. All refused to allow themselves to be examined. 'My heart was going like mad', D'Arcy recalled; 'I was moving in a dream; time was standing still'.[472] But the women displayed exemplary solidarity: none would allow herself to be released until all were freed, and finally they were all told to go. No charges were preferred – apparently. But their names were passed to the press and published, which caused sour problems for some of the women either at work or at home. But still, it appeared to have been a minor incident in the strife-torn six counties, and D'Arcy imagined she would hear no more about it.

But politics were becoming harsher. That same March, the British Conservative spokesman on Northern Ireland, Airey Neave, was assassinated, victim of a car bomb which exploded as he drove out of the House of Commons car park. On 4 May, his friend and fellow Conservative, Margaret Thatcher, was elected Prime Minister of the United Kingdom. And only a matter of months after that Lord Mountbatten, uncle to the Duke of Edinburgh and last Viceroy of India, as well as a former First Sea Lord, was assassinated in County Sligo. The six counties were boiling up to a new frenzy, the focus now centring on the prisoners who had been deprived of their political status. There was increasing agitation, protest marches, and dangerous talk of a hunger strike, all of which were met by the new Thatcher government with stony-faced indifference.

D'Arcy and Arden were now no longer willing to engage with professional theatre. They put together a script called *The Menace of Ireland*, and D'Arcy also created a programme called *The Trial and Prison Experiences of Countess Markiewicz*. *The Menace of Ireland* was staged and performed by the two of them on an open stage or platform, and consisted of a collage of passages from all the Irish plays they had written. It thus dealt with the history of Anglo-Irish relations from the seventeenth century to the 1970s. Its theme was the continuing failure of progressive and radical British opinion to find a consistent position *vis-a-vis* the long-lasting Irish struggle for freedom, and the consequent plethora of 'initiatives' which were designed to placate the Irish, but which actually had the effect of prompting a seemingly inevitable return to violence. The programme lasted something over an hour: it was informally presented, and proved extremely successful, being seen not only in theatres (the Half Moon in London, Nottingham Playhouse, Manchester Royal Exchange), but also in Arts Centres and on University campuses. The programme about Countess Markiewicz, famed for her participation in the 1916 Easter Rising, followed a somewhat similar pattern, with readings from memoirs, letters and so on. These presentations were also shown in USA, where Arden and D'Arcy went both in the autumn of 1979 and also in the following spring. They were partly sponsored by the War Resisters League, and took part in the creation of another 30 hour anti-war piece (perhaps a little like the Vietnam *War*

Carnival) for this group. D'Arcy also gave readings on International Women's Day there in 1980.

The prosecution of the Armagh protesters from Women Against Imperialism came to court on 31 October 1979. D'Arcy was inclined not to recognise the British court's jurisdiction in Ireland, though her fellow accused were unwilling to take this line; and though she prepared to conduct her own defence, her co-accused hired barristers. The barristers were successful in making a series of inroads into the case for the prosecution, and they were followed by D'Arcy who decided that the best method of defence was attack. She asserted her Irish nationality, asked how much the trial was costing, and went on to accuse the witnesses of lying. Basil McIver, the presiding magistrate, became increasingly flustered by her tone, and finally banged his gavel on the table and dismissed the court. As he hurried away, D'Arcy could be heard shouting republican slogans at his back. RUC officers tried to arrest her, but were prevented when one of the barristers intervened, and the court room descended into a shambles.

Though not all the women in the group were happy, all agreed that when the trial was resumed – or re-started – in January 1980, D'Arcy would make her case first, trying by non-legal, perhaps naïve, means to prise open the case for the prosecution before the lawyers attempted to drive home the advantage. D'Arcy wanted to invoke the Charter of Human Rights, various official reports and even the speech made by the Pope at Drogheda during his visit to Ireland three months earlier on 29 September 1979: 'On my knees I beg you to turn away from the paths of violence', he had said. 'Return to the ways of peace'. With this as the thrust of her argument, she intended this time to write out her questions, and show them to the lawyers in advance of the hearing. Before this, however, the 'Armagh Eleven' tried to gather as much support, particularly from other women's groups, as possible, and with some success. At any rate, at New Year 1980, as the Eleven gathered in Belfast, there were representatives from many other women's organisations, and meetings and demonstrations, which however often focused at least as much on the ongoing struggles in the H Block gaols as on the upcoming trial.

On 2 January 1980, the eleven accused Women Against Imperialism were heading for Armagh when they were stopped on the road by British soldiers who ordered them from their coach. At first the women refused to obey, but finally they did clamber down, giving their names and addresses, but singing loudly and clapping their hands to annoy their antagonists. But nothing much happened, and after an hour the coach was allowed to drive on to Armagh, where, after further delays and searches, the women entered the court house. However, it was discovered that the lead barrister was sick at home, and not present. The trial could not proceed. Once again, the presiding magistrate, Basil McIver, postponed the hearing. But D'Arcy leapt to her feet – after all, she was not represented by a barrister – and protested: 'Try us now, or dismiss the charges'. McIver refused, whereupon all the women dismissed their barristers. McIver was dumbfounded, and when the women then started again to sing their protest songs, clapping their hands and rocking in rhythm, he left the court room in high dudgeon. But still, another adjournment was hardly acceptable. When the hearing was finally held on 9 April 1980, over a year after the alleged offence had occurred, D'Arcy was in USA. But in her absence, D'Arcy was found guilty, and – like the other women who were present – she was fined. Partly because it was not a heavy fine, she was convinced it would in the end be overlooked, and that the case would be allowed quietly to fade away.

Nothing could have been further from what happened. When D'Arcy returned to the United Kingdom in May 1980, she discovered that at least one of the 'Armagh Eleven' had already been arrested and was now in Armagh Gaol for non-payment of her fine. The tariff for non-payment was six months. Knowing that there was a warrant out for her, D'Arcy returned to Belfast to be with her comrades. But by now the group's solidarity was flaking away. Several decided to pay their fines, and at a women's conference in Dublin on 11 May, it was clear that support for non-payment was not as strong as D'Arcy had hoped. Further defections over the next days left her alone determined not to pay the fine and to face the consequences:

> As a writer committed to the integrity of the written word, I felt we had raised the expectations of the young women in Armagh … and they were all expecting us to come and join them. If we failed in our undertaking, they would think we had been manipulating the situation for our own politics. Besides, if I now determinedly refused to pay the British government for the privilege of speaking the truth during a peaceful protest, and kept on refusing till they sent me to jail, at least a few people still concerned for civil liberties might be perturbed at the implications.[473]

At six o'clock on the evening of 15 May, D'Arcy, accompanied by a number of supporters, handed herself in at the local police station. She first complained that she had not received the warrant. When asked whether she had come to pay the fine, she replied that she would not, and certainly not until the warrant had been served. The officer then scurried away to find the unserved warrant. At last he produced it, so that D'Arcy could formally refuse to pay the fine. Whereupon the terms of her imprisonment were made clear to her. It would in fact be only for three months, which would include a second sentence of two months to run concurrently with the first. She was detached from her supporters and taken away to the court house cells. From now until her release she became an 'unperson'. 'When you are put in gaol', she explained, 'what is happening is – society doesn't want you any more. They lock you up – you don't exist'. She added: 'In goal you're not in control of who you are.

Somebody else decides who you are, and their position in society defines your position'.[474]

Armagh Women's Gaol was divided into sections: 'A' Wing housed the republican prisoners who refused to abandon their claim to political status. They had been the first to feel the force of the British Government's animosity towards their attitude, before even the men in the Long Kesh H Blocks had. In February 1980, male warders had been sent from Long Kesh to Armagh to abuse these republican women, both verbally and – more significantly – physically. The women were locked in their cells for three days, and even denied use of the toilets. This in turn had led directly to the 'no-wash' protest. It was a cauldron of confrontation into which D'Arcy was pitched, or into which she pitched herself, in May 1980.

Later she wrote a song about the attack on the Armagh women in February 1980, as a tribute to them:

In Black Armagh of the Goddess Macha,
Last February in the grey cold jail,
The governor Scott in his savage fury
Came down to break the women's will
'Forty jailers, my forty jailers,
From the hell of Long Kesh come down
And help me break these warrior women
Who will not yield to the power of the Crown'.

The forty jailers put on their armour,
Strapped on their helmets, took up their shields,
Then they beat the Armagh women, they beat them down,
They were sure they'd yield.
Three days he kept them locked up in darkness,
Locked up in filth you would not believe
When he released them he was so conceited
That one and all he thought they would yield.[475]

It was clear that in this gaol at this time she would find not a group of anonymous 'unpersons', but a vivid and vibrant group of women who were defining their own positions within their institutionalisation.

At first this might seem contradictory and perhaps surprising. The days were monotonous, the limited events repetitive and apparently insignificant. The cells on 'A' Wing were approximately eleven feet by eight feet, and two women were imprisoned in each. There were two iron bedsteads with thin foam rubber mattresses, three grey blankets and two pillows. There was one plastic chamber pot per cell, and a plastic slop bowl. Each prisoner had a blue plastic mug and a thermos flask, and a toothbrush, toothpaste and a comb. In this bleakness, perhaps only the flies prospered:

Every morning there are hundreds of flies on the walls, on the floors. We
swat them. I feel like the proverbial white hunter. I try to have a truce
with them. 'You can have the walls, but leave my body alone'. No way,
they crawl up my legs, land on my face, I hide under the filthy grey
blanket, they sneak in, no mercy.[476]

Life was, at least on the surface, merely routine: breakfast, exercise, dinner, tea,
supper. Meals, the major punctuation mark in the day, carried their own dangers
because prisoners had to leave their cells when they immediately became vulnerable
to the warders:

The whole atmosphere at meal-times was tense. We were constantly
standing around in our slops, rivers of urine, sanitary towels, and left-
over food floating down the wing. Then there was the ever-thick crowd of
flies over the hotplate. In the beginning I had to nerve myself to walk
through this putrid stench; sometimes my slop would splash up and
splash against my bare leg. I could never look down or I would have
vomited.[477]

The barren emptiness of the day was a consequence of the women's refusal to work.

All that was left was the one hour of exercise. D'Arcy felt the need to 'engage'
her body, so she jogged up and down the exercise yard. At the same time, she
wanted to meet her fellow inmates, to discover them as people, to understand better
the context of what was happening, and the exercise hour was the only time she
could achieve this. So she attached herself to one or two of them and began to talk.
She discovered individuals, women who cared for their families outside the walls,
who thought about ideas and discussed thoughtfully. They cared for each other,
becoming a sort of second family for one another, and dreamed of a better Ireland in
the future. As a group, they were brought together by their republican idealism.
They were led by Mairéad Farrell, a twenty-four year old, Belfast-born IRA
volunteer. She had been arrested in 1976 after a bomb had been planted at a hotel in
Dunmurry. The RUC swooped on those they thought were the perpetrators, arrested
Farrell and shot her boy friend, Sean McDermott, dead. In the gaol, she had from the
first refused to wear prison uniform and it was she in February 1980 who had
instigated the 'dirty protest' in the women's prison in response to the male warders'
attack. Later, in December, after D'Arcy's release, she began a hunger strike to
coincide with the men's hunger strike in the H Blocks, and only ended it after the
men had ended theirs. She was to be assassinated by the SAS in Gibraltar in March
1988.

Farrell organised the prisoners into a proper unit, 'A Wing Company IRA',
with a Second-in-Command, a Quartermaster, Welfare Officer and Entertainment
Officer. All business with the prison authorities was conducted by Farrell, who held
regular meetings with the Governor to discuss the situation. D'Arcy, because she

was not in the IRA, became a sort of 'honorary' member of the group. The regular group meetings, chaired by Farrell, were held in a disciplined but democratic fashion, calmly and intelligently. The group also noted outside events, such as the death of an IRA man shot in a Belfast street by the RUC. After Sunday Mass, they donned black armbands and paraded with the utmost seriousness, while one member sang an Irish lament to commemorate the fallen.

Mairead Farrell in a 'dirty' cell in Armagh Gaol

For D'Arcy, the hardest task for those who joined the 'dirty protest' was the actual physical process of defecating. In her book, *Tell Them Everything*, she records her problems in hilarious detail – one of the funniest sections, surely, of any prison book.

> What are my shitting habits? Not regular; if I eat I will shit. But I can't shit. What will happen if I don't shit for three months? What will happen to the piled-up food in my stomach? Does shit always come out? … Days pass: I remain absorbed in my lack of shit. I am not aware of anything, only the task of shitting … I am a failure. I must. I must. That night I produce a little one, a sheep's one. Is that all? What about all the food I ate before coming in, bacon, sausage, ice cream, two slices of fried bread and an egg in the police station, the food I'd eaten in here, is it all contained in this small, hard nut? I apply it to the wall, I press hard, it falls off. I pick it up again, pressing it more lightly, as though I was touching a glass for a table-rapping session at a séance; let it take itself over the wall; it moves in thin lines. I am proud. The next time I shit I am going to draw pictures.[478]

The 'dirty protest' was its own adventure, and another kind of loose theatre in its own right. 'The most difficult part to decorate was the ceiling, we had to balance on the bed-rail and make broad sweeps across the high arched cells'[479] It helped to hold the group of women together. But it also posed a danger to their health. The faeces used for the 'decoration' of the walls inevitably got into their hair, caused irritation of the eyes and got onto hands and under fingernails. D'Arcy suffered especially from itchy eyes, but there were also problems for the women with menstruation, with broken finger nails, and with pyjamas and T-shirts.

Being from the Republic rather than from the British province of Northern Ireland, perhaps, and being of the intelligentsia, too, perhaps, D'Arcy found herself something of an outsider among these women. They would boast of their drinking in comradely banter, yet their political commitment was paramount. She wondered how near-alcoholics, as they seemed to paint themselves, could be so politically determined. When she confronted them with this conundrum, they bridled, refused to accept the question, and even to an extent ostracised D'Arcy, who had perhaps confused chaffing and mutual joshing of one another with the serious purpose of their lives. It would be impossible to say these women, enduring so much, so courageous and assured in the lives they were living, were anything other than resolute. When Martin Meehan started a hunger strike in the H Blocks, the young women prisoners argued about it fiercely, criticising him for selfish motives. But when D'Arcy dared to join in the criticism, they rounded on her, defending their comrade IRA volunteer to the last. D'Arcy sometimes struggled to understand.

But she promised to tell the world about their struggle when she emerged from the prison in August 1980, and her reportage was published the following year under the title *Tell Them Everything*. It is an evocative narrative, not unfit to rank alongside Dostoyevsky's *Memoirs from the House of the Dead* or Albie Sachs's *Jail Diary*, and truly conjures the life of the prisoner:

> In all probability my mind was becoming unhinged, lying in a cell 23
> hours a day, the walls covered in excrement and then covered with flies,
> the bowl of urine under the bed sending up a powerful stench. Lying on
> my grey blankets, the windows daubed and boarded up outside, no view,
> except high up, a triangle of clouds racing past; on the floor thousands
> and thousands of small flies hopping. Two predatory Roman-Imperialist
> eagles suddenly block out the light. Beside me on my pillow lies an
> enormous severed hand. I close my eyes and open them again: the eagles
> are pigeons, the macabre hand is my own, tucked somehow under my
> neck. There is no relief from the filth except once again to close my eyes.
> Opposite – a 21-year old girl doomed to lie there for the next ten years
> with nothing to read but a Bible.[480]

Yet there were problems with telling the world *everything*, including the libel laws. And for her there was the issue of 'feminism', too, which seemed to involve her own identity. Many feminists, whose ideological positions had seemed close to D'Arcy's own, publicly doubted the appropriateness of the no-wash protest, but the fact these were women engaging in such extreme tactics was to her a central issue. Gradually she came to recognise that her own feminism was inadequate to the situation she was now faced with – even though, ironically enough, it was her feminism which had brought her to Armagh in the first place. Her song, 'The Armagh Women', ends with a stirring call, which was to indicate her new standpoint:

> Women of Ireland, stand up and declare,
> Women of Ireland, understand your power
> Make us see that together we'll do it
> We'll tumble down their stone grey tower.[481]

On 14 August D'Arcy was released into the northern counties which were perhaps in an even worse state than when she went in. She herself was already enervated and low in spirits after her experience, but a whole series of other factors also conspired to depress her: she had received a head injury from the RUC which plagued her for the rest of her life; an English midlands theatre had decided against staging *The Non-Stop Connolly Show* because of her perceived relation to events in Ireland; a projected feature article about her work in the New York *Village Voice* was suddenly and inexplicably abandoned; and she was effectively banned from BBC and from RTE, the republic's national broadcaster.

Two months after her release, the prisoners in the H Blocks began a coordinated hunger strike over their political status. It is true that in December of that year, the hunger strike was called off and a negotiated agreement providing the prisoners with their demands for civilian clothes, as well as visits, and the receiving of letters and parcels, in return for their cells being kept clean, seemed to have been reached. But in January 1981 the authorities backed away from the deal, and in a desperate development, the prisoners were assaulted by the prison officers. On 28 January there was serious rioting in Long Kesh. Two weeks later, the British Government announced a policy of no compromise, and a terrible collision course was irrevocably set. Meanwhile to D'Arcy's horror, Miriam Daly, the Queen's University lecturer who had inspired Galway Theatre Workshop to make *The Hunting of the Mongrel Fox* and other activities, was murdered by the Ulster Defence Association in Belfast on 16 January.

On 1 March, after careful preparation, the Provisional IRA and INLA prisoners in the H Blocks commenced a second hunger strike. It was not supported by Official Sinn Fein, the Workers Party. The strikers decided to stagger the start of the strike, that is, that only one man would begin the strike, and he would be followed after several days by a second man beginning a strike, and then by a third man, and so on. It was felt, probably correctly, that this would maximise the political impact. The first striker was the charismatic Bobby Sands, a writer and poet. Immediately, tension in the six counties began to rise. A vacancy had oc-curred in the Fermanagh and South Tyrone United Kingdom Parliamentary con-stituency, and it was decided as a publicity coup, Sands would fight the bye-election from prison. He won the seat and thus became an M.P. But his hunger strike, which had by now been joined by more prisoners, continued, and on 5 May he died. Predictably his death set off riots across the six counties; and over 100,000 people attended his funeral. As the summer ran on, more hunger strikers died in the gaol, and more people outside also died in the violence and mayhem that accompanied the strike. Emotions in Ireland ran extraordinarily high: clear thinking in this unique situation was almost impossible. On 20 August, the tenth prisoner, Mickey Devine, died. And on 3 October the strike was ended. It was surely the most horrible time in all the years of the Troubles.

In the meantime, in the twenty-six county republic to which D'Arcy had returned and where she had begun writing *Tell Them Everything*, a general election had been held in June, resulting in a hung Parliament and the formation of a new coalition government under Fine Gael's Garret Fitzgerald. Inflation was over 20%, and the price of oil on the world markets had just been given another jerk upwards. When *Tell Them Everything* was published, it addressed a subject still probably too raw for much objective assessment, and reviews were decidedly mixed. Bernard Crick, in *The Guardian*, for example, wrote: 'John Arden once understood in his *Armstrong's Last Goodnight*, the dilemmas of politics … now all is propaganda and there is no thought'.[482] It was a ridiculous attack. As Arden himself pointed out, *Armstrong's Last Goodnight* is actually about a man, Lindsay, who murders in defence of moderation; and to use a misreading of this play to attack D'Arcy's book was hardly 'scrupulous'. As suggested, however, it was not untypical.

But something else happened that summer which had a profound and liberating effect on D'Arcy and Arden. Shortly before he was voted out of office, on 5 March, Charles Haughey, Fianna Fail Taoiseach, had announced the formation of 'Aosdána', a government-backed association of artists. Suggested initially, it seems, by Anthony Cronin, Haughey wanted it to honour those artists whose work had made an outstanding contribution to the arts in Ireland, and to encourage and assist members to devote their energies fully to their art. In pursuance of this, members were to be offered, under certain conditions, a 'cnuas', or stipend, of up to £4000 tax free, which was specifically designed to enable them to continue their artistic work. It was almost like Merlin's College of Bards in *The Island of the Mighty*. Members were to be elected: prominent artists were to nominate those whom they thought deserving of the honour and some two hundred or so thus became founder members. One of them was Margaretta D'Arcy.

To achieve this founder membership was not simple. The very establishing of Aosdána was itself the subject of some controversy. Which artists would be accepted? Would those whose dissidence was well known (as D'Arcy's was) be admissible? Colm O'Briain, once a theatre and television director, now Director of the Irish Arts Council and nominated Rector of Aosdána, vociferously supported the rights of artists who were not necessarily pliant to the state's requirements, and encouraged D'Arcy and others not to let such considerations deter them. Irish culture had always had dissidence at its heart. All she needed was a letter of application and an endorsement from an eligible artist. She hesitated to write, diffident about her own work, but she knew that it was important that women should assert themselves and their values, so she wrote 'an outlandish begging letter'.[483] She found a respected artist, republican poet, biographer, diarist and playwright, Ulick O'Connor, to sponsor her. And thus she was accepted. 'So I'm a legitimate person, allowed to follow my own creative path', she concluded, with some delight. And the stipend was hers, too. Now no longer somebody else's 'unperson', she was of manifest value in the land for whose freedom her father had fought. 'I was an aspiration of the Irish spirit', was how she phrased it, and, prefiguring her own later protest against Aosdána, she added, 'The church had failed the people – so we were the new church'.[484]

It was a turning-point in the lives of Arden and D'Arcy. It signalled the end to genuine poverty, and a new kind of involvement with Irish and world culture and politics.

Eighteen : 'If You Are Beaten Down, You Just Rise Again!'

In 1980 John Arden was fifty years old. His father had died the previous year, and now he realized -- not necessarily with pleasure – that his active career in the professional theatre was effectively over. His life, and his work, were forced to take a different turn. He embarked, as it were, on a second career, still as a writer, but now not as a playwright.

It was the radio which seemed to beckon first. *Pearl* had been notably successful, and it had of course been preceded by the well-thought-of radio plays, *The Life of Man* and *The Bagman* Arden had also created a fifteen minute radio play, called *To Put It Frankly*, broadcast on 19 May 1979. This had been commissioned by Alfred Bradley, a legendary radio producer whom every playwright wanted to work with. It was set in a television studio, and imagined a military coup in Britain by presenting what the viewer would see as the army took over: the programme was interrupted and an announcement made, directing what the viewer was to do. It was a not-too-subtle satire on the BBC's apparently-effortless paternalism. Alfred Bradley, who directed it, had replaced the apparently-malign Martin Esslin as Head of Drama at the BBC, and his support seemed to enable Arden's work for this medium to flourish. Radio ensured that his talent for spoken dialogue and his typical originality and understanding of dramatic form were still fully challenged, and the radio audience was likely to be as numerous and no less discriminating than anything the live theatre could offer. Moreover, one advantage was obvious: the production process lasted for a few days, and then was over. The hassles of weeks, or months, of rehearsing, the problems of disgruntled actors and over-mighty directors, were gone. And the result was often as satisfying.

In 1980, the BBC, in the person of Alfred Bradley, was considering a radio dramatisation of *Don Quixote*. Christopher Hampton was initially invited to script this, but he was unwilling to do the work. He telephoned Arden, who had never read the book, but who was eager to try, his interest in Cervantes having already been manifested in work he had done on *Life Is A Dream* in the 1960s. *Don Quixote*, Arden soon discovered, was as multi-layered as the former work, and as intellectually stimulating. 'Cervantes is telling the story which is told him by somebody else and then a rival writer comes in and attempts to contradict him', he recounted with some amusement years later. It was 'strangely postmodern',[485] and not unlike *The Knight of the Burning Pestle* by Beaumont and Fletcher, which actually, he later discovered, was probably influenced by *Don Quixote*.

Arden's version of *Don Quixote* follows Cervantes fairly faithfully, though he omits some episodes (in Part One, for instance, the whole of chapters 10 to 20), presumably for the sake of length as well as cohesion – the original sprawls irrepressibly. But most pertinently, Cervantes created a novel-within-a-novel: he is not, he says in his Prologue, the story's 'father', but its 'step-father', since it has been told to him. And Arden was, as he admitted, 'less interested in the Don's adventures and more in the way the novel is constructed'.[486] At one point in the original, for example, Cervantes, having lost his source, buys a notebook from a lad in the market-square and by a striking piece of luck, this contains the continuation of the story. More significantly, Cervantes asserts in his Prologue that the story is such 'as one might dream up while in jail'.[487] Arden began working on his adapt-ation while D'Arcy was in gaol, and he uses this to develop his own story-within-the-story. Cervantes was indeed, as he is in Arden's first scene, a former soldier as well as a tax collector, whose excellent plays have – perhaps like Arden's own – failed, or been overtaken by more 'modern' writers, like Lope da Vega. So he invents a 'meagre, shrivelled, fantastical old man',[488] who becomes the Don, and begins to tell his adventures. But Arden's Cervantes is more self-conscious: when one character mentions his beloved Dulcinea, Arden's Cervantes mutters how he must bring her into the story, even though Lope da Vega will mock him for it.

Arden thus reinvigorates the wistfulness as well as the absurdity of the original, and he is able to show how the story *performs* the end of the medieval period. The naiveté of the style subtly underscores the satire of the social problems, and as Arden himself noted, 'Don Quixote's assumption is that the society through which he moves is basically a fair one in which a few occasional wrongs need righting. But the author (Cervantes) drops hints all the time that this is not the case'.[489] This enables Arden to create an ending to the drama which is both affecting and appropriate: when his Cervantes loses his original sourcebook, he must decide what to do. There must be no third volume, which could be written perhaps by Lope da Vega. So he makes Don Quixote renounce knight errantry, make a will, and die. The priest performs the last rites. This version concludes:

'A gallant and deluded fool', we said;

We only knew his wisdom when he lay dead.[490]

The two parts of *Don Quixote*, which each lasted for an hour and a half, were presented by the BBC on 29 September and 6 October 1980, with a cast including Bob Grant as Don Quixote, Bernard Cribbens as Sancho Panza and Ronald Baddeley as Cervantes. It was directed by Alfred Bradley, and was widely admired. Paul Vallely, for example, wrote in *The Listener*, that Arden's 'enormously rich historical imagination' gave the dramatisation 'a winning basis':

The result is vintage Arden: the poetry, of both the ordinary folk and the fantastical knight, is deep, dark and powerful; the canvas is almost Shakespearian in the breadth of his portrait of Cervantes' society and its workings. The sense of theatre is electric and epic, in the Brechtian sense, in style; the humour and wit range from the urbane smile to the belly-laugh; and the themes of anarchy versus order and the relation-ship of the individual to society are fruitfully re-explored.[491]

In 1982, two more radio plays by Arden were broadcast by the BBC. The first was *Garland for a Hoar Head*, a dramatic celebration of the Tudor poet, John Skelton, and surely one of Arden's most spirited works. We have already noted Arden's lifelong delight in Skelton's work, and as writers, the two are not unalike despite the vastly different ages in which they wrote. One critic characterises Skelton's work as that

> of a moralist by turns laudatory and fervent, gracious and courteous, comic and burlesque, jesting and bantering, epigrammatic and puzzling, angry and complaining, severe in judgment and vengeful, loud-mouthed and frenzied, completely unrestrained in his denunciation of the abuses around him. A characteristic common to all his writings is their invariable concern with matters of the hour. Skelton is before all else a man of his time.[492]

The same critic opines that Skelton was guided 'less by an ideal of individual moral perfection than by a vigilant anxiety for the public welfare', and that, as a poet, 'he finally preferred vigour to beauty'.[493] Almost all this could be said of John Arden.

Skelton was born about 1460 and died on 21 June 1529. His life therefore coincides with the last half century of Catholic supremacy in England, when Henry VIII was hailed as 'Defender of the Faith' against Lutheranism, and the country was expanding politically, economically and culturally. He was perhaps a 'poet's poet', whose influence can be seen in Sir David Lindsay's drama, *Ane Satire of the Thrie Estatis* (which Arden maintains is much superior to Skelton's own *Magnificence*), as well as in Ben Jonson's *Cynthia's Revels*, which uses *Magnificence* as a kind of template. John Bale, the later Tudor polemical Protestant dramatist makes considerable play of Skelton's amatory adventures when the latter was Rector of Diss. And one remembers that Skelton's work was much admired by, among others, Robert Graves.

Skelton seems to have come from Yorkshire (again, like Arden), and seems to have been awarded a poetic laurel as early as 1488. He was cantankerous and quarrelsome, but was on occasion also sweet, funny and even sentimental. Politically he inveighed against corruption among the ruling caste, against the turbulent Scots north of England's border, against Lutheranism and most persistently against Cardinal Wolsey, who tried desperately to silence him. By New Year 1523 he was trying to evade Wolsey as the guest of the Countess of Surrey at her splendid home at Sheriff Hutton in Yorkshire, where he was

> the focus of a brilliant female society … this pleasant company decided to offer the poet-laureate a crown of laurel worthy of his fame, and we know that the entire household set to work on this masterpiece of female industry, in which silk and gold embroidery vied with pearls and precious stones.[494]

This is the starting-point for perhaps Skelton's greatest poem, 'The Garland of Laurel'. It is also the starting-point for Arden's play.

In a talk broadcast on 24 February 1982 in association with the play, entitled *The Winking Goose*, Arden discusses Skelton, an enormously versatile poet, he says, in a thriving tradition, 'a sort of fundamentally constructive Mr Punch'.[495] He reads the poetry, which he has loved since boyhood, aloud with great vigour and panache, and while admitting that he 'couldn't understand the sense' of some of it when he was young, 'the very incomprehensibility seemed crystal clear to my imagination'. He points also to the contradictions in Skelton: he is a conservative and a revolutionary, libidinous and austere, and a loyal royalist who seems to hold his king in contempt, before quoting the lines which give his talk their title:

> Yet when the rain raineth and the goose winketh,
>
> Little wotteth the gosling what the goose thinketh.[496]

He imagines the poet

> all alone in the oppressive atmosphere of his sanctuary house, hiding within the shelter of a legally-defined church precinct, relentlessly and ferociously turning his political grievances into surrealist verbal gold, stabbing at the paper with a pen like an engraver's tool.[497]

This becomes one of the vivid scenes in this remarkable play.

It begins with another, equally graphic, image, however. It is winter, 1522, and Skelton is making his way to Sheriff Hutton. He sends his boy on ahead with the horse and baggage, and then becomes lost in the forest. We 'see' the old poet, stooped, rheumatic, limping, at the end of a dark Yorkshire winter afternoon. He is ill shaved, with a lean hooked nose and a tangle of grey hair sticking out from under his hat. The scene is evocative radio at its finest.

The play follows his life, but uses dreams, memories and sudden unexpected close-ups of the 'present', as when he spills his breakfast in bed. There is bitterness, and regret, and there is much anger and even spite in his poetry. But the play ends with the celebration of the ageing poet: there are cakes, wine and music. Wearing Calliope, the muse of epic poetry's name on his shirt, he bows his hoar head and receives from the children his garland. He believes it honours not just him, but also Gower, Chaucer, Lydgate and the others. Trumpets blare, there are tears on his cheek, and he goes to write the Countess, his hostess, a poem which shall not be spiteful or angry. But 'what I have written, I have written', he says, remembering his own couplet:

> When ye think all danger for to pass,
>
> Ware of the lizard lieth lurking in the grass.[498]

It is a moving ending to a expansive play, which uses the medium of radio to particularly powerful effect. It employs two narrators, one male and one female, who interrupt, comment and 'alienate' the action in the Brechtian sense, particularly suitable for a comparatively contemplative play. The poetry echoes and re-echoes as it can only in radio drama, satirical, warm, embittered, comic, and this seems to stimulate Arden's own rich vocabulary. His use of one of Skelton's favourite ejaculations – 'Gup' – is especially amusing. Skelton frequently uses this in his more colloquial poems, such as 'Mannerly Margery Milk and Ale' ('Gup, Colin Clout, gup, Jack of the Vale!'), or 'Why Come Ye Not to Court?' ('That inn is now shut up,/With "Gup, whore, gup, now, gup!"').[499] Arden transfers this to his hero, who exclaims 'gup' whenever he needs a gentle expletive: surely Arden must have taught the actor how to say it!

This is a play for connoisseurs – of Skelton, of Arden, and of English poetry and its relation to society, which vexed question it addresses with urgency and intelligence. The fact that it, like much in Arden's *oeuvre*, resonates with Robert Graves's notion of the white goddess gives it some of its strength. It was broadcast on 25 February 1982, with Freddie Jones (sounding rather like John Arden) an excellent Skelton and Fiona Walker as the Countess of Surrey. It was directed, of course, by Alfred Bradley. The critics were largely favourable. D.A.N.Jones, in *The Listener*, found it 'a dense and broodingly poetic play',[500] while Val Arnold-Forster in *The Guardian* exhorted her readers to 'Be grateful for enthusiasts, they make the world go round. And they make the best radio programmes'.[501] She suggested Arden's enthusiasm for his subject was what made the play so successful, while also commending Freddie Jones's 'marvellously gravel-voiced, richly varied performance' and Alfred Bradley's 'sensibly restrained' production.

Arden himself was enjoying his theatre again. He spoke in the summer of 1982 of 'the most attractive part of the whole business – the assemblage in only two or three days (where it would take as many weeks in the theatre), of one's entire fictional creation from the recorded broadcast'. He added that 'for all the physical distance between yourself and your public, you seem so very much nearer to them than is ever possible in the theatre'.[502]

Two months after this interview, Arden's next radio play was broadcast on 22 October 1982. This was *The Old Man Sleeps Alone*, which won a Giles Cooper Award, and was published in *Best Radio Plays of 1982*. The cast included Ronald

Baddeley again, Christian Rodska, Frank Middlemass and David Calder, and it was directed, again, by Alfred Bradley.

The Old Man Sleeps Alone is almost perfect in its form. It tells the story of the building of the Lady Chapel in Durham Cathedral. When the French master-builder of the Cathedral dies, he leaves the secret of his building to his daughter to pass on to whichever of his two right hand men she wishes to take for her husband. Though she fancies one of these, Nick, she thinks the other, Charlie, is the better craftsman, so she marries him. But when Nick notices the building begin to crack, he does not seize the chance to oust Charlie and become the master-builder himself, rather he says the chapel must be saved for the honour of their trade and to keep the clergy at bay. The Bishop and the Prior, meanwhile, suspect the hand of the devil in the cracking of the building but, to cover themselves, they suggest it is in fact St Cuthbert who does not want the building over his grave, and that it should be moved to the other side of the Cathedral. Nick encourages this, and Charlie gets on with the rebuilding, thus leaving the way clear for Nick to enjoy the favours of the Frenchman's daughter. The body of St Cuthbert, the 'old man' of the title, is no longer disturbed because the chapel is no longer over his grave: he can sleep on alone.

Interestingly, Arden here returns to his architectural beginnings for a story which is both resonant and witty. It reflects on professional secretiveness and incompetence, as well as defensive groupings of workers. It has a spiritual element, as well as a distinctly earthy one, and, as with all Arden's radio plays, employs the strengths of the medium to powerful effect, for instance, in the burial of St Cuthbert with which the play opens. It also includes some of Arden's strongest writing, not only in the dialogue – here is the Frenchman's daughter trying to persuade Nick not to walk away:

> DAUGHTER : You are needed here, Nick, on the work, Charlie Bones
> needs all your quality – and Nick –
> NICK : Charlie Bones needs bloody nowt o' me but an iron toecap up the
> cleft of his rump: if I bide here much longer he'll get it, for all I'm a peace-
> seeking man. [503]

but also in the astonishing pastiche of the alliterative verse of the period at which the play is set:

> Oh and there she had it: hidden beneath the heat:
> Flat box filled to the brim with flowing lines and figures,
> Deployed draft of every detail her father could devise,
> Measurings, mode and module, meticulous proportion
> Of an entire sacred city begotten in the spirit of one man
> And recorded for the rightful reward of whoever could next regulate it
> best –

Me: she was making it mine . . . [504]

Despite all this, the play received mixed notices. Susie Cornfield, in *The Sunday Times*, thought it 'a glorious earthy tale of spiritual dreams and earthly passions messily fractured yet seamlessly patched. It mischievously plaited together the future of a church left half-built ... with the fortunes of a blighted love affair'.[505] But 'M.P.' in *The Listener* found it 'a strangely disappointing work, intensely private and just a little too archaeologically precise to really engage the listener'.[506]

At this time Arden was described as 'wonderfully fit-looking' and having 'a wiry thatch of silver hair cresting a nut-brown, weatherbeaten face'.[507] But however fit he seemed, he was in dire need of finance, and radio drama did not pay vast commissions to authors. But now he was offered a £3000 advance by his publishers, Methuen, for a novel, and in 1982, *Silence Among the Weapons*, was published. He had been 'nervous', about starting it, and filling '300 pages':[508] it was the sight of D'Arcy at work on *Tell Them Everything* which spurred him into action:

> She went into a private room, sat down with pen and notebook, and
> actually began to write – at a steady rate of so many words per day. This
> obsessive process, going on in my own home, infuriated me. I went into
> another room: opened the typewriter ... and began like-wise.[509]

The novel, we are informed on the title page, deals with 'some events at the time of the failure of a republic':[510] specifically, it is set between 91 and 81 BCE, when the Republic of Rome was the bone to be snatched and devoured by either of the two mad-dog generals, Sulla and Gaius Marius. Arden's sources were Plutarch, who wrote lives of both these overweening characters, as well as Petronius and Apuleius. He also relied on the nineteenth century German historian of Rome, and Nobel Prize winner, Theodor Mommsen, for the history of the period. Quotations from Mommsen, indeed, are placed at the head of each of the four books of the novel. Arden was also influenced by Robert Graves and John Masefield, though there is a rumbustiousness and vigour about Arden's writing which neither of these two forbears ever match. Using a chart rather in the way he and D'Arcy had used charts in the making of *The Non-Stop Connolly Show*, with dates in a vertical column and places (Rome, Antioch, etc) horizontally, and with some early en-couragement from Nick Hern, then his editor at Methuen, Arden found the experience of novel-writing brought 'great personal liberation'.[511]

Silence Among the Weapons, which was called *Vox Pop* in USA, is a high-spirited picaresque tale which follows the fortunes of one Ivory, an actor-turned-theatrical agent, whose tangled personal relations, which are inextricable from the political machinations he allows himself to become involved with, take him to various parts of the Roman Republic. The Republic at the time is in turmoil, and struggling towards becoming an empire, but the novel depicts the political manoeuvrings and the often-casual violence of the conflicts 'from below' – a good vantage-point from which to witness how ambition and greed for power and possessions destroy integrity.

Like other of Arden's works, especially those written around this time, *Silence Among the Weapons* also tackles the subject of the artist's relations with the wider society within which he (or she) lives, as the greatness of classical theatre gives way to more spectacular, but less thoughtful, presentations. Does this have a bearing on our own time? Certainly it is inflected through a series of barely-noticed references to the current situation in Ireland, and indeed to Arden's life in Galway. Thus, Horseferry sings of his being 'the shape of Cor an da Eala beside Loch Orbsen', as Corrandulla is beside Lough Corrib; the people's representatives are 'T.P.s' (Tribunes of the People) where in contemporary Ireland they are 'T.D.s' (members of Dáil Éireann); and the CRAC seems remarkably similar to the Irish Republican organisations – 'no-one's supposed to know that there's a secret CRAC as well as an overt one',[512] just as no-one is supposed to know of the link between Sinn Fein and the IRA. These parallels could be pursued, but it should not be thought that this is some kind of *roman à clef*, in which CRAC equates to the IRA, or Irish politicians can be matched to Roman counterparts; rather it is the turmoil of 1980s Ireland that is echoed in the turmoil of the Republic of Rome, with its mayhem, rioting, and tit-for-tat killings. And what is the artist's role or responsibility here? As the actors constantly don new parts, new masks, Ivory confesses his difficulties with people:

I behaved to these people most of the time with what I think was a distant courtesy. I could not bear to encourage an intimate friendship, to have anyone ask me questions about who I was before I became what I was.[513]

Who is he? Who was he? The question here may carry an overtly theatrical perspective, but it also the perspective of a writer (the work purports to be Ivory's memoirs), caught in the toils of personal or professional agitation and social confusion. As Ivory has changed from actor to agent, so Arden has changed from playwright to novelist.

The novel was well received. According to Neil Jordan, the story is 'presented with a verve and baldness that is both fascinating and shocking ... what one gets is a sense of convergence between empires of the present and that empire of the past – terrifying, fascinating and chaotic'.[514] A later critic called it 'a splendidly original imaginative work ... described in the bawdy, extravagantly emotional terms of theatre people'.[515]

And then suddenly, quite by accident, I heard over the wireless – or *thought* I heard – could I believe it? – that *Silence Among the Weapons* was on the shortlist for the Booker Prize.[516]

He had to believe it. The book was so recognised. Unfortunately, it did not win the prize, which was taken by Thomas Kenneally's *Schindler's Ark*; but it was perhaps a measure of Arden's achievement that his first novel had been so acclaimed.

But Arden was not able to go to London, to the televised prize-giving dinner. Despite Methuen's £3000 advance, the money problems which had perhaps reached their climax in the libel trial in 1978, were not over yet. True, the day when the advance copies of *Silence Among the Weapons* arrived at St Bridget's Place Lower was also the day when news came of Aosdána's *cnuas* (stipend) for D'Arcy. It was true also, that the embargo on D'Arcy's work by the BBC and the consequent reluctance of commissioning agencies to place work with her – and hence with Arden – seemed to be coming to an end. But other troubles were still very evident, and the rumours that D'Arcy was a terrorist still pursued her. 'Rumour' is the accurate word here: she never was a terrorist. But, for example, publicity appearances and a radio interview in connection with the publication of *Tell Them Everything* had been cancelled without a reason being given. Ronald Hayman had implied on BBC radio that John Arden was some kind of traitor. In America, invitations given to D'Arcy were unaccountably withdrawn. And even their sons had been caught in the entanglements of rumour and shadowy Special Branch spies: Finn had been found guilty of disorderly behaviour when present at some minor wrangling outside a disco; Adam was stopped coming out of school by the Special Patrol Group fifteen times in three months; Jacob was arrested twice, roughed up gratuitously and accused of having an IRA member for a mother; and Neuss was beaten by a policeman with a torch. As for the parents, 'no-one wanted to touch us', D'Arcy recalled. 'There we were, the thatch falling in, the place damp, and goodness knows what else'.[517] They were living on the £16 per week which D'Arcy earned from her cleaning job at the Galway City Council offices. And when she was in gaol, Arden did her job for her. Any intention to get to London for the prize-awarding ceremony was in any case hobbled by a furious and long-lasting strike by employees of the Irish banks.

'When I came out of Armagh Gaol, I decided I wasn't going to work with men again',[518] D'Arcy said. Instead, she was going to work to develop a specifically woman's perspective, exploring the implications which the idea of woman's culture raised. She was invited to become a member of Women in Media and Entertainment, which was affiliated to the National Women's Council of Ireland. The aims of WIME included celebrating women's culture and building women's resistance to the patriarchal military-industrial complex. In May 1982 WIME organised a conference at the Project Theatre, Dublin, to promulgate these ideas, and it was after this that D'Arcy gathered around her a few mostly deprived or oppressed women, and formed Galway's 'Women in Entertainment'. On 8 July 1982, this group began a series of more or less drama-related activities, variants of her 'loose theatre', perhaps. For instance, one of the first things they did was to read Euripides' *Hippolytus* together; as the women discussed the play, they found in it, two plays, one following the other. First, Phaedra was shown at ease with her sexuality and Hippolytus confused and desperate; but suddenly, Euripides changed course, and Phaedra now discovered that what had seemed natural, was actually unnatural. Was the reason for Euripides' change of direction his need to please the male judges in the City Dionysia? Later Galway Women in Entertainment meetings encompassed subjects including radio, video, Irish dancing and excursions. D'Arcy brought in contentious press cuttings, handed them round arbitrarily, and asked the women to argue from the point of view of the subject of the cutting. They had an all-night midsummer bonfire, and visited ancient sacred sites such as Knock Ma, where the 'little people' were reputed to dwell. Though the mountain belonged mystically to Maeve, legendary Queen of Connaught, 'on the very top ... we saw the grave of General Kirwan', male scion of a prominent Galway family.[519]

Through such activities, D'Arcy hoped that the women – and she herself, as well – would find their own distinctive voice, different from that of the patriarchal hegemony. One commentator noted:

> Instead of creating audiences for her plays, D'Arcy's enterprise now is to make women, whose lives are mired in anxieties, poverty and brutal assault, at one and the same time authors and audiences of their own dramas.[520]

Her aim ostensibly was to find ways of articulating the nature of women's oppressions and then to seek ways of countering it. Michael Etherton placed this pseudo-dramatic work in a wider tradition of dramatic enquiry rooted in the west of Ireland, which also included plays by John B.Keane and M.J.Molloy, the National Folk Theatre of Ireland which was based in Tralee, the theatre of the Gaeltacht and even the Druid Theatre Company of Galway.

But what D'Arcy was moving towards was probably more unusual than these comparatively traditional manifestations of theatre or entertainment. She was seeking something which might still loosely be called 'theatre', but which would allow the hitherto unheard voices of unprivileged women to be heard, and in a forum which would not inhibit the speaker. Her ideas seem to have derived at least partially from an all-day seminar held in London in 1979 which she attended and which addressed the subject of 'Women in Entertainment'. Ideas from this event, notably the uncritical acceptance of sexual type-casting in theatre, were discussed, and at the first Limerick Women's Festival in 1981, she gave a paper, later published in *Awkward Corners*, which crystallised some of her thoughts. What she was seeking was some way of expressing what needed to be expressed, free not only from overt censorship, but also from all forms of stereotyping, such as sexual stereotyping, which were themselves subtle forms of censorship.

At the same time, she began working with Arden on a BBC commission which was to turn into *Whose Is The Kingdom?* some years later, and which provided a chink through which she was also able to resurrect their collaboration. The radio plays of the late 1970s and early 1980s had been written by Arden alone, but by 1981 or 1982, times were changing. Martin Esslin's influence had waned at the BBC, and as far as RTE were concerned, D'Arcy was a founder member of the country's most prestigious organisation of artists, Aosdána, and could therefore hardly be excluded from their airwaves. Consequently, when the chance arose to make a radio version of *Vandaleur's Folly*, she and Arden took it with both hands.

The new version was called *The Manchester Enthusiasts*. It was perhaps a necessary exorcising of the raw memories of the 7:84 Theatre Company's production of the play. The story was re-conceived, this time from the point of view of Edward Craig, the socialist co-operator who with his wife left Manchester to go to Ralahine to assist in the establishment of the rural co-operative on the land of John Vandaleur. It was to become a sort of Owenite collective farm, a Utopian dream commemorated today in the University of Limerick's Ralahine Centre for Utopian Studies. Craig's personal history was fascinating in itself. He had been at Peterloo in 1819, and was a committed Chartist as well as a self-taught scientist. He understood what Arden and D'Arcy most passionately believed about the Irish situation – that without the support of the English working class, the revolutionary struggle of the Irish people could never wholly succeed. So Ralahine in the new play most clearly stands for this dream of progress, an unrealized dream, of course, because Vandaleur himself never gave up his ownership of the land. But perhaps not unrealizable. It is probably Arden and D'Arcy's clearest statement on the need for thoroughgoing, revolutionary change rather than the compromises inevitably involved in all reform movements. In the case of the historical Ralahine, the reform was remarkable, even extreme: there was guaranteed equality between women and men, and all had the vote at a time when the franchise anywhere else in the world was tightly controlled and extraordinarily narrow. But when Vandaleur had to sell his estate, the co-operating peasants (and the Manchester enthusiasts) had nowhere to go.

The Manchester Enthusiasts was broadcast by the BBC in two one-and-a-half hour broadcasts on 18 and 25 June 1984, with Christian Rodska as Craig. It was directed by Robert Cooper. It was then given an entirely new production by RTE. However, for Irish audiences, the title was changed to *The Ralahine Experiment*, and the play was given in three one hour broadcasts.

Meanwhile political developments in Ireland and the United Kingdom seemed to be presenting opportunities for Craig-style progress. The Northern Ireland Assembly elections of 1982 had seen the beginnings of the rise of Provisional Sinn Fein as a potent electoral force; the General Election in the republic that year had seen the Fianna Fail government fall and Garrett Fitzgerald's Fine Gael resume power. Confrontation was sharpening. Though the Republic's 1983 referendum on abortion law reform was lost, and though the United King-dom may have seemed to be turning into a near-police state, as the miners across England, Wales and Scotland were attacked and finally subdued in 1984, the Workers Party in Ireland was moving forward. The 'street politics' of the 1970s was giving place to something which seemed to promise more lasting and deeper success. In October 1982 the party overturned the longstanding policy which said they would not take any seats to which they were elected until Ireland was united and free, and they began to win seats. Equally significant was their moving closer to the Communist Party of the Soviet Union. Fraternal relations were formally established between the two parties in 1983 and classes in Marxism were held for party members across Ireland. The question of the relevance of Soviet-style communism to the problems of Ireland were doubted by some, however, and this forms the core of Arden and D'Arcy's last collaborative staged work for professional performers.

This was an adaptation of Bertolt Brecht's *The Mother* in its shortened cantata form, which was staged at the Queen Elizabeth Hall on 19 January 1984. Brecht's play, translated here by Steve Gooch, is itself an adaptation of Gorky's novel of the same name. It tells the story of Pelagea Vlassova, the ignorant mother of a typically exploited Russian worker, who is gradually drawn into his revolutionary activities, and in the last scene it is she who bears the red flag at the climactic demonstration in the winter of 1916/1917, just before the overthrow of the tsar. The musician John Tilbury now wanted to commission a new version of this story, refocusing the action on Ireland but retaining Brecht's original lyrics with Hanns Eisler's music. D'Arcy and Arden accepted the commission. A brief comparison of the scripts shows how they changed the original. Brecht's opening –

SPEAKER : Beginning of the year 1904 in the Russian city of Tversk. It is early morning, and Pelagea Vlassova, a 42-year-old working class widow, is preparing soup for her son who is leaving for work.[521]

becomes

SPEAKER : 1968 in partitioned Ireland: Derry. Maire Doherty, a forty-four year old catholic working class widow, is making breakfast for her daughter who is leaving for work.

The child in the story has become female in the new version, but otherwise the starting-point is much the same. But the adaptation quite quickly moves uncomfortably closer to home. Brecht's text states: 'Pelagea Vlassova is disturbed to see her son in the company of revolutionary workers'. D'Arcy and Arden's version is subtly more concrete: 'Maire Doherty is disturbed to find her daughter in contact with republicans on the Housing Action Committee'. And this specificity continues: in April 1969

Maire Doherty's daughter has joined the banned republican movement,
is active on demonstrations and in the election of Bernadette Devlin to
Parliament. Immediately after the election, a civil rights march is banned.
Riots erupt in Derry. The police break into catholic houses and beat a
man to death. In fear of her life, the daughter has to leave home. Maire
Doherty makes tea and sandwiches for the beleaguered people behind the
barricades, and helps to prepare petrol bombs. The Northern Ireland
Labour Party, the catholic church, the bourgeois Nationalist politicians,
and trade union leaders all urge the people to repudiate 'extremists'.

Brecht's support for communistic rebellion in a distant land many decades ago was
one thing; this was clearly another. Chambers and Prior ask why in the D'Arcy-
Arden version the IRA should be seen as a development from the Communism of
the first two decades of the twentieth century,[522] and on one level this seems a fair
critique. But the organisers of the production, the Eisler Collective, who had
previously appeared in such ultra-Communist states as North Korea and Albania,
wanted it as a deliberately provocative part of a particular evening. The concert they
planned was to include works by Cornelius Cardew, Christian Wolff, Dave Smith,
Alan Bush and Yaji Takahashi. And the new version of *The Mother* was to be the
climax of the event.

On 17 December 1983 D'Arcy and Arden were aboard the boat for England
heading for rehearsals of this piece. At precisely that time, a bomb exploded near
Harrods Department Store in central London. Apparently planted by the IRA, six
people were killed, including three policemen. There was outrage in England, and
when it was noticed that the poster for the concert at the Queen Elizabeth Hall
flaunted the words 'Long Kesh' in apparent support of the IRA, the anger generated
by the bomb was trained on this event. The promise by the Arts Council of a
guarantee against loss was withdrawn in a panic because of the concert's 'Irish
dimension'. The 'Long Kesh' poster was also withdrawn, but too late. So, although
the Eisler Collective scraped together enough to pay the musicians, D'Arcy and
Arden received nothing. Even *The Times* called the Arts Council's action 'ill-advised,
inexcusable and counter-productive'.[523]

Then the Brecht Estate, which had originally been happy to agree to the
performance, was persuaded to change its agreement and to withdraw the rights to
perform – presumably because Brecht himself, the well-known Communist, would
not have approved of 'terrorism'. Just in time, Stefan Brecht, the playwright's son,
intervened, and insisted that the evening go ahead. Under these clouds the
performance took place. But it was poorly attended, and the atmosphere was
poisonous. Even the cloakroom attendants, it appeared, had been warned to ensure
that no bomb was cunningly concealed in the pocket of an overcoat left with them.
The critics, mistaking their function, attacked the adaptation as promulgating an

alien political philosophy and suggested unsubtly that the authors were the dupes of international Communism. One report, admitting that the cantata had been performed by 'a small, well-blended ad hoc choir', nevertheless spoke of 'the evening's rather insignificant activities'.[524]

But for D'Arcy and Arden, hardened to such puerile criticism, 1984 seemed a long way from the horrors of the late 1970s and earlier 1980s. The last song in *The Mother* is entitled 'In Praise of the Dialectic' and contains the line:

So if you are beaten down, you just rise again!

If in 1980 the forces of reaction had beaten both D'Arcy and Arden down, it seemed that now, slowly, they were rising again.

Nineteen : Artists for Freedom

In the early 1980s John Arden began virtually a new career as a writer when he abjured the stage and devoted his energy to novels and radio dramas. At the same time, Margaretta D'Arcy's career also took a new turn: the traumas of Armagh Gaol and her election to Aosdána together had made her a 'new person'. Political and community action now became her prime focus. She campaigned in the 'Kerry babies' case, and took an official Sinn Fein exhibition of Irish history to West Germany, where she and Arden also worked with students, using *The Non-Stop Connolly Show* as a basis for role play, improvisations, exercises in choral speech and Irish dance. It was typical of several such visits to Europe, where, for instance, their programmes, *The Menace of Ireland* and *The Poisoned Stream*, received a considerably more sympathetic hearing than in Britain.

Then in February 1984, along with Julie Christie, David Hare, Dusty Hughes, Roger Woddis and others, they went as part of a 'cultural delegation' organised by Andy de la Tour and the Nicaragua Solidarity Campaign to the central American republic of Nicaragua. Here an ideological battle was being fought out in the bitterest terms. In 1979 left-wing Sandanistas had overthrown the long-lasting right-wing dictatorship of Anastasio Somoza, and tried to establish a more democratic version of Cuban socialism. Though initially treated with caution by President Jimmy Carter, the Sandanistas came under heavy pressure from Ronald Reagan after he became President in 1981. Reagan financed and trained remnants of the now-dead Somoza's fascist army and bribed other malcontents to join the anti-Sandanista rebels, known as 'Contras', despite Congress explicitly banning such funding. A huge propaganda offensive was also launched by the Reagan administration, so that by 1984 the Sandanista government was under extreme pressure from their huge and powerful neighbour to the north. And it was into this cauldron of political frenzy that the 'cultural delegation' came.

The delegation was official, and therefore followed a government-approved programme, accompanied at all times by an official guide and interpreter. They stayed in a 'luxurious government hostel'[525] and were driven about in an air-conditioned people carrier. However it was plain to them that the Sandanista government was interested in bringing politics and culture together in ways they approved of and that they were promoting popular culture. Arden and D'Arcy talked to the President, Daniel Ortega, as well as the Minister for Culture, Father Ernesto Cardenal, journalists, trades union leaders and the U.N. Commissioner for Refugees. They also met people from the Miskito and Sumo tribal groups on the Atlantic sea coast, anti-Reagan American tourists and a few ordinary individuals. One of these was their fifty-year-old driver, Raoul, who had been a truck-driver decades earlier, but had given it up because of the predations of the Somoza government's agents on anyone driving a vehicle. He fought against the dictatorship and was now back in a job he liked.[526]

They found the Catholic Church resisting the inbuilt conservatism of the Vatican, and a lively 'Liberation Theology' at work:

> There was folk-singing within the mass itself and community
> participation in the service. People were able to get up in church and
> address the congregation. When the priest gave a long sermon about the
> importance of the forthcoming elections and the need to resist US
> intervention and protect Nicaraguan sovereignty the congregation was
> very attentive. After the sermon two catechists, lay members, a man and a
> woman, addressed the congregation.[527]

Unlike in European services, Arden and D'Arcy noted that here:

> No-one knelt to the host and many people left before the communion;
> they had come for the politics. The murals of the church itself showed
> freedom-fighters, reflecting the militarised lifestyle of a people 'not
> menacing' but armed in preparation against invasion.[528]

They also attended a weekend conference on Central American culture organised by the Union of Cultural Workers where groups of participants made improvised plays on the theme of 'America for the Americans', and there were heated discussions between the plays.

For D'Arcy especially, the comparisons with Ireland were enlightening. Like Ireland, Nicaragua was a country trying to break free from imperial domination and exploitation by multi-national corporations, though depressingly it seemed to her that others in their delegation were unable to make this connection. Arden noted the comparison, too, and also likened the situation to Britain in 1940. It seemed that the new Nicaragua was not a Marxist-totalitarian state, that the people were working and not unhappy, that there were no valid atrocity stories and no truth in allegations of secret police knocking on doors and arresting people in the middle of the night. The situation in Nicaragua, in fact, seemed considerably preferable to that of nearby Honduras and Belize, which the group also visited.

The concern with Nicaragua was made all the starker a few months later when Ronald Reagan visited the Republic of Ireland. It was election year and here was a rather crude way for him to collect Irish-American votes. He landed at Shannon Airport in the west of Ireland on 1 June 1984, his first port of call being the University College of Galway to collect an Honorary Degree. There were protests across Ireland, and when later he addressed the Dáil in Dublin, at least three TDs walked out. In Galway, the cleverest protest was by two University lecturers, Pat Sheeran and Des Johnson, former members of Galway Theatre Workshop, who dressed in their academic robes, went out onto the streets of the city and awarded a 'doctorate' to any passers-by who could give a few 'Alice-in-Wonderland' questions suitably absurd answers. 'That must be the most ignorant reply we've had yet – of course it deserves a doctorate!' [529] There were serious consequences to this 'loose theatre', however, especially for Arden. *Serjeant Musgrave's Dance*, which had been a significant success in a recent production at the National Theatre in London with Albert Finney as Serjeant Musgrave, was to be filmed. But a photograph of the authors protesting against Reagan appeared in the British press, and the American producer of the film backed out.

In June the following year, a conference was held at the Royal Court Theatre called 'Methuen 500', to celebrate the fact that this publisher now had five hundred plays in print. On the Sunday, there was a 'Playwrights' Forum' on the topic of 'Theatre Writing: Why and How?' D'Arcy and Arden, along with other prominent playwrights, were invited to be part of an on-stage panel. After two of the other playwrights had spoken, it was D'Arcy's turn. She urged that the theatre as it was practiced effectively condemned actors and playwrights to the status of hunted prey, with the spectators taking the role of hunters. She advocated a much looser, less formal structure for theatrical events, perhaps something like that achieved in Galway's Theatre Workshop's 'immediate rough theatre' (though she did not refer to this). But her point was disparaged, and booing and barracking broke out, until she suggested that those who were interested in more collaborative or spontaneous forms of theatre accompany her upstairs where they could discuss such ideas in a non-threatening atmosphere. Several members of the conference left with her. Arden stood up and walked to the side of the stage from where he viewed the proceedings without taking further part. It was, as Michael Cohen noted,

> emblematic of an increasing isolation but also of an unbreakable courage
> and integrity: if the theatre will not serve what are perceived as the
> highest artistic and political goals, then there will be no compromise.[530]

D'Arcy was attempting to move theatre and the discussion of theatre in new directions; for others, such as *The Guardian* critic, Michael Billington, this was unacceptable. In an uncharacteristically unpleasant article, in which he virtually accused D'Arcy of racism, he made clear that for him, the *status quo* could be improved, but was basically sound. The chasm between the longstanding D'Arcy-Arden vision of some kind of open-ended democratic theatre and the subsidised cultural establishment was as wide – or wider – than ever.

But D'Arcy's position was clarifying. That same year she attended another conference at Bologna University in Italy, convened by Giovanna Morsiani, who 'gave us the freedom to do what we wanted'. For D'Arcy this was an important moment of realization: 'One day we had a performance where everyone expressed themselves in groups in songs, stories or little plays. So all of us were the audience and all of us were the activators'.[531] Rigid compartments began to disintegrate. It was

261

a revolutionary concept, towards which much of her work since 'Kirkbymoorside 63', and even earlier perhaps, seemed to have been leading. It required a different, non-hierarchical approach to the arts and the possibility of leaving work 'open', 'the excitement of imperfection' as she called it in a memorable phrase.[532]

Much of D'Arcy's activity was dependent on the money she received from Aosdána. When it was established it consisted of 89 male members and seven women. D'Arcy read this as a Government endorsement of the idea that leading artists were a sort of male priesthood, with the arts substituting for religion in a godless age. This religion – 'as hierarchical, patriarchal, authoritarian, secretive and class-based as any of the old ones'[533] – was not one D'Arcy could endorse, and she determined to campaign to democratise the institution which was subsidising her. Her first moves involved submitting resolutions against censorship in the arts to the Aosdána Assembly, and though these were passed, the minutes of the meetings, as she later discovered, were censored. In 1986 she brought another resolution forward asking for the publication of uncensored minutes, the dissolution of crippling Standing Orders, and the opening of meetings to the public. This was, she said, an organisation held together by fear – fear of losing one's *cnuas*, fear of being expelled from Aosdána, fear of cultural blackballing. Cliques and factions were forming, the spirit of the free arts was being lost. Her speech, which lasted less than five minutes, was continuously booed and heckled by those with most to lose, those whom she later described with amusing acidity as 'a clutch of misogynist malevolent goblins hunkered over their crock of knowledge'.

Her motion was not carried. D'Arcy decided on direct action.

From 21 April 1986, therefore, she sat outside the offices of the Irish Arts Council, which happened to be in the same building as the offices of Aosdána, in Merrion Square, Dublin, from where she appealed to

> all those who feel as oppressed as I do by the ever-increasing restrictive
> bureaucracy of the arts administration in Ireland, to come together and
> collectively create a cultural event that will expose the dead corpse and let
> free the living spirit.[534]

She sat on the doorstep of the Arts Council building during office hours every Monday to Friday, from where she expounded her view to anyone who would listen that publicly-funded institutions such as Aosdána must be open to the public's inspection. Moreover, she argued, bureaucratic secrecy disadvantaged the radical and the oddball: her protest aimed to open up the debate which had been stifled at the meeting, especially at a time when buskers were being criminalised and local arts festivals – including Galway's – were being starved of funds.

Margaretta D'Arcy outside the offices of Aosdána, May 1986.

This absurd protest completely confounded the authorities. Once again the loosely theatrical nature of D'Arcy's protest gave it an unexpected edge. Adrian Munnally, the Director of the Arts Council, and Theo McNab, the chair of Aosdána, attempted to move her on, first by threatening a legal writ from the building's owners, then by banning her from using the building's toilets, and finally by threatening to confiscate her chair, table and the posters she was displaying if she moved from her seat. Her answer was to put a chamber pot on her head and to continue to sit there. As *The New Statesman* put it, 'Not since the peripatetic scholars of ancient Greece … used to plonk a stool down in a public place and ask questions infuriating to the authorities has there been such fun as Galway playwright Margaretta D'Arcy's one-woman protest against the Irish arts establishment'.[535] The affair soon became organised into a sort of street carnival. On Mondays, supporters were urged to dress up in fancy clothes – be 'Art in Motion' around the streets of Dublin; Tuesdays saw poets reading their work; on Wednesdays, it was the turn of buskers and street musicians to entertain; Thurs-days was a kind of 'Hyde Park Corner' – 'Freedom of speech for all'; and Fridays was devoted to Irish culture – song, dance, poetry, stories. In all these, D'Arcy insisted on positive discrimination in favour of women. On 20 June, the last day of the protest, there was a 'Monster Slogan Competition' when people were invited to compose an appropriate slogan for the event, such as 'Chained expression is no expression' or 'People's culture is not sub-culture'.

D'Arcy called the whole thing the 'Circus Exposé of the New Cultural Church'. People came to 'cook food for a street-party, alternative healers came with oils and massage (and) other people fell in love'.[536] John Arden worked behind her, sending out propaganda on her behalf, informing people of what was happening and cajoling support from any who might give it. The press was amused, reported the action reasonably, and were useful in informing the wider public of what was going on. And the results were gratifying. Aosdána's leaders decided that their minutes should no longer be edited for the convenience of those in power; meetings were opened to the public; and quickly more women members were admitted. It was a campaign which was both fun and – more or less – successful.

It was almost inevitable after her engagements with Aosdána, Nicaragua, Armagh Gaol, and more, that D'Arcy would become involved with the Greenham Common Women's Peace Camp. This was probably women's most important intervention into the social and political process since the time of the suffragettes. In fact, by the time of her first visit to Greenham in early 1983, the Peace Camp had been alive for almost two years. But before taking proper notice of it, D'Arcy had had to overcome a certain impatience with the women's movement of the 1960s and 1970s, when it often appeared to her to focus on child care for ambitious career women, and seemed to have no interest in, for example, the working class women prisoners in Armagh Gaol.

On 12 December 1979, NATO made the decision to base Cruise missiles, each armed with a nuclear warhead, at Greenham Common, near Newbury in Berkshire. Two years later, thirty-six 'Women for Life on Earth' walked from Cardiff to Greenham to deliver a letter to the Commander of the base protesting the decision. They would, they said, await his reply – which was, effectively, that they could wait as long as they liked. His message backfired. The women did wait. They set up a Peace Camp which lasted for nineteen years. In 1982 they held a 'Festival of Life', and on 12 December that year, 30,000 women joined them to 'Embrace the Base', holding hands and encircling the perimeter. The battle between those who held life dear and those who held the means to destroy it was joined.

In January 1983, D'Arcy paid her first visit to the Peace Camp, driven there by a friend in an unreliable and ancient vehicle. It was just the time when Newbury Council was revoking the bye-laws and claiming to be landlord of the site with powers to evict unwanted trespassers, a claim later proved in court to be com-pletely unfounded. D'Arcy was immediately struck by the maturity and good sense of the women at the main gate, who were in the process of a meeting to discuss how to present their case positively to the unanimously hostile Tory British press. By the time she returned towards the end of that year, the Cruise missiles with their nuclear warheads had arrived. It was 12 December, and again the women – now 50,000 strong – marked the anniversary by 'embracing the base'. But D'Arcy, who had arrived with the rest to join the action, was unable to take part: she had tangled with a vigilante thug who had beaten her badly, leaving her with a hairline fracture of the skull. Bleeding profusely, she was taken to hospital. The long-term result of the injury was an uncontrollable 'wobble' of the head, which stayed with her for the rest of her life.

Such an incident was not likely to daunt D'Arcy's spirit. The camp was magnetic for her. There was no electricity, no telephone, no running water; there were too many long, boring hours; there was hassle and evictions from bailiffs and attacks by vigilantes. But there was also an urgent moral problem to be addressed, a wrong to be confronted. Caroline Blackwood described how

> nothing had prepared me for the desolation of the camps the women inhabited. I had visualised camps that looked like the camps of boy scouts, but I discovered nothing of the kind. At first sight, the camps of the Greenham women looked like derelict piles of refuse that had been allowed to collect on the side of the road. The 'benders' they inhabited were like crazy little igloos made of polythene. As tents and caravans had been forbidden by the local council, they had erected these small and eccentric dwellings by draping a sheet of plastic over bending boughs which they had pegged into the mud. Some of the benders were not more than two feet off the ground and had to be entered on all fours. It was astonishing to see a grey-haired woman going into her bender with the scuttling movements of a rabbit vanishing into its burrow.[537]

The camps were usually squeezed up against the perimeter fence to avoid being on the road, and the women frequently decorated the wire with spiders' webs made of wool, or balloons, or flowers, in defiance of a newly-instituted byelaw which forbade the decoration of fences. There was an extraordinary case of a woman who was arrested for criminal damage after hanging a daffodil on the wire.

D'Arcy connected the camp with mythology – the archetypal mother goddess – and history – the persecution of witches. And indeed the barracks on the base were built over the grave of a witch who had been murdered by Oliver Cromwell's men in the 1650s; now the soldiers accused the peace women of being witches and casting spells. D'Arcy also found it in some ways reminiscent of a closed order of nuns. She discovered there were different camps at the different gates to the base, each with its own emblematic colour. The camp at the main gate was Yellow Gate camp, which had been the victim of a 'road-widening' exercise aimed to destroy it – but without success. Green Gate was nearest the missile silos: it was the camp which was exclusively for women – no male visitors, even, were allowed. Blue Gate was the 'new age' gate, Violet Gate had a religious focus, and Red Gate was for artists.

And there was, of course, hostility from many – but by no means all – of the local people. Some, mainly motivated by their perception that property prices were lowered by the proximity of the camp, formed themselves into Ratepayers Against Greenham Encampments (RAGE). There were vigilante groups. Few pubs or restaurants served the Greenham women (D'Arcy herself was turned away from more than one Newbury establishment). And there were of course the ongoing attempts to evict. In April 1984, four hundred policemen surrounded Yellow Gate camp, and herded the women away and along the road. Then earth-moving equipment was moved in and everything destroyed; a fence was even erected to make sure the women did not return. To no avail. The women did return, and by then Mrs Thatcher needed her police force more urgently for her battles with the striking coalminers. Nevertheless, harassment by eviction order continued right through till 1993. D'Arcy recorded: 'The bailiffs would come and they'd put out the fire & take the wood, and we'd have to move everything or it would be put into the "cruncher" and destroyed'.[538]

The Cruise missiles were taken in convoy out of the base and into the countryside, usually to Salisbury Plain, at least once a month all the time they were based at Greenham. These exercises usually happened in the dead of night, but the women would always attempt to disrupt them. They followed them, blocked them, hindered them in whatever way was possible, while the soldiers abused them and hurled objects, even iron bars, at them while they linked arms, chanted and sang, and even built fires in the middle of the approach roads. D'Arcy graphically described such an action in her diary:

> Frost. Clear night ... We lined the road. Some women in the bushes. We waited for the police cars and vans. Heard vans arrive ... we waited and waited; hushly deathly silence; the moon; waiting for the roar and the lights of the convoy ... Then the lights, the noise, motor-bikes, cars, the convoy! Military colour with cloth flags, like Dracula's coffin: very very weird. Sarah was told to put out her torch. Lights flashing in the bushes; the cops picking up women, throwing them down, rolling them over, as the convoy trundled past. It was over. We went back to Yellow Gate, women bruised and sore.[539]

By now – 1986 – D'Arcy had decided to try to make an opera with Maria Lamburn about the Peace Camp, and they both returned to Greenham in September. Until now, D'Arcy had really only been a 'day tripper'; now she intended to settle in for some months. The first thing she discovered was that the context was not conducive to creating an opera. As a 'beginner' in the long-stay camp she was expected to work hard, fetching, carrying, cooking, and she felt insecure in the face of cliques and arguments. She moved from Yellow Gate to Green Gate in search of more compatible companionship. However, it was the 'Ant Action' of December

1986 which made her feel she had really 'come of age'. The Ant Action was a mass trespass on a frosty Saturday night, when the wire was cut and several women entered the base. They ran in and over the grounds, where most, including D'Arcy, were arrested and taken to the 'process room'. After being detained in Newbury till the Monday morning, D'Arcy was finally allowed out, back to Green Gate, then home to Ireland, feeling that at last she had become a 'Greenham woman'.

The cliques and arguments which she had already noticed, however, were about to become much worse when she returned in 1987 to Yellow Gate, which she now recognised as 'the pivot'.[540] Rumblings were heard between different Greenham-based groups (or Gates), and beyond the gates, many members of CND did not see eye-to-eye with many Greenham Peace Women over various incidents, and there were other differences with groups such as the Camden-based Greenham Women Everywhere and Cruisewatch. Many of these disagreements were exacerbated when President Reagan and the Soviet Union's Mikhail Gorbachev announced they were to sign an Intermediate Nuclear Force treaty. Was this the end of Cruise missiles? How should the peace movement respond? The answer often depended on the political alignment of the responder.

A Women's Global Peace Conference in Moscow was announced. Greenham Women Everywhere and Cruisewatch, both groups established to support the Peace Camp, but also sympathetic to Communism, were invited to send delegates, but they failed to pass the invitation to the non-aligned women at the Yellow Gate Peace Camp, who however managed to receive an invitation after writing to Raissa Gorbachev herself. At the conference, these Yellow Gate women – Sarah Hipperson, Katrina Howse and Beth Junor – made a thorough nuisance of themselves. When Gorbachev congratulated them on campaigning against US Cruise missiles, they immediately and publicly corrected him to say that they campaigned against *all* nuclear weapons, including Soviet weapons. They also asked why Gorbachev himself was speaking at a women's conference, while his wife remained silent. And there was a fierce disagreement about a workshop on Greenham. Greenham Women Everywhere tried to hijack the running of this, and then, when Wilmette Brown, the black leader of the King's Cross Women's Centre, spoke against them, the Camden delegates walked out.

Attempts to resolve the dispute back in Britain failed. The Communist Party's newspaper, *The Morning Star*, published a positive, pro-Communist report of the Moscow conference, and when Sarah Hipperson wrote a letter to point out that the Greenham women's position was one of non-alignment, the paper refused to publish it. Some of the Yellow Gate women, including D'Arcy, went to London to picket the paper's offices. Even though the company's chief executive spoke with Sarah Hipperson and Wilmette Brown, the Metropolitan police were called in, and the picket broken up. Shortly afterwards, possibly coincidentally, a particularly brutal raid was made on Yellow Gate camp, with people dragged face down across tarmac roads, handcuffs and sniffer dogs in evidence, and much property seized – including, by the way, the draft of D'Arcy's opera. She herself was thrown to the ground, her ribs badly bruised, one arm lacerated and one leg bruised.

The dispute dragged on. There were unpleasant phone calls, and the Yellow Gate women were ostracised by the women at the other gates. D'Arcy included a brief description of the matter in *Awkward Corners*, published in 1988, and was threatened with legal action, a threat which caused the book to be held back from being sold to the public briefly. The contention continued for years and was never properly settled.

Meanwhile, at her trial in March 1987, D'Arcy began to read her defence statement from the dock, when it was snatched from her hands by a policeman. When she protested, she was hustled out of the dock and the courtroom, and was sentenced in her absence. She was detained in Newbury Police Station, where she had neither change of clothes nor toilet articles, then taken to Holloway Gaol where she was put into solitary confinement. During the two days she was in Holloway, she was strip-searched twice. She refused to take her clothes off for this demeaning procedure, forcing the women warders to do it for her. And when they had done their nasty business, she refused to put her clothes on again. They protested, whereupon D'Arcy declared she was quite happy to remain in the nude. The warders dressed her.

A later trial, in 1988, had a more comical element. She had tripped into a rabbit hole while eating a chocolate biscuit, and broken her leg. It meant that she was unable to stand when the judge entered, something that undoubtedly pleased her as an Irish republican as much as it amused her. Hers were just two of a total of 812 cases of trespass which the court dealt with between January 1987 and April 1988.

1989 brought more drama. First, at Imber, a deserted village on Salisbury Plain from which in 1943 the people had been evacuated and the village handed to the military. Now it had been made to look like a village in northern Ireland, and was being used for house-to-house combat training. This was perhaps the link between Ireland and Greenham Common which D'Arcy had been seeking. At any rate, as a sort of birthday present to her, on 14 June 1989, the women of Yellow Gate crept into the banned village in the middle of the night, and occupied the church. Here, they honoured the memory of Mairéad Farrell, D'Arcy's mentor in Armagh Gaol who had recently been assassinated by British troops in Gibraltar. Of course the women were arrested, but D'Arcy managed to ask one of them why he was going to Ireland. His answer – 'to kill Gerry Adams' – seemed feeble, and she asked whether he would stand by this statement in court.

Margaretta D'Arcy at Greenham Common.

Then, on Hiroshima Day, 6 August, Helen Thomas, a 22 year-old woman at Yellow Gate, was knocked down and killed outside the camp. A white police horsebox drove past too close to her, its wing mirror hit her head and she died immediately. Of course, D'Arcy knew her. She ran to the scene. She wanted to question the horsebox driver, or go to the hospital to be beside Helen. The women stood in a circle holding hands. The next day, D'Arcy held Helen's mother while she wept for her daughter. Later she went to view the body in the morgue:

> Helen is lying there, white towel on brow, no top of head, her tongue is
> twisted in her mouth, her eyes half closed, her ears big, sticking out; I feel
> her body, it is a board. I am too frightened to touch her face.[541]

The twisted tongue seemed to haunt D'Arcy.

It seemed a sickening end to what had often been a sickening decade. One bright spot had been D'Arcy's persuading a number of Greenham women to visit northern Ireland, to see the war conditions there for themselves: she found places for them to stay, introduced them to people whom she thought it would be useful for them to talk to, and extended some conventional concepts of feminism in the way her own concept had been extended by the women of Armagh.

But in Ireland itself things seemed to be moving in what she regarded as the wrong direction on almost all fronts. Fianna Fáil had won back power, with Charles Haughey entering his third term as Taoiseach. Now he moved spectacularly to liberalise the tired Irish economy in imitation of Margaret Thatcher in the United Kingdom. He cut taxes and spending – most notably, and most unpopularly, health spending – and deregulated much of industry. He tempted international investment, as he brought Ireland into the dance of capitalist globalisation. By 2002, it may be noted, Ireland's GDP *per capita* was the fourth largest in the world, and between 1987 and 2002 the private sector expanded by fifteen per cent. However, it seemed that the Workers Party, still the party closest to D'Arcy and Arden, was making progress, and in the European elections of 1989, it polled more votes in Dublin than any other party. But its closeness to the Soviet Union indicated its Achilles heel, and these gains would not last. The Soviet bloc was crumbling away, and on 9 November 1989, the Berlin Wall was smashed. From then, the writing was on the wall for the Workers Party. As for northern Ireland, matters were certainly not improving. In 1984, 72 people were killed in the 'Troubles'; in 1987 the number had risen to over a hundred. For ordinary people walking the streets of Belfast was a terrifying experience. John Rety, a Hungarian-born poet, described one afternoon:

> I was suddenly conscious of a commotion behind me, emanating from
> beyond the Conway Mill. I looked round to see five soldiers with rifles
> and a black and white dog running towards me. The soldiers were
> dressed in camouflage battle dress. I stayed put. They ran nervously past
> me and did not answer when I asked them what was happening. The
> fattest of the five young men was sweating. As they turned the corner,
> two of the soldiers ran backwards, swinging their guns to cover their exit.
> All this while the taxis went past. A pedestrian walked unconcernedly in
> the direction of the retreating soldiers. The woman who was scrubbing
> her front porch now finished and sloshed her bucket of dirty water into
> the gutter. 'What was that about?' I asked her. 'How should I know', she
> answered and went inside her home, banging the door.[542]

It was into this mix that D'Arcy's next cultural intervention, one of her boldest, was aimed. It was *Duchas na Saoirse* ('Artists for Freedom').

Duchas na Saoirse was a kind of festival, a weekend held in Belfast for any artists, writers, readers, academics or others who felt themselves culturally oppressed, to join in whatever activities seemed appropriate or worthwhile. Though it only gained its name in 1988, it was held each spring for five years from 1987. It was in a small way an attempt to turn the minds of northerners, perhaps especially members and supporters of Provisional Sinn Fein, from violence towards something more productive. But it was important that it was open-ended and not prescriptive, the antidote to state-sponsored arts events. 'The state intimidates people who are just having a different experience', D'Arcy said.[543] *Awkward Corners*, Arden and D'Arcy's 1988 collection of essays, was prefaced by its dedication to Gerry Tanner, who hanged himself in August 1987 and who, in June 1986, had read as a contribution to D'Arcy's 'Circus Exposé' outside Dublin's Arts Council building, his 'Manifesto for les Invisibles', with its hammer-blow refrain: 'CHAINED EXPRESSION IS NO EXPRESSION!'[544] *Duchas na Saoirse* declared itself against all forms of censorship, including that of editors and publishers, 'market forces', official censorship, Acts of Parliament (such as the Prevention of Terrorism Act), immigration restrictions, Arts Council subsidies (or the withdrawal of these), private sponsorship, publishers' hype, book pages in newspapers, and book festivals which only glorified the famous and the celebrated. The statement of aims, formulated in 1989, read:

> We are artists and scholars, isolated because of our consistent struggle for cultural freedom. We are not willing to subordinate ourselves or our work to cultural bureaucracies, which either regress or exploit people's creative imagination.
>
> There is no social or political freedom without freedom of the individual imagination. We cannot break the chains that lock us into capitalism and imperialism without first breaking those that inhibit our own creative vision.
>
> At the second *Non-Stop Connolly Workshop* at the Conway Mill, Belfast, the weekend before Easter 1988, we decided to establish *Duchas na Saoirse* to ensure the continuation of this annual event and to widen its impact.
>
> *Duchas na Saoirse*, using its own traditional weapons of music, song, dance, words, images, hospitality and conviviality, celebrates People's Resistance.[545]

The use of Irish for the title was important – Irish was a 'marginal' language which refused to accept its own death. This became even more important in view of the international mixture of people who were attracted to it. It might also be relevant that 'Saoirse' was the name of an Official Sinn Fein campaign for prisoners' rights.

The first *Duchas na Saoirse* meeting came about almost accidentally. Arden and D'Arcy were asked to present *The Non-Stop Connolly Show* at the Old Museum in Belfast, but were prevented from doing this by fire and other regulations. However, Methuen had just published the one-volume edition of the plays, and D'Arcy now used her connections in the north, notably Gerard McLaughlin, an acquaintance of Albert Hunt, to seek an alternative venue where the new edition could be 'launched.' Just Books, a Belfast bookselling collective, in the person of one of their members, Catherine Couvert, proposed a reading, to involve anyone who wished to participate, in the crèche at Conway Mill which had recently been closed by government cuts. Enough people attended to make the reading, which lasted from noon until three o'clock the next morning, successful, and when it was finished some participants performed their own songs or poems. *Duchas na Saoirse* was born.

Initially, Arden had been reluctant to join, but D'Arcy had persuaded him. The fluidity of its programme, its minimal structure and the lack of formal publicity or press coverage (people learned about it from leaflets, or word of mouth, or, occasionally, letter) gave it its special flavour. When D'Arcy and McLaughlin started it, they 'didn't know where it was going to finish, where it was going to go. Each year provided the impetus for the next year'.[546] Activities included not only reading *The Non-Stop Connolly Show*, but also workshops, acting and improvising, discussions, *ceilidhs* and more. 'The whole process', according to Arden, 'was an attempt to find a camp for people who don't fit into a camp'.[547] It was, he said, 'a kind of performance, of a loosely theatrical nature, incorporating other people without falling into the trap of becoming tyrannical about it'.[548] John Rety described the reading of the play, 'each of us taking it in turns to read in a clockwise direction ... we read for an hour, stopped for a breather and started again'. He noted how 'we benefited in three ways. We got to know the history of Ireland; we got to know the play; and we got to know each other'.[549] Esther Salomon found

> the reading of *The Non-Stop Connolly Show* ... extremely moving, due in part to the play's exploration of oppression and the destructive nature of power coupled with the fact that it was read over an entire weekend by up to fifteen people from diverse backgrounds and cultures and accents. It symbolised our collective understanding and power.[550]

This was not the only activity pursued by those who joined *Duchas na Saoirse*. Anna Taylor describes games such as pairing off 'to listen and report back to the group each other's biographical sketches'. They drew a cake with a felt tipped pen, then divided it into slices, each slice to represent ways the drawer spent her time – daydreaming, reading, eating, at work, and so on. There were games of tig, sessions watching films, story-telling, movement games and long breaks when participants talked to each other and got to know each other. It was, as Arden described it,

> small-scale, rather silly even, and why not?, we only came together to 'kick against the goads', not at all to fasten them like 'masters of assemblies', a daft-like desire, surely, in an era of new conformity; a few diverse creative individuals playing games and reading scripts and arguing about this and that (sometimes friendly, sometimes quite spiteful), an opportunity for any of them to give (among equals) portions of their work which otherwise might have found no feedback, in an open-ended friendly sort of establishment (deliberately *not* sponsored by jealous governmental authority) in a city so ghettoised, so categorised, as

to present an intensified image of the shuttered face of contemporary culture.[551]

For the participants, *Duchas na Saoirse* seems to have had remarkable results. Arden said he got 'an enormous breath of fresh air from it'. For Doreen MacBride it 'provided stimulation and a life line', while Esther Salomon felt 'energised' by it. John Rety wrote:

> What then was so exciting about *Duchas na Saoirse* that I should traverse the entire breadth of the civilised world to visit Belfast not just once but twice? In my romantic imagination the visit was worthwhile because I was going to meet artists and writers in a similar situation to me, who have not allowed themselves to be manipulated by external political and financial organisations. It was the fact of coming together and sharing the fruits of our isolation, of knowing that few as we are, we were not entirely alone, which made the repeated visits such a worthwhile experience.[552]

After 1992, the natural life of *Duchas na Saoirse* seemed to have come to an end, and it partially faded into Sinn Fein's community festival. But everyone who had participated in its meetings was invited to contribute to a special issue of *Theatre Ireland*, published in the summer of 1992. The success of the whole enterprise was ultimately due to D'Arcy's vision of unstructured and playful creativity – what she was to call 'loose theatre' at its best.

What is perhaps even more extraordinary is that during these crowded eighties (and they were more crowded than even this chapter has suggested, as will be seen), D'Arcy was able to achieve any written work at all. In fact, with Arden she created the huge BBC series, *Whose Is The Kingdom?*, at which they worked for most of the decade. In 1981, Richard Imison, Deputy Head of Radio Drama at the BBC, commissioned them jointly to create a dramatic series around the story of the development of Christianity. Conscious that it was now forty years since Dorothy L.Sayers' famous and much-loved *The Man Born to be King*, he was seeking something as monumental which would, however, speak to that time, rather than to the Britain-at-war which had been Sayers's audience. Arden and D'Arcy were interested, but insisted they would not do as Sayers had done and retell the story of the life of Christ. Imison agreed, and all withdrew to consider. The first public mention of where their thoughts were going was in a 1981 interview in *The Guardian* in which Arden spoke of the possibility of five plays which tracked the development of the religion from Christ himself through to Constantine. But by the time they met Imison again this had become a series based solely around the life of the Roman Emperor, Constantine, during whose reign (308-337 AD; though Constantine was sole emperor only from 324 AD) Christianity emerged at the centre of world affairs, and the Judeo-Christian outlook became dominant in and beyond Europe.

One of D'Arcy's immediate aims of the series was to 'open up' the radio in the same way she had tried to open up the theatre, and give the listener some sort of voice. This was more difficult than it had been on the streets of Galway or Dublin, or in the crèche at Conway Mill. But still, phone-ins, post-programme debates, and the like did seem possible, and Imison strove to accommodate this, with the result that two live debates were broadcast, considering issues raised by the plays and featuring luminaries such as David Jenkins, who was then Bishop of Durham, Trevor Huddlestone, Frances Young and the journalist and broadcaster, Mary Goldring. As D'Arcy noted,

> This meant that John Arden and I were released from the burden of
> imposed objectivity, and that we were free while writing to come to grips
> with our own experience, our own individual views, and to allow the gaps
> in *our* narrative to be filled in by other voices.[553]

The writers' initial idea was a cycle structured somewhat like *The Non-Stop Connolly Show* whose main flow followed the hero's life from birth through to death, with tributary stories interpolated at appropriate moments, the whole pun-ctuated perhaps by a number of almost-Shavian debates about the development of the empire or the church. But the material soon proved too various and the history too fluid for such a simple approach. D'Arcy's interest, especially, in the 'eddies and backwaters' of history where 'the losers still survive'[554] led towards less easily-answered questions, such as why Constantine had his wife, Fausta, murdered. Research involved reading more than simply the obvious works, like Gibbon's *Decline and Fall of the Roman Empire*; she and Arden needed to get under the skin of the time and the material. They visited places as various as Ballynaspittle on Lough Derg in the east of County Galway and Beijing, capital of China, where to them the bureaucracy seemed as labyrinthine as the bureaucracy of the Roman Empire. D'Arcy attempted to enter the spirit of the play's themes by experiencing some of the 'old matriarchal rituals (which) can still be discerned hidden under the mantle of Roman-Catholic orthodoxy' in Ireland.[555] Her time at Greenham Common helped, too. The story of the plays partially illustrated

> the rivalry between the Goddess-religion and Imperial Christianity, and
> how the latter solved the problem by ruthlessly subsuming the former –
> and what better place to study it than Greenham, where women were
> already immersed in their searchings for the ancient matriarchies?[556]

Even though BBC seconded a researcher, Geoff O'Connell, to the authors for a time, they only began writing in August 1984.

Whose Is The Kingdom? was to be the last major collaboration between the two. It was still not easy. Arden often seemed 'gentle',[557] but he could be steely when it came to how he thought a scene should develop. D'Arcy was never afraid to

274

challenge him overtly, and for instance in a contemporary interview with them both, she frequently interrupts him, so that he is forced to exclaim: 'You never let me finish, do you?'[558] Paul Hadfield suggested that the process of collaboration 'was also the occasion through which they discovered, slowly and painfully, a practical sense of purpose and direction for their personal and professional lives'.[559] Arden's historical approach often contrasted with D'Arcy way of working through fiction; Arden worked a step at a time, whereas with D'Arcy 'the whole thing comes out at the same time';[560] they worked separately, and came together 'to see if we had anything'.[561] In their collaborations, as mentioned above, the leading name was the author who had had the original idea, had organised the material or who had driven the particular project. Though *Whose Is the Kingdom?* was by Arden and D'Arcy, Arden admitted that 'it ought to be Margaretta D'Arcy and John Arden, except that the BBC commissioned it from me in the first place. But in terms of precedence of ideas going into it, it should be the other way round'.[562] Donald Sandley suggests that *Whose Is The Kingdom?*'s subject makes 'an ideal vehicle to combine D'Arcy's political discourse and Arden's moral introspection', and that it is 'a watershed in (their) collaborative careers' because it 'blends the styles more effectively and presents a more unified voice than previous co-authored works'.[563]

Nevertheless there were problems before the first draft was completed in March 1986. D'Arcy recalled that 'the tension between John and myself centred on keeping the balance between my marginalised characters and his "Imperial" strand'.[564] Was Constantine hero, or anti-hero? Each author wrote different scenes, but if one was dissatisfied, that one would usually rewrite it. Arden tended to type the final version, and D'Arcy sometimes did not even check this. The process was also somewhat complicated by the BBC's demand that the plays should be submitted and paid for three at a time, so that the first three plays were sent well before the last three were complete. It did not help to unify the project. Cutting and editing during rehearsals, of which there was much done, did not solve this problem of overall design and balance.

The plays are complex and stimulating. The period in which they are set is one which, as Arden notes in his introductory remarks to the published text, historians have often shied away from, and which is therefore not familiar to many people. The writers deal with this unfamiliarity by telling their tale through the person of Kybele, a rational philosopher and political refugee, and as such perhaps a partial merger of Arden's philosophical approach with D'Arcy's more overtly pol-itical stance. Kybele has herself witnessed the events of the story, and now tries to explain them to an Irish court which is investigating her. The strands intertwine and thread together like ivy on a trellis – war and power politics, expediency and idealism, the place of women in a patriarchal society, religion as either consolation or a means of asserting dominance. There is slavery and freedom, camaraderie and loneliness and at the back of all, the Emperor Constantine's struggle to be the emperor his ambition or his dreams urge him to be. At the heart of the play, therefore, is an examination of the political process, and the interface between the personal and the political: how the empire tends, like so many states, then and later, to fragment, and how the emperor works furiously to try to hold it together, to centralise its workings. The play questions this 'holding together': is central-isation so beneficent, and for whom? It examines, too, how personal ambitions affect decisions, and how policies are checked and compromised by personal de-sires or fears. Thus, Arius's version of Christianity is condemned and he himself is expelled, but his ideas continue to excite people – a little like the influence Trotsky continued to have in the Soviet Union even after Stalin had expelled him. And Constantine, like Tolstoy's Napoleon, seems as much victim as initiator.

Not surprisingly, *Whose Is The Kingdom?* is also notable for its masterly use of the medium of radio, evoking an army on the march at one time, a freezing mountain pass at another, a scene in an echoey bathhouse, and another in the hollow sewers. The authors intercut one scene with another to create a dynamic collision montage, and words, songs and the use of unexpected but appropriate sound effects are brilliantly combined. In particular, the plays move seamlessly from inside a character's head to 'outside', the scene in reality, as it were, culminating with Constantine himself in the last play of the nine:

> Throughout this play CONSTANTINE is speaking directly to the radio
> audience; and there is no specific location for him, except the images of
> his mind conjured up by his discourse.

The nine-part *Whose Is The Kingdom?* was broadcast by the BBC on successive Friday evenings from 19 February 1988. It was directed by Ronald Mason, who was, interestingly enough, a Northern Irish Protestant, though one with a considerably wider world view that that description might imply. He was Head of BBC Radio from 1976 to 1986, and came out of retirement to direct this work. The music was notably successful. It was eclectic and evocative, and was the work of Stephen Boxer, who had created the original music for *Pearl*. Now he sat and worked at the kitchen table in Arden and D'Arcy's house in Galway – 'a fitting location', he asserted, 'for what was to become a mixture of musical styles – a sort of musical casserole, begun in a kitchen'.[565] The strong cast included Mary Wimbush, Elizabeth Spriggs, Timothy West, Angela Pleasance and David Buck, one of the actors with D'Arcy in the Royal Court group in the 1950s.

The critics were divided by this last Arden-D'Arcy epic. Val Arnold-Forster, in *The Guardian*, surprisingly felt the series lacked 'a strong sense of the period' and wondered 'how much was based on recorded history, and how much was the invention of the authors?' adding, 'It shouldn't matter. But it did'.[566] Anthony Vivis was more enthusiastic, noticing that the authors 'concentrate on the elements of good story-telling: pace, variation, suspense, and (listener-friendly) sex and violence'.[567] Discussing the plays perhaps more judiciously some years later, Donald Sandley came to the conclusion that *Whose Is The Kingdom?* 'emerges as the crowning achievement of the writing partnership, allowing for a near complete synthesis of the two differing purposes'.[568] Certainly, it is an extraordinarily powerful portrait of how orthodoxy is asserted, as perhaps might be expected from so unorthodox a woman as had been seen in the Circus Exposé, at Greenham Common and in *Duchas na Saoirse*, and her partner. But it is also possible that the subject matter is too distant from us, too strange, for easy comprehension. It seems perhaps to lack that intangible spark which Arden's lifelong obsession with the Arthurian legends gave to *The Island of the Mighty*, and both authors' passionate fury and sympathy with James Connolly gave to *The Non-Stop Connolly Show*.

Their individual introductions to *Whose Is The Kingdom?* were reprinted in the jointly-authored *Awkward Corners*, a book of essays which also appeared in 1988. Because it included an account of some of the contentious infighting of the Greenham Common Peace Camp, D'Arcy warned the publishers of possible legal action against the book. Methuen's lawyer rather airily dismissed such a possibility, but the review copy sent to *The Morning Star* did indeed spark that paper into threatening libel proceedings. Methuen, relying on the legal opinion they had obtained, pressed on, but one hour before publication, five women from the groups opposing the Greenham Yellow Gate women announced they were going to the High Court to obtain an injunction to stop publication. According to *The Listener*, this threw Methuen into 'quite a state', because 'they are on the point of moving offices and cannot imagine where they are going to store all these returned copies of *Awkward Corners*'.[569] In the event, Arden, always strong in these kinds of situations, refused to accept such censorship. D'Arcy consulted a second legal expert, David Hooper, and he recommended publication and, if necessary, facing the would-be censors in court. At which point the five women backed off, and the book was published without further hindrance.

Awkward Corners is an eclectic collection of articles and essays, and includes Arden's first published short story as well as poetry from D'Arcy. It was respectfully rather than enthusiastically received. Douglas Kennedy was not untypical of reviewers in voicing a certain surprise at the volume: first he was surprised that Arden was 'an exceedingly gifted essayist who writes with passionate erudition', and also 'demonstrates that politically committed writing can be highly individualistic and accessible'; and second, that D'Arcy (for him, as for so many others, a kind of wild Irish fire-eater) 'can frequently hit upon an important truth'.[570] The surprise was because their recent work was so largely unknown to metropolitan commentators, and their earlier achievements perhaps forgotten.

Twenty : Pirate Woman

Busy as Margaretta D'Arcy was in the 1980s with international and Ireland-wide campaigns, arts festivals, writing projects and her local community, her most significant achievement in that decade was almost certainly the creation of Radio Pirate-Woman, which remains a model of genuinely radical cultural practice. The story of how it came about is both fascinating and instructive.

The idea of creating some sort of radio station probably first came to D'Arcy when she was a prisoner in Armagh Gaol. When she returned to society outside prison, she discussed the possibilities with sympathetic people, and was invited to join the newly-established Women in Media and Entertainment. This was founded by Agnes Bernelle and Nora Lever, who realized that women were largely slotted into entertainment patterns devised to suit men, and that the audience expectations to which they were performing were male-oriented. Their new organisation was dedicated to changing this: they demanded an end to stereotyping, an end to racist type-casting, to sexual discrimination in the arts, and for child-care as an essential condition of work. They also campaigned for 50% female participation in live theatre, and the repeal of legislation which excluded the entertainment industry from equal opportunities laws. They aimed to celebrate women's culture and make links with any women's group opposing the patriarchal power bases in the arts and culture. At a conference early in 1982, the group had proposed to make May a month of women's action, and the planned events included a 'Women Live' weekend at the Project Theatre in Dublin which D'Arcy attended.

The programme for this event included, on the Saturday, in the morning, discussion of the history of women in Irish theatre; in the afternoon, self-help theatre and alternative theatre. On the Sunday, in the morning, there were sessions on writing for theatre and media, and music; and in the afternoon, on trade unionism (sexism and consumerism in the context of work), and on community radio and video. It was suggested that radio, rather than being seen as a form of therapy for housebound working women, had the potential for something much greater than this. This was also a spark to light D'Arcy's ambition.

In the meantime, she had founded 'Galway Women's Entertainment', discussed above. Her aim here was for something 'very low-key and informal' which would have 'nothing of a regular structure or organisation'.[571] Despite this, it managed to mount up to four festivals for women each year, open events largely held in D'Arcy's house in St Bridget's Place Lower, Galway, and any women were invited to join in, to make music, sing, talk – to create, in other words, any form of spontaneous entertainment. The first festival was held in December 1982, when there was a games session led by Eileen Murphy and a more intense session when Ann Slattery led a discussion about *Phaedra*.

Galway Women's Entertainment did not limit itself to festivals. When any two or three women wanted a GWE event, a date was agreed , a few posters made and displayed and, as with the festivals, any woman was welcome to attend. In 1983, a speaker from the newly-established National Association for Community Broadcasting was invited to explain their work to the group. This Association aimed to campaign for suitable legislation for community broadcasters, and to support individuals or groups who were keen to develop community radio for themselves. Galway Women's Entertainment were certainly tempted. They knew that local women had no source of information about birth control, abortion, divorce or gender-sexuality; nor could they hear any dissenting political voices, for instance on the subject of northern Ireland. A women's radio station could fill in at least some of these blanks. With D'Arcy in their midst, the information which they might put out in these areas would be likely to be uncompromising. But NACB were a cautious middle-of-the-road organisation, not minded to oppose governmental censorship or have any ideas about specifically women's radio, and they counselled the Galway group to wait until the necessary legislation was in place. So wait the Galway women did.

And time went by. In 1985, at the Methuen conference on the theatre in London, D'Arcy had spoken of theatre as practised as a kind of straitjacket. She expressed her viewpoint later thus:

> The theatre (by which I mean any form of dramatic entertainment that
> involves an audience passively watching performers or 'participating'
> *under the control of performers*), instead of changing society, has actually
> copperfastened the unequal distribution ... of power.[572]

Now she sought an alternative which would create a much more fluid relationship between performer and auditor or spectator which would blur the lines of power. And 'after twenty-seven years' search and breaking through my conditioning, I came to the conclusion that radio is the answer'.[573] But actually, as she points out in her lively account of the whole venture, *Galway's Pirate Women: A Global Trawl*, radio as practiced is like the other media, wholly in the control of the powerful, that is, the male-dominated élite. So how long would she comply with the wishes of NACB and wait for the élite to allow her experiment? In 1986 she lost patience and struck out on her own, taking the Galway women with her.

She acquired a small transmitter and put the aerial on the roof of her house. She already possessed a music centre. Now she was given two microphones and a mixer. She set up her house as a studio, with participants downstairs in the main living room, while upstairs was the radio transmitter. No male engineers or technicians were employed. Everything was done by D'Arcy, Janet Watts and the other women: they learned the technical skills as they needed them. D'Arcy discovered that FM104 was a free airwave, and having satisfied herself with the quality of the transmitter, she was ready to begin.

It was intended that their broadcasting would be part of the Galway Women's Entertainment quarterly Festivals. Thus, the week-long programme for the February 1987 Festival, which was when the radio would come into action, in-cluded a wide range of items, from open discussions to music sessions, dance workshops (tap, African rhythms), videos and alternative health and aromatherapy. And every evening at midnight the radio would broadcast. It was known as 'Women's Scéal Radio', 'scéal' meaning gossip or chit-chat. But despite this apparent inconsequentiality, Women's Scéal Radio had serious aims, which D'Arcy listed as follows:

A. To honour and celebrate women's oral language, because it is women who pass on the spoken word to the children. Without the spoken word there can be no written word. Women are the prime source and custodians of language.

B. To recognise that the three ages of women are a continuity, pre-menstruation, menstruation and post-menstruation. No one of them is more valuable than the others.

C. To let each woman speak freely without being controlled by another woman.

D. To speak freely on all subjects of Article 19 of the UN Charter of Human Rights (Freedom of Speech, Freedom of Expression, Freedom to Impart Information).

E. To promote the concept that a woman has as much right in her own space to have her voice heard via a low-powered radio transmitter as she has to listen to the voice of someone else on a radio receiver.[574]

As D'Arcy herself pointed out, her fourth aim conflicted with such Irish censorship regulations as Section 31 of the Broadcasting Act, as well as the wider ban on providing information on a range of subjects, from abortion to the banning of particular cited books and magazines, usually because of the sexual nature of their content. D'Arcy had deliberately and provocatively stated in 1987 in a letter to the newspaper that she intended to disseminate information on abortion, and the relationship of this area of the radio's work to *Duchas na Saoirse*'s programme is obvious.

This was uncensored, open radio, and women in the area were invited to come to St Bridget's Place and take part. Emma Campbell, one who did take part, remembered 'fascinating people – grandmothers, anarchists, artists …' She continued:

When I could, I'd go down to the station, and oftentimes it was just as simple as that – she (D'Arcy)'d just start a conversation, or ask you a question – she always had a good question – to make you think. It was a challenge. When you see how diverse are the women that she brings together in her kitchen … we can all sit around, drinking tea, having food, you know. From traveller women to women of different sexualities – *all* kinds of women. Catholic types meet people who are very radical, and they have outrageous arguments and conversations. But you leave that house feeling something's happened.[575]

A subtly developing outcome was that the range of viewpoints expressed helped all the women articulate and understand, enabling them and raising awareness of themselves as themselves. It was certainly not the expected orthodox women's radio of the BBC 'Woman's Hour' kind: here any woman could say anything she wanted to say. It was freewheeling, open-ended, unplanned.

The range of the transmitter was only three or four miles, so this was local radio at its most local. On the other hand it enabled D'Arcy and her supporters to leaflet virtually every house within the transmitter's range, informing them of the Scéal station; and the leafleting itself became something of a social activity. The radio not only empowered those on the wrong side of the accepted social structures, it was positively dangerous to those structures. It ignored bans on women who were inadmissible or unwelcome to those in power, such as members of Sinn Fein or travelling people. It turned its back on traditional programme planning, and simply allowed anyone who came to the studio air time. And it paid no attention to audience figures: if no-one listened, those taking part in the *craic* still enjoyed themselves. Because of these policies, the National Union of Journalists instructed its members not to co-operate with it, even to the extent at one point of prohibiting anyone who had appeared on Scéal Radio (or its successor, Radio Pirate-Woman) from being interviewed on national television or radio.

In March 1987, D'Arcy was sent to gaol in England for her activities at Greenham Common. It seemed that Radio Scéal might be finished. But a local survey of opinion discovered the programme's surprising popularity, and in spring 1988, with D'Arcy back in Galway, the Galway Women's Entertainment Festival saw the resurrection of Women's Scéal Radio. And it began to broadcast for three successive weeks, not just one, and besides its midnight broadcasts of music and poetry, including, by the way, music sent in by women on tape, it also went on air at eleven in the morning with its unique mix of women's chat, gossip and argument, having made a special effort to include as many women as possible. D'Arcy even had her telephone adapted so that callers could speak, as in phone-in programmes from larger stations. And even after the three-week Festival period, the radio continued to broadcast for three days each week, twice per day.

Moreover there was a more outgoing or practical side to the radio's work now. It clearly took sides in matters of local concern, supporting unemployed people, arguing against bureaucratic obfuscations and giving time and space to often-persecuted travellers. It raised questions of civic injustice, maladministration, problems with public housing. It discussed marriage difficulties, hire purchase problems, and the authoritarianism of the Catholic church. It gave air time to groups such as Residents Associations, and campaigned on issues as apparently far away as the South African apartheid regime. By now the women's radio was becoming a noticeable feature of Galway's public life. People with old-fashioned or authoritarian attitudes had discovered that they too could voice their opinions on it, for D'Arcy's policy of no censorship was absolute; whereupon many who called themselves progressive objected, saying these people should not be allowed air time. So not only did the radio's campaigning offend business people, politicians, and the establishment generally, its open access policy offended University lecturers, progressive women's groups and the like. But no-one could deny its vitality and its relevance.

Perhaps Radio Scéal became a thorn in too many important sides. In 1988, new broadcasting legislation was announced which would compel all radio stations to apply for a licence. Of course, Women's Scéal Radio immediately applied; but their application was ignored. They could not so easily ignore the new legislation, however, for it threatened a £20,000 fine and two years in gaol for anyone broadcasting without a licence. Meanwhile, a meeting was convened for those Galway groups bidding for a licence under this legislation. But once again Women's Scéal Radio was ignored, and not invited to attend. Consequently, when she was next 'on air', D'Arcy telephoned Charles Lynch of the Regional Development Association, and read out to him, and for the benefit of her listeners, the letter which acknowledged receipt of Scéal Radio's bid for a licence. She asked him bluntly why the station had been excluded. At which point, Lynch was forced to invite her to attend. Even so, at the meeting, the points raised by D'Arcy and her supporters were largely brushed aside and there was a joke made at the idea of a *women's* radio station. Though this meeting resolved little, D'Arcy and her co-movers decided that legally their best response would be to close the radio for the time being and await the outcome of their bid for a licence.

But the following year there was still no licence, and D'Arcy's patience ran out. She decided to resume broadcasting in the teeth of the government. She re-named the station 'Radio Pirate-Woman' and announced with more bravado than logic: 'If we women are asked to open our purses to the advertisers, we equally have a right to open our mouths on the airwaves'.[576] Because of the swingeing punish-ments threatened, she felt she could not ask anyone else to share the risk, and named herself as solely responsible for the station. It should be said, however, that she received plenty of encouragement and support, including from Selma Jones and Wilmette Brown of Wages for Housework and from the women at Yellow Gate,

Greenham Common, who sent her material from Greenham for broadcasting. Perhaps the most significant support came from Lise von Bomm, who ran a woman's radio station in Montreal and who was also on the committee of the World Association of Community Radios (AMARC). She not only brought D'Arcy into AMARC, she also put her in touch with the Women's International Newsgathering Service which gave her access to international news of interest to women, especially women in struggle, from a woman's perspective.

The shocked guardians of the city's prerogatives in Galway tried to mount a campaign against the re-launch of this subversive radio station. But they made surprisingly little headway, and in spite of their campaign, or perhaps because of it, the re-launch became widely known and was largely welcomed by its female audience. The new international dimension which D'Arcy had been able to give it only made Radio Pirate-Woman more popular, and so it continued. There seemed no way in which the station could be brought to heel. D'Arcy would probably have to have been caught twiddling the knobs on the transmitter before it would have been possible for the authorities to close her radio station down, and by the time any interfering policeman had come through the door of the house in St Bridget's Place Lower, the transmitter would have been switched off and D'Arcy would have been in another room. 'The station's upstairs in a small room,' Emma Campbell said. 'Everybody's ready ... I admired the illegal aspect of it', she added.[577] News of the opening of the new Radio Pirate-Woman also stirred the local papers, who in spite of their natural inclination to support the *status quo* and their frequent opposition to anything genuinely innovative, found themselves rather admiring D'Arcy's nerve. They interviewed her and reported what was happening, which clearly helped potential listeners to think of tuning in. The station's own publicity was eye-catching and amusing. 'We have an old pram which we wheel through the town decorated with balloons and streamers. We hang drums and other percussion instruments on it for women to beat'.[578]

The first season of Radio Pirate-Woman took place from the eighth to the twenty-second of March 1990. D'Arcy appealed to AMARC for international tapes to play in case the women of Galway should be intimidated by the law, but she need not have feared. For one thing, the radio resumed during the campaign for the election of a new President of the Republic, when Mary Robinson opposed the Fianna Fail Party's Brian Lenahan. Women could hardly keep out of this, and there were plenty of fierce arguments in the St Bridget's Street Lower kitchen, all transmitted by Radio Pirate-Woman without a whisper of cen-sorship. And the pass-ionate argument strengthened the women's commitment.

Pirate Woman with actress Sabina Higgins, wife of Michael Higgins, later President of Ireland.

The radio station became involved with other issues, too. In 1991 Radio Pirate-Woman flouted the law by interviewing a representative of Provisional Sinn Fein. Members of the party were supposed to be denied access to the media, so that they were starved of 'the oxygen of publicity'. Practical opposition like D'Arcy's to this crass policy was exceedingly rare at the time, however much journalists chafed at their shackles. The next year, 1992, saw a referendum in the Republic of Ireland on the question of abortion. But the referendum was held on the same date as a general election, and was inevitably overshadowed by this contest. Only a few minority institutions, such as Radio Pirate-Woman, made proper time to air the arguments. D'Arcy herself was firmly in favour of the reforms proposed, and she leafleted, campaigned, and put up posters; but on the radio, all viewpoints were aired and argued about in a remarkable piece of self-denying humanity. The fact that the referendum resulted in a partial victory for the forces of progress – now Irish women were to have the right to travel abroad to obtain an abortion, and they also had a new right to information – was perhaps some small consolation.

As for local matters, air time was still provided for Traveller women. 'We never knew when they'd come in', D'Arcy related: 'suddenly they'd be there'. And their contributions, especially those of the children and adolescent girls were particularly memorable:

285

The minute details of their fantasies, weddings, fast cars, Disneyland,
mixed with an extraordinary depth of emotion and love as they put out
their messages to their families and sang songs to them with such
intensity as to be almost unbearable.[579]

One traveller whom D'Arcy was pleased to interview was Margaret Sweeney who in
1988 with her husband and five children had been in their caravan when the site was
attacked by no fewer than three hundred settled people. Margaret had decided to
speak out against this, and indeed was to go on and stand for election to the Dáil.

Another extraordinary incident occurred when a woman told on Radio Pirate-
Woman of how she had been raped and by whom. The man must have been
listening because in a short time he arrived in St Bridget's Place Lower and barged
his way into the house. It seemed as if he was now intent on raping Margaretta
D'Arcy. She managed to evade his clutches and rush outside where she called the
Gardai. But they were in no hurry to eject the man. D'Arcy had to invoke the Irish
constitution, which guarantees that 'the dwelling of every citizen is inviolable and
shall not be forcibly entered save in accordance with the law',[580] before they would
stir themselves to evict the intruder. The pirate women exorcised the place afterwards, including baking in an oven for thirty days a decorative penis, modelled on
one from Pompeii!

As might be expected, Radio Pirate-Woman also celebrated special days in the
women's calendar, such as Women's Disarmament Day and International Women's
Day. They gave space to 'Radio *Duchas na Saoirse*', when men who had supported
that organisation were permitted to speak, and they mounted educational sequences,
such as an examination of Padraig Pearse as an educator and writer. Their range was
frankly remarkable. As they sang:

> Hey, Pirate-Woman, what-u-cooking today?
> I'm airin subversion the radio way!
> Excuse me, Galway women, play a pirate today,
> Join the *craic* on the free air way![581]

What D'Arcy herself stressed about the pirate radio station was its *play*
element. Each day or evening of broadcasting was perhaps a little like a party, with
plenty of games to keep the guests amused, and everyone chipping in to contribute
their mite to the whole. They 'tell stories, sing songs, argue, air their grievances,
recount their herstory', one participant reported.[582] And they enjoyed each others'
company, which was stimulating beyond anything which many of them had known.
Here is one participant:

> From the start the most obvious thing about Radio Pirate-Woman was
> that all women were welcome. Over the years, visiting Margaretta
> D'Arcy's house at St Bridget's Place Lower in Galway, I have met a
> wonderful group of women from totally diverse backgrounds. I feel it

says a lot that Travellers, single mothers, academics, Catholic grandmothers, students, ultra-Right Catholics, black feminists, lesbians, actors, poets, musicians, businesswomen have visited the house and had the freedom to speak and perform on the radio.[583]

And here is another, whose words carry a distant but fascinating echo of Shylock's most famous speech:

As the involvement grew, it opened me up and gave me a confidence and strength I never knew I possessed ... Nowadays I find myself dealing with a very mixed grill of women, yet we all have the same physical attributes, the same capacity for hurt, suffer the same repression and yes – now I tend to think in terms of 'sisters' ...[584]

For these and a huge number of other women, it was D'Arcy who was the catalyst, it was she who effected the liberating change they felt after a few sessions with the Pirate-Woman radio station. The first woman quoted above, Sheila McCrann, went on to say: 'I really appreciate how patient Margaretta has been, allowing each of us to take it at our own pace',[585] and the experienced Selma Jones of the Wages for Housework campaign commented: 'Margaretta was a facilitator, never imposing her own view'.[586]

Caroline Mitchell, examining Radio Pirate-Woman perhaps more objectively than these participants, noted that

The soundscape woven by the women on this radio station is radically different to the 'prattle and pop' promulgated by mainstream radio. The station uses the airwaves to subvert, create and campaign and is active at both parochial and global levels.[587]

She describes the process in strongly positive terms:

Radio Pirate-Woman has no management structure and allows any woman to walk into a studio based in a house and speak into a microphone in order to debate issues without censorship. The station's aim to allow 'each woman to speak freely without being controlled by another woman', seems close to the ideal of Habermas' conditions for a public sphere. The station's programming is more like a translation of daily life over the airwaves. There is no set programme as such: I have observed women walking in off the street and joining in broadcasts – perhaps continuing a conversation that they had been conducting with a neighbour. D'Arcy likens this to the rural tradition of visiting, high-lighting the importance of oral cultural discourse.[588]

But Mitchell is also aware of the danger of this:

The simplicity of this model may also be its main weakness, as it is potentially subject to the control of one woman (who lives in the house)

and as an unlicensed station is vulnerable to closure by the regulatory authorities.[589]

The first objection overlooks D'Arcy's extraordinary history, her determination to find just such a freewheeling and open form, her fierce belief that in allowing every voice to be heard, each of us will gain. And it ignores the fact which one woman expressed pithily: D'Arcy 'is not afraid of the police or gaol'.[590] As for Mitchell's second 'weakness' Radio Pirate-Woman continued well into the twenty-first century. Partly this was because in fact D'Arcy was sponsoring more than simply a radio. As has already been made clear, the radio was tightly locked into her other activities. And this fact perhaps holds the key to its success. The radio was not an end in itself, it was one strand in a whole spider's web of social, political, cultural and artistic discourse.

As D'Arcy herself said: 'We'd talk about it on the radio, then we'd go out into the streets and do things'.[591]

Twenty-one : Undeviating Paths

In the last years of the 1980s and the early years of the 1990s Arden and D'Arcy stuck to their chosen paths as they moved into their sixties. They worked together less and less, but by 1991 they were able to look back on the embargo which had blocked their work through much of the previous two decades with comparative equanimity. It was over, though D'Arcy noted that it had 'obviously caused tremendous tension between the two of us' for some time. But were they going to 'allow our life, work and collaborative efforts to be determined and shaped by the enemy'?[592] It seems, however, that not all their tensions were resolved, for while D'Arcy was receiving her stipend from Aosdána, now £5,000 per year, Arden had only what he earned from his writing. So he continued to write.

Arden had made a considerable name for himself as a playwright in the past, but now with the theatre more or less closed to him, and his own disinclination to write more plays, it was novel-writing which engaged him. 'It's all from the same well; it's all storytelling', he remarked.[593] But of course it was not as simple as that. In a novel 'you've got to fill in the bits between the speeches':

> It doesn't necessarily take longer to write a novel, because a play can take
> a very long time. But a novel has more words, so I find that the amount of
> actual physical work at the typewriter rather than in the head is
> increased.[594]

And there was no possibility of 'communality' in novel-writing.

The first novel of this period was *Books of Bale*, which appeared in 1988. Set in the middle of the sixteenth century, it presents a red-blooded picture of British and Irish society in turmoil, as England throws off Catholicism and takes tentatively to Protestantism. In the book this is symbolised first by the changes in popular drama from mystery and miracles plays ('the Christ-plays in a wide green field'[595]) to the more flexible, less tractable dramas of the late Elizabethan period; and second by the protagonist, John Bale's shift from Catholic Friar to Protestant fanatic. No-one else could have written this book except John Arden: its unique mixture of erudition and exuberance is wholly original, and its ubiquitous use of humour in a serious cause shows the author at his characteristic best. The great ongoing joke which pervades the book springs from Bale's ineffectiveness – he sweats so greatly to achieve so little – but the turbulent comedy of scene after scene makes this one of Arden's funniest works. It is also notably full of voices: the narration is taken over by Anthony Munday, the Elizabethan playwright, by Bale's wife, Dorothy, by Conrad, and Wentworth and the poet Wyatt, and Pronsias Duth and Bale himself at various times, keeping the reader both on her toes and also amazed at the ventriloquial skills of the author. *Books of Bale* has some claim to be regarded as Arden's greatest single work.

The book is historical fiction. As such, Arden's master, Robert Graves's influence is again felt, though to many Arden will be seen here to have transcended his master. However, the *genre* provides a way of understanding history – *how* things happen, rather than merely *what* happened. Fiction is not constrained by any narrative of the known. Byeways open up, you can linger, go back, examine events subjectively, impressionistically and from differing viewpoints. Historical fiction should be seen as a particular process for deconstructing the past. And Arden's action sweeps across the vast acres of England, Ireland and the European continent in ways no historian would dare. Its range is breathtaking: Bale the writer is profoundly interested in Welsh and Scots poets, as well as his English forebears; the rebels of Norwich resist enclosures, those bringers of starvation for the poor; women of London entertain men in their own 'Birdcage'; while the executioner-cum-torturer, Mr Topcliffe, prepares the tools of his trade.

The central character is based on the historical Bishop of Ossary, a significant playwright and compulsive agitator. In the novel, he is a highly compelling character, whose name, meaning 'unhappy' or perhaps 'malign', is the first irony in a book full of ironies. He is first glimpsed by his wife-to-be by the intermittent light of a cloud-washed moon. He is a white friar,

> his cloak clasped about him, his cowl pulled down over his white beret.
> The ear-flaps of the beret were tied around his chin, and altogether he
> gave the appearance of a greedy walking corpse, new-risen from a fresh
> grave. Perhaps too stout and stocky for a true ghost.[596]

He is elusive, hard to pin down from the start. He is an actor – he plays the part of Herod – but like Shakespeare's actor, he has 'many parts': he is Bully Bale, Bull-in-the-Bush, Bale-zebub, Balla, Baal and, most sordidly, Dangle-tool. His wife Dorothy, who provides the novel's complementary and opposite viewpoint, detached, a woman's, and 'from below', is almost as elusive as he is: she is la Haute-jambée, Barbara, Mary, Mrs Bale, Mrs Brewer and Longlegs. At the end, she seems almost to be a witch.

Bale, the zealous Protestant, is sent to Catholic Ireland 'expressly to help restructure the English-speaking sector of the Irish Church in line with the new doctrines';[597] his chosen tool is the drama, a new kind of drama which will enable the mysteries and moralities of the early Tudor period to transform into the chronicle plays of the Elizabethans. He is, however, 'a far from heroic character', according to Michael Cohen,[598] 'cranky' according to the author himself,[599] and 'characterized by his hapless concupiscence' according to Jonathan Wike,[600] who also provides a fruitful comparison with other Arden characters, notably Serjeant Musgrave. Arden in the book relates Bale to John Skelton, his admired predecessor, and to Shakespeare (the Dark Lady of the Sonnets makes an unexpected entrance into the novel at one point), though this Shakespeare is pragmatic where Bale is dogmatic. Bale's problem as a playwright is comparable to Arden's in the 1950s and 1960s. Arden's non-naturalistic dramaturgy then was hard for the patrons of the Royal Court Theatre to cope with. Bale's prospective Irish audiences had similar problems: they were used to 'plays of the old religion, more like fairy-legend' than what he proposes to bring them. 'Their actors are traditional artisans. You cannot ask for them in *your* pieces, they will say you are turning their whole souls inside-out'.[601]

The book questions again the place and purpose of the theatre, and the writer, in society. Is their primary task polemical or is it the telling of a story? In *The Island of the Mighty*, there are three poets arranged almost schematically so that we can see and compare three possible answers to this question. In *Books of Bale*, a second such set of three writers is completed, but this time from across all of Arden's writing, this time the 'real' poets of the Tudor period. The first is Lindsay, the suave courtier of the stage drama, *Armstrong's Last Goodnight*; the second is the cantankerous and roguish Skelton in the radio play *Garland for a Hoar Head*; John Bale, passionate partisan and campaigner in *Books of Bale*, completes the triumvirate. All have something of Arden in them; all have a specific idea of what their primary purpose as writers in their place and their time should be. Arden himself suggested something of that when alluding to 'the battlefield of opposed philosophies' which was being dramatised by playwrights in the mid-sixteenth century, by comparing it to 'exactly the sort of theatre that we at the Royal Court in the 1960s thought we might possibly be inaugurating'.[602] This vivid strand in a book about the life of the theatre, and the theatre's unique ability to absorb the lives, thoughts and emotions of whole groups of people, is extraordinarily strong, deriving as it obviously does from Arden's own experiences. We are reminded of Mr Croke and his company in *The Royal Pardon*, of the Narrator's bagful of 'little men' in *The Bagman*, of Backhouse and Barnabus in *Pearl* and of Ivory and his company in *Silence Among the Weapons*. Once again but with greater intensity, perhaps, we live the problems of play-wrighting, the struggles of acting companies, the horrors and delights of performance, the excitement and sometimes the outrage of the audience. Bale – like Arden – wants something new, and like Arden, he goes to Ireland to try to forge it. Fintan O'Toole sees the whole book as 'a kind of metaphor for his (Arden's) own journey'. 'I thought it was fantastic', O'Toole added.[603]

Three years after *Books of Bale*, Arden's next fiction, *Cogs Tyrannic*, presented four interlinked novellas, each from a different period of history, but each concerned with the impact of technology on social and political life. The title is a quotation from William Blake in a passage asserting that mechanical inventions are 'cogs tyr-

John Arden reads from his own work.

annic' which petrify the human imagination. Actually the stories suggest that technology is harmful when it is in the wrong hands, those of tyrants, but since it usually is in those hands, the book seems profoundly pessimistic.

The first story, 'Slow Journey. Swift Writing' is a kind of deconstruction of the Odysseus myth set in Egypt in the twelfth century BC. Odysseus's ship has sailed round Africa, and the crew have seen the sun to the north of them. For the Egyptian sun-worshippers, not only is this impossible, it is extremely dangerous blasphemy. The subsequent events are seen through the eyes of Harkhuf, a bur-eaucrat out of his depth in the political emergency the arrival of these strangers creates. He knows their leader is called 'Od-diss', and Arden enjoys other well-known figures from Greek mythology: Circe is Kur-kai, Telemachus Tel-emma-cossa, Calypso Kal-p'so, Nausicaa N's-kaa and so on. An obscure byeway in Greek mythology is objectified to bring home the cruelty and the machinations of power politics which in the usual romantic retellings of the ancient myths remain concealed. Harkhuf loses his nerve, or perhaps simply is at a loss to know how to cope with this unprecedented incursion, and himself becomes a kind of tyrannical cog in the imperial machine.

Margaretta D'Arcy had made a story about the persecution of witches and how the book, *Malleus Maleficarum*, aided in this persecution in the late middle ages, and now Arden addressed this in the next story in *Cogs Tyrannic*, 'The Little Old Woman and Her Two Big Books'. This time Arden uses a pseudo-fairy story frame, starting his sections, for instance, with formulaic, almost incantatory, phrases: 'A long long time before this, and a very long time before'; 'A long long time after that, and a very long time after that'[604] in order to deconstruct the dispassionate voice of history as it customarily deals with this subject. Kraemar and Sprenger, the witchfinders general, become the 'lean friar' and the 'square friar' and the priests performing their rites become pseudo-music hall performers:

He clattered a feverish rhythm on a tambourine with little bells, and
Bruder Jakob began to sing. His voice was harsh but very powerful:

> When your money in our box goes jingle-jing
> So the soul in Purgatory gives a spring
> And he jumps straight up to Heaven:
> From the Pope the power is given
> To accomplish here and now this marvellous thing!

(The ironic use of the almost-limerick form, associated with comic nonsense, is typical of Arden.) The mumbo-jumbo of the priests is set against the other 'big book', *The All-Science Book*, or *The Old Wife Book*, which the old woman uses to heal people. The story fiercely questions the treatment of women in western society. It also examines censorship and thinking outside the bounds of accepted limits, as well as the responsibility of the publisher to the writer, and to the reader. Once technology has provided society with the means to print virtually limitless numbers of copies of a book, the printer (or publisher) becomes a new kind of trustee.

The remaining two novellas are 'Uses of Iron' about the coming of the railways, and specifically the first public railway journey from Liverpool to Manchester in 1830, when the M.P. for Liverpool, Thomas Huskisson, was killed; and 'Like a *Dream* of a Gun', set in contemporary Ireland. 'The Uses of Iron' is the funniest tale of the four, and two strands of its story, besides that of the death of Thomas Huskisson, engage the reader. The first concerns the leading actress of the day, Fanny Kemble, who is being pursued by the Prime Minister, the Duke of Wellington, here described by Arden as 'a debilitated pantaloon';[605] the second introduces us to Edward Craig, whom Arden and D'Arcy had already made into a central figure in *Vandaleur's Folly* and *The Manchester Enthusiasts*. He leads the working people of Manchester's protest, and though it ends in violence and he himself is robbed, he still finds a surprising means of returning home to Manchester. The story in the end is one concerned with responsibility: was it the halt at Parkside which was the death of Huskisson? Or the wheels of the Rocket? Or 'the hidden manoeuvres of politics; which indeed may have caused all the misadventures, tragic and trivial, piling one upon the other through the length of the day.[606]

'Like a *Dream* of a Gun' may be the least satisfactory of the four pieces in this book. It enters the impossibly complicated world of espionage and counter-espionage, and while it is often comic and always interesting, sometimes the parts seem more than the whole. The information is not always easy to disentangle from the disinformation, and while Arden has plenty of fun at the expense of the English newspapers, his assertion that 'truth so sensational must needs be untrustworthy'[607] is not really helpful to the reader.

Cogs Tyrannic offers matter for much thought in its well-told tales. Though it is in some senses a sombre book, it is also paradoxically suffused with comedy. This stretches from Arden's Dickensian use of names – the counsel for the Ministry of Defence is Alaric Houndsditch; he defends Lance-Corporal Alfred Truethought – through to his characteristically mordant asides – in 'The Little Old Woman and Her Two Big Books', the witchfinders are set on their course by a complacent Pope who 'let loose his bull (or minotaur); and thought little more of the matter'.[608] And though it deals often with people who struggle to understand or articulate, it is often very beautifully written: a single example is the memorable simile in 'Uses of Iron', when the two young women are found 'helpless with laughter, as though a pair of Bo-Peep's lambs had been caught at the brandy'.[609]

Jack Juggler and the Emperor's Whore, published in 1995, was Arden's last full length novel. It tracks the progress of a love – or lust – triangle, which is also a threesome of artistic ambition and jealousy, involving Jack Pogmoor, a theatre director, Fidelio Carver, a playwright, and his stage designer sister, Leonore. Their struggles to achieve form the main driver of the narrative. It is Arden's longest work, and told with a profligate energy which rarely flags. Like some of his earlier work, this book is Dickensian in much of its scope and manner, though it is considerably more sexually explicit than Dickens ever dared to be. It also carries a sniff of the Jacobean playwrights again, as we may guess from the many tags from Chapman, Webster, Ford and others, from the intricacies of its plot, and from the murders, incest, jealousy, and sex which abound in its pages. There are indeed more murders here than in most Agatha Christie novels, and the unravelling of them is considerably more ingenious. Mostly set in the contemporary period, but with longish excursions into the eighteenth and nineteenth centuries, the book's multiple stories and complex web of characters refract and reflect on one other with prodigal fullness.

The plot of *Jack Juggler and the Emperor's Whore* deals mostly with the machinations and desires of a group of dropouts and inhabitants of the 'fringe' culture of the years between 1968 and about 1990. Mostly the characters' fortunes are bound up with the rise and fall of a number of theatre companies which exist just beyond the world of large building-based companies such as the Royal Shakespeare or the regional repertory theatres. They are serious theatres, however, which wish to engage seriously with contemporary politics and society, and we see them trapped in a virtually insoluble dilemma. They always need money to mount their productions, but without a state subsidy, which clearly compromises their position, they must either rely on a rich capitalist, who will then wish to influence the content of their plays, or get themselves caught up in shady deals which here lead to entanglements with 'terrorism' and the secret services. Thus, Fidelio Carver, the writer, works with Vexaction Theatre Company, which however is somehow involved with gun running for the IRA. Fid pursues his Irish play's theme to Northern Ireland, where he dies. Pogmoor's Maffick Company presents *Deepwater Dread*, his play about the sinking of the Belgrano in the Falklands War: its power prompts the rich Levi Cordwain to offer financial support to the company – but his money comes inevitably with unwanted strings attached.

The theatrical dimension to the novel will thrill anyone who has ever tried to mount any sort of theatrical entertainment, and moves beyond the theatre worlds of Ivory in *Silence Among the Weapons* and John Bale in *Books of Bale*. It brilliantly captures the sheer fun of preparing a play, while the accompanying passions, selfishness, hope, hate and despair are given free rein. The theatre companies Arden invents are a range of what might have been found in this world at this time – his inside knowledge is put to subtle and comic use – and includes not only those mentioned already but also Polly Blackadder's would-be feminist troupe, 'Les Femmes Savantes' as well as Pogmoor's other company, originally called 'Mouth-71' which transmutes into 'Moth'. There is even a theatrical company dominating the world of Eugene Aram in the novel's most successful foray into the past.

It might be argued that the historical sequences, and especially that involving the last years of Napoleon Bonaparte, could be omitted, that such pruning would give the book a faster pace and remove some of the obstacles as well as some longeurs, from its totality. Despite Arden's attempts to make the sections from different historical periods cohere, for instance by using the same names for similar – or very different – characters, the effect is sometimes strained, and parallels between revolutionary France and the pseudo-revolutionary atmosphere of Britain in the 1970s are actually rather thin. Still, and again like some of Dickens's novels, we accept the whole as a generous, full-blown piece of high entertainment. John Spurling wrote in *The Times*:

> Although the characters are almost uniformly unsympathetic and their
> desires, furies, revenges and foul-mouthed rantings and couplings
> unashamedly melodramatic, they hold their audience through thick and
> thin, through dream and retrospect, suicide-note, diary or self-
> justification, for nearly 600 pages in full cry ... This is partly because
> Arden is a smart plotter, but even more because his language is so
> boisterously alive.[610]

It is also clear that *Jack Juggler and the Emperor's Whore* rummages around in Arden's own theatrical experiences, including the prosecution of a play for libel, as already noted above. One play presented by Vexaction in the novel receives a notice remarkably similar to that received by Arden and D'Arcy's *Harold Muggins Is a Martyr*: 'Rarely can a hitherto intelligent playwright have lent his reputation as well as his subfusc person to such crudely unthinking charades'.[611] When the playwright offers the BBC 'a couple of radio plays dealing with Ireland', he receives a reply which echoes that of Martin Esslin two decades earlier: 'Do remember, Mr Carver, our drama will be accessible to listeners in Ulster, we cannot present anything that might *inflame* the situation there'.[612] And Carver will not allow his director to interfere with his text, any more than Arden and D'Arcy would allow David Jones to be responsible for re-writes to *The Island of the Mighty* in 1972. Finally, we are allowed a glimpse of Arden's fear that his own reputation might be sinking: when Carver dies, 'most of the obituaries implied that he had long outlived the probably unjustified fame of his plays in the '60s and '70s'. Some bitterness is allowed to show through: 'Some critics said he had damaged his ageing talent by crude espousal of the propaganda of violence. He had certainly damaged his bank balance; and his agent did not like it at all'.[613]

Arden very frequently worked on his novels in the cottage in Corandulla, especially while D'Arcy's radio station was transmitting from the house in Galway. The cottage itself was becoming run down, with problems in the roof and under the floor, through which water occasionally seeped up. As the years went by, it was cleaned less frequently and the garden was gradually allowed to run wild. For Arden perhaps it was an ideal bolt-hole; for others it was barely salubrious. Perhaps their friend Nancy Coughlan put the situation most succinctly: 'They live very simply, you know, they've no interest in money, they're not materialists, not materialists at all'.[614]

'Writers today sit and brood', Arden said, referring mostly to himself. 'We sit and write all on our own and talk to ourselves while we're doing it'.[615] He gave a vivid glimpse into his working practice when he was alone in Corandulla. His alarm would go off at 6.30 or 6.45, and he would begin the day listening to a radio news programme until about eight o'clock, when he would get up, make coffee so as to be at his desk by half past eight, 'rewriting what I wrote yesterday'. An hour and a half later, perhaps, he would go and buy a newspaper, returning to read it for a while. But he would usually work some more before making lunch and listening to the news again. Then he would return to his desk and continue to work, 'hopefully not on yesterday's text but on today's'. Sometime in the afternoon he would take a break, sometimes merely taking a nap, sometimes going out on his bicycle, sometimes working in the garden. Having eaten his evening meal, he would work again till perhaps nine o'clock, after which he might read or watch television.[616] D'Arcy had an amusing vision of him 'watching TV at Corandulla in wellies cause floods seep in under the floor'.[617] Arden continued:

> At midnight I begin to get cold feet about something I've written in the course of the day. I tell myself, 'if I work on that damned word processer I won't be able to go to sleep'. On the other hand, if a wretched paragraph is nagging at me I won't be able to sleep anyway, so I'll go and work on it and probably end up going to bed at 2. Having done the bit of work at midnight, I've got a bit fazed with the word processer which I can't take for too long. I have to settle down and unwind after that.[618]

Despite his novel's playwright's pessimism about his standing, Arden was still highly enough regarded at this time for *Cogs Tyrannic* to win the 1992 Macmillan PEN 'silver pen' award, and more substantial studies of his and D'Arcy's work were beginning to appear, most notably *Toward a Theater of the Oppressed* by Javed Malick, and *John Arden and Margaretta D'Arcy: a Casebook*, which began to redress the wrongful omission of consideration of D'Arcy's contribution to the partnership. Two essays in this collection should be particularly noted in this connection: 'An Undeviating Path' by Claudia W.Harris and 'Who Wrote "John Arden's" Plays?' by Tish Dace. On the continent of Europe, too, their works were being seriously examined, in books such as Michael Goring's *Melodrama Heute: Die Adaption Melodramatische Elemente Und Strukturen im Werk von John Arden und Arden/D'Arcy* published in the Munich Studies in English Literature series, and *Frauengestalten und Frauenthemen bei John Arden und Margaretta D'Arcy: Mit Vergleichskapiteln zu Anne Jellicoe, Arnold Wesker, John McGrath und Caryl Churchill* by Heike Jüngst. Malick's complaint, however, still had more than a grain of truth in it:

> Even after four decades of an active writing career, the corpus of criticism
> on this major contemporary playwright has remained largely inadequate,
> in both volume and quality, to the historical significance of his work.[619]

And in 2004, Fintan O'Toole was to remark sadly: 'Arden is hugely under-estimated as a novelist'.[620]

Meanwhile D'Arcy's work for women, centred on Radio Pirate-Woman, was continuing unabated. But it was not exclusively devoted to the radio. She contributed a fine story to the series of 'fairytales for Feminists' being brought out by Attic Press in Dublin. 'The Budgeen' owes something to Gogol's *The Nose*, perhaps, but is clever and amusing in its own right, and soars away with its own Irish logic. It concerns Macha, a young girl who lives in a land of fear because of the fragility of people's noses. When she accidentally knocks off her father's nose, she embarks on a quest to change this world. She visits the Morrígan and gets her to stop making noses ('budgeens'). The king is forced to call a council of all the men in the land to discuss how they can take over the making of budgeens. But Macha intervenes: she runs faster than the king's fastest horse to defeat him, and then she swallows him. Having given new birth to him, she makes him crawl to find the budgeen she has made for him, with the final warning:

> 'If men steal women's work, ... and claim it for their own, I will not just
> swallow *one*, but the *lot* of you!' And the men never dared pull such a
> stroke ever again.[621]

In a new initiative at this time the European Union required member countries to work to raise the status of women; in response, the Irish government set up a Council for the Status of Women, which D'Arcy was invited to join, though her main work in this field was done with Western Women's Link, the offshoot of the Council devoted to the position of women in the west of Ireland. However it was in no official capacity that she took on some of the notorious discriminatory regulations which worked against women locally. For example, there was the case of the pregnant woman made homeless by her landlord's eviction and put into a hostel. Perhaps this was a justifiable decision, but it was compromised by the fact that the hostel was closed every day from twelve noon to six in the evening, when the hostel inmates had to be out of the building. Effectively, they (and their babies) were being forced to live on the streets in the day time.

When D'Arcy discovered what was happening, and that it was as a result of cutbacks authorised and voted for by the local politicians of the city council, she took out an injunction against seven of them with the intention of getting the court to force them to keep the hostel open during the day. When the matter was to be heard in the circuit court, she tipped off the local press, radio and television, so that when the visiting judge appeared, the courtroom was packed. There were not only journalists, however, but also a small army of mothers with their babies or toddlers together with all the paraphernalia a baby needs – piles of nappies, feeding bottles, potties and more. But after hearing a single witness, the judge dismissed the case and left. Whereupon D'Arcy stood up. 'Silence in court!' she commanded. 'All be seated! The Women's Court is in session now'. She described what happened next:

> The women stood in a line in front of the judge's bench. The toddlers sat
> quietly on the ... bench ... Each woman bore witness to her story of
> homelessness. There was total silence in the packed courtroom, except
> for the sobbing of shocked listeners. The Gardaí themselves were silent as
> they stood to attention listening.[622]

At the end of the women's declarations, D'Arcy declared the session of the Women's Court over. No-one said a word as they filed out of the room after this piece of theatricalised protest. But within a day or two, the order closing the hostel by day was rescinded and in fact the women themselves were soon found council flats.

Through the 1990s, D'Arcy continued to visit Greenham Common where she stayed at the Peace Camp for varying lengths of time. After the departure of the Cruise missiles, there were arguments as to whether the Camp should be closed, but most of the Yellow Gate women, with whom D'Arcy associated herself, were in favour of continuing the Peace Camp, partly because Trident missiles were expected to replace Cruise, and they too must be protested against, partly also because the Camp was fighting for the restoration of the land as common. Court cases, attempted evictions, gaol sentences and resistance continued. On Christmas afternoon 1991, with two others, Beth Junor and Judith Walker, D'Arcy entered the empty army training mock-village where exercises in Fighting in Built-Up Areas (FIBUA) was practiced, walked to the 'graveyard' and began to 'decorate' (or 'desecrate') the mock gravestones. They had cans of spray paint and used these to write slogans – 'R.I.P. Irish children killed by British troops' and so on – as well as the names of children killed by plastic bullets and a few adults, including Miriam Daly and Mairéad Farrell, particular friends of D'Arcy, who had been assassinated. The women were soon arrested by a Sergeant Moorehouse and charged with criminal damage. In September the following year, their case came up at court. They maintained that the prosecution lied in evidence, but they were found guilty and sentenced. D'Arcy's opera, parts of which had been mounted in the streets of Galway, was still being composed at this time, but unhappily it was never completed.

Other things intervened. In early 1991 she went to Gateshead, in the north east of England, at the invitation of a women's group who wanted to set up their own radio station. Gateshead had still not found an alternative way of making a living after the shutdown of the coalmining and shipbuilding industries, and she found a run-down and depressed town. Her mission was probably doomed from the outset. She discovered too many local women with 'hearts as strong as stone',[623] seeming happy to send their men off to the Iraq war. She was able to visit Full Sutton from here, and recalled handing in her protest letter to the US base commander, protesting at the nuclear weapons there. Now she was still protesting against war: she attended a protest meeting at the Friends Meeting House. Her diary records: 'Poor turnout. Started late'.[624] The women's radio station failed to materialise.

Another excursion to the north of England was to the Yorkshire coalfield, nearly ten years after it was ravaged by the defeat of the miners' strike in 1984. D'Arcy went in response to an appeal for support for a women's camp at Armthorpe where the last skirmishes of the war against pit closures were being fought. The area was depressed, the people angry and frustrated and the moment chosen was not propitious, since there was a strike going on at the nearby Timex watch factory. D'Arcy met two women from Greenham, though she hardly knew them and it seemed they could contribute little practically. And while she was there, there was an attempt to burn the camp out. The people seemed to be reliant on drugs or bingo to keep going. As at Gateshead, D'Arcy's attempts to make a video were not successful. But these experiences taught her more about the English working class's forlorn struggles.

Now nearing her sixtieth birthday, D'Arcy was still energetic and passionately involved. Claudia Harris came to Galway at this time and recorded 'a pleasant afternoon visit' which in the evening turned into a sort of international *ceilidh* in the house at St Bridget's Place Lower. D'Arcy walked briskly and talked with conviction. She was extremely sensitive to the political implications of things said or things done, and her mind sniffed out connections between seemingly disparate actions or ideas. Claudia W.Harris wrote:

Margaretta is a lightning rod whether she's working with *Duchas na Saoirse* in Belfast or Radio Pirate Woman in Galway. She is both tireless and uncompromising in her efforts as an artist, a woman, and an activist. Ignoring her, silencing her is impossible; she merely develops new ways to be heard. She readily scales that wall of indifference to her issues and continues passionately on her undeviating path.[625]

She also spent time and energy in support of the campaign for wages for housework, which she had encountered while at Greenham Common. This was organised by a collective from Kings Cross which had at that time seemed notable for the way it included all kinds of disabled or disadvantaged or victimised women – 'black women, handicapped women, lesbian women.'[626] In 1992 D'Arcy went to Brussels to lobby the European Parliament on behalf of Women in Media and Entertainment. The aim was for the European Parliament to adopt the United Nations Resolution on Counting Women's Work and though Women in Media and Entertainment was the only Irish group present, there were plenty of women's groups from other countries, all part of a determined world-wide campaign to recognize women's work. And the lobby was successful, in that the European Parliament did adopt the resolution in 1993.

The next year, D'Arcy tied this concern into the ongoing work of Radio Pirate Women, and mounted an exhibition in her own house entitled 'Twenty-Four Hours in the Life of a Woman'. The radio surveyed its listeners, asking how much work they did, and for what reward. Women were invited to photograph unwaged work and bring the results to St Bridget's Place. The exhibition included four television monitors, each showing different types of unwaged work women were likely to be found doing in 1994. It moved to Galway's Town Hall Theatre, and was then seen in Waterford, Belfast, London and Philadelphia, USA. It formed part of the world-wide 'platform for action' which led in September 1995 to the Fourth United Nations Women's Conference in Beijing. D'Arcy again represented Women in Media and Entertainment at this conference, and this time the Council for the Status of Women in Ireland, and its western section, Western Women's Link, gave their support. After some heated debate, the conference agreed that women's unpaid work should be measured and valued by all governments. The fact that at the time of writing this has still to happen in most countries, including the United Kingdom and Ireland, does not diminish the importance of the agreement.

And D'Arcy was still active in more obviously artistic matters. In 1995 she presented a staged reading of *The Good People*, a play which she had adapted, originally by Abdel Kadar Alloula, in London, and at the Irish Writers Centre in Dublin. Three years earlier she and Arden had signed an agreement with the BBC for a radio play about the death of Eleanor Marx, the daughter of Karl Marx. This was their first collaboration since *Whose Is The Kingdom?*, and was to be virtually their last. For all that, the process was hardly any easier now than it had been at any time over the thirty-five years since they had started writing together. Arden remarked that presenting each other with their latest pages was somewhat like presenting examination answers to an examiner. 'Each partner disappoints the other with what he turns up with', he said. But D'Arcy came back with: 'I say nice things to John, and he never says nice things to me'. She added 'I wake up and say, oh God, what am I allowing this man to do?' whereupon Arden exclaimed: 'Oh God! Where is she taking this play? I thought I had it all clear in my mind. And suddenly you have a brainwave and the thing is drifting off into sheer horror'.[627] But 'the rows were creative, not destructive', their friend Noëlle O'Hanlon observed.[628] Part of the problem with *A Suburban Suicide* for them was that it was more of a domestic drama than their usual epic. The one and a half hour play, which was broadcast on Radio 3, starred Miriam Margolyes as Eleanor Marx and John Shrapnel as Edward Aveling, and was directed by Ronald Mason.

Set in 1898, the play's personal and political strands interact and reverberate. D'Arcy stated that the play was 'a statement about commitment',[629] but it may be read as being more about feeling oneself besmirched, and consequently unable to live. This is a particular psychological condition. Eleanor feels that her vision of her father has been fatally contaminated, and she is unable to live with it. The play is sometimes difficult for the listener as it moves between Eleanor's thoughts and the objective world about her, and between her private world with its tangled and unsatisfactory relationships, and the disputatious public world of Kautsky, Bernstein, Aveling, Olive Schreiner and others of Marx's 'heirs'. There is a British dimension, too, the trades unionists' typical gradualism, exemplified by the actions of Will Thorne, which seems as much of a betrayal as Engels's revelation that Freddie is Eleanor's half-brother. But the kaleidoscope of memories, voices, fantasies and desires which erupt in her head do not always clarify these complex events as she moves towards her suicide.

The play was broadcast in 1996, when Arden, too, was still engaged in the polemics of everyday controversy, as may be seen in his rapier-like letter to *The Irish Times* in April 1996. In this he challenged one of that paper's regular col-umnists, Kevin Myers, who, writing about Friedrich Engels and Mary Ellen Synon, boasted of his personal revulsion at the promotion of hatred. Arden asked why, if he truly reviled hatred, he was prepared to use such a word of prejudice as 'knackers' for Irish itinerant travellers.[630]

But suddenly it seemed everything was stopped when Arden was rushed to hospital, having suffered a heart attack.

Twenty-two : The Ink Horn Not Yet Dry

Arden's heart attack was serious. It was, perhaps a warning about smoking cigarettes. At any rate, having been a heavy smoker, he decided now to give it up. He recovered, and the following summer he and D'Arcy were in London to celebrate their fortieth wedding anniversary in Camden. There were readings from the works, and the event was attended by many old friends from their earliest London years, including Tamara Hinchco and William Gaskill.

Their affection had withstood the trials and battering which they had endured over years, and remained firm. Thus, in 1992 it was reported that Arden was a thoroughly equable man: 'the only thing that ignited that radical spark in his eye was the thought that Margaretta D'Arcy, his partner and collaborator for thirty years, might not be accorded her due'.[631] A year before this, D'Arcy wrote in her diary of sending him a valentine card from Gateshead, and with it a poem in which she describes receiving a poem from him:

> Your envelope with
> your love feeling poem
> is put through my letter box, drops in the
> cluttered dark mess inside the door
> on top of a thousand bills, ads,
> free newspapers and letters,
> all for someone else who once dropped in to pass the time.

Later the poems says:

> Your poem catches
> my heart
> pushes emotions
> up through my eyes
> so water drops like
> waterfalls.
> The sun cold & hard
> outside to catch
> a welling tear
> & turn it into a thousand
> prisms of colour.[632]

And in an earlier poem, published in 1987, and entitled 'To John Who Complains I Never Write Nice Poems to Him', she is possibly even more revealing:

> If you died
> I
> Would have
> No

302

Past
Or
Future
Only
Now:
No dreams
No time.
Conscious for only each second that passes
As the earth spins
With
Me
On it
With out
You.[633]

After his recovery, Arden concentrated on shorter forms of writing, mostly radio plays and short stories. To begin with he made a series of six radio plays out of *The Little Novels* by Wilkie Collins. This series of novellas, written by Collins at various times throughout his life, were brought together for publication in three volumes in 1887. Arden selected six of them and made each into a one hour play. They were linked by the casting of Ronald Pickup as the cantankerous author, Wilkie Collins, throughout the series. The first five of the 'little novels' were directed by David Blount and broadcast weekly from 31 December 1997.

The first was 'Mr Policeman and the Cook', with John Quinn, Rachel Atkins and Hugh Dickson, in which a policeman confesses on his deathbed that for the love of a woman (the cook), he had shielded a murderer. 'Miss Jeromette and the Clergyman' with a cast including David Brooks and John Rowe, tells the story of Stephen Wheatmeal, a clergyman who once had a relationship with Miss Jeromette: when she dies, Wheatmeal is confronted by a bloodstained apparition. The third story, 'Miss Marmaduke and the Minister', with Peter Kelly and Emma Fielding, is a theatrical tale with a difference, in which Felicia, a minister's daughter, marries a man who disappears each evening … 'Miss Bertha and the Yankee', with Alison Petit and Jenny Lee, concerns two friends, one English, the other America, who clash over the beautiful Bertha Laroche; the Englishman, thinking he has killed his friend in a duel, goes mad and commits suicide, leaving Miss Laroche for the American. The last of the five was 'Miss Morris and the Stranger', broadcast on 28 January 1998, with Deborah Berlin and Alistair Danson. In this, Nancy Morris is a governess who inherits a fortune and a curious suitor who also has claims to the money.

The sixth little novel of Wilkie Collins was 'Mr Percy and the Prophet', but it was not broadcast till 21 November that year. Jonathan Firth and Mark Peyton played the main parts, with Ronald Pickup again as Collins, the narrator, and it was directed by Rosalynd Ward. In this story, Percy Linwood, a sceptic, and Captain

Bervie, a believer, meet in the consulting-room of a clairvoyant, Dr Lagarde. Dr Lagarde predicts – rightly – that Percy will marry Charlotte Bowmore, whom Bervie loves, but after he marries her, Percy becomes embroiled in political intrigues and Bervie virtually forces him and Charlotte to leave England for France. And it is there, some years later, that Bervie comes across the dead body of Dr Lagarde in the street. These stories are often intense and sometimes creep into the realms of the supernatural. Arden enjoyed them, and enjoyed dramatising them. But he was soon engaged on an altogether more ambitious radio play.

This was *Woe, Alas, The Fatal Cash Box*, which was broadcast on 23 July 1999, directed by Jeremy Mortimer and with a cast including Stephen Critchlow, Richard Burke and, as Julius Applewick, Bernard Hepton. The latter was particularly effective 'with his conspiratorial half-whisper'.[634] *Woe, Alas, The Fatal Cash Box* is a masterpiece, a work which could only succeed on the radio because of its subtle use of internal monologue, dreams and the sudden interruptions of 'reality', which in turn sometimes fade into fantasy. Where the interplay between reality, dream and fantasy in *A Suburban Suicide* was strained by the introduction of public events and personalities, here it is confined entirely to the protagonist's personal experience, and is extremely powerful. Closer to *The Bagman* than to Arden's epic or historical work, *Woe, Alas, the Fatal Cash Box* has a haunting, indeed terrifying, immediacy, and the autobiographical elements – the heart attack itself, his problems with the school magazine money in his last term at Sedbergh School a full fifty years earlier, and so on – add a powerful introspective dimension unusual for Arden.

The play opens with an Elizabethan-style musical setting for the song:

You noble poets with wisdom for your word,
Give ear to me who once sang like a bird;
Hear my sad tale of how to my gray age
All my young grief came back in pain and rage.

In an ambulance on a fine spring afternoon is Julius Applewick (J.A.). He has just had a heart attack. He calls himself a 'superannuated literary gent', though forty years earlier he had been a fierce little biting insect, an intractable anarchistic snarler, burning to turn the whole British theatre upside down. Now for the first time in his life he knew he was on the very edge of death.

It soon transpires that the doctors are doing some research on new drugs and he is invited to participate in the trial. He considers himself 'a man of good social conscience', and thinks he probably should, but is worried by possible side effects. He is to remain in intensive care for some days. '1 – 2 – 3 I'm asleep; 4 – 5 – 6 and I'm dead'. He has one hour to decide. But the drug company is a multi-national capitalistic imperialist exploitative consortium – just what makes him anti-imperialist. The nurse becomes wavery, blurred. She is sensuality, sexuality, erotic enchantment ... Then he is being watched by a group of students with notebooks, and the nurse is speaking about 'a ludicrous trauma in his schooldays' which is profoundly buried in his memory. He can make out the nurse's badge on her nipple: THALIA. Perhaps that means 'Terminal Hypnotism And Lethal Injection Administrator'.

He is aware that a clergyman is at his bedside, wondering whether there is anything he can do. He asks whether Julius is in distress because of the grand-children and children he will leave behind, and explains that 'Thalia' is the Greek muse of comedy. Julius worries: comedy? Is he a figure of fun to the 'sniggering riffraff'? At the death of Applewick surely should be Melpomene, muse of tragedy. As he becomes excited the pain attacks him:

> Pricks and prickles,
> Nettles and thistles,
> Sharp upon his heart
> With stabs of pain,
> And now they're gone,
> And now they're back again.

This is 'intermittent delirium', and the clue to his whole life. The test of the new drug was a test of himself, and he'd failed.

The clergyman has somehow become the school chaplain who had taught him Greek at school. He was in his first year, and he was late for class. 'Aristophanes. *The Frogs*. Who shall construe?' The boy Applewick enters. The clergyman turns to him – 'Deceased, are we? No longer extant?' The frog croaks in Aristophanes' play are imitated in a comic-horrific chorus, first by the teacher, then by the whole class together. Applewick remembers a sermon, the story of a cheat, how Gehazi obtained money by telling 'a dirty little lie', how in consequence he became a leper. It was preached by Reverend McFraw, school chaplain, later a headmaster, a government adviser, a bishop, always popping up like an unstoppable jack-in-the-box. He was 'jealous as a wasp' of Mr Sawyer, the English teacher. When Applewick was to go to Oxford to sit his scholarship exam, McFraw had said senior prefects should set an example by entering the big school athletics race. But Applewick was going to Oxford on the day of the race. McFraw now notes that Applewick has been appointed editor of the school magazine by Mr Sawyer. Mr Sawyer oversees the pages, but there is a 'coadjutor' in its affairs, he warns – McFraw himself, who deals with the business side. He admonishes Applewick that the money must be accounted for. Thalia calls this 'canting rant', weak-kneed melodrama, and closes the bed curtains. She is inside in nothing but feathers, rings, bracelets . . .

She announces: 'Your suicide!' There is a fanfare on a trumpet. The Cadet Corps is marching, but Applewick is still in his study. Thalia asks him: 'Why do you frowst like a masturbatory hedgehog on a fine bright spring afternoon?' Applewick's answer: because he's lost his jacket. He looks in his cupboard, then – 'Rigid he stood

– rigid – wide open mouthed – to see – what was not there'. 'The silly devil's lost his cash box', Thalia mocks. The cash box itself is still there in fact, but the contents have disappeared. 'They'll expel me – embezzlement, theft, prosecute me, prison ...' Suicide seems the only solution. Applewick thinks of hanging himself by the window cord. In stretching for it, he knocks a jamjar off the shelf. It breaks, and he cuts himself on the glass, gets blood on his Shakespeare essay. He loops the cord round his neck. He remembers his pride in his Shakespeare essay, compares himself to Hamlet, who was also going to kill himself but that 'the dread of something after death ...' Applewick is paralysed '... no traveller returns'. So is the Ghost a liar? There is something important here, but he falls off the chair, he's strangling. Thalia laughs. He doesn't die – this is just a slapstick routine.

But he feels stronger. He remembers locking the box, and locking it in the cupboard. Then he spent three days in Oxford, and when he got back, McFraw demanded the money. 'How much have you got?' he demanded. Applewick lied. 'Ten pounds, ten shillings in notes. And cash as well'. McFraw told him to bring it to him before bedtime, but Applewick deliberately 'forgot'. He had to finish his essay. He was late for Cadet Corps. He couldn't find his uniform. The cupboard was not locked. Had he forgotten to lock it? How could he forget? Who took the money? 'You could have nicked it', Thalia says. 'Me? Is it possible? Was it me?' His heart pains are bad. Prickles, thistles ...

McFraw told the headmaster, the headmaster told Julius's parents. They and their son were summoned back to school even though it was after the end of term, and Julius had left. Though McFraw called him a dirty little liar, like Gehazi, the headmaster asserts that calling in the police would harm the school's reputation, and besides he (Applewick) is finished with the school. He is a foolish boy. National Service will do him good. The nurse, or Thalia, asks if he is awake. Does he want to participate in the research project? Applewick realizes he couldn't cope with much in life, but on this one day he has refused to be exploited by a multi-national capitalist drug company, and his refusal is responsible. He begins to sing a comic song:

> Four years and more he haunted me at school.
> 'You have not learned', he said, 'I think you never will'.
> Then with his thumb print he jabbed my brow just here,
> Made his reeking mark, I never could be clear.

The nurse begins to waver, she seems to take off her white coat and begin to dance, plumes on her head shaking, bells on her feet jingling. Applewick laughs. 'Did I die? Or did I live? Do you know, I'm not sure any more I'm aware of the difference'.

The whole play is much richer than a description such as this can convey, not least because of the subtle use of music throughout the broadcast. The play is dense, moving and intense. Particularly clever are the interplay between Greek, the Greek lesson and Thalia, the comic muse; the visit of the clergyman leading into the nightmare of the bullying school chaplain; above all, the suspicions about the drug company's profit-making linking with the fatal cash box and the story of Naaman and Gehazi. Some of the 'set scenes', too, are notable: the Greek class, for instance, is a marvellous *coup de théâtre*, ending with the pupils and teacher all croaking like frogs. Then there is the absurd but vivid suicide scene heralded and finished with Shakespearean trumpet flourishes. And the sermon about Naaman and Gehazi which later relates to the silly lie Applewick tells McFraw. And radio can uniquely convey the slipping in and out of consciousness, the way the past drifts into the present and vice versa, and the merging and separating of reality and dreams. The extraordinary occasions for comedy, too, are notable in this harrowing piece: is Arden now, as Aristophanes was then, the 'darling of the immortal Thalia'?

At the millennium, Arden was almost seventy years old, and D'Arcy in her late sixties, but neither seemed to be slowing down. For a number of years around 2000, they sent annual Christmas letters to all their friends and correspondents, not (as most such round robins are) to tell all and sundry of the death of their cat or the triumphs of their children, but to inform their acquaintances of their latest political campaigns and to exhort their readers to join in. Of course there were social reasons as well, because D'Arcy and Arden were sociable people, but there was certainly a distinction between their round robins and most such specimens.

The campaigns often found a voice on Radio Pirate Woman, of course. Here for instance D'Arcy first made her call for a national strike by women. This was in connection with the campaign which reached its climax in 1999 and 2000 for a Women's Mobile Parliament. Denouncing Dáil Éireann as 'a hornet's nest of self-destructive sleaze, moral bankruptcy and political insanity emitting its noxious exhortations and slick insinuations one after the other',[635] they called for a Women's Parliament to meet in Dublin in May 1999. They appealed to all women to 'come and join, for a long time or a short, much work or little work, a smile or a joke',[636] and proposed to meet for several sessions lasting over a week outside the Dáil while that august body was itself sitting. Furthermore, it was suggested that at least some of these sessions should include 'drumming, singing and squalling'. On International Women's Day they proposed to hand in documents of protest against the Balkan War at all NATO embassies in Dublin, and at the end of May a delegation would leave to join others from all over the world in the 'Mother Earth 2000 Walk' outside NATO headquarters in Brussels.

This campaign was supported by, among others, the International Wages for Housework group and the Greenham Common Women's Peace Camp. The latter, of course, was in its last phase. In 1997 the perimeter fence surrounding the base was taken down and the common was restored to the people. Radio Pirate Woman made an audiotape commemorating this event, in association with the Yellow Gate women, and the programme was awarded the Katherine Davenport Award for 'The International Story of the Year' by the American Women's International News Gathering Service. On 5 September 2000 the camp was finally closed, with all the women's objectives achieved, and the airbase was re-named New Greenham Park, with its status protected. In October 2002 a peace garden was inaugurated with four impressive sculptures of earth, air, fire and water, made by Michael Marriott, and a memorial to Helen Thomas, the only woman who was killed during all the years of the camp. Later in 2005 D'Arcy was to make a retrospective film of the whole protest, called *Yellow Gate Women*, an idea first discussed as long ago as 1987.

In 2003 Arden had to have a hip replacement. It failed to stop new work from him appearing, however, and indeed 2003 was a particularly productive year. His first collection of short stories, *The Stealing Steps*, was published by Methuen, and there were two radio plays broadcast by the BBC. There are nine stories in *The Stealing Steps*, three theatrical tales, two about a disreputable Irish woman of a certain age, and three about 'an old-fashioned Englishman' in Galway. The one odd tale, 'Secret Chats,' is in some ways the most intriguing, a child's eye view of adult behaviour, which moves from sex and adultery out into politics, spying and warfare. It is poignant, convincing and sometimes puzzling.

The first story in the book, 'Barbara,' won Arden the prestigious V.S.Pritchett short story prize. It is set in the time of the mythical John Ball's rebellion, and its central character is a writer of mystery plays. It has elusive echoes of old ballads, such as 'The Demon Lover,' and concerns a man who loves what is only perhaps a phantom. The telling is also notable for Arden's latest pastiche medieval verse, which is certainly as much fun as ever it was in *The Old Man Sleeps Alone*. The second story, 'A Breach of Trust' is also about playwrights, but set now in the early nineteenth century. The third theatrical story, 'A Grim All-Purpose Hall' moves us forward to the end of the nineteenth century and depicts a naïve – or perhaps not so naïve – Irish girl adrift in the too-often immoral seas of the English theatre at the time of Oscar Wilde and decadence in the arts. It does have an ending, however, which takes us back to the Jacobean theatre, being at least as bloody and possibly more enigmatic than anything in the work of John Webster or John Ford.

The two stories about Molly Concannon are perhaps a response to some of the women who were attracted to Radio Pirate Woman. In an interview Arden said that this gave his imagination 'a kind of stimulation' and he 'plundered' it.[637] Be that as it may, Molly Concannon is a disreputable, bohemian, energetic woman, who gets caught up in land speculation and illegal immigrant protection, and whose adventures climax in a hair-raising car chase. And the final three stories in the book centre on Spike Oldroyd, a journalist from Yorkshire, who has a satisfyingly sexual relationship with another immigrant in Galway, a German woman, Ute O'Reilly, whose fidelity however tests him to the limit and beyond in the last story. In effect, he has a knack of becoming involved in events which turn into adventures beyond his control and indeed, especially in the second story, we recognise a familiar Arden plot pattern: something odd happens to someone, and soon we are into something much bigger than it seemed at first, a little local difficulty has turned into a global scam.

The stories as a whole display Arden's unflagging energy and inventiveness, not to say his sense of humour. The prim, even primitive, Mr Tumulty, for example, trapped in a sort of prison-hotel, has only a feeble television for amusement, and that only shows either continuous news or continuous pornography. He stares at the pornography for ten minutes. 'I'd prefer to tell no detail, it doesn't bear thinking of. But I can't help thinking of it', he says. To distract himself, he decides to look out of the high windows, but even when he stands on the table he cannot see out. He sets a chair on the table, stands on it, and comes crashing to the floor. Since he is recovering from being in a plane crash, the pain and the humiliation are so much greater – as is the absurdity! Arden's fiction is Dickensian, not just in its wild humour and its vitality, but also in the way he manages to show the type in the individual and the individual in the type. These stories, like his plays, both those he wrote alone and those he wrote with D'Arcy, are therefore more than mere anecdotes and, despite their characteristic lack of an overt political or social 'message', leave us with something to chew on. Fintan O'Toole commented of this collection: 'Although the Irish stories are more contemporary and have an anarchic energy, I think the English ones are the most powerful despite being set in the past. They seem more personal as he deals with ageing writers wrestling with the nature of their lives and their work'.[638] *The Irish Times* suggested that *The Stealing Steps* was more 'broadly popular' than *Cogs Tyrannic*, and suggested that it was 'arguably the best of his (Arden's) output in any genre'.[639]

The first of the three stories about Spike Oldroyd was the foundation for Arden's radio play, *Wild Ride to Dublin*, broadcast by the BBC on Radio 4 on 9 July 2003. It was directed by Roland Jaquarello, with Edward Petherbridge as Oldroyd and Sara Kestelman as his lover, Ute O'Reilly. Oldroyd's apparently-simple truth becomes entangled with the manoeuvrings and double-crossings of the Irish conflict, and his love is outwitted by spies, prejudice and somebody else's political agenda. So he sets out on his wild ride to Dublin late one night in order to save his honour, his love affair and one Irishman's possible (but not probable) innocence. It is a marvellous, mad journey through a terrible night, first by van, then by train, then by bus and finally by taxi. At each stage of the rain-swept journey there is some intransigent hold-up and Spike's urgency becomes more dire with every stop. It is a fine piece of writing, and makes for excellent radio. 'A new play by John Arden', *The Daily Telegraph* remarked, 'has to be an event', and noted warmly how 'sense' is knocked flying 'as (Ute's) past catches him in a sudden conflict with conscience, honour battling with ardour'.[640]

Later that year, on 21 December 2003, the BBC broadcast on Radio 3 an altogether more ambitious radio play, *Poor Tom, Thy Horn Is Dry*, based on the memoirs of a freebooting soldier and adventurer of the Napoleonic period, Thomas Ashe. This play, like *Wild Ride to Dublin*, was directed by Roland Jaquarello, and starred Aidan McArdle as Ashe. Also in the cast were David Calder, Jim Norton, Marcella Riordan, Rakie Ayola and Colum Convey. Ashe, like Julius Applewick in *Woe, Alas, the Fatal Cash Box*, describes himself as a 'literary gent', but he is a very different type to Applewick. He boasts of himself:

I always cut a dash,

Though they told me I was trash

And he swears he never bent his back to prince or peer. Sitting alone, poor and exiled, at the end of his life, he wonders, 'Where has God gone?' He decides to write his memoirs. Will that answer his question? It might earn him a little money.

The play then recounts his adventures from the age of sixteen, in 1787, when his father punished him for his idleness by getting him a commission in the 83rd Foot Regiment about to sail for India. But a mutiny among the regiment tosses Tom into his first adventure. He is apprenticed to a wine merchant in Bordeaux where he seduces his master's daughter and has to flee rapidly back to Dublin. Here he finds a place in Government House, as well as in the bed of a seductive older woman, only to discover that she is the mistress of his current master. Again, he must move on, and by 1790 finds himself in Switzerland where he writes his first book, a pastiche of a famous work on physiognomy. He decamps for revolutionary France, moves to Germany and rejoins the British Army. But by 1796 he finds himself in a French gaol. His means of escape is to join the French Army from whom he deserts and makes it hot foot back to Ireland, and then on to America.

At Austin, Massachusetts, he buys a farm and a couple of slaves, as well as an 'uppity' mulatto woman, Favene, whose 'desolate beauty swooped up at me'. She turns out to be vulnerable, voluptuous and enigmatic. He lives with her for three years and they have two children, one boy and one girl. After three years without profit, Tom wants to sell up and move with Favene somewhere else, but her previous lover, one Corcoran from County Mayo, reappears to claim her. Tom finds a job editing a newspaper for President Jefferson, and loses it, and then, in New Orleans, discovers a valley of dry bones. He takes some of these back to Liverpool, where he sells them to the museum for a good profit. But before he can settle down to enjoy this, he meets an old friend who persuades him to join him in a scam to steal diamonds from a mine in south America. The adventure goes wrong, of course, and Tom loses even the few diamonds he had saved for himself in a shipwreck off the Azores. Back in England he finds himself being paid to write political propaganda, first for the republican cause and then – simultaneously – for the royalists. Political shenanigans, blackmail and 'negotiations' lead to his losing these positions, and he turns his hand to writing more obviously scandalous works, which the victims will pay to have suppressed. Finally he is sent to France, where he will be left alone provided he leaves the British establishment alone. He sings: 'Tom, Tom, the piper's son ...' He has grown old and tells neither truth nor lie: Poor Tom, thy horn is dry!

The whole play is a *tour de force*, wildly comic and enjoyably unlikely – even as we know that it contains more than a kernel of factual truth. One feature that keeps the listener enjoying the work is the way Tom's adventures so frequently bump into the big political events of the time: he is, as it were, tossed about on the stormy waves of history. The many scenes are effectively linked with Arden-style folk ballads, and there is some delightful dialogue, too. His journey may perhaps be seen – as so often in picaresque works – as a journey to 'find himself', and this is particularly true of the scenes in Massachusetts. Or does he find his true self in his writing? And in that sense, perhaps he is comparable to Arden himself. Tom asserts proudly that he has become a 'professional author'. But does he write for more than the cash any patron will give him? Is his final memoir, which we have just enjoyed, at last a 'true' piece of writing? Must he enlighten his readers, or is entertainment enough? What is the difference between 'truth' and 'fiction'? And what is the point of each? These are questions Arden's own career also inevitably poses. Is Thomas Ashe, in Graves's terms, a 'bard' or a 'gleeman?'

Twenty-three : Loose Theatre

A newspaper article about John Arden in September 2003 noted how busy he still was with writing projects, and added: 'He and his wife are also involved with local and national politics'.[641] It details how 'anti-Iraq (war) protests have taken up much of their time', and also mentions their campaign in Galway, whose council had invoked an obscure bye-law to prevent campaigners or protesters handing out leaflets to the public in the street or holding meetings of a hundred or more people in any public park. And there were other campaigns not mentioned, such as the one for a Senior Citizens' Parliament, which had crystallised after an Irish government proposal to remove medical cards from old age pensioners had been greeted with a storm of dissent. The protests led the government to scurry rapidly away from the proposal. D'Arcy and Arden also supported the campaign against a notably tasteless development proposed for the centre of York: 'The ancient structure of the City of York must not be smothered by the ephemeral mudpies of oversized and overhyped development', Arden wrote.[642] Through Women in Media and Entertainment, D'Arcy in particular was involved in other campaigns, too: for a Women's Public Holiday to coincide with St Bridget's Day, for the implementation of United Nations Resolution 1325, which demanded that women be part of all conflict resolution actions, and, more locally, for the repeal of the secrecy clauses in the 2002 Residential Institution Redress Board Act. Probably the most exhausting and passionate campaigns, however, were those against the Corrib Gas project, whereby Shell Oil attempted to bring gas and oil from the Corrib Field in the Atlantic Ocean eighty kilometres north west of County Mayo by pipeline onto the land and to a new refinery which they proposed to build; and that against the violation of Irish neutrality which was inherent in the Irish Government's permission for American forces to use Shannon Airport both as a staging post for troops and war materials on their way to Iraq, and for what were almost certainly rendition flights of prisoners. And for both of these two campaigns D'Arcy made a film.

The Corrib gas and oil field may be worth over 50 billion Euros. It is therefore worthwhile for a company like Shell to exploit it, and inevitably it is likely to do this as ruthlessly as it can. And Irish law seems to give it virtually *carte blanche* to do what it likes. Certainly no tangible benefits seem to accrue to the ordinary Irish citizen, those whose lives and livelihoods are most affected by the developments. The whole of any profit generated goes to the companies concerned: in 1987 the government exempted the oil and gas industry from royalty payments and ab-olished all State participation in the commercial development of natural resources. In 1992, Corporation Tax on oil and gas companies was halved from 50% to 25%,[643] and later compulsory acquisition orders became available for private com-panies.

But from the beginning of Shell's exploration every proposal for a pipeline was opposed by local residents, and for a few years the courts were busy with appeals and counter-appeals, and hearings and inquiries. In April 2005, however, the High Court granted Shell all the rights it wanted to prevent residents obstruct-ing the construction of their pipeline, and the company began work. Five residents of the village of Rossport which was being disfigured by Shell's works refused to comply with the High Court order, whereupon Shell took out an injunction against them and they were gaoled indefinitely until they purged their contempt of court. They were the 'Rossport Five', and their jailing whipped up a storm of indignation and opposition, both nationally and internationally.

In September 2005 Shell, reeling from the fury it had created, backed down. The five men, one of whom, Willie Corduff, was to be awarded the Goldman Environmental Prize, were let out of gaol. But it was too late for Shell to save their reputation. For the Rossport Five and their supporters in County Mayo and beyond, this was

> a tale of resistance to power, of resistance to being treated as objects without a voice. It is tale of a refusal to being exposed to unacceptable levels of risk, a refusal to allow families, community and place to be diminished and threatened for the profits of a multi-national cor-poration. But it is also a tale of the affirmation of community values, of safety, of democracy.[644]

What was at stake, claimed the men's supporters, was

> the quality of Irish democracy, the integrity of Irish administration, the power and responsibilities of global corporations, environmental well-being and the rights of citizens to dissent and protect themselves from threats.[645]

Also at stake, of course, were the unique marine habitat, and the area of outstanding natural beauty in the Irish Gaeltacht land, where the Blue Stack Mountains rose to the north, and Ben Bulben and Knocknarea in the west, a land strewn with prehistoric monuments, megalithic tombs, stone circles and Iron Age field systems.

Nevertheless, and however that may have been, the struggle continued, for Shell were not going to back away from such a potentially lucrative project. From mid-2005 until October 2006, all attempts to start the project works on the land were blockaded, but in October 2006 things changed. The Gardai, previously comparatively neutral in the battle, changed their tactics. Instead of more or less standing by, they decided to enforce Shell's 'right' to pursue their plans. This would entail, they declared, a policy of 'no arrests', that is, the use of violence against protesters to ensure the company's wishes. The upshot was inevitable – running battles, injuries and mayhem. An independent American inquiry carried out by Accufacts in 2005, plainly showed the disastrous consequences of Shell's then-proposed exploitation: it looked for 'all parties to shift into a more responsible dialogue and reach a more informed and balanced decision on this crucial matter'.[646] Shell prevaricated. Maura Harrington, one of their opponents, went on hunger strike in 2008, but was reprieved by a change in Shell's position. Then a local fisherman, Pat O'Donnell, had his boat hijacked out at sea by masked gunmen, and sunk. Finally, in 2009 Shell were ordered to redesign the pipeline. The struggle continues.

It provided a singularly appropriate subject for D'Arcy's film-making. Her film, called *Shell Hell*, is a campaigning work which certainly pulls no punches. Though she shot much more material, and continued to do so after having created this film, which perhaps could be incorporated into it now, the very brevity of *Shell Hell* (it is little over ten minutes long) provides it with part of its effect. It is a montage of song and speech, excerpts from television news, and 'actuality'. It opens with an adapted traditional ballad, spliced into local people talking about how their lives are affected by the project. There are also references to Ken Saro-Wiwo, the Nigerian environmental activist, who had also won the Goldman Environmental Prize, and who was hanged by his own government for his campaign against multinational oil giants in Nigeria. A heavy metal rock band accompanies pictures of earth-shifters and bulldozers, and we cut between protest marchers, people signing petitions and speeches of defiance. The film ends with pictures of the Rossport Five, and their message: 'All we demand is for our families and ourselves to be safe in our own homes – no more and no less'. Then we see the men being freed – but the marches and protests continue. It is a moving film, but also a fighting film, made, as one protester says, 'to keep up spirits.' And because the Corrib gas controversy is still not properly resolved, it retains a burning urgency.

D'Arcy's other film concerns the case of Mary Kelly, a social activist who found that American planes were using Shannon Airport to refuel, as a staging post for troops on their way to Iraq, and for illegal rendition flights. All this was against the Irish Constitution. So she took an axe to one of the planes. Her action caused her to be arrested and tried. D'Arcy's film, called *Big Plane, Small Axe*, subtitled 'The Mistrials of Mary Kelly', follows the case. The opening shots are of the Airport, and of a good-tempered protest march with drums and songs, though it then shows scuffles between the demonstrators and the forces of law and order. The campaign against the American use of this airport began almost as soon as it was clear President Bush was going to war with Iraq. It was immediately apparent that the Irish Government would permit the Americans to use Shannon for their convenience. A women's peace camp was set up – not a permanent camp, as at Greenham Common, but women camped outside the base regularly – and a regular picket was mounted at the entrance to the airport.

The film rapidly moves to the first trial of Mary Kelly. Obviously there is no film from inside the courtroom, but witnesses, including the defence solicitor and international experts such as Daniel Ellsberg, who 'leaked' the Pentagon Papers decades earlier, are interviewed on their way into or out of the court, and those who are keeping vigil outside are also shown. As the interviews continue, the tension begins to build. It emerges clearly that the judge has a view not shared by most of the expert witnesses. Will Mary Kelly be found guilty? Finally, the verdict: a hung jury. The case will have to be re-tried. Before the second trial, it seems clear that pressure is being put on the Irish government, presumably by the Bush Administration, to find Kelly guilty. Before the trial commences, her barrister and her solicitor withdraw, but her files – several box loads of paper – are not handed over. A legal injunction forces them to be given up, but all that Kelly receives is eight photocopied pages. As a consequence of all this, the second trial collapses.

Then, while we await the third trial, we see scenes inside 'the Peace House' of her supporters, and a public meeting where the case is being explained, as well as scenes from the war itself, and George Bush's absurd premature declaration of victory. Then comes her third trial, and now Mary Kelly conducts her own defence. The new judge is unwilling for her expert witnesses to give evidence, and he will not accept the international law, deriving from the Nuremberg trials after the Second World War, that their principles override national law. Indeed he seems bent on making the case as stressful as possible for Kelly. He even seems to mislead the jury. Once the jury is out there is a long, long wait for the verdict. Finally, it comes: she is found guilty, but is given a two-year suspended gaol sentence. As she says at the end of the film, she is not repentant, her conscience is easy and she invites any American soldier coming to Ireland to hop off the plane and become a refusenik!

The film, like D'Arcy's earlier documentary about the Corrib gas controversy, works as a montage of shots and sequences. It is more arresting than the earlier film, however, because it has a natural built-in tension, as we wait to see what will happen to Mary Kelly, and, it seems, trial after trial collapses, and judge after judge hurls his weight against her. The fact that the camera does not see Kelly attack the plane, nor is it allowed into the courtroom during the trial might seem like a fatal handicap. In fact, it strengthens the film, as it shows the campaigners at the airport, and it lingers outside the courtroom, picking up whatever scraps it can from those also waiting. The tension builds, but at the same time, the important wider context to the film become clearer, preventing it from becoming too emotional and too focused on a single person. In other words, the style of the film underlines the 'reality' of what it is showing, and prevents us from responding to it as though it were a sort of Irish *Twelve Angry Men*.

The protests about the use of Shannon Airport by the American military before and during the Iraq war of the early twenty-first century is where *Loose*

Theatre, Margaretta D'Arcy's memoirs, which she published in 2005, begin. She calls this book a 'scrapbook' and indeed it contains an eclectic selection of musings on events in her life. There are family memories, descriptions of her early years in the Dublin theatre, excerpts from her diaries and discussions of some of her struggles, notably at Greenham Common. It is a provocative, partial and fascinating book, which deliberately omits as much as it includes, and still manages to run to well over four hundred pages.

She opens the book with an explanation of the title, 'Loose Theatre'. She describes standing on the traffic island outside Shannon Airport, holding a placard which asks motorists who pass to 'Beep for peace' (she says 'Bleep' but surely she means 'beep'?). Many who drove past did beep their horns, some did not, but

> the whole experience was so enlivening that we took it in turns to stand
> out there most of the night – nothing formally organised: we just took
> our places when the spirit moved. As each car bleeped (*sic*) we all let out a
> roar of approval and delight, saluting them. It soon became a cacophonic
> musical show, shouts and car-horns, exuberance, vitality; cars that had
> hurried past turned round and came back to join in. We had created a
> loose and spontaneous form of theatre; so much so, that as dawn broke
> the Garda patrol ending their shift finally picked up the spirit and
> bleeped in their turn.[647]

And she describes how this 'loose theatre' did not appeal to one woman there:

> She was unable to put herself into the imagination of drivers who had just
> picked up tired relatives coming in on their flights from all over the world
> and who suddenly saw this unexpected dawn vision of a bunch of
> dancing women on a traffic island. How can one judge such a thing? How
> can one know what the effect will be, how can one measure it or evaluate
> it or properly assess it in its full context?[648]

The answer, of course, is – one can't. And so at last D'Arcy had completed her search, begun in the garden in Earls Court half a century earlier, when she and Arden had vowed to each other that they would find and articulate a new kind of theatre. 'Loose theatre', as she describes it, embodies the essence of what they had both been struggling towards since the 'revolution' at the Royal Court Theatre, which actually changed nothing; since the tentative collaboration of *The Business of Good Government* in Somerset, that 'most enjoyable' of theatrical experiences; what they had searched for through *Ars Longa, Vita Brevis*, through Kirkbymoorside '63, the Vietnam *War Carnival*, La Mama, CAST and *Harold Muggins Is a Martyr*, and those searing folk theatre performances in the heat of the Indian night. Each of these had been a stepping stone towards 'loose theatre'. The end had rarely been clear, but it is possible to recognise with hindsight how the dogfight over *The Island of the Mighty*, the Dublin staging of *The Non-Stop Connolly Show*, and the various performances of Galway's Theatre Workshop's 'immediate rough theatre' had further moved towards it. But it had also been shaped by the Merrion Square 'Circus Exposé', by Greenham Common, by the anti-Reagan protests on the streets of Galway, by the protest at Methuen 500, by *Duchas na Saoirse*, by the women's court, and above all by Radio Pirate-Woman. 'Loose theatre' is perhaps the only convincing riposte to the 'society of the spectacle' described by Guy Debord and the 'Situationists,' of the commodification of all forms of culture by the relentless march of capitalism. The Situationists describe a society in which the ruling élite creates a 'spectacle' in order to dazzle and numb the ordinary person, the mass, the majority. 'Loose theatre' debunks and destroys this process.

So how to characterise 'loose theatre'? It is fluid, non-authoritarian, participatory; it has no obvious pre-conceived structure and no boss figure; it is inclusive and needs a relaxed audience, at least some members of which are prepared to 'join in'. It is pre-figured in what Arden had imagined in his Preface to *The Workhouse Donkey*:

> I would have been happy had it been possible for *The Workhouse Donkey*
> to have lasted, say, six or seven or thirteen hours (excluding intervals),
> and for the audience to come and go throughout, assisted perhaps by a
> printed synopsis of the play from which they could deduce those scenes
> or episodes which would interest them partic-ularly, and those which
> they could afford to miss. A theatre presenting such an entertainment
> would, of course, need to offer rival attractions as well, and would in fact
> take on some of the characteristics of a fairground or amusement park;
> with restaurants, bars, sideshows, bandstands and so forth, all grouped
> round a central playhouse.[649]

Loose theatre has something of the theatre, something of community and something of a special event. *The Business of Good Government* and Galway Theatre Workshop's rough theatre plays were theatrical and communal; the Vietnam *War Carnival* was part-theatre and part-special event; 'Circus Exposé' was obviously theatrical and communal; *Duchas na Saoirse* sought to give succour to a particular disenfranchised cultural community and was a special annual event; D'Arcy's H-Block protest was partly theatrical and partly an event. Radio Pirate-Woman seemed to embody all three elements. The fact is that loose theatre needs a loose and indefinite definition. We can see it in different forms and different creative expressions, and attempts to be too precise are self-defeating and contradict the very spirit of the idea.

Where does this leave the written text? In 1975 D'Arcy had said: 'The playwright is the play as the composer is the orchestral music. Without the playwright there is no play. You can put that in huge capital letters'.[650] It might seem that her later practice contradicted this assertion, but it was not quite so simple as that. If we return to Arden's 1963 vision, the scripted play is at the centre of it, and because by about 1980 Arden and D'Arcy had been virtually driven out of the professional theatre, it does not mean that they drove out the written text from any form of loose theatre. On the contrary, their own contributions to the Galway Festivals in the middle and later 2000s were a series of staged readings of their own plays – scenes from *The Non-Stop Connolly Show* in 2006, *The Ralahine Exper-iment* in 2007, *The Happy Haven* in 2008. They gathered a scratch cast from friends and volunteers, and presented the plays in the Town Hall. The plays then usually went on to other venues in the west of Ireland, such as Inishmore in the Aran Islands, and the Festival at Gort. Emma Campbell, who was involved in these productions but was in no sense an experienced actress, described how the show was staged after only one week of rehearsal. No-one was expected to learn their lines, everyone read from scripts and the moves were just blocked in sketchily. 'John and Margaretta were so kind', she said. 'I mean I hadn't a clue'. But they encouraged her at all times. 'You're doing fine … well, maybe a bit more here, with the body … and your inflection here, you know …'[651] After the performance, audience members were invited to stay on and discuss the plays. The poet Fred Johnston, who also acted in some of these productions, remembered: 'One might jump from discussion of Connolly to discussion of the use of Shannon Airport by the US military in a matter of minutes'.[652] It was the essence of 'loose theatre'.

Thus, no definition of 'loose theatre' which excluded the written script could be acceptable, not least because Arden was a writer. And he continued to write throughout these years into the twenty-first century despite reaching the age of seventy when the millennium turned. *Scam* was a radio play first broadcast by the BBC on Radio 4 on 14 April 2007. Directed by Roland Jaquarello again, it had Kika Markham as Cressida Owlglass, Deborah Findlay as Henrietta and also included in the cast Emma Amos and Neil Dudgeon. Cressida Owlglass is the 57 year-old librarian at a respected boys preparatory school. She obviously has an Arden pedigree: she was born in Brent Knoll in Somerset, and the school she teaches at, like that in *Ars Longa, Vita Brevis*, is called St Uncumbers. She writes letters to her friend, Henrietta Clump, the owner of an art gallery and tea shop on Lake Windermere, and these letters form the skeleton of the drama.

The idea for this play came from the scams which were particularly prevalent on the email in the early years of this century. It seemed to Arden that whatever their crooked intent, the authors of these had great imagination and an eye for story-telling. It was those *behind* the emails, not their actual authors, who were the criminals, the money launderers, arms traders, or drug merchants. The play centred on innocent people who became caught in these desperate webs, the lack of accountability of the police and the unspoken alliance which often seems to exist between large crooks and the supposed forces of law and order, connections soon to be notably exposed in Britain by the so-called 'phone-hacking scandal'. In the play, Cressida's school has been disrupted by the installation of computers, and the newly-appointed Mr Hawkshaw, with his 'dark, tangled hair and elegant fingers', has taught her the rudiments of working the machine – an unexpectedly erotic experience. 'Don't oscillate your mouse', he tells her as they seek out Google.

Despite his warnings, she responds to an email apparently from West Africa which has informed her that she is in line to inherit a million pounds. Of course, this may be a decoy for terrorists, but she is intrigued and pursues it tenaciously. Gradually it is revealed that St Uncumbers is in receipt of a large investment from the Euro Equatorial Consortium which seems to be behind some of the emails. Before she has quite comprehended the world she has entered, Cressida's flat is ransacked while she is out. The school is filled with policemen. Parents begin to remove their children. Cressida is taken to Crewe by Mr Hawkshaw in his car, where she is seized. The gutter press is full of the story. To Henrietta, receiving Cressida's frantic letters, everything is running out of control, and she could have helped her friend. Has she failed? Her husband, Charles, tries to find out what is going on, but their telephone is blocked. However, he has photocopied Cressida's letters, wrapped them in clingfilm and hidden them under a boulder half way up Scafell. Henrietta and Charles think they should 'go public' about what they know; meanwhile the headmaster's secretary has betrayed all and then committed suicide. The international order is collapsing, Ms Owlglass is lost and the Euro Equatorial Consortium is somehow linked to the CIA. At two o'clock in the morning, Henrietta's door is smashed in. She tries to defy the marauding police, but they put her in a van and she is taken away. The end.

The play is not as absurd as it may sound, except in a hugely enjoyable surrealistic sense. Hiding the photocopied letters, wrapped in clingfilm, on Scafell is a typically comic Arden episode. But if much of it is comic, it is also undeniably nightmarish. The use of the letter device, common in novels, is notably well deployed here. Once again, Arden shows himself an expert in this medium, and he has discussed how in radio drama he finds a 'linguistic structure' for a piece such as this 'as much as a plot structure. I think of a radio play rather like a musical arrangement, with its rhythm, its *accelerando* and *diminuendo*', he adds.[653]

In 2009 he published *Gallows*, a fat collection of a dozen assorted stories, some quite long, each with its own *timbre* and interest. Four of these in particular – 'The Free Travel', 'A Masque of Blackness', 'A Plot to Crack a Pisspot' and 'Yorkshire Pudding' – are highly accomplished works, and place Arden alongside Rudyard Kipling, D.H.Lawrence and Katherine Mansfield as a master of the *genre*. The title story, 'Gallows', is set in seventeenth century Galway, where a sinister miscreant, reminiscent of the Nazi Dr Mengele, comes back to haunt and disrupt the modern-day radio station. 'The Free Travel' begins with a comic middle-aged couple and turns into something of a horror story as the man becomes obsessed with an apparently-ubiquitous and villainous bus driver. The ending reaches almost to the realms of tragedy. The third Irish story resurrects Molly Concannon, the wild woman in *The Stealing Steps*. Here she finds herself plotting arson against the local police station while most of the force is away guarding the President of the USA on a state visit to Ireland.

There are two 'London' stories, the first of which, 'A Masque of Blackness', is a superb evocation of Jacobean England. It recounts with subtlety as well as gusto Ben Jonson's involvement or rather lack of involvement in the Gunpowder Plot. It also serves, for those who know Arden's work, as an attractive pendant to his Tudor plays and stories. The Gunpowder Plot itself is seen as the final fling of the English Catholics (Jonson being a Catholic), whose presence here had fired Bale's fanaticism but had been a social and religious cornerstone for sweet, truculent Skelton. At the end of the story, Arden's Ben Jonson channels his view of the plotter, Redbeard, (Guy Fawkes, or 'Fox'), into his great stage villain, Volpone, the fox, in what is surely a stroke of genius by Arden.

All the seven following Yorkshire stories are linked, and linked, too, to stories in *The Stealing Steps*. The first returns to Spike Oldroyd, the Yorkshire journalist some of whose later exploits in Ireland were told in the earlier collection; now we learn about his earlier years. And 'A Plot to Crack a Pisspot' returns to Dryght-skerry House, the scene of perhaps the best of that earlier collection, 'Secret Chats'. It is another near-tragic tale of a reclusive Yorkshire writer who is traduced and nearly murdered out of a kind of professional jealousy. The five remaining stories all focus on members of the long-lasting Fouracre family, denizens of Kirk Deerwood, a lightly-disguised form of Beverley where Arden's own father grew up. The earliest chronologically reflects on the cruel effects of the French Revolution and the Irish rebellion of 1798 on sleepy, conventional Kirk Deerwood: it results in the last hanging, drawing and quartering in English history. Next we see another Fouracre, who is the mayor of Kirk Deerwood, putting an end to the popular traditional football game of the town because of his fear that it may be used for political ends by plotters and rioters. In 'Yorkshire Pudding', we re-enter another Arden world, this time the early twentieth century world of the local council or corpor-ation. Frank Fouracre, somewhat resembles Alderman Charley Butterthwaite of *The Workhouse Donkey*, though this story is based in the market town of Kirk Deerwood, rather than the industrial dirt of the early play's city. The story is a comic-disgraceful tale which one can imagine being told in whispers in certain lounge bars, and Arden's prose does it full justice. The remaining stories are more or less contemporary, 'Yorkshire Tyke' being a kind of sequel to 'Yorkshire Pudding', dealing as it does with the hero of that story's illegitimate line, and 'Yorkshire Bluebeard', shorter and more intense than most Arden stories, centred on the descendant of another char-

Launch of John Arden's collection of stories, Gallows, 2009: (left to right) Margaretta D'Arcy, John Arden, Finn Arden.

acter in the Fouracre saga. This story includes brutal sex and graphic violence; it is harsh and undeniably powerful, though like the other stories in the collection this is leavened by some characteristic humour – the central image of what the heroine takes to be Bluebeard's dead victims, but are actually archaeological specimens, is horribly funny.

The book should have been published by Methuen, as had all Arden's previous works, but when they prevaricated he decided to publish it himself – a move which authors are increasingly deciding to take. This allowed for the book to contain a DVD, in which the author discusses his work. He points out how the title refers not only to the executions in two of the stories, but also to the gallows humour he deploys throughout the book. The collection, just over 500 pages long, is subtitled 'Tales of Suspicion and Obsession', and Arden very equably discusses his own paranoia, which he says fuels a resentment at the world at large. He tells how he tries not to let this stand in the way of his personal relations, but tries to sublimate it in his writing. He sees all politicians as corrupt and points to the Catholic Church in Ireland's abuse of children as an example of abuse of authority and of the common tendency to cover things up. He says he finds that Galway people, though likeable, are often obsessive and suspicious, and while he likes as a writer to listen to them talking, he is often soured by the experience. His special worry is the police force: how, even in 'democratic' societies, all forces seem unaccountable.

Also on the DVD are reproductions of Arden's own paintings of scenes from his stories; indeed we see him painting them during the interview. The results are extraordinary. They are bright, colourful, emblematic works, full of life and movement. He himself says he is influenced by George Cruikshank, and Gillray and Rowlandson, the late eighteenth century caricaturists, and these works do have something of their zest – a zest which the stories themselves possess, too. And although Arden says they are more stylized, more 'twopenny coloured' than the actual stories, it may be that he has slightly misjudged the stories, which this reader at least finds blazingly colourful.

'His Worship the Mayor chucks the ball to the Constable; thereby he puts an end, after hundreds of years, to the Kirk Deerwood Football Game'. Water colour by John Arden; Gallows, 2009.

It is a shame that full colour reproductions were not included in the book. The illustrations include Molly Concannon, for instance, burning down the police station. A huge red, orange and yellow swatch of flame whooshes out of the station door while two blue-clad constables lean panicky out of the window. In the foreground are Molly and her companion, but in the midst of the flames there is a vision of Molly in her student days, with her friends dancing naked round an ancient dolmen. The flames form a sort of oval frame round this vision, and give the whole picture an arresting focus. Other pictures show Ben Jonson in bed with his landlord's wife, spied on by the quivering landlord himself – a scene well worthy of Thomas Rowlandson! A sort of companion piece to this is the lovely, amusing picture of Spike Oldroyd and his beloved naked on the moor, discovered by Lee McStarna. And a third picture in the same vein depicts Fouracre and his friends 'playing' in Mrs Kettlewell's garden. There is Henry Pellinore, the 'Pisspot', almost drowning, Mayor Fourscore throwing the football to the Constable, thereby putting an end to the football game, and many more.

The pictures reveal an artist's feel for colour and composition and surprising skill in depicting people engaged in action. They were framed and displayed in Galway city museum on the occasion of the book's launch. This event went virtually unnoticed in England, but it was a cause for rejoicing in Ireland, where there were plenty of reviews, almost unanimous in their praise. 'Arden may be entering his 80s', one commentator wrote, 'but he is still an artist in full in-ventive flight'.[654] Fintan O'Toole wrote in *The Irish Times* that the book was 'fizzing with energy and invention',[655] and Charlie MacBride concurred: 'the collection vividly attests to Arden's continuing vitality as a writer of imaginative force and distinctiveness'.[656] John Kenney wrote that 'Arden's fiction is characteristically unruly ... *Gallows* is simultaneously a declaration of individual freedom and a pro-vocation of collective conscience'.[657]

Still working: John Arden and Margaretta D'Arcy at work on Tea with George Moore, *2011*

The following spring, Arden collaborated again with D'Arcy for *Tea with George Moore*. This was to be presented in four parts. The first part was first presented in March 2011 at 'an informal soirée' at the Forge at Gort Festival, and then at other venues such as the Kilkenny Playwrights Festival. The subject, the writer George Moore, sometimes thought of as Ireland's first modern novelist, was the central character. Despite great wealth (Moore came into a large property when still a very young man), his family had a history of supporting Irish freedom struggles and the Irish peasantry. Though influenced initially as a writer by Emile Zola's naturalism, he joined the Irish Literary Renaissance at the opening of the twentieth century and collaborated with W.B.Yeats on the play *Diarmiud and Grania* in 1901, when it was produced with music by Edward Elgar. His years of involvement with the Irish literary and cultural world before the First World War were the subject of his controversial memoir, *Hail and Farewell*, and this gave Arden and D'Arcy most of the material for their presentation.

Tea with George Moore was presented in spite of difficulties. In 2005 D'Arcy had been diagnosed with bladder cancer, and although this was cleared, there was still grounds for worry about her health. Arden developed cancer at the base of his spine. He was told an operation was possible, but there could be no guarantee of success, and an operation could cause brain damage. He rejected the option, and gradually came to rely on a wheelchair. It was no surprise that before long D'Arcy had discovered how wheelchair users were excluded and discriminated against. Soon she was campaigning for wheelchair users' rights, and with their son Finn making a film on the subject. And there were compensations. Arden's eightieth birthday was celebrated with an evening of his works presented at the Galway Town Hall Theatre, much of it coordinated by Eamon Draper, who had directed the original Irish-language version of *Serjeant Musgrave's Dance* in Galway. Now he staged a number of extracts from Arden's dramatic works, and there were short pieces of film and video shown. One piece showed a youngish Arden trying vainly to understand how to make soda bread, and another had him following D'Arcy down the road, a large wine bottle in his hand from which he was seen to take copious swigs. 'Have you a cork for this, my lady?' he asks flightily.[658] Finally, Arden himself, from his wheelchair, read a number of extracts from his own work, including the speech Charley Butterthwaite makes while robbing the safe in the Town Hall in *The Workhouse Donkey*. Was the evening an example of 'loose theatre'? It was perhaps reminiscent of the presentation at Sheriff Hutton in 1523 of the garland to the ageing John Skelton, who had crept out of London to be warmly greeted in Yorkshire: here was John Arden, almost forgotten in England, rapturously and fittingly acclaimed in his adopted land, Ireland.

And then in November, Arden was elected to membership of Aosdána, though as he and D'Arcy remarked:

> It was extraordinary that in the recent hairshirt budget they took away
> benefits for young people with disabilities, and cut the children's
> allowance for families with more than two children, yet an elderly
> gentleman of no benefit to the economy is actually given money.[659]

There may be some modesty here as well as truth: his commitment to Ireland was recognised, and – perhaps more to the point – his bank balance immediately became more healthy. Aosdána's *cnuas* now amounted to more than €17,000 per year, and it enabled him and D'Arcy to take a holiday cruise along the coast of Norway in the summer of 2011. Was it ironic that while they were on this cruise, a deranged Norwegian pseudo-Fascist gunned down and murdered scores of politically-inclined young people?

Nevertheless, what rings in the head from these latest years is Ronnie O'Gorman's thought, published in 2010 after the eightieth birthday celebration:

> You might imagine that (Arden and D'Arcy) have earned a rest, and time to enjoy the comfort of their home and neighbours. But these two people still passionately care about injustice in the world; the bullying of great nations against a weaker one, the struggle of small people against the stronger one, and are prompted to write, plead, protest and stand in the rain on a wet Saturday asking people to support their latest concern.[660]

Twenty-four : 'This Was Not History. It Has Not Passed'

This chapter's title is the last line of *The Non-Stop Connolly Show* by Margaretta D'Arcy and John Arden. It seems an adequate way to suggest their significance. Their writings, their activism, their aims are still urgently important. When their work is considered, or a play of theirs is produced, it is not out of some antiquarian curiosity, but because it still resonates with us today. When *Serjeant Musgrave's Dance* was revived in the early twenty-first century, its continuing relevance surprised many, and Arden noted how this was a common feature of reactions to this play:

> It became very relevant during the Vietnam war. I saw a highly effective
> American production in 1967 that surrounded the stage with blown-up
> photos of the fighting in Vietnam. It became relevant again in 1972, when
> 13 people were killed in Derry by British soldiers. And what's going on in
> Iraq today makes it even more relevant.[661]

And Michael Billington wrote about a revival of *Armstrong's Last Goodnight* in 1994:

> Watching the play, I kept thinking of the tortuous peace-keeping moves
> in the Balkans and the semantic wrangling over the IRA ceasefire, which
> is a sure sign that Arden's work is infinitely more than a dusty chronicle.
> In short, (this was) a necessary revival of an unfairly neglected play.[662]

At the heart of these plays is a cry for liberty and democracy. The need for hope is built into their every line. The search to make these sing more loudly, resonate more continually, always drove D'Arcy and Arden. At the Royal Court Theatre in the 1950s, the special acting group was to be trained to make plays demand more from their audiences. The plays which Arden wrote in those years were similarly challenging, and were already far ahead of the conventional naturalism of his peers. 'Arden is an incomparably greater figure than Osborne', the critic and commentator Fintan O'Toole wrote in 2009.

> Compared to the dreary, misogynistic and self-pitying *Look Back in
> Anger*, Arden's early Royal Court plays – *The Waters of Babylon* and *Live
> Like Pigs* – still have a ferociously sharp edge of humour, anarchy and
> theatricality'.[663]

But after a decade or more, it became clear that the Royal Court and the other major subsidised national theatres were incapable of fulfilling D'Arcy and Arden's shared dream.

D'Arcy it was who first reached a hand out towards community, the place where she lived, and for a time it seemed that community, or the 'fringe' of the recognised theatrical and cultural circuit, might provide a more satisfactory means to reach their goal. Their joint work in the 1960s is rich, optimistic and full of unexpected delights. They offer in these 'alternative' works, written partly under the influence of radical American playmakers, new kinds of drama, new relationships with spectators, a new freedom from the constraints of convention, whether the convention concerns the length of time a performance may last, the place of a performance or the 'believability' of the action. When they went to India at the end of that decade, they suddenly saw a completely different way in which theatrical activity could reach out to people, affect, amuse, stimulate them. And they brought this home and attempted to apply it to their own work – *The Island of the Mighty* and *The Non-Stop Connolly Show.* If the established British theatre could not take to this enormous shift in perspective, what they learned still spilled out into campaigning drama, like *The Ballygombeen Bequest,* and into their 'immediate rough theatre'. But those ensconced in their comfortable positions of power in the established theatre found all this a little too much for them, and by 1980 this line of experiment was at an end.

From 1980, instead of following their joint path, Arden and D'Arcy's ways became complementary. They were still comrades-in-arms, even when they were involved in different projects. D'Arcy's work especially moved beyond the confines of theatre into wider, often theatricalised social and political arenas. Her career has baffled many British observers, but there is a significant tradition of women, especially German and Russian women, who have combined activism with theatre work in differing proportions. Rosa Luxemburg, for instance, sought 'spontaneity' in the German revolution and criticised the Bolsheviks for suppressing the Constituent Assembly, believing that all voices have a right to be heard. 'Freedom is always the freedom of the dissenter', she argued. Emma Goldman preached 'the propaganda of the deed', and Clara Zetkin took Lenin to task on 'the woman question' in 1920. Then there was Olga Kameneva, sister of Trotsky, wife of Kamenev, who became the Head of the Theatre Department of the Commissariat of Enlightenment and worked with Vsevolod Meyerhold to nationalise all the theatres of Russia – a measure too radical for the faint-hearted political and theatrical establishments. And Alexandra Kollontai who became People's Commissar for Social Welfare and founded the Women's Department (*Zhenodel*) in 1919: her drive to free women from their old shackles was another project too far for the Bolsheviks.

Kollontai's link with the revolutionary theatre was also significant, and she served as the model for Milda, protagonist of Sergei Tretyakov's play, *I Want a Baby,* for the unnamed Woman Commissar who is the heroine of Vsevolod Vishnevsky's *Optimistic Tragedy,* and even for Ninotchka, played by Greta Garbo in the film of the same name. Women in the theatre who fought important political battles included not only Germans, such as Marlene Dietrich and Brecht's collaborators, Margarete Steffin and Elisabeth Hauptmann, but also Zinaida Raikh, Meyerhold's wife. Her promptings led Meyerhold towards a series of plays in the 1930s which addressed the subject of women's rights, even though Stalin had dissolved the Women's Section of the Communist Party at the start of the decade, declaring the 'woman question' was solved. Meyerhold-Raikh argued, in language uncannily similar to D'Arcy's five decades later, that 'women should take over men's roles on the stage, as well as in real life, by acting parts written for male actors'.[664]

Such radicalism was not confined to women in the theatre, either. In the visual arts, for instance, Lyubov Popova and Varvara Stepanova designed 'useful' objects, such as workers' overalls, and argued for the artist as agitator, and pur-veyor of socialist ideas and ideals. The German pacifist, socialist and feminist, Käthe Kollwitz, made her name with her images of Gerhart Hauptmann's revolutionary drama, *The Weavers*. She insisted on the social function of art, and as one critic put it, 'the philosophy expressed in her works anticipated that of some contemporary activist groups, such as the women's peace movement, and departed radically from traditional conceptions and representations of motherhood'.[665]

D'Arcy's work is rooted in this tradition, though her achievements over thirty years and more are not always easy to document, or to evaluate. Her philosophy, she says, was based on 'the three Fs', which she gives as 'Freedom to receive and give information, Freedom of expression, Freedom of speech',[666] and these are certainly what her pirate radio station was single-mindedly devoted to. But she adds to the list – *play*. Play is a means of exploring life. Children learn best through playing. But, as D'Arcy points out, there are always forces trying to channel and control play, or to make play into *games*, which is not the same. Play is free, it has no rules and it changes from cowboys-and-indians to mummies-and-daddies at the merest whim of the player(s). The examples may not be the best, but the fluidity of the process is clear. And those who take life too seriously, and believe in the pro-fundity of their way, are comprehensively undermined by play.

D'Arcy understood that new kinds of democracy become alive and available once false barriers, such as the will to dominate or the will to organise, are broken down, and once false expectations are ignored. And this leads to empowerment. At the Galway Festivals, she advertised 'conversation': if you wanted to have a con-versation, you were welcome to her house in St Bridget's Place Lower. There people could contribute if they wanted to, and how they wanted to. Earlier, at Kirkby-moorside and in Muswell Hill, she created a somewhat similar, if less clearly-defined, frame within which anyone could 'perform' anything.

Her declared aim now was to help people to value themselves, to find their own criteria, and not to accept those foisted upon them. She learned this partly from seeing how unvalued Arden was if he had no play on in London at any given time. And she believed in 'doing things in a small way in small groups'.[667] And these, of course, were always rooted in her own community. Nancy Coughlan, who worked with her, commented:

> She's an inspiration to everyone in Galway ... I mean, she's fighting court
> battles for the underdog, she'll get onto Women's Groups, she helps every
> Tom, Dick and Harry – nothing's too much for her.[668]

But her small local groups were connected with larger groups. In her book, *Galway's Pirate Women*, there is a diagram with Women in Media and Entertainment and Radio Pirate-Woman in the centre, connected by the radio wave band; out from WIME spread Greenpeace, Café (Creativity Activity For Everyone), Council for the Status of Women, Western Women's Link, Yellow Gate at Greenham Common, and Time Off For Women; and out from Radio Pirate-Women are FERL (European Federation of Community Radios), AMARC (World Association of Community Broadcasters), and CPBF (Campaign for Press and Broadcasting Freedom); all these interact, and often through the single person of Margaretta D'Arcy. And this is not simply mechanical or business-oriented. When WIME was launched in Galway, women from all over Europe descended on St Bridget's Place, where their hostess fed and entertained them, provided aromatherapy and even took those who wished to a sauna.

D'Arcy's ability to make links suggests her method may be a model, or a blueprint, for radical social and cultural action, for her work gives a voice to the voiceless and value to those who are overlooked or even despised. Of how many others can this truly be said?

Margaretta D'Arcy is therefore a dissident, which used to be a badge of honour for citizens of the Communist Soviet Union in the period of the Cold War, but was never acceptable in the capitalist west, and still is not. Consequently people are often uneasy with her. She 'challenges' people, her friend Tamara Hinchco said. Partly this was through the little words most people use almost without thinking – 'perhaps', 'maybe', 'rather', and so on – as 'verbal cap-doffing that proves you know your place, and legitimizes the minority in power'. These small words, she argues, show we are manipulable: 'I refuse them, so therefore I cannot be wooed or seduced, I am obnoxious'.[669] And though she is 'obnoxious', and many people have been refused the indulgence of these conventional platitudes by her, she is also held in the highest esteem by those for whom she has cared. Selma James, of Wages for Housework, came to know some of the very ordinary women who participated in Radio Pirate-Woman, and wrote:

> In the course of their involvement they had obviously come to accept
> Margaretta who lives a most non-traditional life – more than accept; they
> clearly love her and feel that she has contributed richly to their lives as a
> friend and as a broadcaster.[670]

Arden's has been a more traditional path than D'Arcy's. He tried and failed to combine his writing with political activism. He discovered that the writer can march, demonstrate, protest and write letters, but his attempts in the 1970s to use his writing directly to intervene politically rarely achieved much. The jointly-authored *The Ballygombeen Bequest* was probably the only work which may be said to have intervened directly, and it was stopped in its tracks. The later version, *The Little Gray Home in the West*, which Arden considered superior to *The Ballygombeen Bequest*, did not have the same inflammatory urgency. The later radio plays, novels and short stories illuminate our dilemmas as social and political creatures, but do not intervene directly, any more than did his earlier plays.

Arden has ploughed a lonely furrow. He seems always to have been difficult to 'place', partly because he is clearly more 'original' than the other 1950s Royal Court dramatists. But he is also, according to Michael Billington, 'the most mysterious' of them,[671] though as Fintan O'Toole pointed out, 'German theatre, for example, seems to have no great trouble treating Arden as a major modern figure'.[672] This, it may be argued, is because Arden has often been known as 'Britain's Brecht', though except for a decade or two around 1980, Brecht was always a 'difficult' figure for British theatre. O'Toole argues that Arden, though a great writer, is somehow marooned between the Eng. Lit. tradition within which he was brought up, and the 'outsider' tradition of Irish writing. However, it may be more accurate to suggest that the difficulty which critics still find in placing Arden is because he has moved during his career from one tradition to the other.

His early work can without too much difficulty be fitted into an English tradition: Skelton, Jonson, Gay, Dickens. It clearly has an allegiance to the drama of the Elizabethans and Jacobeans. There is something of Middleton and Jonson in plays like *The Waters of Babylon* and *The Workhouse Donkey*, as there is of Marlowe or Webster or Ford in *Serjeant Musgrave's Dance* or *Armstrong's Last Goodnight*. We may even detect something Shakespearean in *Live Like Pigs* and *The Hero Rises Up*. And these influences are not completely lost in his later work. It is, for instance, notably present in the fruitful dialogue he conducts across his career with the Tudors – Skelton, Bale and others – and indeed with history in general, recalling Shakespeare and Jonson's fascination with Roman as well as British history. Arden's work spans the ancient world (*Silence Among the Weapons*, *Whose Is the Kingdom?* and the first story in *Cogs Tyrannic*, for example), medieval history (*Left-Handed Liberty*, *The Old Man Sleeps Alone*, 'Barbara', the prize-winning first story in *The Stealing Steps*) and the nineteenth century (*The Life of Man*, *Vandaleur's Folly* and several short stories).

All this may be regarded as part of a classically English literary tradition, but still Arden's work from the first caused English critics headaches. That was because his work also draws on the European tradition of twentieth century Modernism, rather as D'Arcy's does. Arden's plays have a clear relationship to the work of Meyerhold and Eisenstein's playwrights – Mayakovsky, Tretyakov, Erdman, as well as Brecht and Toller and, in the English language, Sean O'Casey and Ewan MacColl. And the Irish influence becomes more pervasive in the later plays written with D'Arcy. The seeds of Irish outsiderism may always have been embedded in his work, in *Live Like Pigs* and *Armstrong's Last Goodnight*, but the affinities between his plays and those of Boucicault, Synge, O'Casey and Behan undoubtedly became more marked from about 1970. Thus, his increasing adoption, with D'Arcy, of a melodramatic form not unlike Boucicault's characterises much of his 1970s output; and the final scene of the wake in *The Ballygombeen Bequest/The Little Gray Home in the West* has its own twist upon one dramatised also by Boucicault and Synge and found in the heart of the Irish folk as well as literary tradition. His novels and stories, which take over from plays in his output around 1980, are from the very beginning much more akin to the rumbustious Irish story telling of James Joyce, Flann O'Brien and perhaps even the Samuel Beckett of *More Pricks Than Kicks* and *Murphy* than the more desiccated work of so many English authors.

At the heart of this shift are what may be regarded as Arden and D'Arcy's greatest works, part English history plays, part extravagant Irish picaresque epics, *The Island of the Mighty* and *The Non-Stop Connolly Show*. These are extraordinarily original works, which neither the British theatre not the Irish has yet come properly to terms with, though they both owe something to each tradition. But they both go beyond these roots, perhaps because of the strong Indian influence detectable in each. There is hope, a new path, an imperative embedded in every line of *The Island of the Mighty*, as there is in Indian versions of *The Mahabharata*; and there is a cry for liberty and democracy at the heart of *The Non-Stop Connolly Show* which echoes that of those Indian peasants sinking in the mud of Bengal. Perhaps these works are closest, in the western tradition, to the spirit of those 'Romantic' outsiders, Blake, Shelley and Ruskin. And indeed Arden has some striking similarities to Blake. Like Blake, Arden had a bent for visual as well as verbal art forms, like Blake he tackled 'big' themes and like Blake he is capable of the most beautiful and stylish writing. He would undoubtedly endorse the prayer Blake puts into the mouth of Brutus at the end of *King Edward III*, that

> Liberty shall stand upon the cliffs of Albion,
> Casting her green eyes over the blue ocean.[673]

He would ask, too, with Blake:

> Is this a holy thing to see
> In a rich and fruitful land –
> Babes reduced to misery,
> Fed with a cold and usurious hand?[674]

But Arden also has much in common with Percy Bysshe Shelley, especially perhaps *The Mask of Anarchy* and his political poems in a time of repressive reaction, which ask:

> Men of England, wherefore plough
> For lords who lay ye low?
> Wherefore weave with toil and care
> The rich robes your tyrants wear?

> Wherefore feed, and clothe, and save,
> From cradle to the grave,
> Those ungrateful drones who would
> Drain your sweat – nay, drink your blood?[675]

Many believe we need a Blake or a Shelley now, in an age of extraordinary greed and corruption, when teenage boys of perfectly good character can be sent to gaol for years for suggesting they should meet and 'riot' somewhere, more in jest than in serious intent, and though their words had no outcome in action. Yet this happened in 2011 in England. This is a society in which bankers and politicians can swindle the public purse and help themselves to whatever they can get, and still complain, as MPs do, that any check on their 'expenses' is not 'value for money'. It is a society where a Prime Minister can be caught trying to fiddle hundreds of pounds in bogus 'expense claims' (and a cabinet minister thousands of pounds), but where all is well when they simply 'hand back' the fruits of their burglary – or some of its fruits. 'Rioters', or the poor, are not afforded such a chance. Where is the Shelley now, to cry for 'Liberty' which is being 'smitten to death'?

Arden and D'Arcy are perhaps the closest we have to such prophets. But like most such, including Blake and Shelley, they seem to be honoured anywhere but in the England which first nurtured their talents. At least some in Ireland appreciate them. 'I admire them', Emma Campbell said. 'They're very kind people, and they're very aware of people's suffering. Galway would be a poor place without them'.[676]

Bibliography

1. Full length books by John Arden and/or Margaretta D'Arcy

(excluding unpublished works, plays and stories published in journals or anthologies, newspaper and journal articles and interviews, chapters in books, etc)

Arden, John (1960), *Serjeant Musgrave's Dance*, London: Methuen

Arden, John, and D'Arcy, Margaretta (1963), *The Business of Good Government*, London: Eyre Methuen (*Note: this book was originally published under the name of John Arden alone.*)

Arden, John (1964a), *Three Plays*, Harmondsworth: Penguin; contains: *The Waters of Babylon, Live Like Pigs, The Happy Haven*

Arden, John (1964b), *The Workhouse Donkey*, London: Methuen

Arden, John (1965a), *Armstrong's Last Goodnight*, London: Methuen

Arden, John (1965b), *Ironhand* (adapted from J.W.von Goethe, *Goetz von Berlichingen*), London: Methuen

Arden, John (1965c), *Left-Handed Liberty*, London: Methuen

Arden, John, and D'Arcy, Margaretta (1965), *Ars Longa Vita Brevis*, London: Cassell

Arden, John (1967), *Soldier, Soldier and Other Plays*, London: Methuen; contains: *Soldier, Soldier, Wet Fish, When Is A Door Not A Door?, Friday's Hiding*

Arden, John, and D'Arcy, Margaretta (1967), *The Royal Pardon*, London: Methuen

Arden, John, and D'Arcy, Margaretta (1969), *The Hero Rises Up*, London: Methuen

Arden, John (1971), *Two Autobiographical Plays*, London: Methuen; contains: *The True History of Squire Jonathan and His Unfortunate Treasure, The Bagman,* or *The Impromptu of Muswell Hill*

Arden, John, and D'Arcy, Margaretta (1974), *The Island of the Mighty*, London: Eyre Methuen

Arden, John (1977a), *Plays: One*, London: Eyre Methuen; contains: *Serjeant Musgrave's Dance, The Workhouse Donkey, Armstrong's Last Goodnight*

Arden, John (1977b), *To Present the Pretence*, London: Eyre Methuen

D'Arcy, Margaretta and Arden, John, *The Non-Stop Connolly Show*: (1977), Pts 1 and 2; (1978), Pt 3; (1978) Pt 4; (1978) Pt 5; (1978) Pt 6, all London, Pluto Press; published in one volume (1986), London: Methuen

Arden, John (1979), *Pearl*, London: Eyre Methuen

D'Arcy, Margaretta, and Arden John (1981), *Vandaleur's Folly*, London: Eyre Methuen

D'Arcy, Margaretta (1981), *Tell Them Everything*, London: Pluto Press.

D'Arcy, Margaretta, and Arden, John (1982) *The Little Gray Home in the West*, London: Pluto Press; also published (1986), London: Methuen

Arden, John (1982), *Silence Among the Weapons*, London: Methuen.

Arden, John, and D'Arcy, Margaretta (1988a), *Whose Is the Kingdom?*, London: Methuen

Arden, John, and D'Arcy, Margaretta (1988b), *Awkward Corners*, London: Methuen

Arden, John (1988), *Books of Bale*, London: Methuen.

Arden, John (1991), *Cogs Tyrannic*, London: Methuen.

Arden, John, and D'Arcy, Margaretta (1991), *Plays: One*, London: Methuen; contains: *The Business of Good Government, Ars Longa Vita Brevis, Friday's Hiding, The Royal Pardon, The Little Gray Home in the West, Vandaleur's Folly, Immediate Rough Theatre*

Arden, John (1994), *Plays: Two*, London: Methuen; contains: *The Workhouse Donkey, The Bagman, Armstrong's Last Goodnight, Left-Handed Liberty, The True History of Squire Jonathan and His Unfortunate Treasure.*

Arden, John (1995), *Jack Juggler and the Emperor's Whore*, London: Methuen

D'Arcy, Margaretta (1996), *Galway's Pirate Women: A Global Trawl*, Galway: Women's Pirate Press

Arden, John (2003), *The Stealing Steps*, London: Methuen.

D'Arcy, Margaretta (2005), *Loose Theatre: Memoirs of a Guerrilla Theatre Activist*, Victoria, B.C., Canada: Trafford

Arden, John (2009), *Gallows*, Dublin: Original Writing.

2. Works cited in this book

Anderson, Michael (1976), *Anger and Detachment: a Study of Arden, Osborne and Pinter*, London: Pitman

Ansorge, Peter (1975), *Disrupting the Spectacle*, London: Pitman

Bethell, S.L. (1944), *Shakespeare and the Popular Dramatic Tradition*, London: Staples

Bigsby, C.W.E. (1981), *Contemporary English Drama*, London: Edward Arnold

Billingham, Peter (2002), *Theatres of Conscience, 1939-53*, London: Routledge

Billington, Michael (2007), *State of the Nation: British Theatre Since 1945*, London: Faber and Faber

Blackwood, Caroline (1984), *On the Perimeter*, London: Heinemann

Brecht, Bertolt (1980), *Life of Galileo*, London: Eyre Methuen.

Brecht, Bertolt (1978), *The Mother*, London: Eyre Methuen.

Brown, John Russell (1969), *Effective Theatre*, London: Heinemann

Brown, John Russell (1972), *Theatre Language*, London: Allen Lane

Brown, John Russell, and Harris, Bernard (1962), *Contemporary Theatre*, London: Edward Arnold

Browne, Terry (1975), *Playwrights' Theatre: The English Stage Company at the Royal Court*, London: Pitman

Burke, Mary (2009), *"Tinkers": Synge and the Cultural History of the Irish Traveller*, Oxford: O.U.P.

Burton, Peter, and Lane, John (1970), *New Directions*, London: Macgibbon and Key

Calder, John (2001), *Pursuit*, London: Calder

Carpenter, Humphrey (2003), *The Angry Young Men*, London: Penguin

Cervantes, Miguel de (2010), *Don Quixote*, trans Tom Lathrup, Richmond: Oneworld Classics.

Chambers, Colin, and Prior, Mike (1987), *Playwrights' Progress: Patterns of Postwar British Drama*, Oxford: Amber Lane Press

Child, Francis James (1965), *The English and Scottish Popular Ballads*, vol III, New York: Dover Publications

Clarke, Peter (1997), *Hope and Glory: Britain 1900-1990*, London: Penguin.

Collingwood, R.G., and Myres, J.N.L. (1936), *Roman Britain and the English Settlements*, Oxford: Clarendon Press

Connolly, Frank (ed) (1984), *The Christy Moore Songbook*, Dingle: Brandon

Connolly, Frank, and Lynch, Ronan (2005), *The Great Corrib Gas Controversy*, Dublin: Centre for Public Enquiry.

Coveney, Michael (1990), *The Citz: 25 Years of the Glasgow Citizens Theatre*, London: Nick Hern Books.

Craig, Sandy (1980), *Dreams and Deconstructions: Alternative Theatre in Britain*, Oxford: Amber Lane Press

Debord, Guy (1994), *The Society of the Spectacle*, N.Y.: Zone Books.

Demastes, William W. (1996), *British Playwrights 1956-1996*, Westport, CT: Greenwood

Duff, Charles (1995), *The Lost Summer: The Heyday of the West End Theatre*, London: Nick Hern Books

Duncan, Ronald (1968), *How to Make Enemies*, London: Rupert Hart-Davis

Eisenstein, Serge (1968), *The Film Sense*, London: Faber and Faber

Etherton, Michael (1989), *Contemporary Irish Dramatists*, London: Macmillan

Fanon, Frantz (1963), *The Wretched of the Earth*, N.Y.: Grove Press

Ferriter, Diarmid (2009), *Occasions of Sin: Sex and Society in Modern Ireland*, London: Profile

Findlater, Richard (ed) (1981), *At the Royal Court: 25 Years of the English Stage Company*, Oxford: Amber Lane Press

Fo, Dario, and Rame, Franca (1981), *Female Parts*, London: Pluto Press

Foley, Timothy P., Pilkington, Lionel, Ryder, Sean, Tilley, Elizabeth (eds) (1995), *Gender and Colonialism*, Galway: Galway University Press.

Foster, Paul (1967), *Tom Paine*, London: Calder and Boyars

Fountain, Nigel (1988), *Underground: the London Alternative Press 1966-1974*, London: Routledge

Fowke, Edith, and Glazer, Joe (1973), *Songs of Work and Protest*, New York: Dover.

Garavan, Mark, et al. (no date), *Our Story: The Rossport Five*, Magheramore: Small World Media

Gaskill, William (1988), *A Sense of Direction*, London: Faber and Faber

Goethe, Johann Wolfgang von (1965), *Götz von Berlichingen: a Play*, trans. Charles E.Passage, New York: Frederick Ungar

Graves, Robert (1955), *The Crowning Privilege: the Clark Lectures 1954-5*, London: Cassell

Graves, Robert (1997), *The White Goddess*, 4th edn, edited by Grevel Lindop, London: Faber

Gray, Frances (1982), *John Arden*, London: Macmillan

Gray, Tony (1994), *Ireland This Century*, London: Little, Brown

Greaves, C.Desmond (1979), *Sean O'Casey: Politics and Art*, London: Lawrence and Wishart

Greer, Herb (1964), *Mud Pie, the CND Story*, London: Max Parrish

Hanley, Brian and Millar, Scott (2009), *The Lost Revolution: The Story of the Official IRA and the Workers' Party*, London: Penguin

Harford, Barbara and Hopkins, Sarah (1984), *Greenham Common: Women at the Wire*, London: The Women's Press.

Harrington, John P. (1991), *Modern Irish Drama*, New York: Norton

Hayman, Ronald (1968) *John Arden*, London: Heinemann

Henderson, Philip (ed) (1948), *The Complete Poems of John Skelton, Laureate*, London: J. M. Dent & Sons

Hipperson, Sarah (2005), *Greenham: Non-Violent Women -v- The Crown Prerogative*, London: Greenham Publications

Hogan, Robert (1967), *Renaissance After the Irish: A Critical History of the Irish Drama Since The Plough and the Stars*, Minneapolis: University of Minnesota Press

Horovitz, Michael (1969), *Children of Albion: Poems of the 'Underground' in Britain*, Harmondsworth: Penguin.

Howe, Stephen (2000), *Ireland and Empire*, Oxford: O.U.P.

Hunt, Albert (1974), *Arden, a Study of his Plays*, London: Eyre Methuen

Hunt, Albert (1976), *Hopes for Great Happenings*, London: Eyre Methuen

Hunt, Albert, and Reeves, Geoffrey (1995), *Peter Brook*, Cambridge: C.U.P.

Imison, Richard (ed) (1983), *Best Radio Plays of 1982*, London: Methuen/BBC.

Innes, Christopher (1992), *Modern British Drama*, Cambridge: C.U.P.

Ionesco, Eugène (1960), *The Killer and Other Plays*, London: John Calder.

Itzin, Catherine (1980), *Stages in the Revolution*, London: Eyre Methuen

Johnson, B.S. (ed) (1973) *All Bull: the National Servicemen*, London: Allison and Busby

Jones, David (1963), *In Parenthesis*, London: Faber and Faber

Jones, Gwyn, and Jones, Thomas, (trans) (1973), *The Mabinogion*, London: Dent

Junor, Beth (1995), *Greenham Common Women's Peace Camp: A History of Non-Violent Resistance 1984-1995*, London: Working Press

Kealy, Máire (2007), *Dominican Education in Ireland, 1820-1930*, Dublin: Irish Academic Press

Kennedy, Andrew K. (1975), *Six Dramatists in Search of a Language*, Cambridge: C.U.P.

Kershaw, Baz (1992), *The Politics of Performance: Radical Theatre as Cultural Intervention*, London: Routledge

Kippen, John (2001), *Cold War Pastoral*, London: Black Dog Publishing

Kitchen, Laurence (1966), *Drama in the Sixties*, London: Faber

Lacey, Stephen (1995), *British Realist Theatre: the New Wave in its Context 1956-1965*, London: Routledge

Leach, Robert (2003), *Stanislavsky and Meyerhold*, Bern: Peter Lang A.G.

Leach, Robert (2006), *Theatre Workshop: Joan Littlewood and the Making of Modern British Theatre*, Exeter: University of Exeter Press

Lee, J.J. (1989), *Ireland 1912-1985*, Cambridge: C.U.P.

Leeming, Glenda (1974), *John Arden*, Harlow: Longmans

Lewenstein, Oscar (1994), *Kicking Against the Pricks: A Theatre Producer Looks Back*, London: Nick Hern Books

Lomax, Alan (ed), (1964), *The Penguin Book of American Folk Songs*, Harmondsworth: Penguin.

Loomis, Roger Sherman (1963), *The Development of Arthurian Romance*, London: Hutchinson

Luckhurst, Mary (ed) (2006), *A Companion to Modern British and Irish Drama, 1880-2005*, Oxford: Blackwell

McGrath, John (1990), *The Bone Won't Break*, London: Methuen

MacLennon, Elizabeth (1990), *The Moon Belongs to Everyone*, London: Methuen

Malick, Javed (1995), *Toward a Theater of the Oppressed*, Ann Arbor: University of Michigan Press

Malory, Sir Thomas (1971), *Works*, Oxford: O.U.P.

Marowitz, Charles, Milne, Tom and Hale, Owen (eds), (1965), *The Encore Reader*, London: Methuen

Marowitz, Charles and Trussler, Simon (eds) (1967), *Theatre at Work: Playwrights and Productions in the Modern British Theatre*, London: Methuen

Matthews, Caitlin (ed) (1990), *Voices of the Goddess: A Chorus of Sibyls*, Wellingborough: The Aquarian Press

Mitchell, Caroline (2000), *Women and Radio*, London: Routledge

Neat, Timothy (2007, 2009), *Hamish Henderson: a Biography*, 2 vols, Edinburgh: Polygon

O'Brien, Conor Cruise (1962), *To Katanga and Back*, London: Hutchinson

O'Casey, Sean (1955), *The Bishop's Bonfire*, London: Macmillan

O'Casey, Sean (1960), *The Drums of Father Ned*, London: Macmillan

ÓhAodha, Mícheál (1974), *Theatre in Ireland*, Oxford: Basil Blackwell

Ó Suilleabháin, Sean (1967), *Irish Wake Amusements*, Cork: Mercier Press

Page, Malcolm (1985), *Arden on File*, London: Methuen

Page, Malcolm (1984), *John Arden*, Boston: Twayne

Patterson, Michael (2003), *Strategies of Political Theatre: Postwar British Playwrights*, Cambridge: C.U.P.

Peacock, D.Keith (1991), *Radical Stages: Alternative History in Modern British Drama*, Westport, CT: Greenwood.

Pollet, Maurice (1971), *John Skelton, Poet of Tudor England*, London: J.M.Dent & Sons

Priestley, J.B. (1934), *English Journey*, London: Heinemann

Rebellato, Dan (1999), *1956 And All That*, London: Routledge

Reid, Christopher (ed) (2007), *Letters of Ted Hughes*, London: Faber and Faber

Ride On Rapunzel: Fairytales for Feminists (1992), Dublin: Attic Press

Rockett, Kevin, Gibbons, Luke, and Hill, John (1987), *Cinema and Ireland*, London: Croom Helm.

Sandbrook, Dominic (2006), *Never Had It So Good*, London: Little, Brown

Shellard, Dominic (ed) (2000), *British Theatre in the 1950s*, Sheffield: Sheffield Academic Press

Spolin, Viola (1963), *Improvisation for the Theater*, Evanston, Ill: Northwestern University Prress

Styan, J.L. (1981), *Modern Drama in Theory and Practice 3: Expressionism and Epic Theatre*, Cambridge: C.U.P.

Sweeping Beauties: Fairytales for Feminists (1989), Dublin: Attic Press

Taylor, John Russell (1969), *Anger and After*, London: Methuen

Thomson, Peter (ed) (1984), *Plays by Dion Boucicault*, Cambridge: C.U.P.

Trewin, J.C. (1971), *Peter Brook: a Biography*, London: Macdonald

Trussler, Simon (1973), *John Arden*, N.Y.: Columbia University Press

Vinson, James (ed) (1977), *Contemporary Dramatists*, London: St James Press

Wager, Walter (ed) (1969), *The Playwrights Speak*, London: Longmans

Wardle, Irving (1978), *Theatres of George Devine*, London: Eyre Methuen

Wesker, Arnold (1994), *As Much As I Dare*, London: Arrow Books

Whiting, John (1957), *The Plays of John Whiting*, London: Heinemann

Wike, Joanthan (ed) (1994), *John Arden and Margaretta D'Arcy: a Casebook*, London: Garland

Williams, David (ed) (1992), *Peter Brook: a Casebook*, London: Methuen.

Willeford, William (1969), *The Fool and His Scepter*, Chicago: Northwestern University Press

Winkler, Elizabeth Hale (1990), *The Function of Song in Contemporary British Drama*, Cranbury, NJ: Associated University Presses

References

[1] Arden (1971), p.9.

[2] Wike (1995), p.ix.

[3] Malick (1995), p.1.

[4] *The Guardian*, 3 January 2004.

[5] *Writing Ulster*, No 2/3, 1991-1992, p.87.

[6] http://www.culturenorthernireland/article/2257/my-cultural-life-martin-lynch (accessed 12 October 2011).

[7] Arden and D'Arcy (1988b), pp.61-64.

[8] *Ibid.*, p.58.

[9] Priestley (1934), pp.154-155.

[10] Arden (1991), p.112.

[11] Arden and D'Arcy (1969), p.6.

[12] Arden and D'Arcy (1988b), p.60.

[13] http://www.lib.rochester.edu/camelot/INTRVWS/arden.htm (accessed 3 June 2010.)

[14] Arden and D'Arcy (1991), p.xiii.

[15] Arden and D'Arcy (1988), p.67.

[16] *Ibid.*, p.243.

[17] Arden and D'Arcy (1974), p.10.

[18] Marowitz and Trussler (1967), p.36.

[19] Arden and D'Arcy (1974), p.10.

[20] Tape recorded interview, 4 September 2009.

[21] Marowitz and Trussler (1967), p.36.

[22] Arden (1965b), p.9.

[23] Billingham (2002), pp.87-88.

[24] Marowitz and Trussler (1967), p.36.

[25] Johnson (1973), p.234.

[26] *Ibid.*, p.258.

[27] *Ibid.*, p.234.

[28] *Ibid.*, pp.31, 137.

[29] *Ibid.*, p.233

[30] Arden and D'Arcy (1974), p.10.

[31] Graves (1997), p.450.

[32] *Ibid.*, p.70.

[33] Bethell (1944), pp.19, 21.

[34] See Arden (1971), pp.10-11.

[35] *Encore*, vol 8, no 4, July-August 1961, pp. 23, 24.

[36] Marowitz and Trussler (1967), p.39.

[37] *The Listener*, 22 July 1971.

[38] Arden (1967), p.9.

[39] Interdisciplinary Studies in the Long Nineteenth Century, 3, 2006, p.2.

[40] Arden and D'Arcy (1988b), p.128.

[41] D'Arcy (2005), p.19.

[42] *Ibid.*, p.25.

[43] Lee (1989), p.177.

[44] Arden and D'Arcy (1988b), pp.122-123.

[45] Arden and D'Arcy (1991), p.ix.

[46] D'Arcy (2005), pp.72-73.

[47] Matthews (1990), pp.69-70.

[48] *Ibid.*, p.84.

[49] Marowitz, Milne and Hale (1965), pp.126, 127.

[50] *Theatre Ireland*, no. 28, summer 1992, p.11.

[51] D'Arcy (2005), p.152.

[52] Gray (1994), p.190.

[53] O'Casey (1955), p.110.

[54] Lee (1989), p.317.

[55] Hogan (1967), p.123.

[56] D'Arcy (2005), p.35.

[57] Saint-Denis (2009), p.192.

[58] D'Arcy (2005), p.209.

[59] *Ibid.*, p.214.

[60] Tape recorded interview, 30 March 2010.

[61] Horovitz (1969), pp.18-20.

[62] Clarke (1997), p.258.

[63] Duff (1995), p.171.

[64] Shellard (2000), p.38.

[65] *New Theatre Quarterly*, Vol XI, no 43, August 1995, p.211.

[66] Findlater (1981), p.16.

[67] Lewenstein (1994), p.38.

[68] D'Arcy (2005), p.215.

[69] D'Arcy (2005), p.225.

[70] Billington (2007), p.115.

[71] Arden (1967a), p.10.

[72] *Ibid.*, p.6

[73] Findlater (1981), p.52.

[74] Wesker (1994), p.626.

[75] Gaskill (1988), p.36.

[76] *Ibid.*, p.25.

[77] *Ibid.*, p.35.

[78] Findlater (1981), p.55.

[79] *Ibid.*, p.22.

[80] Saint-Denis (2009), p.71.

[81] Findlater (1981), p.59.

[82] D'Arcy (2005), p.197.

[83] Tape recorded interview, 30 March 2010.

[84] D'Arcy (2005), p.233.

[85] Tape recorded interview, 30 March 2010.

[86] D'Arcy (2005), p.233.

[87] Tape recorded interview, 30 March 2010.

[88] Arden (1967a), p.102.

[89] *Plays and Players*, vol 19, no 7, April 1972, p.49.

[90] Carpenter (2003), p.191.

[91] Arden and D'Arcy (1988b), p.56.

[92] *The Observer*, 5 October 1958.

[93] *Punch*, 8 November 1958.

[94] Findlater (1981), p.22.

[95] *The Guardian*, 3 January 2004.

[96] Arden and D'Arcy (1988b), p.132.

[97] Tape recorded interview, 3 September 2009.

[98] *New York Times*, 10 April 1966

[99] *Encore*, Jul-Aug 1961, p.26.

[100] *Ibid.*, p.40

[101] Howe (1993), p.231.

[102] Billington (2007), p.117.

[103] *The Sunday Times*, 25 October 1959.

[104] *Punch*, 28 October 1959.

[105] *Manchester Guardian*, 24 October 1959.

[106] *The Guardian*, 3 January 2004.

[107] Wandor (2001), p.73.

[108] *The Guardian*, 23 September 2003.

[109] The Transatlantic Review, no 40, summer 1971.

[110] Taylor (1969), p.89.

[111] Brown and Harris (1962), p.52.

[112] Child (1965), p.253.

[113] Graves (1997), p.23.

[114] Bethell (1948), p.45.

[115] Brown and Harris (1962), p.202.

[116] Marowitz, Milne and Hale (1965), pp.123-129.

[117] Willeford (1969), p.6.

[118] Tynan (1975), p.278.

[119] Wardle (1978), p.212.

[120] Hunt (1974), p.171.

[121] D'Arcy (2005), p.238.

[122] Arden and D'Arcy (1991), p.ix.

[123] *Encore*, vol 8, no.4, July-Aug 1961, p.40.

[124] Marowitz and Trussler (1967), p.47.

[125] Lomax (1964), p.108.

[126] Taylor (1969), p.99.

[127] Arden (1967b), pp.10-11.

[128] *New Statesman*, 2 November 1957.

[129] Greer, (1964), pp.58-59.

[130] Gaskill, (1988), p.38.

[131] Tape recorded interview, 2 September 2009.

[132] *Peace News*, 18 August 1967.

[133] Arden and D'Arcy (1988), pp.103-115.

[134] *The Guardian*, 3 January 2004.

[135] Tape recorded interview, 4 September 2009

[136] Wager (1969), p.200.

[137] *Ibid.*, p.252.

[138] *Encore*, vol 10, No 6, Nov-Dec 1963, p.19.

[139] Tape recorded interview, 16 February 2010.

[140] Calder (2001), p.258.

[141] Arden and D'Arcy (1991), pp.ix-x.

[142] Tape recorded interview, 16 February 2010.

[143] Marowitz and Trussler (1967), p.56.

[144] Tape recorded interview, 30 March 2010.

[145] *Encore*, vol 10, No 3, May-June 1963.

[146] Kershaw (1992), p.107.

[147] *Encore*, vol 10, No 6, Nov-Dec 1963, p.17.

[148] Tape recorded interview, 16 February 2010.

[149] Itzin (1980), p.27.

[150] *Encore*, vol 10, No 6, p.21.

[151] Ibid.

[152] Burton and Lane (1970), p.352.

[153] Marowitz and Trussler (1967), p.57.

[154] *The Sunday Times*, 11 July 1965

[155] Arden (1994), p.xv; D'Arcy (2005), p.429

[156] *Encore*, vol 11, no 4, July-August 1964, p.48.

[157] Marowitz, Milne and Hale (1965), p.75.

[158] Arden (1977), p.5.

[159] Hunt and Reeves (1995), p.63.

[160] Trewin (1971), p.137

[161] Tape recorded interview, 3 October 2010.

[162] Hayman (1968), p.3.

[163] *Encore*, vol 11, No 4, July-August 1964, pp.50, 51.

[164] *Encore*, vol 11, No 5, September-October 1964, p.52.

[165] Arden (1964), p.10.

[166] *Peace News*, 30 August 1963, p.7.

[167] Marowitz and Trussler (1967), p.51.

[168] Malick (1995), p.56.

[169] *The Sunday Times*, 11 July 1963.

[170] The Sunday Telegraph, 11 July 1963.

[171] *Peace News*, 25 October 1963.

[172] *Encore*, vol 10, no 5, September-October 1963, p.52.

[173] Arden (1977b), p.24.

[174] Arden (1994), p.xii.

[175] *The Guardian*, 23 September 2003.

[176] *Encore*, vol 12, no 5, September-October 1965, p.7.

[177] Arden (1965b), p.78.

[178] *Encore*, vol 12, no 5, September-October 1965, p.7.

[179] *The Times*, 13 November 1963.

[180] Arden (1994), p.xv.

[181] Child (1965), p.371.

[182] Programme for National theatre production of *Armstrong's Last Goodnight* (1965)

[183] *Encore*, vol 12, no 5, September-October 1965, p.24.

[184] *Encore*, vol 11, no 4, July-August 1964, p.47

[185] *Encore*, vol 12, no 5, September-October 1965, p.37

[186] Coveney (1990), p.57

[187] Marowitz and Trussler (1967), p.52

[188] Arden (1994), p.xiv

[189] *The Times*, 16 June 1965

[190] *Encore*, vol 12, no 5, September-October 1965, p.8

[191] Graves (1999), p.23

[192] *Encore*, vol 12, no 5, September-October 1965, pp.22, 23.

[193] *Encore*, vol 12, no 4, July-August 1965, p.39.

[194] Taylor (1969), pp.104-105.
[195] *The Guardian*, 3 January 2004.
[196] Williams (1992), p.31.
[197] *The Guardian*, 3 January 2004.
[198] *Peace News*, 30 August 1963.
[199] Arden (1977a), p.7
[200] Brown (1969), p.146
[201] Arden (1964), p.8.
[202] Tape recorded interview, 16 February 2010.
[203] *Peace News*, 8 December 1967.
[204] Tape recorded interview, 8 November 2009.
[205] Tape recorded interview, 3 September 2009.
[206] *The Observer*, 14 February 1965.
[207] Tape recorded interview, 30 March 2010.
[208] Arden and D'Arcy (1991), p.44
[209] *Encore*, vol 11, no 2, March-April 1964, p.12.
[210] *Encore*, vol 12, no 5, September-October, 1965, p.34.
[211] Arden and D'Arcy (1991), p.xi.
[212] *Peace News*, 28 May 1965.
[213] *Peace News*, 18 August 1967.
[214] Arden and D'Arcy (1965), Introduction.
[215] Kershaw (1992), pp.121-122.
[216] *Peace News*, 30 August 1963.
[217] *The Guardian*, 3 January 2004.
[218] Arden (1977a), p.5.
[219] Burton and Lane (1970), p.22
[220] Kershaw (1992), pp.92, 110-111.
[221] Fountain (1988), p.13.
[222] Arden (1977b), p.48.
[223] *The Observer*, 14 February 1965.
[224] Arden and D'Arcy (1991), p.x.
[225] Tape recorded interview, 30 March 2010.
[226] Arden and D'Arcy (1974), p.18.
[227] *Contemporary Literature*, vol 32, no 2, summer 1991, p.159.
[228] Wike (1995), p.52.
[229] D'Arcy (2005), p.229.
[230] Fo and Rame (1981), p.iv.
[231] Wager (1969), p.196.
[232] http://www.lib.rochester.edu/camelot/INTRVWS/arden.htm (accessed 3 April 2010)
[233] *The Guardian*, 3 January 2003.
[234] Tape recorded interview, 3 October 2010.
[235] Arden (1977b), pp.51-60.
[236] *Ibid.*, p.59.
[237] Arden (1977a), p.6.
[238] Puchner (2006), pp.224-225.
[239] *Peace News*, 10 November 1967
[240] Ansorge (1980), p.56.
[241] Itzin (1980), p.343.
[242] Craig (1980), p.47.

[243] *The Drama Review*, vol 13, no 4, summer 1969, p.192.
[244] Itzin (1980), p.20.
[245] Kershaw (1992), p.131.
[246] Itzin (1980), p.21.
[247] Kershaw (1992), p.125.
[248] *The Sunday Times*, 9 June 1968.
[249] *The Drama Review*, vol 13, no 4, summer 1969, p.185.
[250] Ibid.
[251] *The Observer*, 16 June 1968.
[252] Hunt (1974), p.127.
[253] Tape recorded interview, 30 March 2010.
[254] Itzin (1980), p.22.
[255] Hunt (1974), p.127.
[256] Itzin (1980), p.344.
[257] *The Observer*, 16 June 1968.
[258] *Tribune*, 21 June 1968.
[259] *The Drama Review*, vol 13, no 4, summer 1969, p.185.
[260] Arden (1977b), p.83.
[261] Tape recorded interview, 4 September 2009.
[262] Itzin (1980), p.344.
[263] *Contemporary Literature*, vol 32, no 2, summer 1991, p.164.
[264] *The Sunday Times*, 23 June 1968.
[265] *The Observer*, 14 February 1968.
[266] Peacock (1991), p.77.
[267] Arden and D'Arcy (1969), p.6.
[268] http://www.lib.rochester.edu/camelot/INTRVWS/arden.htm (accessed 3 April 2010)
[269] *The Sunday Times*, 9 March 1969.
[270] Arden and D'Arcy (1969), p.6.
[271] Hunt (1974), p.140.
[272] *The Drama Review*, vol 13, no 4, p.188.
[273] *Galway Advertiser*, 19 November 2009.
[274] *Peace News*, 24 January 1969.
[275] Arden (1977b), p.91.
[276] Arden (1971), p.10.
[277] *The Transatlantic Review*, no.40, summer 1971, p.56.
[278] Ionesco (1960), p.111.
[279] *New Statesman*, 10 April 1970.
[280] Gray (1982), p.67.
[281] Arden (1971), pp.16, 17.
[282] *The Guardian*, 28 November 1972.
[283] Hanley and Millar (2009), p.67.
[284] D'Arcy (2005), p.246.
[285] *In Context*, summer 1987, p.12.
[286] *The Guardian*, 28 November 1972.
[287] Tape recorded interview, 8 November 2009.
[288] http://www.lib.rochester.edu/camelot/INTRVWS/arden.htm (accessed 3 April 2010).
[289] *Plays and Players*, vol 20, no 4, January 1973.
[290] Arden and D'Arcy (1974), p.16.
[291] *Plays and Players*, vol 20, no 4, January 1973.

[292] Ibid.

[293] D'Arcy (2005), p.100.

[294] Arden (1977), pp.137-152.

[295] http://www.lib.rochester.edu/camelot/INTRVWS/arden.htm (accessed 3 April 2010).

[296] http://www.lib.rochester.edu/camelot/INTRVWS/arden.htm (accessed 3 April 2010).

[297] Tape recorded interview, 3 October 2010.

[298] Tape recorded interview, 30 March 2010.

[299] Tape recorded interview, 3 October 2010.

[300] Ibid.

[301] Tape recorded interview, 30 March 2010.

[302] Ibid.

[303] Tape recorded interview, 3 October 2010.

[304] Arden (1977b), p.129.

[305] Arden and D'Arcy (1988), p.133.

[306] Hanley and Millar (2009), p.250.

[307] *Ibid.*, p.246.

[308] *Plays and Players*, vol 19, no 3, December 1971, p.14.

[309] Ibid.

[310] *Plays and Players*, vol 20, no 4, January 1973, pp.18-19.

[311] *Plays and Players*, vol 19, no 3, December 1971, p.14.

[312] *Writing Ulster*, no 2/3, 1991/1992, p.88.

[313] *Performance*, vol 1, no 4, September-October 1972, p.12.

[314] Arden and D'Arcy (1991), p.xi.

[315] *Theatre Ireland*, no. 28, summer 1992, p.11.

[316] *Irish Times*, 22 March 2010.

[317] *Theatre Ireland*, no. 28, summer 1992, p.12.

[318] Ibid.

[319] Ibid.

[320] *Plays and Players*, vol 20, no 2, November 1972, p.51.

[321] Chambers and Prior (9187), p.151.

[322] *The Guardian*, 3 January 2004.

[323] Arden and D'Arcy (1988), pp.215-216.

[324] *The Guardian*, 3 January 2004

[325] Ibid.

[326] MacLennan (1990), p.38.

[327] *Ibid.*, p.39.

[328] Arden and D'Arcy (1988), p.134.

[329] Arden (1995), p.124.

[330] *Ibid*, p.125.

[331] *Plays and Players*, vol 20, no 2, November 1972, p.51.

[332] Page (1984), p.118.

[333] MacLennan (1990), p.38

[334] Arden and D'Arcy (1974), p.9.

[335] Ibid.

[336] Collingwood and Myres (1936), p.293.

[337] Jones (1963), p.324.

[338] Loomis (1963), p.125.

[339] Graves (1997), p.18.

[340] Times Education Supplement, 22 December 1972.

[341] *Ibid.*, p.201.

[342] *Plays and Players*, vol 20, no 4, January 1973

[343] Arden and D'Arcy (1974), p.12.

[344] *Ibid.*, p.20.

[345] *Plays and Players*, vol 20, no 4, January 1973.

[346] Ibid.

[347] Ibid.

[348] Ibid.

[349] Ibid.

[350] Arden (1977b), p.159

[351] http://www.lib.rochester.edu/camelot/INTRVWS/arden.htm (accessed 3 April 2010).

[352] *Plays and Players*, vol 20, no 4, January 1973.

[353] Arden (1977b), p.160.

[354] *The Times*, 30 November 1972.

[355] *The Guardian*, 3 January 2004.

[356] Arden (1977b), p.166.

[357] Arden and D'Arcy (1988b), pp.3-4.

[358] Gaskill (1988), p.137.

[359] *Plays and Players*, vol 20, no 5, February 1973

[360] *The Guardian*, 5 December 1972.

[361] *The Times*, 5 December 1972.

[362] *The Times*, 6 December 1972.

[363] *The Guardian*, 8 December 1972.

[364] *The Times*, 13 December 1972 and 16 December 1972.

[365] *The Guardian*, 6 December 1972.

[366] *Flourish*, 1972/73, issue 3.

[367] Tape recorded interview, 16 February 2010.

[368] *The Times*, 15 December 1972.

[369] *The Times*, 7 December 1972.

[370] *The Guardian*, 27 November 1972.

[371] Arden (1967), p.12.

[372] *The Guardian*, 28 November 1972.

[373] Arden (1977b), p.170.

[374] Ibid.

[375] Hanley and Millar (2009), pp.249-250.

[376] Gray (1994), p.266.

[377] Arden and D'Arcy (1991), p.373.

[378] Arden (1994), p.xi.

[379] Tape recorded interview, 3 October 2010.

[380] Arden (1977b), p.108.

[381] Ibid.

[382] Arden and D'Arcy (1991), p.373.

[383] D'Arcy (1996), p.13.

[384] Tape recorded interview, 16 February 2010.

[385] *Plays and Players*, vol 20, no 4, January 1973, pp. 17, 18.

[386] Arden and D'Arcy (1991), p.374.

[387] Tape recorded interview, 30 March 2010.

[388] Arden and D'Arcy (1991), p.375.

[389] D'Arcy (1996), p.14.

[390] Arden (1977b), p.98.
[391] D'Arcy and Arden (1977), p.vii.
[392] *The Irish Times*, 1 April 1975.
[393] Eisenstein (1968), pp.182-183.
[394] Tape recorded conversation, 8 September 2009.
[395] *Plays and Players*, vol 19, no 1, October 1971, p.59.
[396] Arden (1977b), pp.106-107.
[397] Tape recorded interview, 30 March 2010.
[398] *Plays and Players*, vol 22, no 10, July 1975, p.40.
[399] Page (1985), p.56.
[400] *Studies*, vol 96, no 384, winter 2007, p.415.
[401] *Theatre Quarterly*, vol 5, no 20, December 1975-February 1976, p.140.
[402] Arden (1964b), p.8.
[403] *The Irish Times*, 13 March 1975
[404] Tape recorded interview, 3 September 2009.
[405] *Studies*, vol 96, no 384, winter 2007, p.413.
[406] *New Statesman*, 11 April 1980.
[407] *Theatre Quarterly*, vol 5, no 20, December 1975-February 1976, p.140.
[408] *Plays and Players*, vol 22, no 10, July 1975, p.41.
[409] Reproduced in *Theatre Quarterly*, vol 5, no 20, December 1975-February 1976, p.141.
[410] *Plays and Players*, vol 22, no 10, July 1975, p.40.
[411] *Theatre Quarterly*, vol VII, no 25, spring 1977, p.94.
[412] *The Irish Times*, 1 April 1975.
[413] D'Arcy (2005), p.432.
[414] *Tribune*, 28 May 1976.
[415] *Plays and Players*, vol 22, no 10, July 1975, p.40.
[416] *The Guardian*, 3 January 2004.
[417] Ibid.
[418] Chambers and Prior (1987), p.153
[419] Bigsby (1981), p.154.
[420] *New Society*, 18 January 1979.
[421] *The Guardian*, 3 January 2004.
[422] Arden and D'Arcy (1988b), p.134.
[423] *Caoineadh Airt Uí Laoire*, DVD, Cinegael; www.conamara.org.
[424] Rockett, Gibbons and Hill (1987), pp.138-139.
[425] Hanley and Millar (2009), p.315.
[426] D'Arcy (2005), p.275.
[427] *Ibid.*, pp.275-276.
[428] Arden/D'Arcy (1991), p.385.
[429] Ibid.
[430] Arden and D'Arcy (1991), p.387.
[431] Matthews (1990), p.78.
[432] *Ibid.*, p.389.
[433] Burke (2009), p.208.
[434] Arden and D'Arcy (1988), p.182.
[435] Tape recorded interview, 8 September 2009.
[436] McGrath (1990), pp.154-155.
[437] *The Guardian*, 3 January 2004.
[438] Arden (1995), p.127.

[439] D'Arcy (2005), p.21.
[440] Itzin (1980), p.36.
[441] *The Times*, 18 October 1977.
[442] *The Guardian*, 3 January 2004.
[443] Theatre Research International, vol V, p.218.
[444] Vinson (1977), p.46.
[445] *Ibid.*, p.47.
[446] D'Arcy (2005), pp.279, 283, 284, 285.
[447] *Ibid.*, p.275.
[448] *Theatre Quarterly*, vol vi, winter 1976-77, p.36.
[449] Ibid.
[450] *Ibid.*, p.69.
[451] Bigsby (1981), p.147.
[452] Chambers and Prior (1987), p.155.
[453] Arden and D'Arcy (1991), p.432.
[454] Tape recorded interview, 2 September 2010.
[455] Hanley and Millar (2009), p.365.
[456] D'Arcy (1996), p.15.
[457] D'Arcy (2005), p.290.
[458] Arden and D'Arcy (1988b), p.134.
[459] Tape recorded interview, 2 September 2009.
[460] Wike (1995), p.218.
[461] Tape recorded interview, 8 November 2009.
[462] Arden and D'Arcy (1988b), p.185.
[463] *Tulane Drama Review*, vol 11, no 2, Winter 1966, p.42.
[464] International Journal of Scottish Theatre, vol 3, no 2, December 2002.
[465] Tape recorded interview, 3 October 2010.
[466] Arden and D'Arcy (1991), p.xii.
[467] *The Guardian*, 23 September 2003.
[468] Ibid.
[469] D'Arcy (1981), p.16.
[470] Chambers and Prior (1987), p.156.
[471] D'Arcy (1981), p.28.
[472] *Ibid.*, p.20.
[473] *Ibid.*, p.35.
[474] Tape-recorded interview, 3 September 2009.
[475] Connolly (1984), p.132.
[476] D'Arcy (1981), pp.78-79.
[477] *Ibid.*, p.66.
[478] *Ibid.*, pp.49, 50, 51.
[479] *Ibid.*, p.81.
[480] *Ibid.*, p.113.
[481] Connolly (1984), p.132.
[482] *The Guardian*, 12 November 1981.
[483] D'Arcy (1996), p.19.
[484] Tape-recorded interview, 3 September 2009.
[485] Tape recorded interview, 3 October 2010.
[486] Tape recorded interview, 4 September 2009.
[487] Cervantes (2010), p.7.

[488] Arden, The Adventures of the Ingenious Gentleman, Don Quixote of La Mancha.

[489] *The Radio Times*, 25 September 1980.

[490] Arden, The Adventures of the Ingenious Gentleman, Don Quixote of La Mancha.

[491] *The Listener*, 9 October 1980.

[492] Pollet (1971), p.xviii.

[493] *Ibid.*, pp. 186, 202.

[494] *Ibid.*, pp. 136, 137.

[495] John Arden, The Winking Goose.

[496] Henderson (1948), p.390.

[497] John Arden, The Winking Goose.

[498] Henderson (1948), p.33.

[499] *Ibid.*, pp.24, 143, 315.

[500] *The Listener*, 18 February 1982.

[501] *The Guardian*, 27 February 1982.

[502] *The Sunday Times*, 22 August 1982.

[503] Imison (1983), p.40.

[504] *Ibid.*, p.37.

[505] *The Sunday Times*, 24 October 1982.

[506] *The Listener*, 14 October 1982.

[507] *The Guardian*, 26 August 1982.

[508] Arden and D'Arcy (1988b), p.43.

[509] *Ibid.*, p.44.

[510] Arden (1982), title page.

[511] Arden and D'Arcy (1988b), p.44.

[512] Arden (1982), p.137

[513] *Ibid.*, p.191.

[514] *The Guardian*, 26 August 1982.

[515] *The Guardian*, 18 April 1983.

[516] Arden and D'Arcy (1988b), p.47.

[517] *Writing Ulster*, No.2/3, (1991-1992), p.86.

[518] Tape recorded interview, 3 September 2009.

[519] Arden and D'Arcy (1988a), p.xxx.

[520] Etherton (1989), p.82.

[521] All quotations from unpublished scripts relating to this performance.

[522] Chambers and Prior (1987), p.155.

[523] *The Times*, 21 January 1984.

[524] Ibid.

[525] Arden and D'Arcy (1988b), p.89.

[526] *Ibid.*, pp.98-99.

[527] *Red Letters*, no.17, March 1985,p.22.

[528] Ibid.

[529] Arden and D'Arcy (1988b), p.10.

[530] Wike (1995), p.176.

[531] Arden and D'Arcy (1988b), p.138.

[532] *Ibid.*, p.137.

[533] D'Arcy (2005), p.307.

[534] *Ibid.*, p.308.

[535] *The New Statesman*, 13 June 1986, vol III, no 2881.

[536] Arden and D'Arcy (1988b), p.138.

[537] Blackwood (1984), p.2.
[538] D'Arcy (2005), p.375.
[539] *Ibid.*, p.342.
[540] *Ibid.*, p.358.
[541] *Ibid.*, p.372.
[542] *Theatre Ireland*, no. 28, summer 1992, p.31.
[543] *Ibid.*, p.6.
[544] Arden and D'Arcy (1988b), dedication.
[545] *Theatre Ireland*, no. 28, summer 1992, inside front cover.
[546] *Ibid.*, p.6
[547] Ibid.
[548] *Writing Ulster*, no 2/3, 1991-1992, p.86.
[549] *Theatre Ireland*, no. 28, summer 1992, p.32.
[550] *Ibid.*, pp.57-58.
[551] *Ibid.*, p. 45.
[552] *Ibid.*, pp. 6,70, 58, 29.
[553] *Ibid.*, p.xxxii.
[554] Arden and D'Arcy (1988a), p.xxvi.
[555] *Ibid.*, p.xxix.
[556] D'Arcy (2005), p.320.
[557] Wike (1995), p.64.
[558] *Writing Ulster*, no 2/3, 1991-1992, p.92.
[559] *Ibid.*, p.86.
[560] *Ibid.*, p.103.
[561] *Ibid.*, p.100.
[562] *Ibid.*, p.98.
[563] Wike (1995), p.180.
[564] *Writing Ulster*, no 2/3, 1991-1992, p.101.
[565] Arden and D'Arcy (1988a), p.xv.
[566] *The Guardian*, 19 April 1988.
[567] *Drama*, 1988, vol 3, p.48.
[568] Wike (1995), p.186.
[569] *The Listener*, 21 April 1988, p.14
[570] *Ibid.*, p.28.
[571] D'Arcy (1996), p.17.
[572] *Ibid.*, p.56.
[573] Ibid.
[574] *Ibid.*, p.3, 5.
[575] Tape recorded interview, 3 September 2009.
[576] D'Arcy (1996), p.38.
[577] Tape recorded interview, 3 September 2009.
[578] D'Arcy (1996), p.49.
[579] *Ibid.*, p.58.
[580] *Ibid.*, p.52.
[581] *Ibid.*, Preface.
[582] *Ibid.*, p.85.
[583] *Ibid.*, p.71.
[584] *Theatre Ireland*, no. 28, summer 1992, p.77.
[585] D'Arcy (1996), p.71.

[586] *Ibid.*, p.92.

[587] Mitchell (2000), p.114.

[588] *Ibid.*, p.196.

[589] *Ibid.*

[590] *The Advocate*, 7 March 1991.

[591] Tape recorded interview, 3 September 2009.

[592] *Writing Ulster*, no, 2/3, (1991/1992), p.87

[593] *The Guardian*, 3 January 2004.

[594] Wike (1995), p.56.

[595] Arden (1988), p.103.

[596] *Ibid.*, p.64.

[597] Arden and D'Arcy (1988b), p.17.

[598] Wike (1995), p.173.

[599] *Theatre Ireland*, no. 28, summer 1992, p.45.

[600] Wike (1995), p.228.

[601] Arden (1988), p.28.

[602] Arden and D'Arcy (1988b), p.17.

[603] *The Guardian*, 3 January 2004.

[604] Arden (1991), pp.158, 195.

[605] *Ibid.*, p.247.

[606] *Ibid.*, p.260.

[607] *Ibid.*, p.395.

[608] *Ibid.*, p.198.

[609] *Ibid.*, p.251.

[610] *The Times*, 17 September 1995.

[611] Arden (1995), p.88.

[612] *Ibid.*, p.151.

[613] *Ibid.*, p.54, 50.

[614] Tape recorded interview, 4 September 2009.

[615] *Theatre Ireland*, no. 28, summer 1992, p.43.

[616] *Writing Ulster*, no, 2/3, (1991/1992), p.108.

[617] D'Arcy (1996), p.50.

[618] *Writing Ulster*, no, 2/3, (1991/1992), p.108-109.

[619] Malick (1995), p.1.

[620] *The Guardian*, 3 January 2004.

[621] Rapunzel Rides Again (1992), p.124.

[622] D'Arcy (1996), p.52.

[623] D'Arcy (2005), p.412.

[624] *Ibid.*, p.417.

[625] Wike (1995), p.64.

[626] D'Arcy (2005), p.337.

[627] Wike (1995), p.53.

[628] Tape recorded interview, 8 September 2009.

[629] Wike (1995), p.54.

[630] *Irish Times*, 20 April 1996.

[631] Wike (1995), p.64.

[632] D'Arcy (2005), p.418.

[633] Arden and D'Arcy (1988b), p.217.

[634] http:/web.ukonline.co.uk/suttonelms/jarden.html (accessed 27 March 2011).

[635] Publicity leaflet.

[636] Ibid.

[637] *Writing Ulster*, no 2/3, 1991/1992, p.92.

[638] *The Guardian*, 3 January 2004.

[639] *The Irish Times*, 28 November 2009.

[640] *Daily Telegraph*, 11 July 2003.

[641] *The Guardian*, 23 September 2003.

[642] Castle Area Campaign against Coppergate II, publicity leaflet.

[643] Connolly and Lynch (2005), pp. 4, 10-11.

[644] Garavan (2006), p.12.

[645] Ibid.

[646] Connolly and Lynch (2005), p. 40.

[647] D'Arcy (2005), pp.1-2.

[648] *Ibid.*, p.2.

[649] Arden (1964b), p.8.

[650] *The Irish Times*, 13 March 1975.

[651] Tape recorded interview, 3 September 2009.

[652] *Studies*, vol 96, no 384, 2007, p. 412.

[653] http://www.fictionfactory.co.uk/page4.html (accessed 13 August 2011)

[654] *Galway Advertiser*, 19 November 2009.

[655] *The Irish Times*, 14 November 2009.

[656] *Galway Advertiser*, 5 November 2009.

[657] *The Irish Times*, 28 November 2009.

[658] *Galway Advertiser*, 7 October 2010.

[659] Arden and D'Arcy, Christmas greeting message, 2011

[660] *Galway Advertiser*, 7 October 2010.

[661] *The Guardian*, 23 September 2003.

[662] *The Guardian*, 5 September 1994.

[663] *The Irish Times*, 14 November 2009.

[664] Leach (2003), p.194.

[665] Witzling (1992), p.152.

[666] D'Arcy (1996), p.56.

[667] Ibid.

[668] Tape recorded interview, 4 September 2009.

[669] Arden and D'Arcy (1988b), p.123.

[670] D'Arcy (1996), p.92.

[671] *The Guardian*, 23 September 2003.

[672] *The Irish Times*, 14 November 2009.

[673] Yeats (1983), p.44

[674] *Ibid.*, p.67.

[675] Hutchinson (1960), p.572.

[676] Tape recorded interview, 3 September 2009.

Index

Indigo Dreams Publishing
132 Hinckley Road
Stoney Stanton
Leicestershire
U.K.
www.indigodreams.co.uk